CRIMES AND COVER-UPS
IN AMERICAN POLITICS

—— 1776–1963 ——

THE HISTORY THEY DIDN'T
TEACH YOU IN SCHOOL

DONALD JEFFRIES

FOREWORD BY RON PAUL

Skyhorse Publishing

Skyhorse Publishing books may be purchased in bulk at special discounts for sales promotion, corporate gifts, fund-raising, or educational purposes. Special editions can also be created to specifications. For details, contact the Special Sales Department, Skyhorse Publishing, 307 West 36th Street, 11th Floor, New York, NY 10018 or info@skyhorsepublishing.com.

Skyhorse® and Skyhorse Publishing® are registered trademarks of Skyhorse Publishing, Inc.®, a Delaware corporation.

Visit our website at www.skyhorsepublishing.com.

10 9 8 7 6 5 4 3 2 1

Library of Congress Cataloging-in-Publication Data is available on file.

Cover design by Qualcom

ISBN: 978-1-5107-6910-6
Ebook ISBN: 978-1-5107-4148-5

Printed in the United States of America

This book is dedicated to my son, John, who is also a seeker of truth, a lover of justice, and a student of real history.

CONTENTS

ACKNOWLEDGMENTS IX
ABOUT THE AUTHOR XI
PREFACE TO THE 2021 EDITION XIII
FOREWORD BY RON PAUL XXI
INTRODUCTION XXV

CHAPTER ONE   THE BIRTH OF THE REPUBLIC 1
The Slandering of Jefferson 4
Sacrifices of the Founders 11
Benjamin Franklin 13
Thomas Paine 17
Shays' and Whiskey Rebellions 19
Adam Weishaupt and the Illuminati 24
Our Revolutionary Legacy 27

CHAPTER TWO   PRE–1860: JACKSONIAN DEMOCRACY 36
Meriwether Lewis 36
The War of 1812 40
Freemasons and Anti-Masons 42
Andrew Jackson 45
Remember the Alamo 49
The Mexican-American War 50
John Brown 53

CHAPTER THREE   HONEST ABE 56
Clement Vallandigham 66
The Invention of Total War 73
Lincoln the Racist 84

Lincoln the Warmonger   88
Lincoln the Atheist   93
Lincoln's True Legacy   96

CHAPTER FOUR   **THE LINCOLN ASSASSINATION**   112
The "Trial" of the Conspirators   121

CHAPTER FIVE   **POST–CIVIL WAR AMERICA**   142
Reconstruction   142
The 1876 Election   155
The Garfield Assassination   157
Reconstruction Fallout   159
The Populists   164
Spanish-American War   166

CHAPTER SIX   **THE 1900s–1920s**   169
The McKinley Assassination   170
Bully for Teddy Roosevelt   172
The 1913 Federal Reserve Act   176
Cowboys and Indians   182
Anti-Union Violence   184
World War I   186
The Death of President Harding   200
Prohibition   203
Sacco and Vanzetti   205

CHAPTER SEVEN   **THE DEPRESSING 1930s**   210
The Bonus Army   212
The Lindbergh Kidnapping   214

CHAPTER EIGHT   **FDR CHANNELS LINCOLN**   232
Pearl Harbor   240
Jeannette Rankin   248
Crushing Domestic Dissent   249
Mussolini   258
Allied War Atrocities   260

CHAPTER NINE   **POSTWAR AMERICA**   264

The Alleged Suicide of Hitler 265
More Allied Atrocities 267
Glenn Miller 275
Eddie Slovik 277
The Nuremberg Trials 279
Truman Drops the Bomb 288
The Creation of Israel 295
Robert Taft 297
War is a Racket 298
The Cancer Explosion/Vaccinations/
   Government Experimentation 302

CHAPTER TEN   THE FABULOUS FIFTIES 315
Senator Joseph McCarthy 315
The Central Intelligence Agency 321
Korean War 325
The Reece Committee to Investigate
   Tax-Exempt Foundations 329
The Rosenbergs 332
The True Cost of Communism 335
World Government 338

CHAPTER ELEVEN THE HISTORY OF UN-AMERICANISM 342

CHAPTER TWELVE CONCLUSION 352

BIBLIOGRAPHY 361
NOTES 368
INDEX 379

ACKNOWLEDGMENTS

I would like to thank the following people who helped me during the course of writing this book: Meriwether Lewis descendant Howell Bowen, Cathy Vallandigham, John Wilkes Booth descendant Joanne Hulme, Peter Secosh, and Lincoln assassination expert Nate Orlowek. Talk show host Tim Kelly was interested enough to interview me about the subject of this book, a few years before it was even published. American Free Press and Lew Rockwell were kind enough to publish my articles, some of which touched upon the sort of hidden history described in this book. I am grateful for all my newfound cyber friends: *Midnight Writer News* host S. T. Patrick provided encouragement and support and published my article on Abraham Lincoln in his *Deep Truth Journal*; talk show hosts Richard Syrett and Meria Heller; courageous whistleblower Heidi Weber, who was featured on CBS's "Whistleblower with Alex Ferrer" and associate producer and consultant to Season 2; JFK assassination researcher William Law; especially Billy Ray Valentine, host of the *Infinite Fringe* radio program; and the wonderful Eyerly Felder, host of *Whistleblower Heroes* and other shows, who led me down the new path of talk radio hosting. A special thanks to show business legend and important JFK assassination researcher John Barbour, who was consistently supportive, and to my delight has become a good friend. I am also indebted to my hard-working editor at Skyhorse,

Michael Campbell. And as always, I want to say how much I appreciate my family for their encouragement and support, especially my lovely wife Jeanne, for her unending positivity. Last but not least, my children John and Julianna, who I am so proud of, and feel blessed to be their father.

ABOUT THE AUTHOR

Donald Jeffries has been researching the JFK assassination since the mid-1970s, when he was a teenage volunteer for Mark Lane's Citizens Committee of Inquiry. His 2007 sci-fi cult classic "The Unreals" was lauded by the likes of multi-awardwinning author and former Harvard professor Alexander Theroux and screenwriter ("Night at the Museum") and actor ("Reno 911") R. Ben Garant. His 2014 book *Hidden History: An Expose of Modern Crimes, Conspiracies, and Cover-Ups in American Politics* became a bestseller, featured a foreword from Roger Stone, and received praise from Cindy Sheehan, former Rep. Cynthia McLinney, and Jerome Corsi. His next book, *Survival of the Richest: How the Corruption of the Marketplace and the Disparity of Wealth Created the Greatest Conspiracy of All*, received unanimous critical acclaim, from leading feminist author Naomi Wolf to Jimmy Carter's Chairman of the National Advisory Council on Economic Opportunity Arthur Blaustein to Ron Paul's former Chief of Staff Lew Rockwell. Jeffries is also the host of the weekly program "I Protest," which airs on the IHeartRadio network.

PREFACE TO THE 2021 EDITION

But a Constitution of Government once changed from Freedom, can never be restored. Liberty once lost is lost forever.

—*John Adams*

America, and the world, has changed dramatically since this book was first published in 2019. It could probably be argued that no other two year period in our history, with the possible exception of the end of the American Revolution and the beginning of the republic, or the final stages of the Civil War, Lincoln assassination, and beginning of Reconstruction, featured such significant and long-lasting change.

In 2020, the entire world was shut down in a matter of a few weeks. Not a single police officer was needed to enforce the lockdown, and no military troops were in the streets (yet). I believed that our leaders had finally overplayed their hand, and gone too far in banning spectator sports, movies, plays, and concerts, and closing churches and schools. But I was wrong. Most Americans adjusted to the increasingly Orwellian strictures as easily as they'd adjusted to the suspension of the writ of habeas corpus and death of nearly a million youngsters in the 1860s. Or the imprisonment of WWI protesters, with the Supreme Court justifying it by putting the "fire in a crowded theater" asterisk on free speech. Or the assassinations (and laughable explanations for them) of progressive leaders in the 1960s.

Or to the mass murder of American citizens at Waco. Or countless other examples I could cite. In other words, I shouldn't have been surprised.

While small businesses were forcibly closed, and millions thrown out of work, all the big chains were allowed to stay open. The "science" cited was contradicted by the Centers for Disease Control and Prevention (CDC) and the World Health Organization (WHO) themselves. And yet most Americans clung to their masks, dutifully followed "social distancing" guidelines, and the most extreme reported rule breakers to the police. Then the summer of 2020 featured mass protests across the country, with historical statues being torn down and monuments desecrated, while authorities stood idly by and let it happen. The coronavirus somehow wasn't deadly at *these* protests, we were told, but rallies for Donald Trump were "super spreaders." Buildings were burned, stores looted, and people died, yet the state controlled media kept justifying it and calling the protests "mostly peaceful." Then came the election. Voter fraud is nothing new, as readers of this book and its predecessor *Hidden History* know all too well, but the 2020 election was in a class of its own. A solid Trump lead in all the crucial swing states disappeared overnight, and Joe Biden won an implausibly large majority of all remaining votes. There were over a thousand sworn affidavits filed by post office employees and poll workers, testifying to witnessing clear electoral fraud. But the media, which openly cheered for Biden, kept declaring "there's no evidence!" Social media giants clamped down on all speculation about the election, and Donald Trump himself was "canceled" from Twitter. Putting an authoritarian exclamation point on the fiasco, every court Trump's defense team appealed to refused to even hear their case. The Supreme Court, with a supposed conservative majority thanks to Trump's three selections, wouldn't even look at the evidence.

Now we are confronting the possibility of a vaccine passport. Those who opt out from taking any COVID-19 vaccine face the prospect of second-class citizenship. Already, the virus and the lockdown have shattered familial relationships and ended long friendships, as happened during the Civil War. Getting the vaccine has become an emotional issue, especially for the elderly. At the very least, the unvaccinated will be shunned by polite society, including their own family members. At worst, they will be openly discriminated against by most employers and unable to attend cultural events. It is entirely possible we will see separate seating for those who haven't been vaccinated. Perhaps they'll be charged more for tickets, or their insurance premiums will rise due to the increased "risk" they represent. Is it possible we may see a new kind of apartheid, with the unvaccinated relegated to separate restrooms and water fountains?

With the wild overreaction to what was in reality mostly a meandering through the Capitol Building in Washington, DC on January 6, the authoritarianism has been ramped up to a record level. Everyone who attended Donald Trump's "Stop the Steal" rally that day is a potential "insurrectionist" or "seditionist" in the eyes of our draconian leaders. The censorship on social media and the burgeoning "cancel culture" have resulted in a diminishment of free speech that our Founders would be appalled by. The "commie" witch hunt of the 1950s was child's play compared to the persecution those labeled "White Supremacists" or "conspiracy theorists" now are subject to. At least five thousand US military troops remain stationed in our nation's capital, and we still haven't been provided any justification for it beyond the fact they may be there until the Fall of 2021.[1] Illinois Gov. J.B. Pritzker, upon activating five hundred members of the National Guard to join the forces in Washington, DC noted, "Ultimately, we must root out the dark forces of racism, white supremacy and disinformation that have created this moment, but until we do that, our extraordinary troops will deploy with honor."[2] Stationing troops in the streets of an American city, especially in a time of peace, is unconstitutional and contradicts everything this country was founded on. Even Lincoln could grasp at the rationale he was "countering the rebellion." To those who run America now, criticizing them and exposing their corruption is "disinformation," subject to punitive legal measures, or perhaps even military force.

The Bill of Rights is in grave danger at this moment in our history. The Democratic Party, which is in complete control of the machinery of government, the media, and the culture, doesn't remotely believe in free speech. The concept of "hate speech," which they tout constantly to justify censorship, contradicts any notion of free speech. Hate is a human emotion and in the eye of the beholder. One person's "hate" is another's justified outrage, much as one person's "terrorist" is another's "freedom fighter." "Hate speech" epitomizes identity politics, which relies on emotion, not reason. The Founders would have been mortified at this kind of abridgement of rights. They didn't risk their lives, their fortunes, and their sacred honor to fight the British throne, only to cede power to a far more insidious form of home-grown tyranny. It is only a matter of time until the First Amendment is officially altered, so that it reads something like "Congress shall make no law....abridging the freedom of speech, or in the press; or the right of people peaceably to assemble; except where the words and actions are motivated by hatred, racism, or disinformation," or abolished altogether. The saddest part of all this is that most Americans would unquestionably be in favor of something like that.

This book, despite its especially controversial nature, has received less negative attention than all my other works. The material is irrefutable; I quote the Abraham Lincolns and Franklin Roosevelts and use contemporary sources that have been largely "canceled" by the court historians. I have no particular theory, other than that history shows us repeatedly that we are being run by a vicious mixture of corruption and incompetence, which has gone largely unpunished in every era. Lincoln's tyranny has been whitewashed into a sacred legacy that one must obey as surely as follow the political correctness of our modern age. Lincoln, Woodrow Wilson,

Theodore Roosevelt, and FDR remain the highest ranked presidents by the court historians. The record shows that they should be considered the worst, with their administrations leaving behind a dangerous record that paved the way for today's authoritarian nightmare. Genuinely heroic figures from Thomas Jefferson to Andrew Jackson to Smedley Butler to Huey Long to Robert Taft to John F. Kennedy are either smeared, slandered, misrepresented, or ignored by the court historians and professional academics. Mahatma Gandhi's quote, "First they ignore you, then they laugh at you, then they fight you, then you win" used to resonate with me. It gave me inspiration. But the events of the past year have disillusioned me further. I frankly don't see any way we can win against this kind of tyrannical power, without more people at least recognizing that the tyrannical power exists.

In a just world, people at this point would be patting every veteran "conspiracy theorist" on the back, and telling them, "You were right—we should have listened to you!" But this isn't a just world, and COVID-19 has further demonized "conspiracy theorists." I lost many friends on social media, some of them big supporters of mine who wrote glowing reviews of my books and lauded me in interviews. I was called "dangerous" and worse for my open skepticism about the virus, and condemnation of the unconstitutional lockdown. I have been shocked to learn, after talking to so many whistleblowers of all kinds, just how infrequently even close family members supported them. Jim Garrison's wife left him, and it is unclear now how many of his five children still support his investigation into the assassination of John F. Kennedy. But Garrison left a sterling example to us all, especially those fighting great powers with little or no support; he summoned his ex-wife to his deathbed and remarried her, just so she would qualify to receive his pension. Now *that's* a profile in courage. Julian Assange, Edward Snowden, and Chelsea Manning remain unfree, because whistleblowers are not welcome where corruption rules. Everyone

I communicate with who has attempted to expose corruption in a business, at the local level, or about some national political scandal, is met with the same fierce opposition from a rotten and rigged system. And the public usually is against them, as well. After Edward Snowden revealed that the National Security Agency (NSA) had been illegally surveilling Americans, polls found that only 24 percent of respondents supported his actions.[3] After Julian Assange was arrested in April, 2019, 53 percent of Americans were in favor of him being extradited back to America, where he was certain to be prosecuted. Less than half (44 percent) had a favorable opinion of Wikileaks.[4]

The false flags delineated in this book, beginning with the Spanish-American War of 1898, and the demonization of foreign leaders as a prelude to senseless war, continue to be accepted without skepticism by the public. Russia's Vladimir Putin is the latest in what H.L. Mencken called "an endless series of hobgoblins," to frighten the American public into not only supporting endless conflicts abroad, but ignoring glaring domestic needs like the massive disparity of wealth and collapsing infrastructure. The same Left which advocated for détente with the Soviet Union at the height of its imperial expansionism, now lusts for war with a Russia that certainly seems less dangerous and more reasonable.

George Orwell warned about what could happen when authoritarianism gets out of control. We may not have a literal Big Brother figure, but in many ways, America is becoming Oceana. The "cancel culture" is very similar to the "unpersons" in Orwell's classic novel *1984*. "Hate speech" and "hate crime" are concepts that border perilously close to Orwell's Thoughtcrime. Newspeak and Doublethink are everywhere. And tossing inconvenient parts of history down the memory hole is essentially something every court historian and mainstream reporter does routinely.

Only by learning the truth about history can we understand the present and assure a better future. We didn't arrive at this sad state of affairs by happenstance. The signs were there for a very long time. Americans are woefully unknowledgeable about their own history. This is not exactly their fault; our school systems churn out McHistory, with the few topics examined at all done so through a superficial, politically correct lens. The court historians write terribly inaccurate but impressively-worded books and articles, which are targeted toward educated people interested in history. The problem is, as Thomas Jefferson observed, those who are misinformed about things know less than those who know nothing about them. The average Ivy Leaguer with a doctorate in History is about as misinformed as it gets. Jefferson also reminded us, "Educate and inform the whole mass of the people. They are the only sure reliance for the preservation of our liberty." This book, and my other historical work, is my very small attempt to educate people about our hidden and distorted history.

—Donald Jeffries, April 2021

FOREWORD

by Ron Paul

My late friend Murray Rothbard, founder of the modern libertarian movement, saw historical revisionism as one of the three pillars of libertarian scholarship, along with Austrian economics and natural rights theory. Revisionism is important because the "official" history promulgated by the court historians who dominate America's education system—from K-12 to graduate schools, as well as the mainstream publishing industry, the so-called "news media," and Hollywood—present a version of American history where far-sighted, selfless leaders expand federal power to benefit the people—especially those oppressed by greedy one-percenters and the capitalist system. Those who stood against these attempts to expand government are either smeared or ignored. The fact that Thomas Jefferson, whose first draft of the Declaration of Independence condemned slavery, is routinely smeared as a racist and a child molester by mainstream historians and journalists while Alexander Hamilton, father of America central banking, is a Broadway sensation tells us everything need to know about the biases of America's political, academic, and cultural elites.

Revisionism counters the official narrative with the truth about the real agendas and actions of those behind the transformation of America from a republic to a gigantic welfare-warfare state. Therefore revisionism—along with a knowledge of sound economics and an embrace of the non-aggression principle—is one of the keys to convincing individuals to embrace the ideas of liberty but actively work to bring about the free society.

Therefore, every lover of liberty should be thankful for Donald Jeffries's *Crimes and Cover-Ups in American Politics*. Jeffries presents hidden facts and inconvenient truths about many major events in American history from the revolution era to the early days of the Cold War. Jeffries also tells the unfriendly and oftentimes ugly truth about the establishment's heroes and rehabilitates many forgotten and/or smeared champions of liberty.

Jeffries goes where even many revisionists fear to tread—addressing the racist views of Abraham Lincoln, Ulysses S. Grant, and other northern leaders while exploring the anti-slavery views of Confederate leaders Robert E. Lee and Stonewall Jackson. Jeffries also challenges the myth that World War II was the "good war" by exposing how allied forces engaged in what—by the allies' own standards as applied at the Nuremberg trials—can only be called war crimes, oftentimes with full knowledge and support of top military commanders and leading government officials.

Jeffries also discusses how Franklin Roosevelt was so desperate to get popular support for US entry into the war that he ignored intelligence regarding the impending Japanese attack on Pearl Harbor. This is particularly important since the official versions of the Civil War and World War II are the founding myth of the American empire and its global crusade for democracy and human rights.

Pointing out how Lincoln violated civil liberties and the Constitution or how FDR deceived the public about the government's prior knowledge of, and desire for, Pearl Harbor does not make one "pro-Nazi" or "proslavery." These slurs are used by the war party to avoid debate of the merits of an interventionist foreign policy.

I do not agree with all of Jeffries's conclusions. For example, I am not anti-vaccine. However, I do believe the medical profession—as well as

Congress and the Food and Drug Administration (FDA)—has been captured by the pharmaceutical industry and needs to address the many legitimate health risks vaccines instead of silencing and smearing so-called "anti-vaxers." Government should never force an individual to get a vaccine against their will or force a child to be vaccinated against the parent's wishes.

Crimes and Cover-Ups in American Politics is an eye-opening look at the real history of how the political class, aided and abetted by special interests, has betrayed the principles of America's founding for their own power and gain. I can't imagine anyone reading this book and not wanting to join the ongoing peaceful revolution to restore individual liberty, free markets, and a foreign policy of peace, friendship, and trade with all.

INTRODUCTION

I'm not a conspiracy theorist—I'm a conspiracy analyst.

—Gore Vidal

S ince the publication of my book *Hidden History: An Expose of Modern Crimes, Conspiracies, and Cover-Ups in American Politics*, readers have often pointed out that the corruption didn't start on November 22, 1963. They are certainly correct, and that is the purpose of this book.

There is only so far we can go back and still record what happened at a particular moment in history with any real accuracy. The great library of Alexandria, which held an unimagined amount of knowledge, was tragically lost thousands of years ago. The Dark Ages, or the Middle Ages from the collapse of the Roman Empire until the fourteenth century Italian Renaissance, left comparatively little for historians to sift through, especially alternative historians who understand the corrupt reality of politics. When Johannes Gutenberg introduced the printing press in 1440, only about 30 percent of adult Europeans were literate. Things had improved by the time the US Constitution was signed in 1787, but still less than 60 percent of adults in America could read. History has always been written by the victors, and for a very long time it was consumed by a limited audience of adults who were able to read and understand it.

According to Edward Gibbon, author of *The Decline and Fall of the Roman Empire*, "History is indeed little more than the register of the crimes, follies and misfortunes of mankind." Napoleon Bonaparte declared, "What is history but a fable agreed upon?" Leo Tolstoy said, "History would be a wonderful thing, if only it were true." "History will be kind to me," Winston Churchill quipped, "for I intend to write it." Henry Ford called history "bunk." Mark Twain said, "The very ink with which history is written is merely fluid prejudice." Edward Bernays, certainly a conspirator if ever there was one, acknowledged that "The conscious and intelligent manipulation of the organized habits and opinions of the public . . . this unseen mechanism of society constitute an invisible government which is the true ruling power of our country." British Prime Minister Benjamin Disraeli famously disclosed, "For you see, the world is governed by very different personages from what is imagined by those who are not behind the scenes." US Supreme Court Justice Felix Frankfurter echoed these sentiments with "The real rulers in Washington are invisible and exercise power from behind the scenes." Another person who certainly should have known, President Woodrow Wilson, once said, "There is a power so organized, so subtle, so complete, and so pervasive, that they had better not speak above their breath when they speak in condemnation of it." Theodore Roosevelt, yet another knowledgeable insider, described a nearly identical phenomenon: "Behind the ostensible government sits enthroned an invisible government owing no allegiance and acknowledging no responsibility to the people." Teddy's cousin Franklin Roosevelt would admit, "The real truth of the matter is, as you and I know, that a financial element in the large centers has owned the government of the US since the days of Andrew Jackson." Even Bill Clinton reported, "There's a government inside the government, and I don't control it."

But despite even those at the pinnacle of power referencing these shadowy, unseen forces behind the scenes, Americans are by and large reluctant to confront this frightening, ugly reality. As Charles Mackay put it, in his absorbing 1841 book *Extraordinary Popular Delusions and the Madness of Crowds*, "Men, it has been well said, think in herds." As long ago as the 1500s, Sir Thomas More declared, "Everywhere do I perceive a certain conspiracy of rich men seeking their own advantage under that name and pretext of commonwealth." In the 1700s, Sir William Pitt acknowledged, "There is something behind the Throne greater than the King himself."

There are basically two views of history. Well-known establishment historian Robert Dallek set forth the standard view concisely in the following statement: "George Washington sets the nation on its democratic path. Abraham Lincoln preserves it. Franklin Roosevelt sees the nation through depression and war." That is conventional history in a nutshell: supposedly great, heroic figures triumphing over random forces and cardboard, caricatured villains. Certainly that's an attractive, simplistic approach that appeals to those who are reluctant to think outside the boundaries. On the other hand, as maverick Libertarian Murray Rothbard once described it, some of us prefer to study *"who* our rulers are, of how their political and economic interests interlock." Or, in the words of author Gary Allen, "We believe the picture painters of the mass media are artfully creating landscapes for us which deliberately hide the real picture." Thomas Jefferson once said that people who didn't read the newspapers of his day knew more than those who did. In a similar vein, it might be said that those who get their historical information from the History Channel, or the most widely-promoted historians, are farther from the truth than those who aren't interested in history at all. Is it better to be uninformed or misinformed?

David Aaronovitch's book *Voodoo Histories: The Role of the Conspiracy Theory in Shaping Modern History* typifies the mindset of establishment historians. Aaronovitch didn't set out to sift through data, conduct independent research, or honestly investigate anything. As a January 30, 2010 NPR piece described it, Aaronovitch was incensed when a coworker expressed doubts that we had really landed on the moon, and "he wasn't prepared with evidence to counter his co-worker's claim." Spurred on, Aaronovitch "spent six years looking into the details behind top conspiracy theories such as the faked Apollo moon landing and has come out with a new book to forensically debunk them." Aaronovitch was apparently incredulous that educated people can believe "perfectly ridiculous things." Aaronovitch, like every other court historian, attributes any questioning of official accounts concerning important events to "conspiracy theories." Robert C. Williams, in his *The Historian's Toolbox: A Student's Guide to the Theory and Craft of History*, advised his impressionable young readers, "Conspiracy theories are . . . usually based on highly selective and sometimes discredited evidence. You should avoid assuming a conspiracy theory unless you have hard evidence to back it up." Williams revealed the breadth of his ignorance and the extent to which he is devoted to "evidence" by recommending Gerald Posner's thoroughly discredited lone-assassin manifesto *Case Closed* as a "good introduction" to the assassination of John F. Kennedy. In the mind of the court historian, there is no room for skepticism, unless it is directed at the skeptics themselves. All doubt and skepticism of authority are transformed into easily demonized "conspiracy theories," and all those who question the predominant view are derided as "conspiracy theorists"—whether warranted or not. That's the term I'll use in this book for those who challenge the accepted norm, but as I've told interviewers numerous times, if you can find a "theory" in anything I write, please let me know what that theory is.

The anti-conspiracy mindset is strong in those who have attained success of any kind in our civilization. The late Steve Jobs, who certainly benefited greatly from the established order, once said, "When you're young, you look at television and think, there's a conspiracy. The networks have conspired to dumb us down. But when you get a little older, you realize that's not true. The networks are in business to give people exactly what they want." Tell that to Jesse Ventura, whose *Conspiracy Theory* television show was the highest-rated program TruTV ever had. They still canceled Ventura's show, which contradicts the popular notion that it's all about the ratings, or all about the profits.

Clearly, there are other, more important agendas to consider—at least for those with a public platform. Establishment journalist Chris Matthews reacted to questions about President Obama's birth by exclaiming, "It's almost like an addiction to being afraid." His supposed ideological opponent, Bill O'Reilly, countered doubts about the official Boston Bombing narrative with, "I think that this internet stuff, with this access people have, has made more crazy people, because people who were borderline crazy now go in there and become crazy." Despite O'Reilly's overt anti-conspiracy bias (which included authoring the monstrously inaccurate recent book *Killing Kennedy*), President Obama would still blast O'Reilly and Fox News for pushing "conspiracy theories" in their reporting on Benghazi and other subjects. It was reminiscent of Obama's ideological opponent, his immediate presidential predecessor George W. Bush, who angrily lashed out at 9/11 "Truthers" by saying, "Let us never tolerate outrageous conspiracy theories concerning the attacks of September 11th; malicious lies that attempt to shift the blame away from the terrorists, themselves, away from the guilty." Bush would summarize the new draconian, post-9/11 chic by also warning, "Either you are with us, or you are with the terrorists." This was very similar to the slogan used against the hippies (and Bush's generation overall): "America—love it or leave it." All this is to show that there is a disconcerting lack of tolerance for dissent, especially in wartime, in a country founded upon freedom of speech.

"Daring" comedian Doug Stanhope had this to say on the subject: "I love conspiracy theories. . . . You know it's all just hype and garbage . . . it's fun entertainment." "Controversial" comedian Bill Maher is, shockingly enough, dismissive of "conspiracy theorists," and directs curt rebuttals to them such as, "Come on, nutjobs, get your bullshit straight." Comedian turned "conservative" journalist Dennis Miller once declared, "The biggest conspiracy has always been the fact that there is no conspiracy. Nobody's out to get you." Conservative columnist Charles Krauthammer sounded a very familiar theme when he explained, "Whenever you're faced with an explanation of what's going on in Washington, the choice between incompetence and conspiracy, always choose incompetence." Liberal Jeff Greenfield echoed this with his quote, "More things happen in politics by accident or exhaustion than happen by conspiracy." One of our greatest modern conspirators, Zbigniew Brzezinski, mimicked this oft-repeated response with, "History is much more the product of chaos than conspiracy." I can't calculate the number of journalists and historians I've heard react to any doubts about any official historical narrative with, "you couldn't get all those people to stay quiet," and/or "you can't keep a secret in Washington." Honest researchers understand that a great number of people have indeed attempted to expose official crime and corruption. They usually can't find anyone interested in hearing their story, outside of those dreaded "conspiracy theorists." While our leaders are undeniably incompetent, they are also mired in perpetual corruption and regularly conspire against the interests of the general public. Power doesn't come with the trappings of intelligence, or even competence. Conspirators can be powerful without being rocket scientists.

Conspiracies in general have become such a big topic that the mainstream media can't ignore them any longer. Their disinformation has grown more polished, but it remains totally predictable disinformation. A great example of this is the television show *Brad Meltzer's Decoded*. In each episode, bestselling author Meltzer's team of "investigators" confronts a particular topic, a specific "conspiracy theory." To no educated observer's surprise, the "investigators" always find little evidence to support *any* conspiracy. Meltzer admitted, "I think if you blame everything on the government, you're not just wrong, you're being reckless. It's as silly as blaming everything on the Freemasons, or the Illuminati, or insert-bad-guy-here." The show *Mythbusters* essentially debunks the conspiratorial "myths" that counter establishment history. It would more accurately be titled "Conspiracy Busters." *Penn & Teller: Bullshit* serves a similar purpose. Again, we see celebrities advertised as "daring" or "anti-establishment," who just happen to support the official accounts of 9/11, the JFK assassination, etc.

Online, Snopes is the establishment's favorite "debunking" site. Snopes has a clear agenda, as well as a totally undeserved reputation for accuracy within the establishment. It is regularly cited as an infallible source by the likes of CNN and MSNBC, while *National Review* calls it "indispensable." Republican senator Jon Kyl, erstwhile "opponent" of Barack Obama, in dismissing the concerns of "birthers," wrote the following to a constituent: "Rumors pertaining to (Obama's) citizenship status have been circulating on the internet, and this information has been debunked by Snopes.com."[1] At best, Snopes is a terribly biased site, getting their information from surfing the internet and trusting the sources they choose to trust. At worst, they are being funded by someone or something powerful for nefarious purposes. If Snopes was promoting "conspiracy theories," or even discovering that any of them have the slightest amount of validity, you can bet that they wouldn't be considered "trustworthy" and would instead be ridiculed by the same establishment voices who are singing their praises.

I prefer the perspective espoused by the intriguing iconoclast Charles Fort, who wrote, "The proper authority saw to it that the proper belief should be induced, and the people behaved properly." The independent-minded Gore Vidal summed things up well: "I say, they [those at the top] don't have to conspire. . . . They all tend to think quite alike, otherwise they would not be in those jobs." That's it in a nutshell; while the names and faces change, those in charge keep promoting the next generation of like-minded leaders.

It's crucial for any people to accurately know their history. As George Orwell wrote, in 1984, "Who controls the past controls the future: who controls the present controls the past." And the philosopher George Santayana reminded us, in words that many repeat but few seem to heed: "Those who do not remember the past are condemned to repeat it."

Americans, like people all over the world, are woefully uninformed about history. In my earlier book, I covered what I consider to be the all-important Baby Boomer-era of the past fifty years. By doing what the court historians, tenured professors, and professional journalists don't—by assessing events without a modern bias and a healthy skepticism towards authority—we can easily decipher a pattern of self-serving, rather obvious disinformation. We can learn to recognize that we've been lied to. To paraphrase Victor Lasky, one of the countless liberals and conservatives who despised John F. Kennedy, it didn't start with the JFK assassination.

CHAPTER ONE

THE BIRTH OF THE REPUBLIC

Those that can give up essential liberty to purchase a little temporary
safety, deserve neither liberty nor safety.

—Benjamin Franklin

The American Independence movement was not born in Philadelphia's Independence Hall, in that oppressively hot summer of 1776. It wasn't born when silversmith Paul Revere rode through the streets of Lexington and Concord, warning "The British are coming!" It actually was born a decade earlier, when bands of anti-tax activists loosely referred to as the Sons of Liberty began holding clandestine meetings up and down the east coast, often in taverns run by sympathetic owners. Their efforts are most dramatically remembered today for 1773's Boston Tea Party.

The early leaders of the Sons of Liberty were men like Samuel Adams, John's less-remembered second cousin. John Hancock was one of the wealthiest men in America, with much of his wealth apparently accrued through smuggling. For quite a long time, Hancock and Adams were forgotten figures in American history; as the historian Alfred Young noted, "Boston celebrated only one hero in the half-century after the Revolution:

George Washington." John Adams complained that his cousin and Hancock had been "almost buried in oblivion." Young attributed the tearing down of Hancock's Beacon Hill home in 1863 to the state's leaders being "not comfortable with a rich man who pledged his fortune to the cause of revolution."[1]

If Hancock and Adams were forgotten figures for decades, Dr. Joseph Warren was a figurative historical MIA. Warren played a prominent role in the Patriot organizations of Boston, and was responsible for directing Paul Revere and William Dawes on their legendary night ride. No armchair warrior, Warren participated in the battles of Lexington and Concord, and died at Bunker Hill on June 17, 1775, at only thirty-four years old. Another little-recalled figure is *Boston Gazette* publisher Benjamin Edes, whose newspaper was one of the loudest voices for independence in the colonies. Isaac Sears, no relation to the retail store chain, was a leading figure in the often-violent patriotic mobs of New York. John Lamb was another Sons of Liberty figure who walked the walk, serving with distinction as a military officer during the War for Independence. Eventually fired by President John Adams, he died in poverty in 1800.

James Otis coined the phrase "taxation without representation is tyranny," and was an early, important figure in the patriotic movement. John Adams was only one of those who recognized his greatness, claiming he was "a flame of fire." Otis's early writings protesting British actions later would prompt Adams to say, "I have never known a man . . . who suffered so much, never one whose service for any 10 years of his life were so important and essential to the cause of his country as those of Mr. Otis from 1760 to 1770." His works like *The Rights of the British Colonies* influenced his friend Thomas Paine, who would pen the crucial pamphlet *Common Sense.* Injured when a British tax collector hit him in the head, Otis suffered mental problems for the rest of this life, and died at only fifty-eight when he was struck by lightning while standing in a friend's doorway, purportedly after expressing a wish to die in just that manner.

It is not generally publicized that another early leader in the Sons of Liberty was merchant Benedict Arnold, later to become a reviled figure whose name is synonymous with treason. Patrick Henry was the most prominent voice of the patriot cause, and his "Give me liberty, or give me death" speech still resounds with audiences today. In conjunction with Thomas Jefferson and Richard Henry Lee, he started up Virginia's own Committee of Correspondence, the name given to groups organized by patriots to communicate with each other in the immediate years before the Revolutionary War. Henry was a vocal opponent of the Constitution, which supplanted the original Articles of Confederation. He refused to attend the Constitutional Convention of 1787, remarking that he "smelt a rat in Philadelphia." Alarmed that the Constitution granted too much power to the federal government, he was instrumental in getting the Bill of Rights enacted.

The cultural overlords who drive public opinion in America have never been fond of the greatest historical figures this nation ever produced. As a child in the 1960s, I remember how our schools still passed on the largely mythical anecdotes about George Washington chopping down a cherry tree and then being unable to lie about it, or throwing a coin across the Potomac River. But films and television shows largely ignored the Father of our Country, and all the other Founders, with astonishing openness. Filmmakers like Michael Moore scrutinize the Founding Fathers by modern-day standards, and label them as forgettable "racists." Young children have been subjected to this same propaganda, with the most extreme example being a pamphlet created by the Nation of Islam depicting the Founders as racists, distributed by at least one Tennessee elementary school.[2] A similar project in an Oklahoma school system, termed "flocabulary," involved teaching "at risk" students using rap music, but it was scrapped after a huge controversy erupted over one of the lessons referring to the Founding Fathers as "old dead white men."

There has never been a full-length motion picture devoted to the life of Washington, or Thomas Jefferson, or Benjamin Franklin, or any other legendary figure from the revolutionary era, with one exception: the 1931 biopic of the bankers' favorite Founding Father, Alexander Hamilton. This is decidedly odd, considering that during the Golden Age of film, Hollywood lavished big-budget attention on the likes of Henry the Eighth, Queen Elizabeth, Benjamin Disraeli, Napoleon, Marie Antoinette, Andrew Johnson, Annie Oakley, Buffalo Bill, Woodrow Wilson, and the mistress of Andrew Jackson. This was during a conservative, highly patriotic period in our history, with a plethora of World War II films produced, almost as soon as America entered the conflict. Lincoln and the Civil War weren't exactly shunned either. Where was the *Gone With the Wind* of the War for Independence? It's obvious the powers that be are reluctant to even discuss the revolutionary era, because to do so is to speak favorably of anti-government movements, tax protests, and citizens taking up arms to revolt. It's not the Founders themselves; it's what they represented that remains so threatening to those who misrule us.

THE SLANDERING OF JEFFERSON

In some ways, Thomas Jefferson invented racism in America.

—Paul Finkelman, *Thomas Jefferson and Antislavery: The Myth Goes On*

In recent years, there has been an intense campaign to diminish the reputations of the Founding Fathers, with a special emphasis on Thomas Jefferson. Jefferson was probably the most talented, impressive statesman that this country has ever seen. As John F. Kennedy remarked, during an April 29, 1962 state dinner honoring Nobel Prize winners, "I think this is the most extraordinary collection of talent, of human knowledge, that has ever been gathered together at the White House, with the possible exception of when Thomas Jefferson dined alone." Jefferson was an outstanding writer, politician, inventor, and farmer. His Declaration of Independence will be remembered long after most American leaders, and all of his critics, have been forgotten. Despite the fact that Jefferson abhorred slavery, and in fact his original draft of the Declaration included a strong condemnation of it as "an assemblage of horrors," he is increasingly pictured as an *advocate* of human bondage. An October 2012 article in *Smithsonian* magazine, titled "The Dark Side of Thomas Jefferson," typified this revisionist view. Irish historian and politician Conor Cruise O'Brien wrote an earlier hit piece in the October 1996 issue of *The Atlantic*, headlined "Thomas Jefferson: Radical and Racist," which argued, "His flaws are beyond redemption. The sound you hear is the crashing of a reputation."

The Thomas Jefferson-Sally Hemings controversy began in 1802. His former ally, journalist James Callender, felt spurned by Jefferson, whom he believed owed him political favors following his work as a propagandist against John Adams in the highly contentious 1800 election. In retaliation, Callender published a series of articles alleging that Jefferson had been having a long-term affair with one of his slaves, Sally Hemings.[3] Fawn Brodie revived this long-forgotten rumor in her 1974 "psychobiography" *Thomas Jefferson: An Intimate History*. The 1998 DNA tests, which found a match between one of the Hemings's descendants and the Jefferson family line, seemed, on the surface, to suggest that there had been some kind of relationship there. Remarkably, the Thomas Jefferson Memorial Foundation, which owns and operates Jefferson's Monticello home, unquestioningly bought these arguments and declared, in a January 2000 report, that there was a "high probability" that Jefferson fathered one of Hemings's children, and mostly likely all of them.

What was not reported by a media anxious to discredit Jefferson was the fact that a full-spectrum DNA test had not been performed. The results could only demonstrate that one of the estimated twenty-five male Jefferson family members living at the time in Virginia had fathered one of Hemings's children. Just as ignored was the fact that these same ballyhooed tests disproved what was considered the strongest bit of oral tradition, from a branch of Hemings's family that could not be matched with Jefferson family DNA. Despite the lack of specific results of the tests—which couldn't conclusively identify Thomas Jefferson or any other member of the family as the father of a Hemings child—the "scientific" journal announcing the results trumpeted them with the headline, "Jefferson fathered slave's last child." The foundation that is allegedly devoted to honoring Jefferson's legacy ignored, and continues to ignore, any evidence which contradicts the notion of an affair between the Founding Father and Hemings. The foundation even suppressed a minority dissent to the report. A group of Jeffersonian scholars formed the Thomas Jefferson Heritage Society, Inc. and wrote a rebuttal to the report, in which they stated there was "serious skepticism about the charge to a conviction that it is almost certainly false." By one of those miraculous coincidences, the misleading conclusions of the DNA tests were published shortly before the House voted to impeach President Bill Clinton, and played nicely into the hands of impeachment opponents, who had maintained that Clinton's indiscretions were nothing new historically.

Despite the fact that DNA tests proved conclusively that Jefferson could not have been the father of the child Sally Hemings bore at sixteen, he continues to be vilified as a "child rapist." Typical of the dishonest mainstream media coverage surrounding this issue was an October 7, 2015 story in the *Columbia Missourian*. The story recounted demonstrations at Missouri University, including demands to have a statue of Jefferson removed from the campus. The newspaper unquestioningly quoted graduate student Maxwell Little thusly: "Little said Jefferson was also a slave owner and rapist of a 16-year-old slave named Sally

Hemings." Students had posted sticky notes all over Jefferson's statue, with epithets like "racist," "rapist," "misogynist," and "slave owner." A petition on change.org had failed to get the expected number of signatures, but seniors Aliyah Sulaiman and Bryant Hill created a Twitter campaign to "engage people in critical conversation" about racism and sexual assault.[4] The fact that Jefferson is being routinely portrayed now as a "rapist" as well as a "racist" was hammered home in this inflammatory and wildly inaccurate statement from student Reuben Faloughi: "Every day that it sits on campus, students are affected. . . . We talk about wanting to fix the culture of sexual violence and racism on campus, but that sits here." Lin-Manuel Miranda's hit 2015 Broadway musical *Hamilton*, lovingly named for the bankers' favorite Founding Father, depicts his enemy Jefferson as a racist villain. This kind of refusal to confront the emotional misinformation about Jefferson being promulgated everywhere resulted in CNN anchor Ashley Banfield exclaiming, "There is a monument to him in the capital city of the United States. No one ever asks for that to come down." Banfield's proposal was based exclusively upon the fact that, of course, Jefferson owned slaves. Fellow anchor Don Lemon chimed in, "There may come a day when we want to rethink Jefferson."[5] And the mainstream media continued to disseminate disinformation, inferring that Jefferson had indeed raped an underage girl, with the following statement: "Jefferson owned slaves and had children with one of them, Sally Hemings, who is believed to have been a teenager when she first gave birth."[6] Notice also the matter-of-fact reportage of "had children with one of them," when in fact that has not been proven. The DNA tests demonstrated that Jefferson could only possibly have been the father of one of Hemings's children, and he was only one of many potential candidates.[7]

An October 4, 2012 *Slate* magazine article was titled "Founding Fathers Fetish." As a November 2002 article by Stephen Ambrose in

Smithsonian Magazine bluntly put it, in dismissing Thomas Jefferson, "He was a racist." High-profile historian Eric Foner typifies the establishment's view of the Founders, which judges them primarily through the prism of slavery. In a January 4, 1987 op-ed in the *New York Times*, Foner expressed admiration for Benjamin Franklin and Alexander Hamilton, perhaps the least-liberty-minded Founding Father, referring to them both as "abolitionists." Foner, like most modern historians, concentrated his vitriol on Jefferson, writing that he "all his life owned slaves, bought and sold them like any other planter, and believed them innately inferior." Foner's admiration of Abraham Lincoln, however, has not been affected by Honest Abe's own racist, white supremacist statements, uttered during the presidential debates with Stephen Douglas and on other occasions. Interestingly, Gettysburg College professor Allen C. Guelzo claimed that Abraham Lincoln "hated Thomas Jefferson," directly quoting Lincoln's longtime law partner William Henry Herndon as his source, in a July 3, 2015 op-ed piece in the *New York Times.* The mainstream media's flagship newspaper had referred to Jefferson as "the Monster of Monticello" in a 2012 book review of Henry Wiencek's predictably negative portrayal of Jefferson in his *Master of the Mountain: Thomas Jefferson and his Slaves.*

Establishment historians have painted a new, unflattering portrait of Jefferson as a hypocritical racist, perhaps even a rapist and a pedophile, which even the foundation devoted to his memory supports. In reality, Jefferson was the quintessential classic liberal, and one of the strongest voices in America *against* slavery. The following bold charge was deleted from the Declaration of Independence: "He [King George] has waged cruel war against human nature itself, violating its most sacred right of life and liberty in the persons of a distant people who never offended him, captivating & carrying them into slavery in another hemisphere, or to incur miserable death in their transportation thither." Was there any other man alive in 1776 who could have or would have issued a stronger condemnation of the slave trade? It is true that Jefferson, unlike George Washington, didn't free his slaves upon his death. However, this was largely out of concern for their welfare. He recognized how difficult it was going to be for these mostly illiterate former slaves to enter mainstream society. Like many others, he wanted them to be assimilated gradually, and advocated that all born into slavery after a specific date would be declared free, followed by an absolute abolition. Like many whites of his time (and future historical icon Abraham Lincoln), he thought that blacks should eventually be colonized out of the country.

The Democratic Party in Connecticut recently caved in to political correctness, and vowed to rename its annual Jefferson Jackson Bailey fundraising dinner. The party voted unanimously to remove the names of Thomas Jefferson and Andrew Jackson, in light of their ties to slavery. "I see it as the right thing to do," said state party chairman Nick Balletto. NAACP Connecticut chapter head Scot X. Esdaile lauded "the symbolic first step and striving to right the wrongs of the past." Robert Turner, a law professor at the University of Virginia, which was founded by Jefferson, was aghast. "It is a sad and short-sighted decision based upon tragic ignorance," Turner declared. In referencing the Thirteenth Amendment to the Constitution, which abolished slavery, Turner noted, "The authors of that amendment purposely chose language drafted by Jefferson in an unsuccessful effort to outlaw slavery in the Northwest Territories as a means of honoring Jefferson's struggle against slavery. . . . If (Democrats) understood Jefferson's lifelong opposition to slavery, they would have reached a different conclusion." Exemplifying the confused nature of our civilization, the party left untouched the name of John Bailey, who was a powerful but historically insignificant Democratic Party figure behind the scenes in the 1960s.[8]

Why is so much vitriol reserved for Thomas Jefferson, when other presidents like Washington, James Madison, and James Monroe were slave owners as well? Madison, especially, receives increasingly positive coverage from mainstream historians and I am aware of no protest movements against his name or image. In its winter 2011 issue, the *Journal of the Abraham Lincoln Association* would ludicrously compare Jefferson and Jackson to "intolerant" Supreme Court Justices Antonin Scalia and Clarence Thomas.

While the attacks on Jefferson in particular have really heated up in recent years, criticism of the Founding Fathers is nothing new. Nineteenth-century abolitionist leader William Lloyd Garrison denigrated the Constitution as "a covenant with death and an agreement with hell," and publicly burned a copy to emphasize his point. Historian John P. Diggins maintained that Abraham Lincoln had "an acute estrangement" from the Founding Fathers. *The Atlantic* argued that we are too deferential to the Founding Fathers in a September 2003 article titled "Founders Chic." Incredibly, the author of the piece, H. W. Brands, claimed that the Founding Fathers "were no smarter than the best their country can offer now."

Obviously, slavery was an unfortunate reality of the revolutionary era and remained an integral part of American life until the end of the Civil War. It was an ugly component of most every culture on earth, not just the United States, and if our leaders are to be judged on this issue alone, then nearly all pre-1865 politicians should be given failing marks and consigned to the dustbin of history. Is this really an intellectually honest way to assess the past? I'm sure all those "dead white males" were homophobic as well, would have insisted that men and women were different, and would have had little tolerance for transgender issues. We need to recognize them as the products of their times. But beyond that, the principles and issues they fought for are timeless, and trump any kind of political correctness. But instead, we seem to be on the verge of declaring history itself racist.

Speaking of slavery, why don't we hear any public castigation of India, which *still has* an estimated 14 million people enslaved? The 1860 census recorded fewer than 4 million slaves in America by contrast. Slavery still exists in China, and Pakistan, and Nigeria, and Ethiopia, and Russia, and Thailand, and the "Democratic Republic" of Congo. There remain some 40 million slaves around the world.[9] Instead of constantly harping on long-eradicated slavery in America, why aren't any "activists" demanding that countries which *still have* human slaves be picketed? Why aren't any Hollywood "liberals" making movies about present-day slaves? Instead, they actually celebrate India's "Bollywood." Most incredibly of all, the first black president of the United States, Barack Obama, vetoed a Senate amendment to the odious Trans Pacific Partnership trade deal, which would have made it difficult for countries engaging in human slavery to be a part of the TPP, essentially giving his stamp of approval to modern-day human slavery.[10] And in the United States, the prevalence of sex and human trafficking caused the FBI to admit, "It's sad but true: here in this country, people are being bought, sold, and smuggled like modern-day slaves." An estimated 100,000 child sex slaves are forced into prostitution in the US each year. Human trafficking has become a $150 billion industry.[11] But the truly outrageous thing, which we must never forget, is that Thomas Jefferson had slaves two hundred years ago.

SACRIFICES OF THE FOUNDERS

We've all read about how the Founding Fathers swore on their lives, their fortunes, and their sacred honor when they signed the Declaration of Independence. These were many of the wealthiest men of their time, and it is impossible to imagine a gaggle of present-day billionaires risking a single stock option, let alone their very existence, for the cause of human liberty. Although the legend attributing his act to a desire for King George to be able to read it without his spectacles is probably apocryphal, John Hancock's audacious boldness in signing his name in huge letters exemplified the spirit of that generation. Fifty-six men signed the Declaration of Independence in the summer of 1776. Few Americans realize the awful price that many of them wound up paying.

Seventeen of those who signed the Declaration lost everything they owned. Nine of these men lost their lives in the conflict. Rhode Island's William Ellery's estate was burned to the ground during the war. William Floyd of New York suffered the same fate. Fellow New Yorker Francis Lewis saw his estates destroyed by fire as well, and he was imprisoned and died during his incarceration. One of the richest of all those who signed, William Livingston, died impoverished a few years after the war. John Hart of New Jersey risked not only his fortune, but his family ties. His wife was dying as he signed the Declaration, and he was forced to flee from the British when he headed home to say goodbye. He never saw his thirteen children again and died in 1779. New Jersey judge Richard Stockton was another British prisoner, and he too died a pauper. Wealthy banker Robert Morris gave away his fortune in an effort to finance the revolution. He also died penniless. Imagine any banker doing something remotely like that today. Virginia's Thomas Nelson, in a perhaps implausible anecdote, allegedly turned a cannon on his own home, which had become General Cornwallis's headquarters, and destroyed it. He, like so many of the others, died in poverty. South Carolina's Thomas Lynch, along with his wife, simply disappeared at sea.[12]

While patriotic themes have been drummed home to Americans by their government for a very long time, this genuinely inspiring example of self-sacrifice gets short shrift in our schools and our media. It also demonstrates how the wealthiest among us can act like noble statesmen. Our present-day, narcissistic One Percent could learn a great deal from them.

BENJAMIN FRANKLIN

Evil doth not exist.

—Benjamin Franklin

Like Thomas Jefferson, Benjamin Franklin was a brilliant man of many diverse talents. He discovered electricity, and his numerous inventions include bifocal lenses, the lightning rod, flippers for swimming, and the Franklin stove. His *Poor Richard's Almanack* made him famous and left behind a slew of quotations like "A penny saved is a penny earned," which are still widely remembered today. However, in addition to being the powerful Grand Master of Masons of Pennsylvania, Franklin was also an unrepentant libertine and a member of the notorious Hellfire Club, the nickname given the Medmenham Monks, a secret society for the elite that was located far below the ground under England's Medmenham Abbey. Rumors at the time and those routinely dismissed as "conspiracy theorists" to this day insist that the club engaged in orgies and occult rituals, including sacrifices, in these underground caverns. The club's founder, Francis Dashwood, was described by one historian as having "far exceeded in licentiousness of conduct any model exhibited since Charles II."[13] Some think that forerunners of modern black masses were held there. During the orgies, prostitutes were allegedly dressed blasphemously as nuns. These profane "monks" were evidently the first to use the satanic credo "Do what thou wilt," which Aleister Crowley would later adopt as his own. Franklin's personal religious beliefs were best expressed when he declared, "I have found Christian dogma unintelligible. Early in life, I absented myself from Christian assemblies." Franklin, like some other Founding Fathers, was a Deist, or someone who believed that God created the universe and then basically abandoned it.

It has become accepted that Franklin, despite his bald, portly, grandfatherly appearance, was a ravenous womanizer. He was quite open about it, once writing a letter to a friend titled "Advice to a Young Man on the Choice of a Mistress" and attempting to seduce a married woman forty years his junior while serving as United States commissioner in France. As Albert Henry Smyth remarked, in a 1907 biography of Franklin, "the taint of an irredeemable vulgarity is upon much of this man." He had at least one acknowledged illegitimate son, the little boy who helped him fly the kite during his celebrated electricity experiment. William Franklin would grow up to become the colonial governor of New Jersey and a steadfast loyalist to England. In 1782, he left America for Britain, never to return home. The war caused an irreparable split between father and son; William tried to reconcile with his father, but Ben Franklin refused to forgive his son. When Franklin died he left practically none of his substantial fortune to William, stating in an addendum to his will that "The part he acted against me in the late War . . . will account for my leaving him no more of an Estate he endeavored to deprive me of." A crushed William reacted by calling this a "bitter injustice."

Ignoring his own timeless advice, Franklin was an extravagant personality who spent money on every luxury imaginable, especially when he was in London. His privileged lifestyle came courtesy of the taxpayers, as he tended to charge everything to the people of Pennsylvania.[14] Although Franklin was married for some forty-four years to Deborah Read, it seems to have been largely one of convenience; he was away from home for nearly half that time, and when she died in 1774, they hadn't seen each other for ten years. Like one of the present era's most visible womanizers, Bill Clinton, Franklin is somehow still considered by many to be an early-day feminist. As Jill K. Conway explained, in the spring 1974 *History of Education Quarterly*, "Franklin was willing to abandon the Christian view of the female—as a lesser creation marked by greater impulsiveness and less able to use reason in control of the emotions than men—and to put in its place a view of the female as a rational being engaged in the pursuit of happiness." One of Franklin's more clever pickup lines was said to be, "Care to join me in the pursuit of happiness?"

Ben Franklin made the headlines again on February 11, 1998, when it was reported in the *London Sunday Times* and other newspapers that "Workmen have dug up the remains of ten bodies hidden beneath the former London home of Benjamin Franklin, the founding father of American Independence." The remains of four adults and six children were discovered during the restoration of Franklin's old home at 36 Craven Street, close to Trafalgar Square. The story detailed, "Researchers believe that there could be more bodies buried beneath the basement kitchens." The bones were estimated to be around two hundred years old, and corresponded to the time period when Franklin was living at the house. Most showed signs of having been dissected or cut, and one skull "has been drilled with several holes." Westminster coroner Paul Knapman stated, "One cannot totally discount the possibility of a crime. There is still a possibility that I may have to hold an inquest."

As might be anticipated, a convenient culprit was found, and determined to be one William Hewson, a fellow of the Royal Society (as was Franklin), who was associated with one of the founders of British surgery. Supposedly, Hewson lived in the basement of the home, and in the authoritative words of Dr. Knapman, "It is most likely that these are anatomical specimens that Dr. Hewson disposed of in his own house." One Brian Owen Smith was quoted as saying, "The discovery represents an important insight into very exciting years of medical history." Or, to express an alternative perspective, does it perhaps connect Benjamin Franklin to murder and/or human sacrifice? Hilaire Dubourcq, spokesman for the Friends of Benjamin Franklin House, provided a desperate excuse for an allegation no mainstream journalist or public figure was about to make, saying, "It is possible that he has an alibi. It seems likely that he actually let Dr. Hewson have use of the whole house for his school. . . . He did not necessarily know what was happening below stairs in the house during his absence." We learn here that Dr. Hewson died an unnatural death at the early age of thirty-four, when "He accidentally cut himself while dissecting a putrid body, contracted septicemia and died in 1774."

The mainstream media was quick to accept this innocent official narrative, illustrated by *The Guardian's* August 11, 2003 report that "The most plausible explanation is not mass murder, but an anatomy school run by Benjamin Franklin's young friend and protégé." In one of the few updates on the case, *Smithsonian* magazine reported, in an October 3, 2013 article, that the search had actually turned up "1200 pieces of bone from at least 15 people." So the story is being presented as one in which the unfortunate Hewson, before dying a premature death, relied on the "resurrection men" of the day—grave robbers who sold cadavers to medical researchers—for his grisly material, and simply buried the leftovers. It seems hard to believe that the always intellectually curious Franklin wouldn't have known what was going on. The official mantra of the Friends of Benjamin Franklin House appears to be that while he may have been aware, he certainly didn't participate. How they can know this, of course, is something best left for the court historians to explain.

Unlike Jefferson, Ben Franklin is fondly remembered by establishment historians. This is in spite of his controversial personal life, and the fact that he too owned slaves as a young man. He also carried advertisements for the sale of slaves in his newspaper, *The Pennsylvania Gazette*, and really never spoke out against slavery until very late in life, when he became president of an abolitionist group founded by the Pennsylvania Quakers. In addition to this, Franklin strongly objected to the German immigrants who "suffered to swarm into our settlements, and, by herding together, establish their language and manners, to the exclusion of ours? Why should Pennsylvania, founded by the English, become a colony of Aliens?" The kid-gloves treatment his memory receives, as compared to Jefferson, was exemplified in a puff piece for PBS titled "Citizen Ben," in which it was stated, "Slavery was an accepted way of life in early colonial America. Without the work of slaves and indentured servants, the growing economy of the colonies would have been limited." Sounds reasonable. How come that doesn't apply to Thomas Jefferson?

THOMAS PAINE

Without the author of Common Sense, *the sword of Washington would have been raised in vain.*

—John Adams

The opening words "These are the times that try men's souls" are some of the most famous in the history of literature. The modest pamphlet *Common Sense*, written by Thomas Paine, who grew up poor and quit school at age twelve, had tremendous influence on the other Founding Fathers and a great impact on American public opinion. He exemplified the revolutionary spirit more than any other prominent man of his era. Paine left America shortly after the War for Independence and became embroiled in the French Revolution, where he hoped his vision of liberty would be extended to Europe. In 1792, he would argue in vain against the execution of deposed King Louis XVI, while at the same time he was being tried in absentia in England for propagating "seditious libel." After the Jacobins took over in France, Paine was imprisoned with all the other "traitors" to the revolution, shortly before his *The Age of Reason* was published.

Returning home in 1794 and living with James Monroe for over a year, Paine penned an inflammatory "Letter to Washington." In it, he described the Federalist Party as "disguised traitors . . . rushing as fast as they could venture, without awakening the jealousy of America, into all the vices and corruptions of the British Government." Of Washington himself, Paine wrote, "the world will be puzzled to decide whether you are an apostate or an imposter; whether you have abandoned good principles, or whether you ever had any." Paine was excoriated in the press over his comments; labeled "a drunken atheist" and a "lying, drunken brutal infidel," among other things. He was even denied the right to vote. President Jefferson boldly ignored public opinion, and invited Paine frequently to dine at the White House, informing his daughters that the pamphleteer was "too well entitled to the hospitality of every American, not to cheerfully receive mine." Paine never forgave Washington for not pleading for clemency with Robespierre after he was imprisoned; Robespierre respected Washington and would have acceded to his request if only not to offend him. Upon hearing of Washington's death, Paine suggested the following lines be carved upon his tombstone:

> Take from the mine the coldest, hardest stone,
> It needs no fashion: it is Washington.
> But if you chisel, let the stroke be rude,
> And on his heart engrave-Ingratitude.

Bertrand Russell would write of Paine, in his 1957 essay "Why I Am Not a Christian," "It was his fate to be always honored by opposition and hated by governments: Washington, while he was still fighting the English, spoke of Paine in terms of highest praise; the French nation heaped honors upon him until the Jacobins rose to power; even in England, the most prominent Whig statesmen befriended him and employed him." One of Paine's sayings, that "Government, even in its best state, is but a necessary evil," has become a commonplace expression, dear to the hearts of libertarians everywhere. Paine epitomized the classical liberals of his era.

The members of his generation recognized the impact and significance of Paine. John Adams, despite personally loathing him, said, "History is to ascribe the American Revolution to Thomas Paine." General Nathaniel Greene told him, "America is indebted to few characters more than you." Marquis de Lafayette declared that "Free America without her Thomas Paine is unthinkable." Nevertheless, after Thomas Paine died, on June 8, 1809, he had become so forgotten or despised that only six people showed up at his funeral, two of them free black men, and none of them public dignitaries. He had no surviving wife or children. The Quakers denied his request to be buried in their New Rochelle, New York cemetery, so he was buried on his farm. In a bizarre footnote, his bones were exhumed by radical journalist William Cobbett, who hoped to have Paine interred to great fanfare in England, but never did. Cobbett kept the bones for twenty-five years, and no one knows what happened to them. His skull is rumored to be in Australia, and buttons in England might have been made from his bones. The Thomas Paine Historical Association keeps his mummified brain stem and a lock of his hair in a secret location.[15]

SHAYS' AND WHISKEY REBELLIONS

The seeds of war are now sown.

—Daniel Shays

While there is obviously much to admire about the Founding Fathers, as has been the case throughout the history of civilization, the concerns of the average soldiers in the War for Independence tended to be lost in the shuffle. The recollections of Private Joseph Plumb Martin (*Memoir of a Revolutionary Soldier*) became celebrated by historians when rediscovered in the 1950s, describing firsthand the incredible hardships the average Revolutionary War soldier went through. They were rarely paid, often went days without food or sleep, never received the large land grants they were promised, and had to fight for years to get any kind of pension. Martin later became embroiled in a land dispute with war hero and George Washington's Secretary of War Henry Knox, which Knox not surprisingly won. By 1783, the mostly very young men serving in the Continental Army had grown so weary of not being paid and surviving on meager provisions that an anonymous foot soldier in the Newburgh, New York ranks penned a letter to George Washington, in which their concerns were detailed and a threat to lay down their arms was included. Earlier that year, Pennsylvania soldiers had mobbed the state house. After falsely promising to address their complaints, delegate Alexander Hamilton headed a secret congressional meeting, and instead a message was delivered to the Pennsylvania Council asking for protection from the protesters. All of this percolating discontent came to a head in 1786 with a rebellion led by war veteran Daniel Shays.

Shays' Rebellion was defeated militarily by a private Massachusetts militia. Ironically, the primary motivating forces behind the rebellion were taxes and debt forfeiture. The oppressive measures instituted by the Massachusetts authorities resulted in farms being foreclosed on and struggling citizens being hounded into court by tax collectors. To his credit, Massachusetts governor John Hancock remained true to the spirit of the Revolution, and refused to prosecute citizens for delinquent taxes.

Daniel Shays had good reason to be bitter. After serving at the battles of Lexington and Concord, Bunker Hill, and Saratoga, former farmhand Shays resigned from the army in 1780 without being paid. He returned home only to face charges of nonpayment of debt. While Shays himself would be pardoned after the rebellion was quelled, he was vilified by the mainstream media of his day and moved to New York, where he died broke and obscure in 1825. Two of the other alleged ringleaders of the rebellion, John Bly and Charles Rose, were hanged. Sadly, one of those who advocated such punitive measures was Founding Father Samuel Adams, who declared, "Rebellion against a king may be pardoned, or lightly punished, but the man who dares to rebel against the laws of a republic ought to suffer death." Thomas Jefferson, on the other hand, would write to James Madison in 1787 that "A little rebellion, now and then, is a good thing." Jefferson's famous remark that "The tree of liberty must be refreshed from time to time with the blood of patriots and tyrants" was also in response to Shays' Rebellion. Federalists like George Washington cited Shays' Rebellion in their promotion of a stronger central government. This dream of the Federalists came to fruition after the Constitutional Convention of 1787, tempered only by the reluctant inclusion of the Bill of Rights. In 1927, a monument erected in Petersham, Massachusetts celebrated the defeat of Shays' Rebellion and concluded, "Obedience to Law is True Liberty." However, a new monument in Petersham was erected in 1987, with a diametrically different message: "True Liberty and Justice may require resistance to law." In many ways, Daniel Shays was the first American populist.

Gore Vidal, whom *The Nation* once referred to as the last of the Founding Fathers, wrote a wonderfully radical essay in 1972, titled "Homage to Daniel Shays." Vidal stated:

Massachusetts veterans of the revolution . . . thought that they had been fighting a war for true independence. They did not want London to be replaced by New York. They did want an abolition of debts and a division of property. Their rebellion was promptly put down. But so shaken was the elite by the experience that their most important (and wealthiest) figure grimly emerged from private life with a letter to Harry Lee. "You talk of employing influence," wrote George Washington, "to appease the present tumults in Massachusetts. I know not where that influence is to be found, or if attainable, that it would be a proper remedy for the disorders. Influence is no government. Let us have one by which our lives, liberties and properties will be secured or let us know the worst at once." So was born the Property Party and with it the Constitution of the United States.

21

We have known the "best" for nearly 200 years. What would the "worst" have been like?

In 1791, farmers in western Pennsylvania became incensed over the new Whiskey Tax, and their angry protests eventually turned into what became known as the Whiskey Rebellion. Many of these rebels, like the ones involved in Shays' Rebellion, were war veterans who naturally objected to the hypocrisy of the new government, which had ignited their own rebellion largely in protest against taxation, imposing unjust taxes upon its citizens. It was especially grating to some that these excise taxes had been devised by banker-friendly Alexander Hamilton in order to pay down the war debt. President Washington suppressed the rebellion with a strong military force, composed of militiamen from several states. In a long-forgotten 1796 book, Congressman William Findley fingered Alexander Hamilton as having provoked the rebellion. Predictably, establishment historian Jacob Cooke would, nearly 170 years later, accuse Findley of promulgating a "conspiracy thesis." Hamilton had evidently gone so far as adopting a false persona, known as "Tully," to denounce mob violence associated with the Whiskey Rebellion in the Philadelphia newspapers and lobby for military action. I have often thought of Hamilton as the one Founding Father who would be right at home in the Council on Foreign Relations, or at the yearly Bilderberg get-togethers. Evidently, he had the mindset of a modern-day internet troll, and would probably have wholeheartedly supported the Orwellian proposal of Obama aide and Harvard professor Cass Sunstein to infiltrate internet forums in order to shut down "conspiracy theorists." The establishment press of the day was clearly in support of the government's crackdown on the rebels, and afterwards a popular play called *The Volunteers* celebrated the militia who shut down the Whiskey Rebellion. It is said that President and Martha Washington attended one of the performances. The Whiskey Tax was repealed once Jefferson's party took power in 1801.

Alexander Hamilton was different from the other Founding Fathers. Born illegitimately, Hamilton spent his youth in the Caribbean. General George Washington took a liking to the young Hamilton, and he quickly rose to become the general's chief of staff and closest confidante. At least one historian, Jonathan Katz, has interpreted the sentimental letters Hamilton wrote to the Marquis de Lafayette and others during the war as being homosexual in nature. Of particular interest were letters written to John Laurens, his fellow aide-de-camp to George Washington, one of which included the lines, "Like a jealous lover, when I thought you slighted my caresses."

Hamilton was the first advocate for a national bank in the United States, and as the nation's first secretary of the treasury became George Washington's most trusted cabinet member. According to so-called "conspiracy theorists" like David Icke, Hamilton was an agent for the powerful Rothschild international banking family. He and fellow Washington cabinet member Thomas Jefferson became bitter political foes over banking and other issues. Hamilton was also in favor of the establishment of public debt, and largely because of his lobbying a national bank was established in 1791, with a charter for twenty years. Some Federalists understood the issue as well; John Adams would write, in a 1787 letter to his friend Jefferson: "What allowed the bankers to finally obtain the complete monopoly of the control of credit in the United States? The ignorance among the population of the money question." Because of the influence of Jefferson, Madison, and other Democrat-Republicans, the bank's charter wasn't renewed in 1811. The battle between Jefferson's Democratic-Republican Party, which favored a decentralized government, and Hamilton's Federalists, who wanted a strong national government, would define American political discourse for decades to come.

Predictably, the same court historians who vilify Thomas Jefferson adore Alexander Hamilton. Despite having made jokes about God at the Constitutional Convention, Hamilton believed that Jews were the "chosen" people and proposed the formation of a Christian Constitutional Society. He was killed by Jefferson's vice president Aaron Burr in 1804, the victim of perhaps the world's most famous duel. Burr was at the center of an acknowledged conspiracy to create a new independent country within the United States. A year after the duel with Hamilton, Jefferson ordered Burr to be arrested, and he was tried for treason but acquitted.

ADAM WEISHAUPT AND THE ILLUMINATI

Of all the means I know to lead men, the most effectual is a concealed mystery.

—Adam Weishaupt

The earliest genuine "conspiracy" book that I know of carried the lengthy title *Proofs of a Conspiracy Against All Religions and Governments of Europe Carried on in the Secret Meetings of Free Masons, Illuminati and Reading Societies.* Written by Edinburgh Professor John Robison, it was published in 1797. The book was the first to focus on the Bavarian Illuminati, founded allegedly on May 1, 1776 by University of Ingoldstadt professor Adam Weishaupt, and its supposed infiltration of Freemasonic lodges. While the establishment views the Illuminati as a seldom noted, innocuous organization designed to enlighten the masses, conspiracy theorists consider it as one of the leading candidates for the unseen power behind everything. *Proofs* was widely read, and a copy was even sent to George Washington. Washington commented on the book in a letter to Rev. George Washington Snyder, dated October 24, 1798. A well-known Freemason himself, Washington attempted to refute the contention that Masonic lodges in America had been widely infiltrated by the Illuminati, although he admitted that "It was not my intention to doubt that, the Doctrines of the Illuminati, and principles of Jacobinism had not spread in the United States. On the contrary, no one is more truly satisfied of this fact than I am." Thomas Jefferson, however, seemed naively supportive of Weishaupt (whose name he misspelled as Wishaupt) in a January 31, 1800 letter, labeling him "an enthusiastic philanthropist." Jefferson dismissed the fears of those like Robison towards "the spreading of information, reason, & natural morality among men." In addition to George Washington, many other Founding Fathers were Masons, such as Joseph Warren, James Otis, John Paul Jones, Samuel Adams, John Hancock, and Benjamin Franklin. So was the Marquis de Lafayette, the French nobleman who fought with the American colonists.

Even at that early date, the inclination was strong among establishment voices to discredit any "conspiracy theories." Robison had been a "respected" figure in intellectual circles prior to writing *Proofs*, and had contributed many valuable scientific articles to the Encyclopedia Britannica. After his controversial book was published, however, the Encyclopedia Britannica critiqued it with the following comment, "It betrays a degree of credulity extremely remarkable in a person used to calm reasoning and philosophical demonstration." That sentence could easily have fit into any *New York Times* review of an anti-Warren Commission JFK assassination book.

Few conspirators have left the kind of transparent confessions on the record that Adam Weishaupt did. Consider this quote from Weishaupt:

> The great strength of our Order lies in its concealment; let it never appear in any place in its own name, but always covered by another name, and another occupation. None is better than the three lower degrees of Free Masonry; the public is accustomed to it, expects little from it, and therefore takes little notice of it. Next to this, the form of a learned or literary society is best suited to our purpose, and had Free Masonry not existed, this cover would have been employed; and it may be much more than a cover, it may be a powerful engine in our hands. By establishing reading

societies, and subscription libraries, and taking these under our direction, and supplying them through our labours, we may turn the public mind which way we will.

Does this sound like the philosophy of an innocent free-thinker? Weishaupt, in another statement, appeared to openly advocate assassination, as he reminded his followers, "No man is fit for our Order who is not a Brutus or a Catiline, and is not ready to go to every length." Scoffing at the religious leaders who thought his movement innocuous, Weishaupt remarked, "The most wonderful thing of all is that the distinguished Lutheran and Calvinist theologians who belong to our order really believe that they see in it (Illuminati) the true and genuine sense of Christian Religion. Oh mortal man, is there anything you cannot be made to believe?"

Weishaupt's Illuminati drew the attention of many prominent Americans. On the significant date of July 4, 1812, Joseph Willard, then president of Harvard University, delivered a speech in which he declared:

> There is sufficient evidence that a number of societies, of the Illuminati, have been established in this land of Gospel light and civil liberty, which were first organized from the grand society, in France. They are doubtless secretly striving to undermine all our ancient institutions, civil and sacred. These societies are closely leagued with those of the same Order, in Europe; they have all the same object in view. The enemies of all order are seeking our ruin. Should infidelity generally prevail, our independence would fall of course. Our republican government would be annihilated.

Although the mention of his name is scoffed at in polite society, Adam Weishaupt was a very real person: as noted, a professor of canon law at the University of Ingolstadt. Robison's interpretation of Weishaupt's plans as "scheming the establishment of an Association or Order, which, in time, should govern the world" was well reasoned. His theory would lead inevitably to the concerns present-day conspiracy researchers have regarding the "New World Order," which always seems to be on the minds of those who lead us. Robert Shea and Robert Anton Wilson used Weishaupt with great dramatic license as a character in their wonderful *Illuminatus* science-fiction trilogy in the 1970s. They even claimed that Weishaupt had killed George Washington and assumed his identity. As was mentioned earlier, Weishaupt founded the Illuminati officially on May 1, 1776, which is of great interest considering that "May Day" also came to be celebrated as International Workers' Day, and is dear to the hearts of socialists and communists everywhere. It was an official holiday in the Soviet Union, with elaborate parades held in Red Square in Moscow and in other major cities. The establishment's view on Weishaupt was expressed by Dr. Tony Page, who explained, in his translation of *Supplement to the Justification of My Intentions by Adam Weishaupt*, "His project was utopian and naively optimistic . . . but neither he nor his plan was evil or violent in and of themselves. It is one of the deplorable and tragic ironies of history that a man who tried to inculcate virtue, philanthropy, social justice, and morality has become one of the great hate-figures of 21st-century 'conspiracy' thinking."

OUR REVOLUTIONARY LEGACY

Three millions of people, armed in the holy cause of liberty, and in such a country as that which we possess, are invincible by any force which our enemy can send against us.

—Patrick Henry

Delusional Republican Rep. John Linder once declared, "If the Founding Fathers and other patriots who fought during the Revolutionary War could see the United States today, I believe they would be proud of the path that the thirteen colonies, now fifty strong states, have taken since then." This is about as distorted an interpretation as there could be, of both the philosophy of our Founders and the present disastrous state of this country. In reality, the Founding Fathers would be mortified at what has become of their Republic, and would be marginalized as "wacko" extremists by the mainstream media and their political descendants. This was illustrated by Department of Defense training documents, released through a Freedom of Information Act lawsuit filed by Judicial Watch. The Defense Equal Opportunity Management Institute training guide advised its recruits that "In US history, there are many examples of extremist ideologies and movements. The colonists who sought to free themselves from British rule and the Confederate states who sought to secede from the Northern states are just two examples." The guide also warned that participation in any "extremist" organization is "incompatible with military service and is therefore prohibited." Alex Jones and other alternative researchers have publicized a disturbing FEMA video, which teaches law enforcement personnel that the Founding Fathers were terrorists. Both the far left and the far right claim to be ideological heirs to the Founders, but there is very little chance that any of them—outside of Alexander Hamilton and perhaps Benjamin Franklin—would have achieved much power or influence in today's establishment.

The Founding Fathers left a great deal behind on the public record, in their comments and their writings. It takes very little research to comprehend how utterly opposed they would be to virtually anything our leaders have done for the past century or more. It is only because of the massive ignorance most Americans have about their history, which permits the disinformation of the establishment historians and mainstream media to go unchecked. Thomas Jefferson succinctly expressed the way most of the Founders felt about placing too much power in the hands of any individual or group of individuals when he said, "In questions of power, let no more be heard of confidence in man, but bind him down from mischief by the chains of the constitution." Patrick Henry famously declared, "Give me liberty or give me death!" Joseph Warren echoed this with "We determine to die or be free." The significance of the American War for Independence cannot be exaggerated; as James Madison immodestly but accurately stated, it was indeed "a revolution which has no parallel in the annals of human society." Anyone who looks at present-day America and believes that *this* is what was intended, and fought for, is more clueless than I can describe. Despite the assurances of the professional historians, a 2013 Gallup Poll found that 71 percent of those polled thought that the Founding Fathers would be ashamed of modern America.[16]

We have often been told that the Second Amendment of the Constitution was meant to apply only to state-regulated militias. George Mason, one of the most extreme Founding Fathers and a principal driving force behind the Bill of Rights, delineated the debate in a speech before the Virginia Ratifying Commission on June 14, 1778, in which he exclaimed, "I ask, Sir, what is the militia? It is the whole people. To disarm the people is the best and most effectual way to enslave them." Richard Henry Lee, in the September 8, 1788 *Charleston State Gazette*, boldly spoke of the right of "freeholders, citizen and husbandman, who take up arms to preserve their property, as individuals, and their rights as freemen." In 1788, Samuel Adams told the Massachusetts Commission that nothing should "prevent the people of the United States, who are peaceable citizens, from keeping their own arms." Thomas Jefferson described our present-day situation perfectly when he noted, "Laws that forbid the carrying of arms . . . disarm only those who are neither inclined nor determined to commit crimes. . . . Such laws make things worse for the assaulted and better for the assailants . . . an unarmed man may be attacked with greater confidence than an armed man." Patrick Henry, during the debates over adoption of the Constitution, argued with his typical eloquence that "Are we at last brought to such humiliating and debasing degradation that we cannot be trusted with arms for our defense? Where is the difference between having our arms in possession and under our direction, and having them under the management of Congress? If our defense be the real object of having those arms, in whose hands can they be trusted with more propriety, or equal safety to us, as in our own hands?" Even Alexander Hamilton, who predictably lobbied in *The Federalist Papers* for mandatory military service, acknowledged "the advantage of being armed, which the Americans possess over the people of almost every other nation."

The Founders would have been aghast at what Dwight Eisenhower christened the military-industrial complex. They were fiercely against the concept of a standing army, as Elbridge Gerry explained during the Constitutional debates: "What, sir, is the use of a militia? It is to prevent the establishment of a standing army, the bane of liberty. Whenever governments mean to invade the rights and liberties of the people, they always attempt to destroy the militia, in order to raise an army upon their ruins." Noah Webster, father of the modern dictionary, recognized this as well, warning, "Another source of power in government is a military force. But this, to be efficient, must be superior to any force that exists among the people, or which they can command: for otherwise this force would be annihilated, on the first exercise of acts of oppression. Before a standing army can rule, the people must be disarmed; as they are in almost every kingdom in Europe. The supreme power in America cannot enforce unjust laws by the sword; because the whole body of the people are armed, and constitute a force superior to any band of regular troops that can be, on any pretence, raised in the United States." Roger Sherman, during the debates over the 1790 Militia Act, reminded us that it was "the privilege of every citizen, and one of his most essential rights, to bear arms, and to resist every attack upon his liberty or property, by whomsoever made." George Washington said, "Firearms stand next in importance to the Constitution itself." There is no doubt about what the Founders meant by "the people's right to bear arms" in the Second Amendment, and those who irrationally insist upon a different interpretation are obviously motivated by a political agenda. In one of his rare lucid moments, California governor Jerry Brown once said that he was in favor of the people having the right to bear arms, because the police and the military have them.

Needless to say, those who wrote the First Amendment would be flabbergasted by all the modern assaults upon it. They would have been repelled by "free speech zones." In her book *The Silencing: How the Left is Killing Free Speech*, Kirsten Powers demonstrated, among other things, that "Campuses across the United States have become ground zero for silencing free speech." Recently, a majority of students at Yale University signed a satirical petition to repeal the First Amendment, some of them with great enthusiasm.[17] Jefferson, Madison, George Mason, Patrick Henry, and company would not have understood "hate speech." In May 2015, CNN reporter Chris Cuomo declared that "hate speech" is not protected by the First Amendment. Cuomo tweeted, with astonishing ignorance, especially considering he is an attorney: "Don't just say you love the Constitution . . . read it." There are, of course, no references whatsoever to "hate" in the Constitution, and none of the Founders would have supported the notion that civil liberties should be restricted based upon some subjective interpretation of it.

George Washington's farewell address would have the same effect upon our modern lawmakers as a crucifix does to a vampire. Could American foreign policy of the last hundred years possibly be less consonant with Washington's advice of "Harmony, liberal intercourse with all nations, are recommended by policy, humanity, and interest. But even our commercial policy should hold an equal and impartial hand; neither seeking nor granting exclusive favors or preferences?" His admonition that America adopt "Peace, commerce and honest friendship with all nations—entangling alliances with none" represents the antithesis of modern-day American foreign policy. If he were alive today, how could the father of our country be anything other than dumbfounded by our perpetual bombings, invasions, embargoes, and occupations of other sovereign nations? But this is merely the continuation of a disturbing trend that violates not only Washington's philosophy, but also the spirit of the Revolution itself; by many estimates, the United States has been at war for 93 *percent* of the time since it declared its independence from Great Britain. Incredibly, America has never enjoyed even a single decade of uninterrupted peace. James Madison, although forced into an unavoidable conflict with Great Britain in 1812, reflected the general perspective of the Founding Fathers with the following statement:

> Of all the enemies to public liberty war is, perhaps, the most to be dreaded, because it comprises and develops the germ of every other. War is the parent of armies; from these proceed debts and taxes; and armies, and debts, and taxes are the known instruments for bringing the many under the domination of the few. In war, too, the discretionary power of the Executive is extended . . . The same malignant aspect in republicanism [the advocacy of a republic as a means of government] may be traced in the inequality of fortunes, and the opportunities of fraud, growing out of a state of war, and in the degeneracy of manners and of morals engendered by both. No nation could preserve its freedom in the midst of continual warfare.[18]

The separation of powers, delineating equal roles for the three branches of the federal government, have become so lopsided in favor of the executive and judiciary that the Founders would be reloading their muskets if they were around. As James Madison reminded posterity, "none of them ought to possess, directly or indirectly, an overruling influence over the others." The consolidation of power that we see today in the executive and judicial branches represents what Madison called "the very definition of tyranny." More specifically, when Madison wrote, "the opinion which gives to the judges the right to decide what laws are constitutional, and what are not, not only for themselves in their sphere of action, but for the legislature and executive also, in their spheres, would make the judiciary a despotic branch," he was basically describing what has taken place in America for at least a century. Thomas Jefferson early on argued with the Federalists about the role of the judiciary, declaring in a September 1820 letter, "You seem to consider the judges the ultimate arbiters of all constitutional questions; a very dangerous doctrine indeed, and one which would place us under the despotism of an oligarchy. Our judges . . . and their power [are] the more dangerous as they are in office for life, and are not responsible, as the other functionaries are, to the elective control." There is nothing in the Constitution that permits the Supreme Court to strike down a law, but John Marshall simply asserted the right of "judicial review" in 1803 and the rest is history. Jefferson would be shocked and saddened to learn that nearly everyone with any power now firmly holds that the courts are, indeed, the "ultimate arbiters of all constitutional questions." Judicial tyranny has gone far beyond anything envisioned even by Alexander Hamilton and the other early supporters of a strong judiciary.

Although the Founders were quite clear about what their intentions were, beginning especially with the administration of Abraham Lincoln, the establishment of this unprecedented form of government would gradually come to be viewed as an "experiment in democracy" by all the best and brightest scholars. Benjamin Franklin compared a democracy with a constitutional republic thusly: "Democracy is two wolves and a lamb voting on what to have for lunch. Liberty is a well-armed lamb contesting the vote!" Unfortunately, the perspective of our leaders would evolve from Jefferson's ringing "When governments fear the people, there is liberty. When people fear the government, there is tyranny" to Abraham

Lincoln's plutocratic "Let reverence for the laws . . . become the political religion of the nation, and let everyone sacrifice unceasingly upon its altars." Woodrow Wilson would ultimately declare that "The American Revolution was a beginning, not a consummation." Larry Sabato, a quintessential court historian who wrote a particularly awful book recently on the JFK assassination, expressed the prevailing view of our corrupt oligarchy when he said, "The failure of the nation to update the Constitution and the structure of government it originally bequeathed to us is at the root of our current political dysfunction." Yes, if only we'd just get rid of that pesky Bill of Rights thing, and all the limitations placed upon state control of the people. One of Sabato's numerous suggestions on ways to "improve" the Constitution is to require all able-bodied young Americans to perform two years of "national service."[19]

Historians, politicians, and the mainstream media simply cannot focus much on the heart of the revolutionary drama, which involved American citizen activists throwing off the yoke of British oppression. Considering how handsomely they've profited under the present system, it really isn't in their interests to do so. When they pay attention to the subject at all, they avoid the essential matter of motivation, of *why* the colonists were compelled to such drastic actions. More importantly, they ignore how blatantly similar our situation is today to 1776, and how the usurpations of power on the part of today's government have wildly exceeded the tyranny experienced under King George III. If they spoke favorably of this revolutionary spirit, they couldn't in the next breath produce piece after piece of draconian legislation, designed explicitly to prevent this generation and future generations of Americans from ever rebelling against *them*. Would we really expect leaders who throw brave whistleblowers like Chelsea Manning into prison, and desperately want to do the same thing to "traitor" Edward Snowden, to side with the Sons of Liberty, with George Mason, and Patrick Henry, and Thomas Jefferson? This is really the only plausible explanation, for instance, of why the revolutionary era and its most prominent figures have been so scrupulously ignored by Hollywood. While the so-called "Tea Party" movement was clearly co-opted early on, the very name itself invokes the wrath of the establishment for the most obvious of reasons. The unpleasant reality is that virtually everyone with a public voice in today's world would stand solidly in opposition to the Founding Fathers.

In recent years, the World War II generation, thanks to the promotional efforts of former NBC news anchor Tom Brokaw and others, has come to be hailed as "the greatest generation." I think this is about as preposterous a claim as most mainstream media claims are. If any generation deserves such a distinction, it would be the generation that fought for and attained American independence. With all their human faults, the Founding Fathers took the concepts of enlightened thinkers like John Locke and Edmund Burke, and the cherished tradition of the Magna Carta, and developed as perfect a form of government as can be developed. The separation of powers, the balance between the three equal branches, the limitations placed upon the government, the protections granted to freedom of speech, freedom of assembly, freedom of religion, and freedom of the press were landmarks of intellectual and philosophical brilliance.

If only subsequent generations had followed their lead.

CHAPTER TWO

PRE-1860: JACKSONIAN DEMOCRACY

The highest glory of the American Revolution was this: it connected in one indissoluble bond the principles of civil government with the principles of Christianity.

—John Quincy Adams

MERIWETHER LEWIS

I am not a coward, but I am so strong. So hard to die.

—Meriwether Lewis

A merican schoolchildren still learn about the Louisiana Purchase of 1803, and the expedition of Meriwether Lewis and William Clark. In recent years, even the mainstream media has begun delving into the mysterious death of Lewis, who supposedly committed suicide on October 11, 1809. An episode of the History Channel's *America Unearthed* revealed that the bloodstains on Lewis's Masonic apron were not his, and actually belonged to two other persons. Even the normally staunch anti-conspiracy writer Brad Meltzer seems to have jumped on the Lewis-was-murdered bandwagon. As Xaviant Haze, co-author of the book *The Suppressed History of America: The Murder of Meriwether Lewis and the Mysterious Discoveries of the Lewis and Clark Expedition*, wrote on his blog, "Both Lewis and Clark were masons. . . . In fact Lewis was a Master Master known for achieving high rank among American Masons in almost record time." Haze also makes the extraordinary claim that George Washington had been indebted to the Rothschilds, "who were instrumental in helping him obtain his position as a land surveyor."

Much of the official story of Meriwether Lewis's death hinges on the testimony of James Neelly, who accompanied Lewis on the trip but wasn't at the scene of his death. According to Kathryn Moore of the History News Network, "Family tradition among Clark's descendants, however, holds that he later voiced doubts that his friend would have committed such a desperate act." One of those deeply involved in assembling the journals of Lewis and Clark and getting them published was Nicholas Biddle, a powerful financier who served as the second and last president of the Second Bank of the United States. Because of the inadequate investigation into the death of this heralded man, who was Thomas Jefferson's private secretary and considered a young political figure on the rise, "conspiracy theories" have emerged over the years. The official suicide theory also rests on the curious notion that Lewis shot himself more than once.

In 1994, a book called *The Jefferson Conspiracies: A President's Role in the Assassination of Meriwether Lewis* was published. The author, journalist David Leon Chandler (who had worked on JFK assassination stories for *Life* magazine and even got a mention in the Warren Report), had the dramatic sense of timing to die just prior to its publication. While mainstream historians are perfectly content to destroy Thomas Jefferson's reputation, the critical response to Chandler's book was decidedly lukewarm. Chandler's theory held that notorious General James Wilkinson, whom Jefferson had removed as governor of Louisiana in favor of Lewis, had sent agents to assassinate his rival. The aforementioned "witness" James Neelly was a close associate of Wilkinson's. Another Wilkinson ally, Captain Gilbert Russell, wrote letters to Jefferson that became the foundation for the official suicide narrative. According to author Haze, these letters were proven to be forgeries by handwriting experts in 1996. Chandler went a step farther, however, and suggested that Jefferson participated in a cover-up of his young protégé's death, for fear of his own connection to some of Wilkinson's dubious activities being exposed. *Publishers Weekly* was quick to provide the establishment spin, stating, "Chandler's reconstruction rests heavily on poorly documented inferences."

Much as the descendants of John Wilkes Booth have been unable to get the body buried in Baltimore's Greenmount Cemetery exhumed, Meriwether Lewis's family heirs have been trying unsuccessfully for over a decade to get his body exhumed. As a September 25, 2010 story in the *Wall Street Journal* explained, "A recent letter from the US Department of the Interior turning down the exhumation request is just the latest in a string of rejections handed down to the Lewis family—all distant relatives of Mr. Lewis's sister Jane, because the explorer didn't marry or have children." Actually, the Department of Interior had initially approved the exhumation, but as a June 27, 2010 article in *Think Progress* reported: "The National Park Service has reversed a previous decision allowing Meriwether Lewis' body to be exhumed in an attempt to determining how he died. The decision, backed by Department of the Interior officials, cites policies prohibiting disturbing graves that are not 'threatened by destruction.' 'We're terribly disappointed,' said Howell Lewis Bowen, an Albemarle County resident and direct descendant. 'We've worked with the park service through three administrations—Clinton and Bush and now Obama—and we thought we were finally getting somewhere.'" We only seem to encounter this kind of firm mindset not to honor an exhumation request when the body in question is a historical figure that may disprove a typically inaccurate piece of establishment history. For instance, a spokesman with West London's Brompton Cemetery declared, "If a family wants to exhume the remains of a relative then obviously we try to help as much as possible."[1] In America, news reports indicate that moving bodies from one cemetery to another is becoming much more commonplace. While most states require special permits and licenses to do so, it generally doesn't seem to be difficult. The main issue routinely seems to be the cost involved.

I had a telephone conversation with Howell Bowen on November 5, 2015. Bowen was obviously still frustrated by his long efforts to establish the truth about his illustrious ancestor's death, but also seemed a bit weary of the subject. He reminded me that the grave had been opened once before, in 1847, and that their conclusion then was that "it looked like he died at the hands of an assassin." Bowen shared his personal suspicion that the body interred in Lewis's grave may not actually be that of Meriwether Lewis. Bowen provided the following statement to me:

It has been a very frustrating 19 years since 1996 when a Tennessee Jury recommended exhumation to determine cause of death of my fourth great uncle, Meriwether Lewis. His unfortunate death has long been a topic of discussion among his family. While there is much speculation, and many theories, we only want to know the truth, whatever it is. We would also like to give his remains a Christian burial, which he never received. . . . Excellent attorneys gave their time and expertise to get permission for an exhumation. There was to be no cost to the United States Government. The Interior Department, and in particular, the National Park Service under Interior Department jurisdiction, set up road blocks all along the way. Even after receiving permission, and working to fulfill all requirements with no cooperation from Park Service as promised, the decision was abruptly reversed with change in National administration. It appears the Park Service, and certain historians, are afraid the truth may change history books, and their reputations. Perhaps it would not, but I do not believe we will ever know. I do not believe the family's wishes will ever be fulfilled. The mystery will continue. I believe Meriwether Lewis would greatly appreciate the enormous work done by many on his behalf to verify, or correct, history, and would be greatly disappointed in his beloved Country's noncooperation.

From what I've been able to determine, the family seems to be the final arbiter in determining if a body can be exhumed. Unless the body can solve a historical mystery, that is.

THE WAR OF 1812

War should only be declared by the authority of the people, whose toils and treasures are to support its burdens, instead of the government which is to reap its fruits.

—James Madison

When Americans think of the War of 1812, they usually picture Washington, DC being burnt down, including the White House, and First Lady Dolley Madison heroically rescuing the Gilbert Stuart portrait of George Washington. That is, if they think of it at all; an increasing number of people would probably know nothing more than that it began in 1812.

Some conspiracy theorists believe that the War of 1812 was ordered by Nathan Rothschild, in retaliation for the First National Bank's charter not being renewed in 1811. The First National Bank had been dominated by foreign investors, first and foremost of these being the Rothschilds. This is acknowledged by even mainstream historians, even though they instinctively reject the hypothesis that Alexander Hamilton was an agent for the Rothschilds, or that he actually married into the Rothschild family. In a

January 8, 2013 story in *Business Insider*, the following quote is attributed to Nathan Rothschild, although the article notes it hasn't been verified: "Either the application for the renewal of the charter is granted, or the United States will find itself involved in a most disastrous war."

Court historians attribute the causes of the War of 1812 to the same conglomeration of non-conspiratorial reasons that are trotted out to explain every war. Alternative views hold that the war was fought for the typical reason of further enriching the bankers. If Rothschild's goal was to increase America's debt, he was certainly successful, as the country's debt surged during 1812–1815. As a result, President James Madison authorized the creation of the Second Bank of the United States in 1816. Foreign shares in the new bank soared from 1824 to 1832, with James de Rothschild of France rumored to be a principal investor. It was no "conspiracy theorist," but *Business Insider*, that acknowledged, "The Rothschilds would go on to perfect the strategy of lending to countries on each side of a conflict over the following century of chronic warfare."

Ironically, considering how secession would be viewed some fifty years later, a serious secession movement in New England began in response to Thomas Jefferson's embargo against Great Britain, their primary trading partner. In this case, it was the Federalists, gradually to become the Republicans under the leadership of Abraham Lincoln, who were unhappy with federal policy and aspired to a separatist movement. During the Civil War, of course, it would be these same Federalist/Republicans that would vehemently deny that the southern states had any such right. As we can see so clearly today, our political world has always been full of this kind of partisan hypocrisy.

One of the most astounding historical coincidences involved the passing of Founding Fathers John Adams and Thomas Jefferson at around the same time. Many Americans felt that the date of their deaths was in fact divinely inspired. They had become intense political rivals, with Jefferson's vehement opposition to Adams's Alien and Sedition Acts being the primary impetus for the mud-slinging 1800 presidential election between them. The old friends, however, graduated to a friendly truce and left behind a treasure trove of correspondence to each other. Both men died on July 4, 1826, the fiftieth anniversary of the signing of the Declaration of Independence. In a letter written shortly before his death to Roger C. Weightman, Jefferson had declared: "May [our Declaration of Independence] be to the world, what I believe it will be (to some parts sooner, to others later, but finally to all), the signal of arousing men to burst the chains under which monkish ignorance and superstition had persuaded them to bind themselves, and to assume the blessings and security of self-government." In a lesser known correlating death, former president James Monroe died five years later, also on July 4th.

FREEMASONS AND ANTI-MASONS

Freemasonry is deceptive and fraudulent . . . Its promise is light—its performance is darkness.

—John Quincy Adams

When Captain William Morgan of New York mysteriously disappeared in 1826, after announcing his intention to write a book exposing the secrets of freemasonry, the incident sparked public outcry and led directly to great distrust and suspicion about the secretive organization. Powerful publisher and Whig Party figure Thurlow Weed was inspired to found the new Anti-Masonic Party in response, which ran a presidential candidate in 1832 against Mason Democrat Andrew Jackson.

Morgan, who had been a member of the Masons in Canada, was arrested on September 11, 1826 on bogus charges for nonpayment of a loan and stealing a shirt and tie. A badly decomposed body washed ashore on Lake Ontario in October 1827, but was identified as another missing person. Some freemasons claimed that Morgan had been paid to leave the country, and eventually three Masons were convicted of kidnapping him, but their light sentences outraged the public. There were allegations that powerful Masons had covered up the crime. Morgan's book, *Illustrations of Masonry*, was published posthumously and became a bestseller. In 1881, a grave was discovered on a New York Indian reservation that bore indications it could be Morgan's, but this was never proven. A year later, the National Christian Association, a group opposed to all secret societies, erected a memorial to Morgan in New York's Batavia Cemetery.

John Quincy Adams, sixth president of the United States, became the most prominent figure among the Anti-Masons. The only president to serve in Congress after his term of office, he was elected to the House of Representatives on the Anti-Mason ticket in 1830. Adams was among the most brilliant of all US presidents—he could speak and write seven languages and had memorized Shakespeare and the classics by the time he was ten years old. Adams's opposition to masonry appears to have been fueled by his devout Christianity; he attended church so dutifully that he often worshiped twice on Sunday and was said to start each day by reading several Bible chapters. Adams's keen interest in the subject led to his *Letters on the Masonic Institution*, which was originally published in 1847. Adams objected to the oaths administered to members, declaring, "The Entered Apprentice's oath was sufficient to settle in my mind the immoral character of the institution . . . was in itself vicious—and such as ought never to be administered by man to man."

Adams, understandably concerned with how these vows could conflict with the law, further stated:

> The Entered Apprentice promises never to reveal to any person under
> the canopy of heaven, that which the laws of his country may . . . make

it his duty to reveal to any court of justice before which he may be summoned to appear . . . the Master Mason promises to keep the secrets
of a brother Master Mason . . . murder and treason excepted. . . . The
naming of them emphatically (murder and treason) leaves all other
crimes included in the promise and excluded from the exception. . . . I
do conscientiously and sincerely believe that the order of Freemasonry,
if not the greatest, is one of the greatest moral and political evils under
which the Union is now laboring . . . a conspiracy of the few against the
equal rights of the many. . . . Masonry ought forever to be abolished. It
is wrong—essentially wrong—a seed of evil, which can never produce
any good.

Another president, Millard Fillmore, would say, "The Masonic fraternity
tramples upon our rights, defeats the administration of justice, and bids
defiance to every government which it cannot control." As a strong man
of faith, John Quincy Adams worried that "If the candidate has been educated to a sincere and heart-felt reverence for religion and the Bible, and if
he exercises his reason, he knows that all the tales of Jachin and Boaz, of
Solomon's Temple, of Hiram Abiff and Jubela, Jubelo, and Jubeluem, are
impostures—poisons poured into the perennial fountain of truth—traditions exactly resembling those reprobated by Jesus Christ, as making the
word of God on none effect." Perfectly expressing the concerns many have
with the excessive secrecy of the organization, Adams wrote that a Mason
is "sworn to keep secret what he does not know." The ominous threats
delivered to the Apprentice Mason of "having my throat cut across from
ear to ear, my tongue torn out by its roots, and my body buried in the rough
sand of the sea, at low water mark," and to the Master Mason of having
"his body severed in two in the midst, and divided to the north and south,
his bowels burnt to ashes in the center, and the ashes scattered before the
four winds of heaven" as penalties for revealing Masonic secrets appalled

Adams and ought to stun any rational person. They are frightening, even in a symbolic sense. Adams even mentioned that this violates the passage in the Constitution against "the infliction of cruel and unusual punishments" for what he termed "the breach of an absurd and senseless secret."

Like almost all of America's early leaders, John Quincy Adams would be smeared as a hopeless "isolationist" if he attempted to enter the world of politics today. Reflecting the reality of his time, Adams reminded the world that "America does not go abroad in search of monsters to destroy." Less than a century later, that kind of sentiment would become an anachronism, and be virtually unheard of within the corridors of power.

ANDREW JACKSON

I have always been afraid of banks.

—Andrew Jackson

Andrew Jackson wasn't perfect. He had a taste for violence and war that was far too strong for my liking, as indicated by his quote: "No one need think that the world can be ruled without blood." His treatment of the American Indians was disgraceful, especially the forcible removal of tribes from their lands, where thousands of them died during the drive west that came to be known as the "Trail of Tears." But he was a tremendous foe of the bankers, and the most populist president this country has ever seen, outside of perhaps Thomas Jefferson.

Jackson, popularly known as "Old Hickory," invited a swarm of less than genteel supporters into the White House following his 1828 inauguration. Legendary anecdotes persist about the rowdy, uncouth crowd and how they muddied the carpets and smashed crockery and glassware. Eventually, the punch bowls had to be moved outside onto the White House lawn. Jackson was roundly criticized for harboring a "reign of King Mob."

Arthur J. Stansbury, a contemporary of Jackson's, described the scene: "No one who was at Washington at the time of General Jackson's inauguration is likely to forget that period to the day of his death. To us, who had witnessed the quiet and orderly period of the Adams administration, it seemed as if half the nation had rushed at once into the capital. It was like the inundation of the northern barbarians into Rome." It was the first and only time that the common American riffraff would be granted such free, unfettered access to the halls of power.

Andrew Jackson disliked banks for personal reasons; he'd lost everything on land speculation and worthless banknotes during the time of the first National Bank of the United States. The Second Bank of the United States had been rechartered in 1816, and its credit policies led to mortgage foreclosures, widespread unemployment, and falling prices that negatively impacted agriculture and manufacturing, which eventually resulted in what was called the Panic of 1819. In a bold move, Jackson vetoed the proposal to reauthorize the charter of the Bank of the United States, declaring in his July 10, 1832 speech that he was "deeply impressed with the belief that some of the powers and privileges possessed by the existing bank are unauthorized by the Constitution, subversive of the rights of the States, and dangerous to the liberties of the people. . . . Every monopoly and all exclusive privileges are granted at the expense of the public, which ought to receive a fair equivalent. The many millions which this act proposes to bestow on the stockholders of the existing bank must come directly or indirectly out of the earnings of the American people."

It probably isn't surprising that Andrew Jackson was the first president to be the victim of an assassination attempt, on January 30, 1835. The supposed assassin was unemployed house painter Richard Lawrence, who was pummeled viciously by the sixty-seven-year-old Jackson's walking cane after his gun misfired. One of those who pulled the president away from Lawrence was Congressman Davy Crockett. The conventional view of historians is that Lawrence was, like so many future "lone nuts," a mentally disturbed individual who attacked Jackson for no political or even rational reason. Jackson, on the other hand, more logically viewed the incident as an effort on the part of his opponents in the Whig Party, who were infuriated at his attempts to dismantle the Bank of the United States, to silence him. Interestingly, Jackson's vice president Martin Van Buren subscribed to this theory as well, and thereafter always carried two loaded pistols with him whenever he entered the Senate chamber. Lawrence certainly played the role of psycho well, claiming to be King Richard III and even dressing like a member of royalty at his trial. He was found not guilty by reason of insanity and spent the rest of his life in a mental institution. There was enough evidence of some kind of conspiracy to kill Jackson to produce a congressional investigation, with two witnesses claiming they'd seen Lawrence at the home of Jackson's powerful adversary, Senator George Poindexter of Mississippi. As usually is the case with such congressional investigations, no "credible" evidence linking Lawrence to Jackson's enemies was discovered.

Recently, there has arisen a widely publicized movement, dubbed "Women on 20s," to remove Andrew Jackson's image from the twenty-dollar bill. In the words of the group: "We believe this simple, symbolic, and long-overdue change could be an important stepping stone for other initiatives promoting gender equality." The group established a list of predictable, politically correct names, and Americans had the opportunity to vote online for their choice.[2] As it turned out, it was actually the beloved Alexander Hamilton in danger of being replaced instead, on the ten-dollar bill. When mainstream media outlets questioned why Hamilton, his pro-banker and pro-debt background making him a palatable figure to the establishment, was suffering this ignominy instead of the generally despised Andrew Jackson, Treasury Secretary Jack Lew called it a "happy coincidence" that the redesign would now include a woman's image being placed on the ten-dollar bill, so soon after the campaign to have Jackson's image replaced with a woman.[3]

The establishment press was mortified over the prospect of Hamilton's image being replaced. The most histrionic example of this was a June 18, 2015 *Washington Post* article headlined "Why the US Government needs to Remove Andrew Jackson From the $20 Bill." "Wonkblogger" Steven Mufson went on to declare, in this terribly biased, pro-banker piece, "Hamilton—who will remain on the bill in a presumably diminished role—was a founding father, co-author of the Federalist Papers, Revolutionary War staff aide to George Washington, first Treasury Secretary and architect of the early American economy. He established the nation's first national bank, a very rough forerunner of the Federal Reserve that would spur industry, lend the government money and hold its deposits. Hamilton also advocated a national currency instead of relying on multiple ones issued by various state governments. Jackson didn't even like paper money and he pursued wrong-headed and disastrous economic policies. Yet the Tennessee frontiersman, land speculator, lawyer, slave-owner, war hero and seventh president—will continue to gaze out from the $20 bill. . . . What did Jackson do wrong when it came to the economy? Lots. Among other things, Jackson dismantled the second Bank of the United States (which he called a 'monster institution')." The public relations department at Goldman Sachs couldn't have said it any better.

As could have been easily predicted, in April 2016, it was announced that it was indeed Andrew Jackson who was going to be removed from our currency. Harriet Tubman was selected to be the new face on the twenty-dollar bill. Alexander Hamilton, still endearing to bankers and the rest of the establishment, remains safely ensconced on the ten-dollar bill.

REMEMBER THE ALAMO

I call on you in the name of Liberty, of patriotism & everything dear to the American character, to come to our aid, with all dispatch.

—Lt. Col. William Barrett Travis, in a letter to General Sam Houston

Traditionalists have long depicted the two hundred valiant souls who defended San Antonio, Texas's Alamo Mission in February–March 1836 against an insurmountable onslaught by the much larger forces of Mexico's president, General Santa Anna, in the most idealistic light imaginable. It is estimated that the Mexicans outnumbered the Texans by nearly 6,000. James Bowie, co-commander of the Alamo and inventor of the Bowie knife, was one of my cherished boyhood heroes. There was a vigorous debate back then, in the 1960s, about who was the last to die at the Alamo: Bowie or legendary politician and Walt Disney cash cow Davy Crockett. Depending on the source, Crockett either surrendered and was executed by Santa Anna's men, or his body was found surrounded by at least sixteen Mexican corpses. Establishment historian Gary Wills termed the image of Crockett dying in battle "patriotic hokum." The Mexicans burned almost all the bodies of the victims. Although it is popularly believed there were no survivors at the Alamo, William Travis's slave and several others survived.

Did the small band of Texans at the Alamo fight courageously for thirteen days, as has been conventionally taught, or are revisionists like Phillip Thomas Tucker correct in maintaining that the battle was a complete rout, and over in some twenty minutes? Tucker, in his book *Exodus From the Alamo: The Anatomy of the Last Stand Myth*, claimed that the dimwitted Texans were caught unaware and bolted from the mission like cowards, to be cut down by Mexican cavalry. Tucker also suggests, with some believability considering what we now know about the frequency of such incidents, that at least half of all Mexican casualties were the result of friendly fire. Tucker places great significance on the fact that the Texans were by and large slaveholders. As we have seen, being associated with slavery isn't good for one's historical reputation. As one favorable review of the book gleefully exclaimed, "What the textbooks then, and most histories still now, don't mention is what a lot of scoundrels, greedheads, and sorry hustling-assed lowlifes the Texas Republic leaders were. They were all, every last one of them, dreadfully militarily incompetent and only a few of them were even marginally capable of the political leadership that a successful revolt requires."

It is, of course, impossible to tell how much of the conventional account of the battle at the Alamo is myth, conjecture, exaggeration, or lies. We do know, however, that Davy Crockett's record as a US congressman reveals him to have possessed generally populist principles. For instance, he consistently championed the rights of poor farmers, who were overtaxed and had to deal with Tennessee's complex system of land grants. He also introduced legislation to abolish the West Point military academy, on the grounds that it benefited only the children of the wealthy. Finally, he labeled the banking system "a species of swindling on a large scale." Despite their shared antipathy towards banks, Crockett clashed with fellow Tennessean Andrew Jackson, most notably when he bravely opposed the 1830 Indian Removal Act. Like so many other notables (including Andrew Jackson), Crockett was a freemason.

THE MEXICAN-AMERICAN WAR

The world has nothing to fear from military ambition in our government.
—President James K. Polk

A decade after the battle of the Alamo, genuine war broke out between the United States and Mexico. Ironically, this was primarily a Democratic party-driven war, led by President James K. Polk, while abolitionists and

Whigs (soon to be Republicans) in particular were strongly opposed to it. Slightly more than ten years later, those political roles would be reversed, as the abolitionists and Whig/Republicans, led by new president Abraham Lincoln, were the ones pushing the War Between the States, while many Democrats opposed it.

The shortest reign in the White House belonged to William Henry Harrison, who became the first president to die in office, after only thirty-two days, on April 4, 1841. Harrison obviously had little chance to do much of anything, but he left a couple of intriguing comments in the public record. Sounding very much like a garden-variety conspiracy theorist, Harrison once said, "I believe and I say it is true Democratic feeling, that all the measures of the Government are directed to the purpose of making the rich richer and the poor poorer." On another occasion, in a comment that seemingly suggested the history of this country might have been vastly different had he served two terms in office, he declared, "The chains of military despotism, once fastened upon a nation, ages might pass away before they could be shaken off."

The Mexican-American War was one of conquest, as the United States was able to annex a great deal of new territory, including the huge state of California. Mexico's borders were significantly altered. As they have during every war America has ever been involved in, opponents astutely pointed out the high cost financially and in terms of American lives lost. American state volunteers established an unfortunate pattern that the Union troops would hone to perfection during the Civil War; memoirs from American combatants reported the looting and murder of Mexican civilians. Unlike the armed forces that would fight under the likes of Sherman and Sheridan, however, regular American troops recognized this immoral behavior for what it was, and regarded with contempt those who "robbed Mexicans of their cattle and corn, stole their fences for firewood, got drunk, and killed several inoffensive inhabitants of the town in the streets." Ulysses

S. Grant, serving as a young lieutenant in the war, made these remarkable comments in his 1885 *Memoirs:* "For myself, I was bitterly opposed to the measure, and to this day regard the war, which resulted, as one of the most unjust ever waged by a stronger against a weaker nation. It was an instance of a republic following the bad example of European monarchies, in not considering justice in their desire to acquire additional territory." Grant, aping Abraham Lincoln's desperate, belated claims that the Civil War was some kind of bizarre "punishment" from God, also declared, "Nations, like individuals, are punished for their transgressions. We got our punishment in the most sanguinary and expensive war of modern times." Considering the abominable manner in which the Civil War was waged, it must have been extraordinarily difficult for Grant to write these lines with a straight face.

Much as George Washington and Andrew Jackson had converted their military success into political careers that led to the White House, General Zachary Taylor was the high-profile hero in this war, who went on to become president of the United States. Taylor would die suddenly from a stomach ailment on July 9, 1850, just two years into his presidency. The legend goes that he consumed too many cherries and iced milk after attending a fundraiser for the Washington Monument, which was still under construction. Conspiracy theories arose, with the most popular naturally being that Taylor had been poisoned by his political opponents. The country was still young, and yet to discover that American political figures, according to the historians, are never killed for political reasons. On June 17, 1991, Taylor's remains were exhumed, after obtaining the permission of his closest living descendant. The reader may instantly wonder again why the descendants of Meriwether Lewis and John Wilkes Booth have been denied the same right, and whether such legal inconsistencies are indicative of a political motive. To no real surprise, neutron activation analysis of Taylor's remains revealed no substantial traces of arsenic or any other poison. Author and researcher Michael Parenti was among those who questioned the credibility of the tests conducted on Taylor's remains, and in the 2010 book *Killing the President* by Willard M. Oliver and Nancy E. Marion, the authors conclude on page 189 that, while there was no clear proof Taylor was assassinated, "nor would it appear that there is definitive proof that he was not."

JOHN BROWN

John Brown's body lies a-mouldering in the grave
His soul is marching on.

Author Herman Melville called him "the meteor of the war." As the National Archives *Prologue* magazine put it, John Brown represented to southerners "the embodiment of all their fears—a white man willing to die to end slavery." In 1856, the strident abolitionist Brown, accompanied by four of his sons and three others, abducted five unarmed men and boys from their Pottawatomie Creek, Kansas homes and butchered and dismembered their bodies. When Brown and his party killed a planter and freed eleven slaves in Missouri a few years later, he followed his familiar pattern of stealing wagons, mules, harnesses, and horses in the process. During his infamous 1859 raid on Harpers Ferry, West Virginia, seventeen people were killed, including a black railroad baggage handler. Despite this murderous legacy, John Brown was considered a heroic martyr in the decades following the Civil War, and is still revered by many Americans.

One of the songs that inspired the Union troops was "John Brown's Body." There were July 1861 newspaper accounts of soldiers singing it in the streets of Boston. The tune would later be used for the classic "Battle Hymn of the Republic." One of the most charming of the lyrics in the song refers to hanging Confederate president Jefferson Davis from a sour apple tree. Brown left his own epitaph; as he stood waiting on the gallows to be hung, he handed a note to a guard that read, "I, John Brown am now quite certain that the crimes of this guilty land will never be purged away but with blood." Abraham Lincoln, ever the crafty politician, accused the Democrats of politicizing Brown's hanging, declaring, "You rejoiced at the occasion, and were only troubled that there were not three times as many killed in the affair . . . you were rejoicing that by charging Republicans with this thing you might get an advantage on us."

Henry David Thoreau was an unusually enlightened thinker, but his reaction to John Brown's death was absurd. "Some eighteen hundred years ago Christ was crucified," Thoreau stated. "This morning, perchance, Captain Brown was hung. These are the two ends of a chain which is not without its links." Victor Hugo was another noted literary figure that responded with misguided fervor, exclaiming, "John Brown is grander than George Washington!" Because Brown was passionately against slavery, and devoted his life to this cause, anything else becomes secondary in the eyes of his supporters. It's a classic case of the ends justifying the means. Presumably, Brown could have slaughtered entire villages, and as long as he freed slaves, his actions were justified. John Brown's cohort James Redpath issued this violent statement: "Let nations be dismembered, let dynasties be dethroned, let laws and governments, religions and reputation be cast out. . . . If only one [black] man survived to relate how his race heroically fell, and to enjoy the freedom they had won, the liberty of that solitary negro . . . would be cheaply purchased by the universal slaughter of his people and their oppressors." Both Redpath and Ralph Waldo Emerson compared the gallows on which John Brown was hung to the cross Christ was crucified on. Malcolm X, when asked once if there had "ever been any good white people," quickly thought of John Brown.

The now forgotten iconoclastic historian James C. Malin viewed John Brown quite differently than the court historians. Rejecting what he called "the ideological fashions of the hour," Malin argued that Brown was no more than a murderer, swindler, and petty thief. He charged that Brown had little genuine interest in the plight of slaves. Even preeminent establishment historian Bruce Catton stated that Brown was "unbalanced to the verge of outright madness." Marxist historian Herbert Aptheker, on the other hand, characteristically claimed that Brown's antislavery fervor was the result of his anger at capitalism. More modern biographers gloss over his vicious acts as being "ultimately noble," because they supposedly assisted the cause of liberty for slaves. One of Brown's heroes was Oliver Cromwell, another violent figure who has often been lauded by historians.

Each June, the residents of tiny Osawatomie, Kansas commemorate the murder of their innocent citizens by holding a pageant to select a lucky high school girl to be the new "John Brown Queen." Perhaps this is the logical continuation of the celebrating that began shortly after he and his sons killed those innocent people, with a Broadway play titled "Osawatomie Brown." John Brown died, but he got his wish for a bloody war. Despite the persistent claims of the court historians, it really wasn't about slavery. It was about as bloody as can be, however.

CHAPTER THREE

HONEST ABE

It would not be easy to state what Lincoln conceived to be the limit of his powers.

—James G. Randall

Abraham Lincoln is universally considered the greatest president in American history by all the most influential "experts." Although he was scorned and lambasted by northerners and southerners alike as a tyrant, an uncouth buffoon, and an ape, among other things, upon his assassination he almost instantaneously was converted into "Father Abraham." There is no other historical figure that is so beloved by historians and academics. Perhaps the height of this excessive worship was reached with the 1992 publication of Gary Wills' book *Lincoln at Gettysburg,* which argued that the brief Gettysburg Address had "remade America." Lincoln is the secular saint of our corrupt and decaying civilization. As such, he should be scrutinized honestly.

Lincoln was our greatest president, the historians tell us, because he held the Union together and freed the slaves. He was chronically depressed because of all those deaths this unavoidable conflict was causing. A gentle, kindly soul, Lincoln was a self-educated genius whose poetical phrases still ring clearly and resonate in the hearts of the people. Anything he did was done for the good of the country, and to save the Union. He didn't have a malicious bone in his body. This is the remarkably naïve, conventional view of Abraham Lincoln. Those who dare to criticize this deified figure do so at their own peril, as writers like Thomas DiLorenzo and Charles Adams have learned in recent years. In a typical establishment hit piece that skewered both DiLorenzo's *The Real Lincoln* and Adams's *When in the Course of Human Events*, Herman Belz predictably dismissed their "simple-minded understanding of the relationship between politics and economics, between moral ends and productive entrepreneurial activity."[1] In Belz's review, and in all other rebuttals by court historians to the few brave souls who dare to criticize Lincoln, the underlying theme is one of astonishment. How could *anyone* take issue with the man who saved the union? How could *anyone* cast disparagement upon the man who freed the slaves?

This fawning over Lincoln is probably best exemplified by *New York Times* neocon writer David Brooks. "I have two presidential traditions," Brooks has stated. "I begin covering each campaign by reading a book about Abraham Lincoln, and I end each election night, usually after midnight, at the statue of the Lincoln memorial." As Thomas DiLorenzo describes it, "Being a 'Lincoln scholar' means fabricating *an excuse for everything.*" In an April 15, 2015 column for LewRockwell.com, DiLorenzo pointed out that Doris Kearns-Goodwin, whom he dubs "the high priestess of the Lincoln cult," in her book *Team of Rivals*, uncovered the fact that Lincoln was the promoter of the Corwin Amendment to the Constitution, which would have prohibited the federal government from interfering with slavery. Any other historical figure being exposed as a supporter of something like that would earn the collective scorn of the scholarly community. In this case, however, Kearns-Goodwin actually *praised* Lincoln for a political maneuver that helped "save" the Republican Party.

In a similar vein, Joshua Wolf Shenk revealed in his book *Lincoln's Melancholy* that Lincoln's depression had caused wild mood swings that forced him to take a mid-nineteenth-century medicine containing large doses of mercury to counteract it. Instead of expressing alarm that the leader of our nation had suffered from a mental disorder that required strong medication, the award-winning author actually claimed that this somehow fueled Lincoln's greatness and made his accomplishments all the more remarkable. Compare this curious perspective, for example, to all the critical scrutiny that has been directed at the Kennedy family for "covering up" JFK's Addison's disease. There is no debate permitted here; as the *Detroit Free Press* put it, "Abraham Lincoln is so far above every other man in human history, that to compare him to others seems sacrilege. Nowhere on earth is there a historic character to compare our sainted martyr, Abraham Lincoln."

According to the court historians, Lincoln was such an exceptionally honest man, so scrupulous in all his ways, that he was christened with the moniker "Honest Abe." There are a myriad of far-fetched anecdotes like the one regarding Lincoln walking six miles to return a three-cent overcharge to a customer, or perhaps three miles to give a customer the tea he'd been inadvertently shortchanged. The amount and miles vary, but each tale is identically implausible. There is even a legend that young Lincoln once visited a prostitute, and when she asked for five cents, he only had three cents to his name, so he left out of chivalry and honor. Others have suggested, if the story were true, that it might be another indication that Lincoln was gay. It is said that Lincoln slept in the same bed with Joshua Speed for four years, and also spent many nights together with Captain David Derickson at the Soldier's Home, when Mary Todd Lincoln was out of town. Rumors claimed that Derickson had been seen wearing Lincoln's nightshirt, and the president reportedly stated, "The captain and I are getting quite thick." Lincoln's law partner William Hendon's great-great-niece told author Sylvia Rhue that it had been common knowledge for generations in her family that Hendon "was gay, and he was Lincoln's lover."[2]

Lincoln's opponents, on the other hand, tended to view the "Honest Abe" nickname as indicative of a characteristic he *didn't* have, in the same way one might call a fat person "slim" or a bald man "curly." One clear indication of Lincoln's base instincts as a politician, and his lack of integrity, came in a letter to Norman Judd in 1858. "I have a bare suggestion," Lincoln wrote. "When there is a known body of these voters, could not a true man of the 'detective' class, be introduced among them in disguise, who could, at the nick of time, control their votes?" Lincoln was happy to work with the anti-Catholic, nativist group the Know-Nothings, even though he seemingly was appalled at their politics. Lincoln was elected with strong support from the Know-Nothings, who melded with the Whigs to produce the new Republican Party. Lincoln never had any kind of mandate, or even received significant public support. Most people don't realize that Lincoln's 39.8 percent of the popular vote in the 1860 election remains the lowest total for any winning candidate in American history. Nearly every losing candidate in other presidential elections received a higher percentage of the popular vote.

Upon attaining the office of president, Lincoln wasted little time in wielding an unprecedented amount of power. One of many journalists who felt the brunt of "Honest Abe's" dictums was John Hodgson, Pennsylvania editor of the small newspaper *Jeffersonian*. As detailed in the book *Lincoln's Wrath: Fierce Mobs, Brilliant Scoundrels and a President's Mission to Destroy the Press*, by Jeffrey Manber and Neil Dahlstrom, at first Hodgson's newspaper office was broken into and all his equipment destroyed. Only one event in what came to be known as 1861's "Summer of Rage," not long afterwards federal marshals under the direction of President Lincoln simply shut the paper down. Some antiwar newspaper editors and writers were tarred and feathered. The ones who weren't thrown into makeshift prisons without a trial were ordered to print glowing articles extolling the virtues of Lincoln and his administration. Attorney General Edward Bates supported the closing of newspapers. *The New York Times* set the standard for an ensuing century-plus of lapdog "journalism" by declaring, "speech is only free when loyal." The courageous Hodgson launched a long-forgotten lawsuit against the Lincoln administration and actually won, when a similarly brave judge named Walter Lowrie ruled in his favor in 1863.

A vivid example of the real character of the "great emancipator" can be found in the firsthand account of Mrs. Robert Tansill. Her husband, a captain with the US Marine Corps, had attempted to resign his commission after reading a copy of Lincoln's inaugural address in 1861. Secretary of the Navy Gideon Welles refused to accept his resignation and fired him on the spot. Later that same evening, Capt. Tansill was arrested and sent to jail at Fort Lafayette. He wrote letters to Lincoln, asking to be made aware of the charges against him, to no avail. One of Tansill's letters, dated October 3, 1861, expressed his objection to participating in "an unnatural war against my blood relations, kindred and friends." Tansill noted that his letters to the Navy Department had been ignored, as had been the case with others there. Tansill described how:

> Letters to and from my wife are subjected to the inspection of the commanding officer of this fort, and my dearest friends are denied permission to visit me on the most important business. Under such extraordinary circumstances. . . . I have no other resource but to appeal directly to the President . . . and respectfully ask that I may be brought to trial as soon as possible on the charges against me whatever they may be, or released from this imprisonment which can find no sanction in the laws of war nor in the Constitution or laws of the country which the President has solemnly sworn to support.

Finally, after a great deal of effort, his wife was granted a personal interview with Lincoln. She recounted:

> He spoke, still looking me full in the face, "I did receive that letter and it has got all the answer it will have." Mr. President, I said, you are aware of the circumstances under which my husband was arrested—of his having just returned from sea after an absence of two years from his family and of his being hurried off like a common felon to prison, without giving him any reason for it. . . . His face then turned perfectly livid. He jumped up from the table at which he was sitting, and brought his clenched hand down hard upon it with an oath. . . . He began to walk the room in violent excitement, stamping his feet, and averting his head from me. . . . Mr. Lincoln, you understand, I hope that the only object of my call upon you was to ask if my husband's letter had reached you, and I have received my answer! "You have most positively!" was his reply, with head turned from me. I took my little son by the hand, and closed the door, and thus shut away from my sight, I trust for evermore, the greatest despot and tyrant that ever ruled a nation.[3]

There is no way of knowing the actual figures, but some critics of Lincoln have estimated that the number of political prisoners he had incarcerated was as high as 40,000. They were held indefinitely, without bail and without the services of an attorney, without knowing the charges against them, and in such secrecy that many of their families didn't know where they were. Lincoln shut down more than three hundred newspapers and journals by executive order. Secretary of State John Seward bragged to the British Ambassador Lord Lyons that "he could ring one bell on his right hand, and arrest a citizen in New York, and another bell on his left, and arrest a citizen in Ohio."[4] Rushmore G. Horton detailed the wretched conditions in one such prison, where rats were prevalent. He also recounted the laughingly trivial nature of many arrests. Michigan's David C. Wattles, for example, was arrested because his children had dyed an old shirt with blackberry juice, and raised it high on a pole. Some patriotic citizen interpreted this as the raising of a secessionist flag, and poor Wattles was sent all the way to Fort Lafayette for *five months*. Evidently one of the cases in which Seward used his bell was when Dr. L. M. Ross of Illinois was arrested after being seen in the street drawing his finger under his nose, in what was absurdly claimed to be a private signal of disloyalty. Ross served months in Washington's Old Capitol prison as a result. One of the most prominent of Lincoln's detainees was Frank Key Howard, grandson of Francis Scott Key, who was arrested after midnight on September 13, 1861. Howard was the editor of the *Daily Exchange*, and drew the ire of Lincoln and Seward because of his editorials criticizing both the suspension of the writ of habeas corpus and Lincoln's declaration of martial law in Baltimore. In a bitter irony, Key was imprisoned at Fort McHendry; his grandfather had written "The Star-Spangled Banner" forty-seven years earlier, inspired by the bombing of the same Fort McHendry by a British warship. In an interesting corollary event, in 1859 the son of Francis Scott Key, Philip Barton Key II, was killed by Congressman Daniel Sickles, who had discovered he was having an affair with his young wife. Among his defense attorneys was Lincoln's future secretary of war, Edwin Stanton, who successfully employed the temporary insanity defense.

Lincoln arrested nearly the entire Legislature of Maryland shortly after being elected, along with the police commissioner of Baltimore, several newspaper editors, and other prominent citizens. Some of them served nearly two years in various "Bastilles," as they were derisively referred to. In 1869, John A. Marshall wrote the moving book *American Bastille: A History of the Illegal Arrests and Imprisonment of American Citizens in the Northern and Border States on Account of Their Political Opinions During the Late Civil War*, which described his own arbitrary arrest and unconstitutional internment in Fort Lafayette, one of Lincoln's makeshift prisons. One of the many stories recounted by Marshall was that of *New York Daily News* editor James W. Well, whose editorials condemning the war and Lincoln's countless unconstitutional actions formed the basis of his "crime." Exemplifying the state of absolute tyranny that existed was a December 3, 1861 announcement from Seth C. Hawley, Chief Clerk of the Metropolitan Police Commissioners of New York, that declared, ". . . the Department of State of the United States will not recognize any one as an attorney for political prisoners, and will look with distrust upon all applications for release through such channels; and that such applications will be regarded as additional reasons for declining to release the prisoners."

In 1862, Congress passed the Enrollment Act, which authorized the drafting of young men into the Union Army. It was the first form of national conscription in American history. The Act was rife with inequities, such as the provision which allowed a man to pay $300 to hire a substitute to take his place. For those families of means that couldn't find a substitute, there was a convenient "Commutation" provision whereby a payment of $500 bought an exemption from the draft. This hated "Rich Man's Exemption," as it was called, angered the average American of military age, especially the young Irish immigrants of New York City. A riot erupted in New York in 1863 as a result, and President Lincoln, as was his wont, used some extraordinary executive powers to quell the disturbances. He diverted troops from Gettysburg to the area, and only a lack of manpower stopped him from declaring martial law. Predictably, while Lincoln extolled all poor and lower-middle-class youngsters to lay down their lives on "the altar of freedom" to save the "Union," Lincoln's oldest son, Robert, remained far from the battlefields at Harvard University. The president eventually, when the war was nearing an end, found Robert a relatively safe position on General Grant's staff, where he was commissioned as a captain and assistant adjutant general on February 23, 1865.

Coal miners in Pennsylvania rioted and attacked officials who tried to force them to enlist in the draft. Soldiers were sent to Pennsylvania to quell the riots. Farmers in Ohio who opposed the draft attacked soldiers who were sent to fight them. The July 1863 New York draft riots were the largest insurgent revolt in American history, outside of the secession of the southern states itself. The lottery system, which as noted included a provision that permitted those of means to pay a poorer substitute to take their place in battle, had already angered many, and the passage of the Emancipation Proclamation really lit the fire. Antiwar newspaper editors had fueled the outrage, with coverage that was certain to appeal to poor and working-class whites. The $300 "rich man's" exemption was bitterly compared by many to the $1,000 paid for southern slaves. Often these immigrants, according to Pat Buchanan, "some right off the boat, were put into uniform and sent into battle, where many died never coming to know the land 'where the streets are paved with gold.'"[5] The initial targets of the rioters' wrath were military and governmental buildings, and the mobs only attacked those who interfered with them. But the more extreme rioters soon began focusing their anger on every black person, including a poor fruit vendor, before setting fire to the Colored Orphan Asylum on Fifth Avenue. Eventually eleven black men would be lynched, and hundreds of blacks were forced from the city. Herbert Asbury, author of the book *Gangs of New York,* put the total death toll at some 2,000.

The list of Lincoln's atrocities is long. When there was a delay in paying the Sioux Indians in Minnesota their yearly allowance during the War Between the States, they began attacking the nearby white settlements. Lincoln sent in a Union force under the command of General John Pope and Col. H. H. Sibley, and the Indians were decisively defeated on September 23, 1862. More than 2,000 Sioux were taken captive, and a military tribunal sanctioned by Lincoln authorized the public hanging of thirty-six tribal leaders. Guilt or innocence was immaterial, and the Minnesota Sioux were moved to reservations in Dakota. Incredibly, Lincoln even ordered the arrest of Supreme Court Chief Justice Roger Taney, who had ruled against Lincoln's outrageous suspension of the writ of habeas corpus, citing the ancient rule of English liberty and the Constitution's delineation of this power exclusively to Congress. Taney was never formally arrested, but Lincoln's tyrannical actions continued. Taney was an independent spirit who respected the Constitution. A memorable anecdote about him maintains that he would have refused to administer the oath of office if his political enemy John Seward had been elected president. Lincoln's philosophy was exemplified by what he once told a Chicago clergyman: "As commander in chief of the army and navy, in time of war, I suppose I have a right to take any measure which may best subdue the enemy." Much as the Bush and Obama administrations extended this definition of an "enemy" to include critics of their policies, Lincoln clearly felt that those who opposed his policies were allied with the confederates.

Renowned writer Edgar Lee Masters would later comment that Lincoln "was to call for and send troops into the South, and thus stir that psychology of hate and fear from which a people cannot extricate themselves, though knowing and saying that the war was started by usurpation. Did he mean that he would bow to the American people when the law was laid down by their courts, through which alone the law be interpreted as the Constitutional voice of the people? No, he did not mean that; because when Taney decided that Lincoln had no power to suspend the writ of habeas corpus, Lincoln flouted and trampled the decision of the court."

Antislavery "copperhead" Judge Henry Clay Dean, who charged that the Civil War was being directed by international bankers, experienced the "better angels" of Lincoln's nature firsthand, when his outspoken antiwar views landed him in one of Honest Abe's unconstitutional prisons. "The Postmaster General has for the last five years been violating the mails. The Secretary of the Treasury has been squandering the public wealth. . . . The Secretary of War all crimsoned with innocent blood is employing the army for the destruction of the Country. The Secretary of State has been subverting Constitutional law and disgracing our form of government at home and abroad," Dean charged. "The Attorney General is gravely burlesquing nonsense itself by defining Constitutional construction of unconstitutional laws and is in conspiracy with military commissions to murder innocent women. The President is administering the government through military satraps in a manner unknown to Republican systems and disgraceful to despotism's, which regard the character of those entrusted to power. . . . The courts of the Country are infamously corrupt. The state Legislatures and Congress are flagrantly accessible to bribes."

CLEMENT VALLANDIGHAM

We have, as all will agree, a free Government. . . . In this great struggle, this form of Government and every form of human right is endangered if our enemies succeed.

—Abraham Lincoln

There was surprisingly little effort expended by the top statesmen of the era to avoid the unnecessary bloodbath. In April, 1861, former president Franklin Pierce wrote to all the other living ex-presidents and asked them to consider using their collective stature and influence to attempt a negotiated end to the war. He specifically requested that Martin Van Buren, as the most senior past chief executive, issue a formal declaration on the matter. In an astonishing but familiar display of petty politics, Van Buren replied that Pierce, as the originator of the idea and more recent president, should be the one to do it. There is nothing further on the matter in the recorded historical literature.[6]

Lincoln's most vocal northern critic was Congressman Clement L. Vallandigham of Ohio. As early as July 1861, he took to the floor of Congress to excoriate the president for "the wicked and hazardous experiment of calling thirty millions of people into arms among themselves, without the counsel and authority of Congress." On the subject of Lincoln's claim that the south had no right to secede, the indignant Democrat roared, "He [Lincoln] omits to tell us that secession and disunion had a New England origin, and began in Massachusetts, in 1804, at the time of the Louisiana Purchase; were revived by the Hartford [Secession] Convention in 1814; and culminated during the [War of 1812] in [New Englanders] sending Commissioners to Washington, to settle the terms for a peaceable separation of New England from the other States of the Union." Vallandigham colorfully summarized Lincoln's tyranny as something that "would have cost any English sovereign his head at any time within the last two hundred years."

Vallandigham, as the initial voice in Congress opposing the war, was attacked and criticized as might be expected. On April 24, 1862, he responded angrily to Radical Republican senator Benjamin F. Wade's denouncing him as a traitor by exclaiming:

Now, Sir, here in my place in the House, as a Representative I denounce ... the author of that speech as a liar, a scoundrel, and a coward. His name is BENJAMIN F. WADE.

An unsuccessful effort was launched to censure Vallandigham over these remarks. Undaunted, the brave congressman gave a particularly bold speech in the House on January 14, 1863, in which he declared,

Soon after the war began the reign of the mob was . . . supplanted by the iron domination of arbitrary power. Constitutional limitation was broken down; habeas corpus fell; liberty of the press, of speech, of the person, of the mails, of travel, of one's own house, and of religion; the right to bear arms, due process of law, judicial trial, trial by jury, trial at all; every badge and monument of freedom in republican government or kingly government—all went down at a blow; and the chief law-officer of the crown—I beg pardon, sir, but it is easy now to fall into this courtly language—the Attorney General . . . proclaimed in the United States the maxim of Roman servility: Whatever pleases the President, that is law! Prisoners of state were then first heard of here. Midnight and arbitrary arrests commenced; travel was interdicted; trade embargoed; passports demanded; bastiles were introduced; strange oaths invented; a secret police organized. . . . The right to declare war, to raise and support armies, and to provide and maintain a navy, was usurped by the Executive.

On September 24, 1862, Lincoln first declared martial law and authorized the use of military tribunals to try civilians who were suspected of being "guilty of disloyal practice" or providing "aid and comfort to rebels." Lincoln ordered ministers arrested in their churches; a priest named Kensey Johns Stewart was arrested for treason because he had refused to pray for the president. A year later, on April 13, 1863, General Ambrose Burnside, indignant over rampant anti-administration fervor in Cincinnati, Ohio, issued infamous General Order Number 38, which authorized the death penalty for those who "declared sympathies for the enemy." Clement Vallandigham blasted Lincoln's act of declaring war without the consent of Congress and charged him with "contemptuously" violating the Constitution by suspending the writ of habeas corpus. Vallandigham described it as "an offense to the intelligence" for Lincoln to argue that "gross and multiplied infractions of the Constitution and usurpations of power were done by the president . . . out of pure love and devotion to the Constitution." After a May 1, 1863 speech in which Vallandigham reacted to Burnside's order by spitting on it and trampling it under his feet, and said, among other things, that "the present war was a wicked, cruel, and unnecessary war, one not waged for the preservation of the Union, but for the purpose of crushing out liberty and to erect a despotism," 150 soldiers were sent to the ex-congressman's home at 2:40 in the morning. When refused entrance, they broke down Vallandigham's door and hauled him off to a military prison in Cincinnati.

Public outrage followed this arrest of such a prominent and distinguished citizen. The *Albany Atlas & Argus,* in its May 24, 1863 edition, suggested that the arrest was an experiment to see how much the public would tolerate, and reported, "The blow that falls upon a citizen of Ohio to-day, may be directed at a Democrat of New York tomorrow. The blow, therefore, is a threat at every Democrat." Mobs of New Yorkers assembled at the state capitol in protest. A letter from Governor Horatio Seymour was read to the crowd. Seymour said, in part, "The transaction involved a series of offences against our most sacred rights. It interfered with the freedom of speech; it violated our rights to be secure in our homes against unreasonable searches and seizures; it pronounced sentence without a trial, save one which was a mockery, which insulted as well as wronged. The perpetrators now seek to impose punishment, not for an offence against the law but for a disregard of an invalid order, put forth in an utter disregard of principles of civil liberty." The attendees, including Congressman Francis Kernan and former New York mayor and congressman Erastus Corning, drafted a series of resolutions to be sent to President Lincoln. As the resolutions pointed out, "[the] assumption of power by a military tribunal, if successfully asserted, not only abrogates the right of the people to assemble and discuss the affairs of Government, the liberty of speech and of the press, the right of trial by jury, the law of evidence, and the privileges of *Habeas Corpus,* but it strikes a fatal blow at the supremacy of law."

Lincoln's twenty-page reply to the Albany, New York Democrats was filled with ridiculous justifications. In defending the use of military tribunals, Lincoln defiantly (and ungrammatically) wrote, "a jury too frequently have (sic) at least one member, more ready to hang the panel than to hang the traitor." This was an admission that such "trials" were for show only, as there was not the slightest pretense that anyone charged would be found not guilty. Corning showed admirable resolve in his strong response, charging Lincoln with "pretensions to more than regal authority." President Franklin Roosevelt would use Lincoln's actions as a precedent to try German detainees before military tribunals. The Supreme Court, already fully accustomed to unconstitutional decisions, upheld FDR's right to do so in 1942. After the inaccurately reported events of September 11, 2001, President George W. Bush would again cite these unconstitutional precedents to justify the trying of "jihadists" before military tribunals. Former Bush deputy assistant attorney general John Yoo described Lincoln's tyranny in unique language, terming it "a vigorous and dynamic view of his right to advance an alternative vision of the Constitution." In direct reference to Clement Vallandigham's arrest, Lincoln had famously responded by saying, "Must I shoot a simple-minded soldier boy who deserts, while I must not touch a hair of the wily agitator who induces him to desert?" George W. Bush's declaration that those who opposed his perpetual "war" on terror were supporting the terrorists is a direct descendant of this remarkably statist sentiment of Lincoln's.

Vallandigham fared better than most enemies of the Lincoln administration. He wound up being banished to the Confederacy. However, since Vallandigham merely wanted peace, and didn't support the Confederacy, the Confederate leaders eventually decided to release him, and the former Ohio lawmaker made his way to Canada. Vallandigham had been nominated in absentia for the governorship of Ohio by the Democrats, and he ran his election campaign from Windsor, Ontario. The great believer in "democracy" Abraham Lincoln injected himself into the election, cautioning voters that if they supported Vallandigham, it would be "a discredit to the country." Exhibiting his usual brand of crass party politics, Lincoln also offered to revoke Vallandigham's deportation order if several Ohio congressmen would support some of his policies. On the coattails of recent northern victories, Vallandigham was defeated in the election, but told his supporters, "You were beaten, but a nobler battle for constitutional liberty and free popular government never was fought by any people." Although he and George McClellan disagreed on the Democratic Party's peace platform in the 1864 presidential election, Vallandigham was still named as the nominee for secretary of war on McClellan's ticket.

Lincoln helped establish the fine American tradition of voting fraud by ordering Republican soldiers to be furloughed by their commanders, so as to be able to make it to the polls. Lincoln instructed that soldiers who were suspected Democrats, however, were to be kept in the field, and thus unable to vote. Union soldiers also intimidated voters at the polls. As even ironclad Lincoln cultist David Herbert Donald admitted, "Under the protection of federal bayonets, New York went Republican by seven thousand votes" in the 1864 election.[7] In a 1904 essay titled "How Lincoln Secured His Re-Election," George Edmonds detailed how Lincoln, Stanton, and company had been particularly worried about New York, as signs indicated it would go overwhelmingly for McClellan. General Benjamin "Beast" Butler was sent with five thousand western troops into New York, to "control" the voting process. The New York militia, alarmed at this huge military presence, naturally objected and informed Butler that they were under the authority of the governor of the state. Butler scoffed at this, and told them, "I shall not recognize the authority of your governor. From what I hear of Governor Seymour I may find it necessary to arrest all I know who are proposing to disturb the peace on election day."[8] Butler admitted the true purpose of his presence there in a November 7 letter to Edwin Stanton, in which he said, "I have done all I could to prevent secessionists from voting."

Clement L. Vallandigham's travails supposedly inspired Edward

Everett Hale's famous short story "The Man Without a Country." Like so many others we encounter when researching these events, Vallandigham died a decidedly unnatural death. At only fifty years of age, he accidentally shot himself while demonstrating to other attorneys in his hotel room that the man his client was accused of murdering had accidentally shot himself, and died the following day on July 17, 1871. This called to mind how perhaps the South's greatest military leader, General Thomas "Stonewall" Jackson, died eight days after allegedly being mistakenly shot by his own troops on May 2, 1863.

There were even some "conspiracy theories" revolving around Jackson's death, which postulated that he had grown more strongly antislavery and even voiced doubts about the wisdom of the "lost cause." A primary suspect, an officer named John Barry, was even named. Fortunately, two astronomers in 2013 researched the phases of the moon on the night the general was killed, and somehow were able to determine that "the moon was so dim it would only have revealed his silhouette." The mainstream media bought this weak debunking attempt, trumpeting the conclusions as inviolable in articles like the one in the May 3, 2013 *UK Daily Mail*. Jackson, by the way, was only one of the Confederate leaders who was more racially enlightened than most of his northern contemporaries. He ran a Sunday school for black children, and strongly encouraged their literacy.

Even many of Lincoln's political kinsmen doubted the constitutionality of his actions. Thaddeus Stevens, perhaps the most radical Republican of them all, said, "I will not stultify myself by supposing that Mr. Lincoln has any warrant in the Constitution for dismembering Virginia." Charles Sumner, another extremely radical Republican, declared: "When Lincoln reinforced Fort Sumter and called for 75,000 men without the consent of Congress, it was the greatest breach ever made in the Constitution and would hereafter give the President the Liberty to declare war whenever he wished without the consent of Congress." Powerful financier J. P. Morgan stated, "I supported President Lincoln. I believed his war policy would be the only way to save the country, but I see my mistake. I visited Washington a few weeks ago and I saw the corruption of the present Administration and so long as Abraham Lincoln and his Cabinet are in power, so long will the war continue, and for what? For the preservation of the Constitution of the Union? No! But for the sake of politicians and governmental contractors." Massachusetts abolitionist Lysander Spooner ridiculed Lincoln's concept of "consent" by saying, "The only idea . . . ever manifested as to what is a government of consent, is this—that it is one to which everybody must consent, or be shot."

THE INVENTION OF TOTAL WAR

We are not fighting armies but a hostile people, and must make old and young, rich and poor, feel the hard hand of war.
—General William Tecumseh Sherman

The concept of "total war," and the "scorched earth" policy, was born during Sherman's March to the Sea and Sheridan's Shenandoah Valley campaign. Under this new morally relative philosophy, anything was fair game. Crops were burned, homes were destroyed, and civilians were raped and killed. The Union's notion of "total defeat" included leaving nothing behind for the surviving population to eat. Its brutality was summed up in Sherman's famous quote that "War is hell." Sherman ordered his troops to arrest everyone in the towns he invaded, and to destroy the products of their mills and factories. In a September 17, 1863 letter to the War Department, Sherman wrote: "The United States has the right, and . . . the . . . power, to penetrate to every part of the national domain. We will remove and destroy every obstacle—if need be, take every life, every acre of land, every particle of property." President

Lincoln was so impressed by Sherman's letter that he declared it should be published. In contrast to the angelic portrait painted by establishment historians of Abe Lincoln as being deeply saddened and depressed over the death and destruction from the war, Sherman himself claimed in his memoirs that Lincoln wanted to hear the gory details of his March to the Sea, and laughed uproariously at the stories about how all those women and children had suffered.

Sherman's command to remove the entire population of Atlanta was met with incredulity by his fellow general John Bell Hood, who replied, "This unprecedented measure transcends in studied and ingenious cruelty all acts ever brought to my attention in the dark history of war." But Hood, being a good soldier, obeyed his orders. Sherman instructed Brigadier General Louis Douglass Watkins to "burn 10 or 12 houses of known secessionists, kill a few at random and let them know it will be repeated every time a train is fired upon." He would tell General Philip Sheridan, "the present class of men who rule the south must be killed outright" and urged him to "make bloody results." Sherman advised Grant that the country "would rejoice to have this army turned loose on South Carolina to that state, in the manner we have done in Georgia." Sherman's "Bummers," as his marauding soldiers were referred to, were alleged to have given one-fifth of their stolen property to Sherman himself. Sherman's concept of liberty was best illustrated in a January 31, 1864 letter to Major R. M. Sawyer, in which he attributed the war to "the result of a false political doctrine that any and every people have a right to self-government." In the same letter, this American hero referred to freedom of the press and states' rights as "trash." In her book *South Carolina Civilians in Sherman's Path: Stories of Courage Amid Civil War Destruction*, Karen Stokes recounted numerous incidents of rape on the part of Union soldiers. During that Victorian era, sexual crimes were not discussed in polite society, as noted by Southern historian William Gilmore Simms, who wrote in 1865, "There are some horrors which the historian dare not pursue. They drop the curtain over crime which humanity bleeds to contemplate."

In August 1864, Ulysses S. Grant instructed Sheridan to "do all the damage to railroads and crops you can . . . if the war is to last another year, we want the Shenandoah Valley to remain a barren waste." Sheridan was only too eager to obey, informing his men "the people must be left nothing but their eyes to weep with over the war . . . Winchester or Staunton will have but little in it for man or beast." Some Union soldiers balked at this reprehensible "work." A Pennsylvania cavalryman lamented that "It was a hard-looking sight to see the women and children turned out of doors at this season of year." An Ohio major expressed remorse that the burning and pillaging "does not seem real soldierly work. We ought to enlist a force of scoundrels for such work." When Sheridan's favorite aide was shot by Confederates, he ordered all the houses within a five-mile radius burned in retaliation. Even the homes and barns belonging to the Mennonites, who were pacifists and opposed both slavery and secession, were destroyed. Historian Walter Fleming quoted a local farmer, in his 1919 book *The Sequel to Appomattox*, as saying, "From Harper's Ferry to New Market, which is about eighty miles, the country was almost a desert . . . . The barns were all burned; chimneys standing without houses, and houses standing without roof, or door, or window." President Lincoln congratulated both Sheridan and Sherman on their dastardly deeds, one of which Sherman would lovingly report in a telegram to Honest Abe thusly: "I beg to present you, as a Christmas gift, the city of Savannah." How festive.

In Vicksburg, Mississippi, an ostensibly sympathetic northern journalist nevertheless reported that Sherman's army "left the entire business district section in ruins, burned most of the better residences, dragged furniture into the street to be demolished and looted homes, churches and the state library . . . in summing up his impression of the sack of the town, he stated that such complete ruin and devastation never followed the footsteps of any army before." Following the bombardment of the town and the theft or destruction of their food supply, the residents of Vicksburg were forced to eat all their horses, mules, and even rats. As Sherman explained to Grant, the southern population "cannot be made to love us, they can be made to fear us, and dread the passage of troops through their country . . . all adherents of their cause must suffer for these cowardly acts."[9] In Mississippi, Sherman ordered that any boat fired upon could stop and burn the nearest houses and farms. When his troops weren't stealing, Sherman's heroic boys simply destroyed valuable food. In the Yazoo Valley, a half million bushels of corn were burned. Sherman proudly elaborated on his men's "work" in Meridian, Mississippi: "For 5 days 10,000 men worked hard and with a will in that work of destruction, with axes, clawbars, and with fire, and I have no hesitation in pronouncing the work as well done. Meridian with its depots, store-houses, arsenal, hospitals, offices, hotels and cantonments no longer exists." In Roswell, Georgia, Sherman ordered all the women and children who had worked in the cotton mills his men had burned to be forced to march ten miles to Marietta. Sherman snickered, " . . . the poor women will make a howl." In a classic "might makes right" argument, as well as an acknowledgement of the north's war of attrition, which George McClellan objected so strongly to, Sherman declared, "If we can, our numerical majority has both the natural and constitutional right to govern. If we cannot whip them, they contend for the natural right to select their own government." That's certainly a sentiment every future eugenicist would love. In a stunning case of projection, Sherman told the mayor of Columbia, South Carolina, "It is true our men have burnt Columbia, but it is your fault." Sherman used prisoners of war to clear land mines, and there were rumors that he also used civilians.

In 2007, the History Channel aired a remarkably inaccurate apologia for the atrocities perpetrated by Sherman's army. Much as the Warren Report was contradicted by every piece of evidence it used to reach its conclusions, this documentary was contradicted by every bit of real information that managed to seep through in the horribly biased program. The fact is an army of 60,000 "conquered" a vast territory which was defended by only a few thousand cavalry. In pure military terms, it was more of a farce than the Gulf War; Sherman's brave army faced little opposition other than terrified women and children. Sherman ordered everything destroyed, even if it held no military value whatsoever. Even using the twisted, amoral logic of the "scorched earth" policy, why did churches have to be burned, for instance? And, contrary to the notion that Sherman and his soldiers were a liberating force of abolitionists and not the common terrorists they appear to have been, the black population they encountered was not instantly freed from their servitude. On the contrary, eyewitness accounts reported that the Union army preyed mercilessly upon both the white and black southerners. They seemed to hold a special predilection for turning their lust towards black females. Sherman's descendant S. C. Sherman celebrated the general in a May 31, 2014 post shared on social media, which he titled "General William Tecumseh Sherman: What's Not to Love About Him?" Sherman's descendant wrote, "I'm proud of what he stood for. He literally freed the slaves. Like literally killed their masters and broke off their chains." It is hard to imagine a more inaccurate statement. I realize blood is thicker than water, but S. C. Sherman should read the personal accounts of those who encountered Sherman's heroic army. They didn't free any slaves, although they appear to have physically abused a lot of them, and raped many of the females.

Infrequently, the mainstream media addresses this issue critically. One of the few articles honestly examining the conduct of Union troops appeared in the October 7, 2014 *Counter Punch*. Written by the independent-minded James Bovard, it was titled, "The Civil War and 150 Years of Forgotten US Military Atrocities." Connecticut College professor Jim Downs's book *Sick From Freedom* examined how the chaotic situation both during and after the war resulted in the deaths of hundreds of thousands of newly freed slaves. William Sherman was psychotically proud of the "Sherman sentinels," or chimneys left without their houses, and "Sherman neckties," the railroad rails that had been twisted around trees. While deluded defenders of the barbaric Sherman maintain that crowds of excited, grateful slaves joined his "march" gleefully, Sherman's own orders to his troops advised, "Negroes who are able-bodied and can be of service to the several columns may be taken along." In his *Memoirs*, Sherman described how moved he was by the Fourteenth Corps' rendition of "John Brown's Body" as they looked down on Atlanta, "smouldering and in ruins, the black smoke rising high in air, and hanging like a pall over the ruined city." Lincoln, in his reply to Sherman's letter offering him his gruesome "Christmas gift," after thanking him, lauded the fearless leader who had terrorized all those defenseless women and children by saying, "the honor is all yours."

Lincoln presided over a bloodthirsty lot of Union officers. One of the most savage and corrupt of all was the "Russian Thunderbolt" Ivan Turchaninov, better known as Col. John B. Turchin. Turchin commanded the Eighth Brigade, Third Division, of the Army of the Ohio. Turchin's activities were questioned early on in the war. Brig. Gen. Stephen A. Hurlbut, commanding Headquarters Brigade of the Illinois Militia, notified Col. Turchin on July 16, 1861 that some of his troops "violated private rights of property and of persons." On June 30, 1862, Maj. Gen. Ormsby M. Mitchel informed Gen. Don Carlos Buell, commander of the Army of the Ohio, that "The pillage of the town of Athens (Alabama) by the troops under the command of colonel Turchin is a matter of general notoriety." Gen. Buell issued orders to have Turchin court-martialed. On August 6, 1862, Buell published the findings of the court-martial:

> (He) allowed his command to disperse and in his presence or with his knowledge and that of his officers to plunder and pillage the inhabitants

. . . they attempted and indecent outrage on a servant girl . . . destroyed a
stock of . . . fine Bibles and Testaments. . . . A part of the brigade went to
the plantation . . . and quartered in the negro huts for weeks, debauching
the females . . . Mrs. Hollingsworth's house was entered and plundered . . .
The alarm and excitement occasioned miscarriage and subsequently her
death. . . . Several soldiers committed rape on the person of a colored girl.
. . . It is a fact of sufficient notoriety that similar disorders . . . have marked
the course of Colonel Turchin's command wherever it has gone.

Turchin scoffed that his superior officers "want the rebellion treated ten-
derly and gently." Even though Col. Turchin was found guilty, Lincoln promoted him to the rank of general of the United States Volunteers![10]

"Honest Abe" was presented with solid evidence that former Radical
Republican senator James H. Lane, by then a Union brigadier general, was
responsible, or his troops were, for all manner of pillaging and plundering.
Major General Henry W. Halleck wrote General George B. McClellan about
this on December 19, 1861, stating, ". . . I receive almost daily complaints of
outrages committed by these men . . . and the evidence is so conclusive as to
leave no doubt of their correctness. It is rumored that Lane has been made
a brigadier-general. I cannot conceive of a more injudicious appointment. . . .
Its effect . . . is offering a premium for rascality and robbing generally."
McClellan presented this letter to Lincoln, and he responded by turning
the letter over and writing: "An excellent letter, though I am sorry General
Halleck is so unfavorably impressed with General Lane."[11] General Ulysses
S. Grant stopped exchanging prisoners with the South for the most basic
of mathematical reasons: waging a war of attrition, he knew the numbers
were on his side. Grant and other northern leaders even refused to accept
northern prisoners that the South wanted to release, *without exchanging any
southern prisoners in return.* The South pleaded in vain to release their sick
prisoners, or for the North to at least send medicine and doctors to administer to them. It was incredibly unjust to claim that the atrocious conditions

at Southern prisons like Andersonville were the result of inhumane, cruel prison officials. The South couldn't feed its own troops; how could they have hoped to feed and provide for their prisoners of war? Grant was no military tactician by any measure. He freely acknowledged his horrific strategy, saying his goal was "to hammer continuously against the armed force of the enemy, and his resources, until by mere attrition, if in no other way, there should be nothing left to him."

The North invented yet another unheard of concept when it tried Andersonville Commander Captain Henry Wirz for "war crimes" and summarily hung him. Prior to this time, the term "war crime" was unknown, and it was unheard of for the victors to legally sentence the losers following a war. Even after a similar internal conflict, the English Civil War of the mid-seventeenth century, King Charles I was tried and executed for treason, not "war crimes." One of Wirz's "crimes" was sending thousands of his prisoners to Jacksonville, Florida, which was occupied by Union troops, in an effort to release them. Incredibly, Union officers rejected his offer and they were forced back to Andersonville. Wirz demonstrated more courage and principles than those who executed him; his life would have been spared if he'd merely testified that Jefferson Davis had ordered the murder of prisoners under his command. However, he refused to falsely testify and incriminate Davis. The United Daughters of the Confederacy, with great justification, issued a proclamation in 1908, charging that Wirz had been the victim of "judicial murder." Journalist Edward Wellington Boate was only one of the former Andersonville POWs who attributed the conditions at the prison to the actions of the federal government. The guards at Andersonville had little to eat, let alone the prisoners. Boate called Wirz "as kind-hearted a man as I ever met." According to author James Bovard, this was not an isolated event; he wrote that "The northern armies treated Confederate soldiers who resisted the barn-burning and crop-burning as war criminals and hanged them."

Senator Orville H. Browning, who'd tried many cases with and against Lincoln in Illinois and was a trusted confidante, gave another glaring example of Old Abe's "malice." Sometime in 1864, Browning met with the president on behalf of one Mrs. Fitz, a loyal Mississippi widow who'd been robbed of all her slaves and corn crop by the US Army. In Browning's words:

> She is now a refugee in St Louis, reduced to indigence. She asks no compensation . . . but wishes the government to give her a sufficient number of negroes out of those accumulated upon its hands to work her farm the ensuing season . . . she to pay them out of the proceeds the same wages which the government pays those it employs. I made the proposition to the President thinking it reasonable and just . . . . He became very much excited, and did not discuss the proposition at all, but said with great vehemence he had rather take a rope and hang himself than to do it. There were a great many poor women who had never had any property at all who were suffering as much as Mrs Fitz—that her condition was a necessary consequence of the rebellion, and that the government could not make good the losses occasioned by rebels. I reminded him that she was loyal, and that her property had been taken from her by her own government, and was now being used by it, and I thought it a case eminently proper for some sort of renumeration, and her demand reasonable, and certainly entitled to respectful consideration. He replied that she had lost no property—that her slaves were free when they were taken, and that she was entitled to no compensation. I called his attention to the fact that a portion of her slaves, at least, had been taken in 1862, before his proclamation, and put upon our gun boats, when he replied in a very excited manner that he had rather throw up, than to do what was asked, and would not do anything about it.[12]

It is interesting how similar this foul, unreasonable attitude of Lincoln's, attested to by a longtime friend, was to his encounter with the imprisoned officer's wife, described earlier.

On the Yankee War Crimes blog, the list of ugly, nearly incomprehensible anecdotes of Union atrocities is lengthy. It is difficult to determine the worst of them. The bedridden old man in Lafayette, Louisiana, whose every worldly possession—including his bed covers—was stolen by Yankee soldiers? The ninety-year-old in Louisiana from whom Union troops took everything—even his clothes? The Goulas family in St. Mary Parish, whose babies' clothing and bedding were stolen by soldiers? Mrs. Vilmeau of Louisiana, whose wedding ring was *bitten* off her finger, and pierced earrings torn from her ears? The relatives of those in New Iberia burial vaults, who had to witness Yankees scattering their loved ones' bodies on the ground, and then using the tombs for cooking? Louisiana's Dr. Brashear, whose body was torn from his grave and his metal coffin stolen by soldiers? The citizens of Opelousas, Louisiana, who watched a Massachusetts Army unit turn the local Methodist Church into a brothel? The Catholics in New Iberia, who saw Union troops dance in the robes of their priest and steal the chalice from their Catholic Church? The citizens of Franklin, Louisiana, who witnessed Lincoln's heroic boys tear up the Methodist Church there, and use the pews and other wood from the church as furnishings for a pool parlor? The grandchildren of Theodore Fay of Franklin, Louisiana, whose little toys were stolen by Yankee soldiers? And all that was from just one state. Yankee troops burned family Bibles that contained precious family records. In Chesterfield, South Carolina, Sherman's troops torched the courthouse, destroying all the marriage, property, and other irreplaceable historical records.

When New Orleans became "occupied" in 1862 under the command of Benjamin "Beast" Butler, a reign of terror ensued. An enthusiastic young rebel named William Mumford was hanged for tearing down a Union flag.

Butler sent women, preachers, and priests to jail for refusing to welcome the military invaders. Continuing the clear anti-religious pattern, Butler also closed churches in New Orleans and prohibited church attendance. Butler's infamous General Order No. 28, issued in response to the women of the city insulting Union troops, instructed that every woman thereafter be treated as "plying her avocation"; in other words, as common prostitutes. The order was widely viewed in the south as a legalization of rape. Nancy Emerson of Staunton, Virginia wrote a moving diary about the horrific things she witnessed during the Shenandoah Valley "campaign" of Sheridan and other Yankee officers. "Nothing ought to astonish us," she declared about "this unjust and abominable war." Taking this "campaign" to the next level, Grant issued the memorable order to Sheridan to "eat out Virginia clear and clean." In her diary, which evoked far less interest from the court historians than Mary Chestnut's well-known recollections, Emerson recounted all the atrocities she experienced firsthand, including the very real invasions of private homes by federal troops, where they confiscated food and property.

In denying the right of the southern states to leave the union, Lincoln had apparently forgotten his own words; in the congressional records of 1847, then Rep. Lincoln said, "Any people whatever have a right to abolish the existing government and form a new one that suits them better." The public reads the following quote from Lincoln, and the court historians nod solemnly in appreciation of it, without the slightest understanding of its irony: "This country, with its institutions, belongs to the people who inhabit it. Whenever they shall grow weary of the existing government, they can exercise their constitutional right of amending it, or exercise their revolutionary right to overthrow it." Thomas Jefferson, in the Declaration of Independence, had written, "Whenever any form of government becomes destructive of the ends for which it was established, it is the right of the people to alter or abolish it, and to institute new government." This passage, in fact, was quoted verbatim in South Carolina's Declaration of Secession from the Union. Even Horace Greeley's *New York Daily Tribune* recognized this right, in a December 17, 1860 editorial: "We do heartily accept this doctrine, believing it intrinsically sound, beneficent, and one that, universally accepted, is calculated to prevent the shedding of seas of human blood. And, if it justified the secession from the British Empire of Three Millions of colonists in 1776, we do not see why it would not justify the secession of Five Millions of Southrons from the Federal Union in 1861." On January 12, 1861, the *New York Journal of Commerce* stated that coercing any states to remain in the union by force would change the nature of our government from "a voluntary one, in which the people are sovereigns, to a despotism." Our entire movement for independence was based upon the notion that people have a right to consent, or not to consent, to those who govern them. Clearly, by 1860, the southern states no longer consented. I think there is little doubt that Jefferson, Washington, Patrick Henry, and other revolutionary-era leaders would have supported the South, and would have been mortified by the actions of President Lincoln.

LINCOLN THE RACIST

In the language of Mr. Jefferson, uttered many years ago, "It is still in our power to direct the process of emancipation, and deportation, peaceably" . . . *Our republican system was meant for a homogeneous people. As long as blacks continue to live with the whites they constitute a threat to the national life. Family life may also collapse and the increase of mixed breed bastards may some day challenge the supremacy of the white man.*

—Abraham Lincoln

Some little-known facts about the respective racial enlightenment of southern and northern leaders should be noted. Few Americans have ever heard, for instance, that heroic northern General Ulysses S. Grant was not only a slaveholder, but he continued to hold a slave for almost a year after the war ended, and only freed him when an act of Congress forced him to. Snopes.com, predictably, disputes the fact that Grant owned any slaves except perhaps the one he freed in 1859, but the National Park Service, hardly a bastion of neo-Confederate thought, acknowledges that his wife continued to hold slaves until forced to free them in 1866, after the Thirteenth Amendment was passed. Grant responded to criticism of his wife acting so belatedly and begrudgingly by saying, "Good help is so hard to find."[13] Grant's fellow Union general William Tecumseh Sherman was also a slave owner, and had been arrested numerous times for savagely beating his slaves.[14] General Robert E. Lee, on the other hand, had freed all his slaves prior to the start of the war. Snopes, always anxious to tout the establishment line, disputes this, but makes Lee look even better by claiming there is no evidence he ever owned slaves. Confederate president Jefferson Davis actually adopted a boy of mixed race and treated him as a son. He was separated from the Davis family during the forced abandonment of Richmond to Union troops in April 1865. The southern states, like the rest of the world where the odious practice was common, would have abolished slavery on their own. Indeed, Virginia, considered the "Cradle of the Confederacy," had its state legislature wind up just a single vote short on a bill to abolish slavery *years before the Civil War*. Jefferson Davis tried to get the British government to recognize the Confederacy on the basis of its abolishing slavery.[15] The 1860 census revealed that only *4.8 percent* of Southerners owned slaves. The rebels who fought against the Federal invaders were almost all non-slave owners.

The Great Emancipator himself left some truly staggering comments about blacks on the public record. The most famous of these came from one of his debates with Stephen Douglas, when he stated, "I am not, nor ever have been in favor of bringing about in any way the social and political equality of the white and black races, that I am not nor ever have been in favor of making voters or jurors of negroes, nor of qualifying them to hold office, nor to intermarry with white people; and I will say in addition to this that there is a physical difference between the white and black races which I believe will forever forbid the two races living together on terms of social and political equality . . . while they do remain together there must be the position of superior and inferior, and I as much as any other man am in favor of having the superior position assigned to the white race." It is difficult to imagine a Grand Wizard of the Ku Klux Klan saying anything more racist.

Like many whites at the time, Lincoln was in favor of colonizing blacks back to Africa. On August 14, 1862, Lincoln told a group of free black ministers visiting the White House that "You and we are different races. We have between us a broader difference than exists between almost any other two races" and went on to advise them that *his* race "suffers from your presence." In a 1857 speech addressing the Supreme Court's *Dred Scott* decision, Lincoln declared, "There is a natural disgust in the minds of nearly all white people to the idea of indiscriminate amalgamation of the white and black races. . . . A separation of the races is the only perfect preventive of amalgamation, but as an immediate separation is impossible, the next best thing is to keep them apart where they are not already together. If white and black people never get together in Kansas, they will never mix blood in Kansas." Even in his second Annual Message to Congress in 1862, Lincoln said, "I cannot make it better known than it already is that I strongly favor colonization."

Lincoln could have freed all the slaves in the North at any time. Instead, his Emancipation Proclamation only freed those within the confines of the seceded states. Even Lincoln's loyal secretary of state William Seward realized the absurdity here, acerbically remarking, "We show our sympathy with slavery by emancipating slaves where we cannot reach them and holding them in bondage where we can set them free." Lincoln's Proclamation was a typically pragmatic political act, issued in response to the fact that both Great Britain and France were on the verge of recognizing the Confederacy. Lincoln freely admitted this, saying, "I view the matter [Emancipation Proclamation] as a practical war measure, to be decided upon according to the advantages or disadvantages it may offer to the suppression of the rebellion."

Lincoln had long stressed that his desire was to save the Union, whether that included freeing all of the slaves, some of the slaves, or none of the slaves. "My paramount object in this struggle is to save the Union, and is not either to save or destroy slavery," Lincoln admitted. It wasn't until the time of the Proclamation that Lincoln talked about slavery as a root cause of the conflict. In his first inaugural address, Lincoln said, "I have no purpose, directly or indirectly, to interfere with the institution of slavery in the States where it exists. I believe I have no lawful right to do so, and I have no inclination to do so." The word "slavery" didn't appear in Lincoln's First Annual Message (what is now called a State of the Union address) to Congress. On September 15, 1862, Lincoln told a delegation from Chicago, "What good would a proclamation of emancipation from me do. . . . Would my word free the slaves, when I cannot even enforce the Constitution in the Rebel states?" Unbelievably, just seven days later, Lincoln issued his initial Proclamation. By his second annual message, in December 1862, shortly before passage of the Emancipation Proclamation on January 1, 1863, Lincoln was declaring that the rebellion couldn't have existed without slavery, and "without slavery, it could not continue." Mary Chestnut, in her still marvelously sharp *A Diary From Dixie*, cogently remarked, "The Yankees, since the war has begun, have discovered it is to free the slaves that they are fighting. So their cause is noble."

The Emancipation Proclamation of 1862 was hardly met with universal approval in the North. *The Chicago Times* called it "a monstrous usurpation, a criminal wrong." Ohio's *The Crisis* editorialized, "Is this not a death blow to the hope of union . . . we shall have a dictator proclaimed, for the

Proclamation can never be carried out except under the iron rule of the worst kind of despotism." Lincoln's secretary spoke of all the angry letters sent to the president, some of them from outraged journalists. There was a common theme to the letters, where the writers stressed that they "never gave him any authority to run it as an Abolition war." Because of his executive action, one letter declared, "he is a more unconstitutional tyrant and a more odious dictator than ever he was before." A *New York Herald* reporter, an early precursor to those journalists "embedded" in more recent wars, spoke of the dissatisfaction of the troops and the "large promise of a fearful revolution." The midterm elections were a disaster for Lincoln and the Republicans, and the number of Democrats in Congress nearly doubled. There were thousands of soldiers who deserted from the Union ranks, and rumors that the Proclamation could spark the secession of northwest states like Illinois, Indiana, and Ohio.

LINCOLN THE WARMONGER

I mean simply to say that the war will cease on the part of the government,
whenever it shall have ceased on the part of those who began it.
—Abraham Lincoln, 1864 Annual Message to Congress

Union stalwarts like writer Ralph Waldo Emerson were far more vicious and spiteful than the rebels they condemned. Consider the following comments from Emerson: "If it costs us ten years, and ten to recover the general prosperity, the destruction of the South is worth so much."[16] Incidentally, the great-grandfather of this noted "liberal," Cornelius Waldo, was a slave merchant in Boston, Massachusetts.[17] The authors of *The South Was Right* report on the case of Union general Harry Truman were, in the summer of 1864, tried and found guilty of murder, arson, and larceny, and sentenced to be hanged. Secretary of War Edwin Stanton ordered Truman released and returned to his old rank and status.[18] The curious thing is not only the name, but the fact that this odious officer was located in northern Missouri. Given that the future US president shared his name, and his locale, one wonders if they were related. The authors say nothing about this, and I could find no documented connection. Another renowned writer, Nathaniel Hawthorne, wrote to his wife, just after the shots were fired on Fort Sumter, "Though I approve the war as much as any man, I don't quite understand what we are fighting for."[19] It's educational to know that this kind of mindless patriotism is not a modern phenomenon, even among the most creative spirits. Yet another gifted writer, Boston poet and critic James Russell Lowell, wrote in a private letter: "Mr. Lincoln seems to have the theory of carrying on the war without hurting the enemy. He is incapable, of understanding that they *ought* to be hurt."[20]

Lincoln's inflexibility and unwillingness to negotiate a settlement was best revealed in an incident that occurred at the time of the battle of Gettysburg. "Honest Abe" refused to permit Confederate vice president Alexander Stephens and a companion to pass through a Union blockade and enter Washington. Stephens and his fellow rebel had hoped to hold a conference, but Lincoln's telegram to the blockading admiral said it all: "The request of A. H. Stephens is inadmissible. The customary agents and channels are adequate for all needful communication and conference between the United States forces and the insurgents."[21] It is illuminating to quote from the letter Jefferson Davis sent to Stephens just before his trip, in which he stated, "My whole purpose is, in one word, to place this war on the footing of such as are waged by civilized people in modern times, and to divest it of the savage character which has been impressed upon it by our enemies, in spite of all our efforts and protests. War is full enough of unavoidable horrors." Davis went on to note the North's refusal to exchange prisoners, and the "unheard of conduct of Federal Officers in driving from their homes entire communities of women and children. . . . The putting to death of unarmed prisoners." It is impossible to escape the notion, when reading the respective words and thoughts of Confederate leaders and Union leaders, that nowhere else in American history have the court historians affixed "good" and "bad" labels more dishonestly.

Lincoln's central strategy overall was to capitalize on the huge northern advantage in numbers; to wage, as noted previously, a war of attrition. This was the primary reason behind the schism between Lincoln and General George McClellan. McClellan, whom Lincoln derisively chided for having "a case of the slows," was loath to sacrifice his men in such a war of attrition. As McClellan wrote in a letter to the president, echoing the same theme as Jefferson Davis:

> This rebellion has assumed the character of a War: as such it should be regarded; and it should be conducted upon the highest principles known to Christian Civilization. It should not be a War looking to the subjugation of the people of any state, in any event. It should not be, at all, a War upon population; but against armed forces and political organizations. Neither confiscation of property, political executions of persons, territorial organization of states or forcible abolition of slavery should be contemplated for a moment. In prosecuting the War, all private property and unarmed persons should be strictly protected.

In light of what was to come later, under the command of generals like Sherman, Grant, and Sheridan, this was quite a noteworthy observation, and revealed a tremendous contradiction in philosophies.

George McClellan was slandered constantly behind the scenes, especially by Lincoln's young aides John Hay and John Nicolay. In a letter to Nicolay, Hay wrote, ". . . the little Napoleon sits trembling before the handful of men at Yorktown afraid either to fight or run. Stanton feels devilish about it. He would like to remove him if he thought it would do." Like the bold, present-day "Chicken Hawks" who are so fond of sending others to war, both Hay and Nicolay were among the favored few males of their generation who managed to avoid the tremendous battle for the "Union" being waged by their social inferiors. Hay would leave overt evidence of his animosity towards McClellan in a letter not meant for publication; referring to the ten-volume biography of Lincoln he was writing, he said of McClellan: "I think I have left the impression of his mutinous imbecility, and I have done it in a perfectly courteous manner. It is of the utmost moment that we should seem fair to him, while we are destroying him." After the disastrous 1862 defeat in the Peninsula Campaign, McClellan pulled no punches in his letter to Washington: "I again repeat that I am not responsible for this and I say it with the earnestness of a General who feels in his heart the loss of every brave man who has been needlessly sacrificed today. . . . I have seen too many dead and wounded comrades to feel otherwise. . . . If I save this Army now I tell you plainly that I owe no thanks to you or any other persons in Washington—you have done your best to sacrifice this Army." McClellan's remarks were considered so inflammatory they were deleted by telegraph operators before being forwarded to Stanton and Lincoln.[22] In contrast to the low opinion those in Washington at the time held of him, and his subsequent poor reputation among establishment historians, Robert E. Lee was only one of the Confederate leaders who rated McClellan as the best Union general he fought against, "by all odds." I attempted to locate descendants of McClellan while writing this book. It is a testament to the fates of those who are on the "wrong" side of history that essential facts, birthdates, names of children, etc., about his *grandchildren* aren't in the public record.

Establishment historians persistently promulgate the notion that "Honest Abe," unlike Radical Republican cronies such as Thaddeus Stephens, wanted to welcome the Confederate states back into the Union with open arms and a spirit of reconciliation. This is, however, contradicted by virtually every action Lincoln undertook as president, and his true beliefs were best expressed in his last annual message to Congress, delivered in December 1864. Besides a typical statist reminder that "Taxation should be still further increased," in a crass and tactless gesture even for him, Lincoln seemed to downplay the massive losses of human life in his noble war with a reference to the fact that ". . . we have more men now than we had when the war began; that we are not exhausted, nor in process of exhaustion; that we are gaining strength, and may, if need be, maintain the contest indefinitely." Of any effort at negotiation, Lincoln said: ". . . it seems to me that no attempt at negotiation with the insurgent leader could result in any good." Even an ultra-loyal northern propaganda organ like *Harper's Weekly* categorized the speech as very "unconciliatory."[23] In early 1865, when the Confederacy was in its final waning days, Lincoln curtly replied to yet another attempt to engage him in negotiation by declaring that three things were indispensable to peace: "1. The restoration of the national authority throughout all the States. 2. No receding, by the Executive of the United States on the Slavery question, from the position assumed thereon, in the late Annual Message to Congress, and in preceding documents. 3. No cessation of hostilities short of an end of the war, and the disbanding of all forces hostile to the government."[24] In other words, there was to be absolutely no flexibility on Lincoln's part.

In a highly symbolic final gesture towards the defeated South, Lincoln and his son Tad—on April 4, 1865, the boy's twelfth birthday—walked a mile or so through the burned-out shell of Richmond, Virginia, the capitol of the Confederacy. Lincoln must have felt giddy over all the blacks he encountered, who literally went down on their knees before him, proclaiming him their savior. The Union troops yelled out, "Three cheers for Uncle Abe!" Then, Lincoln strode into the Confederate White House, sat triumphantly in Jefferson Davis's chair, and put his feet up on the desk. Incredibly, this arrogant gesture of Lincoln's has been interpreted by mainstream historians as evidence of his humility, and his reckless visit (certainly endangering the welfare of his son) to Richmond has been portrayed in a heroic light, where Lincoln boldly and bravely risked the wrath of any remaining rebels in the city. No historian appears willing to accept it for what it was: a victorious tyrant celebrating the defeat of a vanquished foe. Reports even persisted that the Great Emancipator, fresh from being hailed as a messiah by worshipful blacks, told a racist joke while seated in Davis's chair![25]

LINCOLN THE ATHEIST

My earlier views on the unsoundness of the Christian scheme of salvation and the human origin of the scriptures, have become clearer and stronger with advancing years and I see no reason for thinking I shall ever change them.

—Abraham Lincoln

Lincoln's closest friend William Herndon admitted that Lincoln was "at times, an atheist." He told someone who asked about Lincoln's religious beliefs that the less said on that subject the better. Lincoln once said, "The Bible is not my book nor Christianity my profession." Lincoln attributed his Thanksgiving message to "some of Seward's nonsense, and it pleases the fools." The words "under God" were not in Lincoln's Gettysburg Address, and were added later. Even his wife Mary Todd Lincoln acknowledged that her husband "never joined any church" and "was not a technical Christian." Legend has it that Lincoln, in his youth, penned a rebuttal to the divinity of Christ. One of those who testified to this, Judge James M. Nelson, an intimate friend of Lincoln's, said "so far as I have been able to find out, he remained an unbeliever." The *New York World* would admit, a decade after his assassination, that Lincoln "was no disciple of Jesus of Nazareth. He did not believe in his divinity." The newspaper, ever anxious as all mainstream media was and still is to perpetuate the heroic myth of Lincoln, justified "the partial concealment of his individual religious opinions" because "it was a conscientious and patriotic sacrifice." According to a February 15, 1998 story in *The New York Times*, John T. Stuart, Lincoln's first law partner, claimed that he "went further against Christian beliefs . . . than any man I ever heard." Lincoln, of course, was free like anyone else to choose his religious beliefs, and this is mentioned only as an illustration of his political hypocrisy.

One little-pondered historical question is just why Lincoln went to a theater on a Good Friday. Certainly, he was no Catholic, but in those times the day was generally considered a somber, if not holy one. And theaters were still considered dens of vices to many Americans. Even a typical worshipful journalist like George Alfred Townsend would write, "The Chief Magistrate of thirty million people—beloved, honored, revered, lay in the pent up closet of a play-house, dabbling with his sacred blood the robes of an actress." John Wilkes Booth's sister, despite coming from such a renowned acting family, remarked that "It desecrated his idea to have his end come in a devil's den, a theater." Missing the point entirely, reliable establishment historian Harold Holzer, one of the most devout of Lincoln's disciples, attempted to impart religious significance to the fact the assassination occurred on Good Friday. Holzer did share the interesting tidbit that Lincoln had "received a suggestion from a bishop in Rhode Island a few weeks before reminding him that he ought to declare that day a day of fasting and mourning. He simply ignored it and went to the theater."[26]

One of Lincoln's most irrational devotees was Robert G. Ingersoll, a leading politician and orator known as "The Great Agnostic." Ingersoll actually wrote the following about Lincoln:

Abraham Lincoln was, in my judgment, in many respects, the grand-est man ever President of the United States. Upon his monument these words should be written: "Here sleeps the only man in the history of the world, who, having been clothed with almost absolute power, never abused it, except upon the side of mercy." Think how long we clung to the institution of human slavery, how long lashes upon the naked back were a legal tender for labor performed. Think of it. With every drop of my blood I hate and execrate every form of tyranny, every form of slavery. . . . I love liberty.

Presumably, "The Great Agnostic" loved the suspension of civil liberties and the mass arrests of those who disagreed with his hero's policies. He evidently didn't believe in the consent of the governed. It is hard to imagine a more inaccurate assessment of an individual than Ingersoll's homage to Lincoln.

For a seeming religious skeptic, to put it mildly, Lincoln invoked the name of the Almighty freely when it served his purposes. One clear transformation we see in Lincoln's speeches, as analyzed so thoroughly in *When in the Course of Human Events* by Charles Adams, is his attempt, during the last period of his presidency, to shift the responsibility for the war onto God. There was an earlier fragment, written by Lincoln in September 1862, preserved by John Hay, who nevertheless said it was "not written to be seen of men," in which Honest Abe declared, "I am almost ready to say that this is probably true—that God wills this contest, and wills that it shall not end yet. By His mere great power, on the minds of the now contestants, He could have either saved or destroyed the Union without human contest. Yet the contest began, And, having begun He could give the final victory to either side any day. Yet the contest proceeds." His second inaugural address really stressed this theme. "Yet, if God wills that it continue until all the wealth piled by the bondsman's two hundred and fifty years of unrequited toil shall be sunk, and until every drop of blood drawn with the lash shall be paid by another drawn with the sword, as was said three thousand years ago, so still it must be said 'the judgments of the Lord are true and righteous altogether.'" Evidently, in Lincoln's mind, it was God who held such a rigid stance against those who wanted to govern themselves, refusing to negotiate and even refusing to accept the South's humanitarian gesture of releasing their prisoners of war. And it was God who demanded that over half a million mostly white lives be lost in a battle to free people that Lincoln himself didn't believe were his equals.

LINCOLN'S TRUE LEGACY

Nearly all men can stand adversity, but if you want to test a man's character, give him power.

—Abraham Lincoln

Acknowledging Abraham Lincoln for what he was did not always result in social and professional ostracization. Renowned author Edgar Lee Masters, in his long-forgotten 1931 book *Lincoln the Man*, accurately noted that "Honest Abe" had "crushed the principles of free government." Masters portrayed Lincoln as a tool of the bankers, who wanted to establish a new bank of the United States. Masters summed up the beliefs of many conspiracy theorists when he wrote, "The political history of America has been written for the most part by those who were unfriendly to the theory of a confederate republic." Masters brilliantly stated that Lincoln "was to inaugurate a war without the American people having anything to say about it." Cogently recognizing the awful precedent that Lincoln had established, Masters wrote, "The World War added to the proof, for Wilson did many things that Lincoln did, and with Lincoln as authority for doing them." Lincoln's overreaching, imperialistic actions have been used as a model by most of the presidents who followed him in office. More than any other historical figure, Abraham Lincoln is responsible for the undue influence of executive power.

In 1932, elderly Virginian Lyon Gardiner Tyler, son of President John Tyler, said of Lincoln. "I think he was a bad man, a man who forced the country into an unnecessary war and conducted it with great inhumanity."[27] Tyler was one of a dying breed, perhaps the last of the anti-Lincoln brigade who personally lived through Lincoln's tyranny. As Don E. Feherenbacher wrote, in *The Anti-Lincoln Tradition*, "the Confederate image of Abraham Lincoln in the 1860s bears a striking resemblance to the American image of Adolf Hitler in the 1940s." It is sobering to consider how Lincoln would be viewed historically if the South had won the War Between the States. As we should always remember, history is written by the victors.

While Lincoln attained the status of a secular saint, a veritable "Father Abraham," throughout much of America following his assassination, the south remembered him differently and was in a celebratory mood. "The world is happily rid of a monster that disgraced the form of humanity," crowed the *Texas Republican*. Some northerners celebrated, too; an unfortunate man in Swampscott, Massachusetts who rejoiced over Lincoln's assassination was tarred and feathered. A man in Astoria, New York was heard celebrating the assassination, and was strung up "as long as was safe without utter strangulation." The editor of the *Seattle Weekly Gazette* wrote, "There are about two dozen of the same sort in this vicinity who deserve the same treatment—except that they ought not to be taken down so soon." Even fellow Republican, Senator Benjamin Wade, regarded Lincoln's assassination as a political blessing. Marcus M. Pomeroy, editor of a small Wisconsin paper, had declared, on the eve of the 1864 election, "The man who votes for Lincoln now is a traitor and murderer. . . . And if he is elected to misgovern for another four years, we trust some bold hand will pierce his heart with dagger point for the public good."

When we celebrate Abraham Lincoln, what are we celebrating? A man who relentlessly pushed an internal conflict that eventually claimed over 620,000 lives, more than the losses Americans have suffered in nearly all other wars combined? A leader who imprisoned an unknown number of citizens, without charges, for simply opposing his policies? A crafty politician who converted the public rationale for the war, halfway through the conflict, into a struggle against slavery, while he personally harbored white supremacist views? A supposedly spiritual savior who was in actuality probably an atheist, who nevertheless late in the war overtly attempted to attribute all the bloodshed to the will of God? A politician so betrothed to big bankers that he once jumped from the second floor window during a hearing of the Illinois House of Representatives, in order to break a quorum when Democrats had called for a vote to cripple the state bank? A man who didn't attend his own father's funeral? Upon being informed of his father's declining health, Lincoln refused to visit him and asked his stepbrother to "Say to him that if we could meet now, it is doubtful whether it would not be more painful than pleasant." What does it say about us as a people, or about the civilization we've created, that *this* tyrannical leader, with more blood on his hands than any other ever elected to the office of the presidency, is considered the crown jewel of our nation's history?

In a 1949 essay, future John F. Kennedy aide, historian Arthur M. Schlesinger Jr., expressed the conventional view that the Civil War was an unavoidable, necessary conflict. Along with World War II, the Civil War is almost universally considered now to have been a "good" war, one that only "racists," perhaps even aspiring slave masters, could have opposed. In Schlesinger's words, there are simply times when a society works itself "into a logjam; and that logjam must be burst by violence." Juxtaposed against Schlesinger's simplistic perspective, the staggering numbers from Lincoln's bloody war boggle the mind. The total deaths from the war, adjusting for today's numbers, would be about six million Americans lost, or 2 percent of the entire population. There were 23,000 casualties during the one-day battle of Antietam alone, and 51,000 casualties at Gettysburg. As H. L. Mencken put it, in honestly dissecting Lincoln's Gettysburg Address: "But let us not forget that it is poetry, not logic; beauty, not sense. Think of the argument in it. . . . The doctrine is simply this: that the Union soldiers who died at Gettysburg sacrificed their lives to the cause of self-determina-tion—'that government of the people, by the people, for the people,' should not perish from the earth. It is difficult to imagine anything more untrue. The Union soldiers in that battle actually fought *against* self-determination; it was the Confederates who fought for the right of their people to govern themselves." The decidedly leftist Mencken went on to note, "What was the practical effect of the battle of Gettysburg? What else than the destruc-tion of the old sovereignty of the States, *i.e.*, of the people of the States?" Demonstrating how honest liberals once viewed Reconstruction, Mencken declared, "The Confederates went into battle free; they came out with their freedom subject to the supervision and veto of the rest of the country—and for nearly twenty years that veto was so effective that they enjoyed scarcely more liberty, in the political sense, than so many convicts in the peniten-tiary." And *that* misleading speech is considered the greatest in American history by establishment scholars. Mencken summed up the war thusly: "The American people, North and South, went into The War as citizens of their respective states, they came out as subjects of the United States. And what they lost they have never got back."

Northern abolitionist Lysander Spooner echoed this theme:

The principle, on which the war was waged by the North, was simply this: That men may rightfully be compelled to submit to, and support, a gov-ernment that they do not want; and that resistance, on their part, makes them traitors and criminals. No principle, that is possible to be named, can be more self-evidently false than this; or more self-evidently fatal to all political freedom. Yet it triumphed in the field, and is now assumed to be established. If it really be established, the number of slaves, instead of having been diminished by the war, has been greatly increased; for a man, thus subjected to a government that he does not want, is a slave. And there is no difference, in principle—but only in degree—between political and chattel slavery. The former, no less than the latter, denies a man's ownership of himself and the products of his labor; and asserts that other men may own him, and dispose of him and his property, for their uses, and at their pleasure.

Speaking of Gettysburg, the Confederate dead there weren't accorded proper Christian burials. They were instead shoved into trenches, buried alongside roads, or left in unmarked graves. A newspaper at the time reported, "The poor Confederate dead were left in the fields as outcasts and criminals that did not merit decent sepulture." While Lincoln spoke of brave soldiers "consecrating" the ground, he might have requested that they all be shown at least a bit of respect. Fund-raising efforts after the war finally resulted, in 1872, in bodies of dead rebels being sent back to Richmond for burial in Hollywood Cemetery. One of those never identified, but presumed to be among these Confederate corpses, was Brigadier General Richard B. Garnett, who was killed while leading what became known as "Pickett's Charge." Some 20 percent of the soldiers Honest Abe sacrificed on the "altar of freedom" were under eighteen years old. Forty percent of the poor souls who perished on the battlefields were never identified. The estimated cost of the war, in today's dollars, ran to approximately $146 billion. Before the war, the government was spending more than one third *per year* less than what it would be spending *per day* during the conflict.

The court historians interpret what is commonly referred to as Lincoln's "Blind Memorandum" in their customary manner. Some even call it Lincoln's "finest moment." This short note that Lincoln wrote on August

23, 1864 stated, "This morning, as for some days past, it seems exceedingly probable that this Administration will not be re-elected. Then it will be my duty to so cooperate with the President elect, as to save the Union between the election and the inauguration; as he will have secured his election on such ground that he cannot possibly save it afterwards." Lincoln went on to fold the note and demand that his cabinet members sign and date the back of it, *without reading it*. To the court historian, this is somehow another example of Honest Abe's mystical magnificence. To an impartial observer, it indicates that Lincoln meant to continue the war indefinitely, and "win" it before allowing his successor to take office. Considering what was already happening at the hands of federal troops by then, it isn't unfair to ask if Lincoln might have been so desperate to "save" the union that he would have simply murdered the remaining southern population. But establishment scholars have ignored the fact that Lincoln oversaw the first blatant voting fraud in American history, not to mention wrote this curious memo and ordered his cabinet to approve it unseen, and actually laud him for permitting the 1864 election during wartime.

In *War Crimes Against Southern Civilians* by Walter Brian Cisco, we learn that "Robbery was common, as was sexual abuse of black women by Yankee soldiers. A US cavalry regiment recruited from among East Tennessee Unionists and described by one girl as 'the meanest men I ever saw' rode into Gallatin in May 1864 and began a reign of terror. They torched two newly established schools for black children, murdered one freedman, and swore they would—as soon as they could—kill every black in town." Witnesses claimed that General John Hunt Morgan was murdered by Union troops in Greenville, Tennessee after surrendering. In the book *In Between the States: Bristol Tennessee/Virginia During the Civil War* by V. N. "Bud" Phillips, stories are recounted of Bristol citizens, including women and children being abused, beaten, and shot by Yankee invaders. In one December 1864 case, a slave in the home of a Mrs. Seabright was watching the Seabright's one-year-old baby as it slept on a blanket near an open fireplace. General Burbridge's goal in Bristol, Tennessee was to put "holy fear" into the local citizens as he visited their homes. A Yankee soldier entered the Seabright home, and seeing the sleeping child, jerked the blanket from beneath it while yelling, "Wake up, you little bastard rebel, and see what a real Yankee looks like." In Gallatin, Tennessee, scores of Confederate soldiers were murdered by the occupying Union soldiers, simply for wanting to see their families.

In Loudoun County, Virginia, the September 10, 1863 *Clarke County Journal* reported that "the Yankees are behaving with greater fiendishness than has heretofore characterized their conduct else where, and that they have in several instances violated the persons of some of the most respectable ladies in the county. Three sisters, young, intelligent, and of excellent social position, have been made the victims of their lust, because a brother of theirs was a Captain in the Confederate service." And in the familiar pattern, in Columbia, South Carolina, the same newspaper edition stated that "The churches were pillaged, and afterwards burned. St. Mary's College, a Catholic institution, shared their fate. The Catholic Convent . . . was ruthlessly sacked. The soldiers drank the sacramental wine, and profaned with fiery draughts of vulgar whiskey the goblets of the communion services. Some went off reeling under the weight of priestly robes, holy vessels and candlesticks." Bringing to mind the recent distressing reports of US soldiers killing dogs "for sport" in Iraq and Afghanistan, the newspaper added that "A soldier, passing in the streets and seeing some children playing with a beautiful little greyhound, amused himself by beating its brains out." For six weeks, a huge pile of sixty-five dead horses and mules, shot by Sherman's marauding heroes, filled Columbia's streets with a deadly stench. It was impossible to bury them since the Union forces had stolen all the shovels, spades, and other farming instruments.

A remarkable letter to his wife from Union lieutenant Thomas J. Myers, dated February 26, 1865, described Union exploits in embarrassingly stark terms, and specified the extent of the criminal activities going on, which as noted earlier included the likes of William Sherman: "We have had a glorious time in this State. Unrestricted license to burn and plunder was the order of the day. . . . Gold watches, silver pitchers, cups, spoons, forks, &c., are as common in camp as blackberries. The terms of plunder are as follows: Each company is required to exhibit the results of its operations at any given place—one-fifth and first choice falls to the share of the commander-in-chief and staff; one-fifth to the corps commanders and staff; one-fifth to field officers of regiments, and two-fifths to the company. Officers are not allowed to join these expeditions without disguising themselves as privates. . . . Officers over the rank of Captain are not made to put their plunder in the estimate for general distribution. This is very unfair, and for that reason, in order to protect themselves, subordinate officers and privates keep back every thing that they can carry about their persons, such as rings, earrings, breast pins, &c., of which, if I ever get home, I have about a quart. . . . General Sherman has silver and gold enough to start a bank. His share in gold watches alone at Columbia was two hundred and seventy-five. . . . All the general officers and many besides had valuables of every description, down to embroidered ladies' pocket handkerchiefs." Near the end of the letter, Myers wisely counsels, "Don't show this letter out of the family."

Union rapes were so rampant during Christmas 1864 in Georgia that Mary S. Mallard, in her journal, wrote, "the servants scarcely had a moment to do anything for us out of the house. The women, finding it unsafe for them to be out of the house at all, would run in and conceal themselves in our dwelling. The few remaining chickens and some sheep were killed. These men were so outrageous at the Negro houses that the Negro men were obliged to stay at their houses for the protection of their wives; and in some instances, they rescued them from the hands of these infamous creatures." Just spreading the Christmas spirit, I guess. She described in another entry how a despicable Yankee soldier stole the chain from the bucket of their well, leaving them without access to water. A September 14, 1865 letter, written to President Jefferson Davis by Rev. Dr. John Bachman, then pastor of the Charleston, South Carolina Lutheran Church, detailed more of Sherman's troops' monstrous crimes. Bachman wrote, "I happened to be at Cash's Depot six miles from Cheraw. The owner was a widow, Mrs. Ellerbe, seventy-one years of age. Her son, Colonel Cash, was absent. I witness the barbarities inflicted on the aged widow, and young and delicate females. Officers, high in command, were engaged in tearing from the ladies their watches, their ear and wedding rings, the daguerreotypes of those they loved and cherished. A lady of delicacy and refinement, a personal friend, was compelled to strip before them, that they might find concealed watches and other valuables under her dress. A system of torture was practiced towards the unarmed and defenseless, which, as far as I know and believe was universal throughout the whole course of that invading army. Before they arrived at a plantation, they inquired the names of the most faithful and trustworthy family servants; these were immediately seized, pistols were presented at their heads; with most terrific curses, they were threaten to be shot if they did not assist them in finding buried treasures. If this did not succeed they were tied up and cruelly beaten. Several poor creatures died under the infliction. The last resort is of that of hanging, and the officers and men of the triumphant army of General Sherman were engaged in erecting gallows and hanging up these faithful and devoted servants."

Following the war, tens of thousands of families, with one in thirteen Civil War survivors returning home missing at least one limb, were forced into financial destitution. With the South burned and devastated, the economic situation was perilous. Official unemployment rates weren't kept until the Department of Labor was created in 1888, but there must have been huge numbers of unemployed males after the war, especially in the South. In recent years, there have been new estimates, which claim that war deaths were dramatically underestimated, and that as many as 850,000 Americans could have died. If these new figures are correct, then one in ten white males of military age in 1860 perished. Nearly a quarter of young southern males lost their lives in Lincoln's "total war." The generation of American males born between 1835–1845 truly became a lost one. The *Southern Literary Messenger* published a letter from a young woman in 1864, which illustrated a disturbing new reality. "The reflection has been brought to mind with great force that after this war is closed, how vast a difference there will be in the numbers of males and females." The young lady wrote, "Having made up my mind not be an old maid, and having only a moderate fortune and less beauty, I fear I shall find it rather difficult to accomplish my wishes."

The only reason the Confederates aren't viewed sympathetically today, as a scrappy underdog fighting an insurmountable foe, is because of slavery. Slavery was an ugly reality all over the world, and yet every other society managed to eradicate it without a disastrous war that claimed over half a million lives. As Ron Paul said, during a 2007 *Meet the Press* appearance, "Every other country in the world got rid of slavery without a civil war." Slavery was on the way out everywhere, and if it had ended peacefully, American society could have avoided what Ron Paul described as "hatred lingered for 100 years." And as was mentioned earlier, India and several other countries continue to enslave human beings *today* without a peep of protest from human rights groups. The historians would have us believe that only Americans ever enslaved human beings, and that our particular form of slavery was so much different, and so much worse than the forms of slavery being practiced worldwide at the time and throughout history, that we must continue to dwell on it, apologize for it, and let it infect our own present politics. And significantly, slavery is the sole excuse given by apologists for the monstrous actions of Lincoln and his criminal military officers like Sherman.

As Steven Spielberg's fanciful 2012 film *Lincoln* showed, the passion within what Thomas DiLorenzo calls the "Lincoln Cult" shows no signs of diminishing. Based on Lincoln worshiper and rumored lover of Lyndon Baines Johnson Doris Kearns-Goodwin's book *Team of Rivals: The Political Genius of Abraham Lincoln*, the movie paints a predictable portrait of Lincoln as an iconic, saintly figure. Lincoln has almost become the antithesis of Adolf Hitler; whereas it is impossible to note anything positive about Hitler without arousing the scorn of the scholarly world, it is just as impossible to point out Lincoln's numerous acts of tyranny, or even his obvious character flaws. As Thomas DiLorenzo noted, in a November 15, 2012 column on LewRockwell.com, "If Lincoln was such a political genius, he should have used his 'genius' to end slavery in the way the British, French, Spaniards, Dutch, Danes, Swedes, and all the Northern states in the US did in the nineteenth century, namely, peacefully." Because Lincoln's legacy is inexorably entangled with the Civil War, any revisionist views on the war itself are considered an attack upon Lincoln. Merely suggesting that slavery wasn't the primary cause of the conflict, or even stating that there were multiple causes, is enough to arouse the ire of the establishment. Northwest Vista College adjunct professor Dale Schlundt was so incensed over Ron Paul's remark, years earlier, about slavery not being the only cause of the war, that he began starting each semester of his history class with a video of Paul's television interview, and then based his entire class around disproving it. It doesn't matter how many comments from prominent rebels, delineating that they *weren't* fighting for slavery, are left in the public record. Without slavery, the barbarity of the "good guys" cannot by any stretch of the imagination be justified. As the leader of the Confederates, Jefferson Davis, said, "The war . . . must go on till the last man of this generation falls in his tracks . . . unless you acknowledge our right to self-government. We are not fighting for slavery. We are fighting for Independence and that, or extermination, we WILL have." Ulysses S. Grant, one of the leading "good guys" here, according to the court historians, declared, "If I thought this war was to abolish slavery, I would resign my commission, and offer my sword to the other side."[28]

As the 150th anniversary of the end of the Civil War, and the Lincoln assassination, approached, the tributes to "Father Abraham" grew even more fantastic. An article in the UK's *Telegraph*, on April 15, 2015, written by Professor Richard Carwardine, lionized Lincoln thusly: "Lincoln had lastingly touched the nerve of British progressive sentiment. Here was the humane emancipator of his country's slaves, the re-unifier of the broken American republic, the advocate of democracy and representative government, and the man of the people. Here, in sum, was the welcoming doorkeeper to the modern world. He inspired liberals, radicals, socialists and all those who challenged ancestral privilege, celebrated the dignity of labour, and worked to widen life chances." *Business Insider* summarized Lincoln in the usual simplistic terms: "Abraham Lincoln kept the US united and freed black Americans from slavery." An eighty-one-year-old gay activist was quoted in *National Geographic* as exclaiming, "He died for me! God bless him!" That's how this supremely flawed man has come to be viewed by historians and most of the public: part Christ-like figure, and part superhero. Americans even envision him as an ultra-cool vampire killer, resulting in a bestselling book. On the website DC Cool, new, even more unlikely anecdotes were revealed about the saintly Lincoln, such as the one claiming he "helped a friend win a bet by lifting a completely full barrel of whiskey over his head and drinking from the middle opening." which came from the book *Abe Lincoln and the Frontier Folk of New Salem* by Thomas P. Reep. Mechanic Dave Kloke and some two dozen volunteers built an exact replica of the train car that carried Lincoln's body across America, in an elaborate act of national mourning that had never been seen before in America. "This really is a project that is of the people, by the people, for the people," the project's public relations director Shannon Brown declared.[29]

Superhero fans have boasted that, if Captain Fantastic and Mr. X were implausibly to have a baby, "it would be Abraham Lincoln." Legend has it that when Lincoln's shirt was stripped off following his assassination, the onlookers were astonished by his chiseled, powerful physique. Well, I guess you need to be strong to be a legendary vampire killer. The absurd mythology began immediately after the assassination; the *New York Times* informed its readers, on April 19, 1965: "Everything which made Abraham Lincoln the loved and honored man he was, it is in the power of the humblest American boy to imitate."

William Herndon, who was Lincoln's law partner in Springfield and, if his descendants are to be believed, Lincoln's lover, wrote the following:

> For fifty years God rolled Abraham Lincoln through his fiery furnace. He
> did it to try Abraham and to purify him for his purposes. This made Mr.
> Lincoln humble, tender, forbearing, sympathetic to suffering, kind, sen-
> sitive, tolerant; broadening, deepening and widening his whole nature;
> making him the noblest and loveliest character since Jesus Christ . . . I
> believe that Lincoln was God's chosen one.

J. T. Duryea of the US Christian Commission, apparently completely ignorant about Lincoln's religious beliefs, showered him with praise: "In temper he was Earnest, yet controlled, frank, yet sufficiently guarded, patient, yet energetic, forgiving, yet just to himself; generous yet firm. His conscience was the strongest element of his nature. His affections were tender & warm. His whole nature was simple and sincere—he was pure." The Marquis de Chambrun, a French writer who knew Lincoln, echoed this grandiose praise: "Such a nature was admirably constituted to direct an heroic struggle on the part of a people proud enough to prefer a guide to a leader, a man commissioned to execute the popular will but, as in his case, strong enough to enforce his own." Someone might have informed the Marquis that the North was engaged in a "heroic struggle" to prevent their countrymen from forming the new government they desired.

One of the nineteenth century's most enlightened thinkers was British historian and writer John Dalberg-Acton, popularly known as Lord Acton, perhaps most famous for his timeless quote, "Power corrupts. Absolute power corrupts absolutely." He epitomized what used to be called a classical liberal. Acton recognized that it was southerners who were fighting for the right of self-government, while Lincoln's troops were the oppressive aggressors. In a poignant November 4, 1866 letter to Robert E. Lee, Acton wrote, "I saw in State Rights the only availing check upon the absolutism of the sovereign will, and secession filled me with hope, not as the destruction but as the redemption of Democracy. The institutions of your Republic have not exercised on the old world the salutary and liberating influence which ought to have belonged to them, by reason of those defects and abuses of principle which the Confederate Constitution was expressly and wisely calculated to remedy. I believed that the example of that great Reform would have blessed all the races of mankind by establishing true freedom purged of the native dangers and disorders of Republics. Therefore I deemed that you were fighting the battles of our liberty, our progress, and our civilization; and I mourn for the stake which was lost at Richmond more deeply than I rejoice over that which was saved at Waterloo."

Once Lincoln became historically deified, only a few critical books about him were published. One of the most notable appeared in 1962, *Patriotic Gore*, written by leftist Edmund Wilson. Wilson wrote that Lincoln sought to "crush the South not by reason of the righteousness of its cause but on account of the superior equipment which it was able to mobilize and its superior capacity for organization." Wilson was able to empathize with his political opponents; recognizing, in the midst of the Civil Rights struggle, how:

> Southerners remember the burning of Atlanta, the wrecking by Northern troops of Southern homes, the disfranchisement of the governing classes and the premature enfranchisement of the Negroes.

Despite his politics, Wilson discovered historical soul mates in Southern secessionists who had risked all in the name of a slaveholding republic. Wilson was a pacifist who stopped paying his taxes in protest of the Cold War, and had been against WWII. His book was published during the height of what Wilson called "this absurd centennial.[30]

The idea that Americans would fight a bloody, internal battle over a group of states' collective desire to secede from the Union would have been unthinkable to the Founding Fathers. As Thomas Jefferson said in his first inaugural address: "If there be any among us who would wish to dissolve this Union, or to change its republican form, let them stand undisturbed as monuments of the safety with which error of opinion may be tolerated, where reason is left free to combat it." The American colonies' independence movement was the most famous act of secession in the history of the world. Throughout *The Federalist Papers*, written largely by James Madison and Alexander Hamilton, which argued for passage of the US Constitution, the United States are consistently referred to as "the Confederacy" or "a confederate republic." The Union clearly was considered a voluntary one by those who established our independent government. It took an Abraham Lincoln to vilify whole states as "treasonous" and launch a vicious war of aggression in order to establish, forever thereafter, that this Union is definitely not voluntary.

I firmly believe that if Lincoln had merely let the original small group of southern states leave peacefully, the others would never have joined, and the Confederacy would probably have folded within a short period of time. But instead, the man who would tell the New Jersey General Assembly in 1861 that "The man does not live who is more devoted to peace than I am," would do everything in his power to push and prolong the unprecedented carnage of the War Between the States. The South merely wanted to be left alone; it is far more accurate to call the conflict the War of Northern Aggression. From shutting down all opposition, to an unwillingness to negotiate, to the usurpation of unprecedented, unconstitutional power, to the promotion of a barbaric, "scorched earth" style of warfare, Abraham Lincoln was akin to some present-day chronic warmonger, like a John McCain or a Lindsay Graham, mixed in with a healthy dose of Julius Caesar. He would have clashed constantly with the Founding Fathers, and would mesh perfectly with today's politically corrupt world. As an unscrupulous, hypocritical, crass party politician, Abraham Lincoln is a fitting symbol for our decrepit, decaying civilization.

CHAPTER FOUR

THE LINCOLN ASSASSINATION

People are just fascinated by assassinations.

—Representative Louis Stokes, Chairman of the
House Select Committee on Assassinations

While Abraham Lincoln has been revered by historians like no
other president, few of them have been willing to honestly delve
into the circumstances surrounding his death. The court historians tell us
that the great martyr was shot by a crazed Southern sympathizer who just
happened to come from the most distinguished acting family in the country, incompetently assisted by a ragtag band of misfits and fans, but the
available evidence as usual suggests otherwise.

The first thing one discovers when analyzing the events of April 14,
1865, is just how reluctant certain powerful figures were to attend Ford's
Theatre with the president that Good Friday evening. General Ulysses S.
Grant was expected to accompany the president, and it was even advertised, in the April 14, 1865 issue of the *Washington Star*, that he would be
attending the play. The general's name, curiously, was even mentioned
first, ahead of the president's.

The official excuse for Grant's absence in the theater box that night is that he wanted to visit his children in New Jersey, but that explanation makes little sense. Even by leaving on the six o'clock train, as he did, Grant didn't arrive in New Jersey until the next morning. Had he attended the play, he still could have caught the morning train, without all the discomfort of an overnight trip, and have seen his children by early afternoon. It is simply hard to accept the premise that Grant, who had been educated at West Point and attained the highest rank the military had to offer, could break an invitation at the behest of his commander in chief on such flimsy grounds. Certainly he would have been influenced, as well, by the fact that this outing was considered to be something of an official victory celebration for the union forces. His presence had been much ballyhooed, and it is not logical to expect that Grant would have been guilty of such a blatant breach of protocol.[1] Historians have come to attribute his reluctance to attend the theater to his wife Julia's dislike of notoriously volatile and jealous First Lady Mary Todd Lincoln.

Grant wasn't the only one to turn Lincoln down. Speaker of the House Schuyler Colfax couldn't make it, either. During a visit to the War Department the afternoon of April 14, Lincoln requested that Secretary of War Edwin Stanton ask Major Thomas T. Eckert, who was Stanton's chief aide, to accompany him to the theater that night as an escort. The President was a great admirer of Eckert's strength, having related how impressed he'd been after witnessing him break pokers over his arm. Stanton refused the President's request, claiming that he had some important work for the major and could not spare him. Lincoln then asked Eckert directly, but the major begged off, pleading that he had work which could not be delayed. That such a request would be denied the President of the United States by the secretary of war is odd enough, but for a major to refuse when asked by the President himself is unbelievable. This suspicious incident is one of many that fueled early conspiracy theories fingering Stanton as a key player.[2] Eventually, the president and Mrs. Lincoln would have to settle for Major Henry Rathbone and his future wife Clara Harris, daughter of US Senator Ira Harris, as their guests in the presidential box at Ford's Theater.

From the outset, the performance of the press in ferreting out the truth about Lincoln's murder was almost as inexcusable as it would be a century later following the Kennedy assassination. The Washington newspapers, in particular, shared a curious reluctance to name the suspected assassin in the earliest editions after the shooting. This was hard to comprehend, inasmuch as the eyewitness testimony identifying the familiar figure of John Wilkes Booth was overwhelming. As Corporal James Tanner, who took the shorthand notes of the testimony at the Petersen house following the shooting, was to state: "In fifteen minutes I had testimony enough to hang Wilkes Booth . . . higher than Haman hung."[3] The Washington Daily Morning Chronicle (April 15, 1865 edition) even went so far as to state that revealing the identity of the suspect would not aid in his apprehension!

In not naming John Wilkes Booth as the gunman when he had been recognized by so many at Ford's Theatre, the press was merely following the lead of Secretary of War Stanton, who neglected to send out a dispatch until 1:30 a.m., more than three hours after the shooting, and in finally doing so did not mention Booth's name. This, in light of the testimony that Stanton himself had heard previous to sending the belated dispatch, was certainly questionable conduct on his part, and can only have hindered the pursuit and capture of the assassin.[4] John Wilkes Booth was a genuine celebrity; his name and face was familiar to most Americans. Noted historian and author Terry Alford has said Booth was "kind of like Brad Pitt. He was that popular." His distant ancestor John Wilkes, radical journalist and politician, was a member of the Hellfire Club, which as mentioned earlier boasted Ben Franklin and other notables among its membership. Booth's father Junius Brutus had once sent a letter to President Andrew Jackson, threatening to slit his throat. For inexplicable reasons, even though Booth left his correct name and return address, it was dismissed as a hoax. In another of those cosmic coincidences, John Wilkes's brother Edwin Booth supposedly saved the life of the president's son Robert Todd Lincoln when the Harvard student fell off a train platform in Jersey City not long before the assassination.

A great deal of controversy has swirled around the actions of John F. Parker, the policeman assigned to guard the president that fateful evening. Parker had enjoyed a mediocre career as a Metropolitan Police officer, and had been summoned before the Police Board on numerous occasions for various transgressions. Amazingly enough, it appears that he was suddenly elevated to the position of White House guard at the behest of First Lady Mary Lincoln herself. In a letter written on April 3, 1865, to James R. O'Beirne, provost marshal of the District of Columbia, Mary Todd Lincoln wrote:

> This is to certify that John F. Parker, a member of the Metropolitan Police has been detailed for duty at the Executive Mansion by order of,
> Mrs. Lincoln

Parker was a man of unsavory character, who had been charged with things like sleeping in a streetcar while on duty, visiting a house of prostitution while intoxicated, and firing a pistol through the window in the process. How he could have been granted a promotion of this stature, at the personal request of the president's wife, is something historians should have questioned a long, long time ago.[5] This man of dubious background was Lincoln's sole security that night, and when he abandoned his post, he left him totally unprotected. Parker has been variously described by critics and mainstream historians alike as leaving his position outside the presidential box to find a better seat elsewhere in the theater or to visit the saloon next door. Regardless, his dereliction of duty was obvious.

Parker was, however, never reprimanded for his actions the night of the assassination. The only available records show that the officer was brought before the Police Board on May 3, 1865, and the complaint was dismissed on June 2, 1865. If any transcripts from Parker's hearing ever existed, they have not been discovered. Since Parker, in a preview of what would be standard operating procedure for the Warren Commission a century later, was never called before the military tribunal which tried the alleged conspirators, the minutes of this Police Board hearing would have been of great interest to researchers.[6]

Although he had often engaged in conduct that involved charges of a serious nature, and repeatedly brought him before the Police Board, Parker continued to escape punishment until 1868. On August 13, 1868, he was promptly discharged from the Metropolitan Police Force for "gross neglect of duty." He had, on this occasion, been found asleep on duty by his sergeant. This last offense of Parker's was probably the least serious among the many he was accused of during his tenure on the force. It is interesting, in light of this, to note that Secretary of War Stanton had been ousted from his position only a few weeks prior to Parker's sudden dismissal. Whether or not this indicates that the man many have theorized was behind the assassination had been protecting Parker over the years is a worthy point to ponder.[7]

White House guard William Crook commented in his memoirs: "I have often wondered why the negligence of the guard who accompanied the President to the theatre on the night of the 14th has never been divulged. So far as I know, it was not even investigated by the police department. Yet, had he done his duty, I believe President Lincoln would not have been murdered by Booth."[8] According to Mary Todd Lincoln's dressmaker, Elizabeth Keckley, the First Lady was overheard screaming at Parker after he was rather strangely assigned security detail at the White House after the assassination: "So you are on guard . . . after helping to murder the

President." Mrs. Lincoln supposedly told Parker that she would always hold him responsible.[9] Perhaps fittingly, John Parker was buried in an unmarked grave, and there are no known images of him.

Another matter that establishment historians have left needlessly enigmatic is the message delivered to President Lincoln in the presidential box only twenty minutes or so before the assassination. The editor of the *Washington National Republican*, Simon P. Hanscom, reported in the June 8, 1865 edition of his daily newspaper that he had gone to Ford's Theatre on the night of the assassination to deliver a message to the president at the request of the White House. He stated that "... At that time there were no guards, watchmen, sentinels, or ushers about the door of the President, and any one could have passed in without molestation." There was a great deal of conflicting testimony from Major Rathbone and Miss Clara Harris, who were seated in the presidential box with Mr. and Mrs. Lincoln, and other witnesses regarding this message. For some unknown reason, editor Hanscom didn't report that he'd delivered the last communication to Abraham Lincoln before this. It is hard to fathom why he waited so long to reveal this exclusive story that involved him personally, when it could have placed his name at the center of such an historic event and almost certainly have increased his newspaper's circulation, not to mention that he should have considered the message a potentially crucial piece of evidence.

Never asked by any journalist or member of the military tribunal that "investigated" the assassination was why this editor was chosen to deliver the message, and more importantly, just what the message was. It must have been of extreme importance to be delivered at such a time and place, but it has never been produced. No mention was made of finding such a message on Lincoln's body, and it is not known (nor did Hanscom choose to disclose in his article) who asked him to act as a messenger. Whatever became of this letter, if it ever existed, is yet another mystery.[10] In recent years, some establishment historians have claimed, not surprisingly, that this note was a totally innocuous request regarding two Confederate officials who wanted to meet with Lincoln. How they know this when the note has never been produced is yet another impenetrable mystery. Information published on the Congressional Cemetery website—where Hanscom is buried—indicates that this journalist was extremely close to Lincoln, free to walk into the president's office at any hour without an appointment. Hanscom was recognized by everyone in Washington as Lincoln's favorite correspondent. The website also repeats the apparently undocumented claim that the note concerned two former Confederate officials.

The official narrative suggests that Booth's original plan had been to kidnap Lincoln, but this morphed into an assassination attempt apparently at the last minute. Booth had assigned his band of conspirators various roles: Lewis Powell/Paine (known by both last names) was supposed to go to Secretary of State John Seward's house and kill him, while George Atzerodt would assassinate Vice President Andrew Johnson in his hotel room. Researcher David McGowan analyzed the improbabilities involved in the Seward attack on his excellent website, Center for an Informed America. Atzerodt, meanwhile, supposedly "lost his nerve" and never attempted to carry out his mission. After shooting Lincoln, Booth escaped into Maryland with a young admirer, David Herold. They were able to cross the Naval Yard Bridge, where Herold's father coincidentally worked as chief clerk of their store, when first Booth (recklessly giving his real name) and then Herold were inexplicably permitted access by guard Silas Cobb. Herold has usually been inaccurately portrayed by historians as a dimwitted Booth worshiper, when in fact he was an extremely well-educated college graduate. After having his injured leg attended to by southern sympathizer Dr. Samuel Mudd, Booth and Herold were eventually trapped on Garrett's farm, where Booth would be shot and killed by a most unusual soldier named Boston Corbett, a religious fanatic who had castrated himself with a pair of scissors in 1858.[11]

John Wilkes Booth, like all good assassins, had a diary. It was supposedly discovered when he was stripped of his belongings as he lay dying
outside Garrett's barn, although its existence was not revealed to the public
until two years later. One sentence in it was particularly intriguing. Booth
wrote: "I have almost a mind to return to Washington and . . . clear my
name, which I feel I can do." General Benjamin Butler, then a congressman, responded to Booth's enigmatic entry by asking: "How clear himself? By disclosing his accomplices? Who were they? If we had only the
advantage of all the testimony, we have been able . . . to find who, indeed,
were all the accomplices of Booth." The House of Representatives would,
in response to the many unanswered questions surrounding the Lincoln
assassination, appoint a special commission to investigate "all the facts
and circumstances connected with the assassination tending to show who
were the persons engaged in the conspiracy, many of whom . . . holding
high positions of power and authority . . . acted through inferior persons
who were their tools and instruments." This investigation, like the one
launched by the House a century later to answer the questions regarding
the Kennedy and King assassinations, was to prove fruitless. After being
locked in the archives for two years, Booth's diary was released, with the
amazing disclosure that eighteen pages were missing from it, whose dates
corresponded with the time immediately preceding Lincoln's assassination. Secretary of War Stanton would claim that the diary was already
missing the pages when he first received it.[12]

After the shooting of the man alleged to be Booth at Garrett's farm,
the corpse was placed on the ironclad USS *Montauk*, which had been used
as a prison and was anchored at the Navy Yard in Washington, DC. An
Identification Commission was formed, which was headed by Stanton's
chief aide Major Thomas Eckert, in order to establish that the body was
that of the assassin's. Secretary Stanton telegrammed the *Montauk*'s com-
mandant, Com. J. B. Montgomery, and decreed that "You will allow no

persons on board the Montauk unless under the joint pass of the Secretary of War and the Secretary of the Navy." Members of the Identification Commission included Judge Advocate Joseph Holt, who would later head the military tribunal that convicted the conspirators; Lafayette Baker, chief of the National Detective Police; and renowned photographers Alexander Gardner and Timothy H. O'Sullivan.

None of the witnesses who were summoned on board the *Montauk* to identify the corpse had known Booth well. The assassin's relatives and fellow conspirators were not called to view his supposed remains, although most were in custody on the adjacent ironclad USS *Saugus*. One of those who was on hand to identify the body was Dr. John Franklin May, who had removed a tumor from Booth's neck two years previously. When Dr. May first saw the dead man's face, he stated, "There's no resemblance in that corpse to Booth, nor can I believe it to be him." After gently being persuaded that this was not the answer they were looking for, Dr. May at length admitted, "I am enabled, imperfectly, to recognize the features of Booth." Dr. May wrote a letter to a relative shortly thereafter in which he said, "The right limb was greatly contused and perfectly black from a fracture of one of the long bones of the leg." This was significant in that Booth was reported to have snapped his left tibia when he jumped from the presidential box onto the stage at Ford's Theater.

Alexander Gardner was rumored to have taken one photograph of the body, which was confiscated by Baker. The government officially denied that a picture was ever taken, but authors David W. Balsiger and Charles E. Sellier state that the Gardner photograph ended up in the personal possession of Edwin Stanton.[13] Supporting the contention that a photo exists or once existed is a report in the *New York Daily Tribune* of April 29, 1865, where it was stated that "a photographic view of the body was taken."[14] Now I'll ask the obvious question that no mainstream historian will: if the body of Booth wasn't photographed, then why were two renowned photographers on board the ship? Author W. C. Jameson would write, in *Return of Assassin,* "Gardner was allowed to take only one photograph and was quickly hastened to a darkroom to develop it. . . . Moments later, Lafayette Baker took the photographic plate. . . . In response to subsequent inquiries, the government denied that any photographs were ever taken of the body."

THE "TRIAL" OF THE CONSPIRATORS

The last act in the tragedy of the 19th century is ended, and the curtain dropped forever upon the lives of four of its actors.
—The *Washington Evening Star*

Eventually, the authorities would arrest David Herold, George Atzerodt, Lewis Paine/Powell, and Mary Surratt and charge them as Booth's primary accomplices. Mary Surratt was "guilty" of owning the boardinghouse where Booth's alleged plot was hatched. Also arrested were Dr. Samuel Mudd, Michael O'Laughlin, Edmund Spangler, and Samuel Arnold. David McGowan cogently pointed out the decidedly non-Confederate, non-Southern background of all Booth's fellow conspirators, with the exception of Powell/Paine, whose murky gaps in his biography lead to natural speculation that he was a northern spy. When a conspiracy is mentioned at all in relation to the Lincoln assassination, it is invariably attributed to the actions of Confederate sympathizers, probably aided and abetted by higher authorities in the rebel ranks.

Secretary of War Stanton outdid himself in his treatment of the alleged conspirators as they awaited their military trial. While the prisoners were being held on board an ironclad ship, Stanton issued an unusual decree on April 23, 1865, which declared that the defendants ". . . for better security against conversation shall have a canvass bag put over the head of each and tied about the neck, with a hole for proper breathing and eating, but not seeing." This barbaric hooding of the prisoners was an especially sadistic method for maintaining their silence. The hoods, which were made of a heavy canvas, fit the heads of the male prisoners (for public relations purposes, the lone female defendant, Mary Surratt, had been spared this) tightly and contained cotton pads which were positioned directly over the eyes and ears. These pads caused intense pressure against the swollen eyes, and the alleged conspirators were not even allowed an occasional washing to temporarily relieve the agony. Special attention was paid to the large, muscular Lewis Powell/Paine, who was personally guarded by Assistant Secretary of War Thomas Eckert. This was probably the only time in American history that such a high-ranking official was utilized in such a curious manner.

The prison surgeon attempted unsuccessfully to intervene with Stanton, maintaining that such devices, especially in conjunction with the summer heat, might eventually provoke insanity. Stanton also arranged for each prisoner to be placed in a cell between empty ones, and saddled the male prisoners with what were known as stiff shackles, handcuffs fastened to each other by a bar of iron about fourteen inches long, which prevented the movement of one arm without the other. Each of the male captors was attended by guards who were not permitted to talk to them. Since all visitors were required to present a pass signed by the secretary of war, there were no visitors. It is remarkable that the pathetic defendants weren't quickly turned into stark raving lunatics. Stanton was a most eccentric, if not mentally unstable, character. He was known to have exhumed the body of his daughter, for instance, and kept it in his home for over a year. Whether these unheard of measures, almost a form of medieval torture, resulted from madness or a more diabolical reason is open to question. What is beyond dispute is that they were inexcusable and had no relation to any brand of justice.

All nine members of the military tribunal that would try the conspirators were handpicked by Secretary of War Edwin Stanton. Interestingly enough, photographs reveal that many if not all members of the commission were Freemasons (because of the hand-in-waistcoat and other Masonic poses). According to David McGowan, so were the prosecutors, some of the defense attorneys, Lafayette Baker, Edwin Stanton, and John Wilkes Booth himself. One of the defense attorneys, Walter Smith Cox, would go on to become a federal judge who presided over the trial where Charles Guiteau was convicted of assassinating President James A. Garfield. Colonel Frederick Aiken was the only attorney among them who appeared to be working diligently for the defendants. Unlike most of the others, he failed to prosper afterwards, dying at only forty-six and buried originally in an unmarked grave. When one of the defense attorneys boldly called President Andrew Johnson as a witness, he merely ignored the summons. Not a single one of those closest to the event, those in the presidential box, were called as witnesses.

After the trial, Stanton would see to it that all the defendants whose lives were spared would continue to be punished beyond all reason. They were sentenced to hard labor at the military prison at Dry Tortugas, Florida, and after a totally bogus "discovery" of an attempt to liberate the prisoners there, the four convicted conspirators (Mudd, O'Laughlin, Spangler, and Arnold) were confined in a small, damp room where, Sam Arnold would later write, "We were denied all intercourse with everyone upon the desolate island."[15] Of all the charges leveled at Stanton by critics, the inhumane treatment he accorded the alleged conspirators is the single hardest to defend. It certainly looks like he was trying to stop them from saying *something*.

While the treatment the alleged conspirators received was overzealous at the very least, the man the government originally proclaimed to be Booth's main accomplice was dealt with quite differently. John Surratt, son of Mary and a closer friend to Booth than any of the others, eluded the grasp of the authorities for two years after the assassination. During the period that Surratt was "on the run," the government seemed to be anything but anxious to find him. For instance, H. Wilding, then vice consul at Liverpool, once wrote to the State Department with the information that John Surratt was in Liverpool and staying at the oratory of the Roman Catholic Church of the Holy Cross. The State Department replied by stating: ". . . it is thought advisable that no action be taken in regard to the arrest of the supposed John Surratt at present." Later Surratt would return to the United States, after traveling unmolested through Europe (including a stint as a Zouave guard in the Pope's service). He was tried in 1867, but the charges against him in the Lincoln case were eventually dropped and he became, incredibly enough, a noted lecturer on the assassination.[16]

At the time, the conspiracy trial was widely criticized. Former attorney general Edward Bates seriously questioned the dubious legality of it, and was amazed at his successor James Speed's opinion that such a proceeding was lawful. "If he be, in the lowest degree," Bates said of Speed, "qualified for his office, he must know better." Of Speed's opinion, Bates wrote in his diary, "This is the most extraordinary document I ever read, under the name of law opinion. This opinion is . . . dated 'July—1865.' After the sentence, and in fact, after the execution of the accused who were condemned to death!" When the findings of the military commission were approved by President Andrew Johnson, on July 5, 1865, Orville Browning, longtime crony of Lincoln's and later secretary of the interior, expressed similar feelings of disgust. "This commission was without authority," he declared in his diary, "and its proceedings void. The execution of these persons will be murder."[17] Wisconsin congressman Charles A. Eldredge wrote a letter of protest to Judge Advocate General Joseph Holt, who headed the military commission, in September 1865. "Do not, I pray you, flatter yourself," Eldredge fumed, "that you and the Secretary of War can, by the circulation of these documents at your own or the people's expense, convince your countrymen that arrests without warrant, imprisonment without trial . . .

and the worse than mockery of your victims in military trials, are anything but crimes." The *New York World*, on May 26, 1865, observed that "The counsel for the accused strike me as being commonplace lawyers. They either have no chance or no pluck to assert the dignity of their profession. Reverdy Johnson is not here. The first day disgusted him, as he is a practitioner of law."[18]

The members of the military tribunal should have made their descendants on the Warren Commission proud. One of them, General Lew Wallace, would later gain renown for writing *Ben Hur*. The proceedings were a sham in all but the most biased, coldhearted eyes. The prisoners were not allowed to testify in their own defense. The charge against them was that of "maliciously, unlawfully, and traitorously, and in aid of the existing armed rebellion against the United States of America . . . combining, confederating, and conspiring together with . . . Jefferson Davis . . . and others unknown, to kill and murder, within the Military Department of Washington, and within the fortified and entrenched lines thereof, Abraham Lincoln . . . and lying in wait with intent . . . to kill . . . Andrew Johnson . . . and . . . Ulysses S. Grant."

As one of the counsels for the defense, General Thomas Ewing, understandably reacted, "The offenses enumerated . . . are separate and distinct, and we, therefore, ask that the Judge Advocate should state . . . of which said offenses . . . he claims they should each be convicted." The response was to claim it was all one transaction, prompting Ewing to request that he be told what code the unheard of crime of "traitorously murdering, or . . . assaulting, or . . . lying in wait" was defined by. Holt replied that the common law of war embraced all these crimes. In his final argument, Ewing boldly stated, ". . . the Judge Advocate said . . . that he would expect to convict 'under the common law of war.' This is a term unknown to our language." Former attorney general Edward Bates commented in his diary, "The laws and usages of war . . . what are they? Who knows them? Are they written in any book? Are they prescribed by any acknowledged authority? There is no such thing as the Laws of War. War is the very reverse of law—and its existence always implies . . . the absence or disregard of all law."[19] In another of those coincidental connections, Ewing's father had helped to raise the future general William Tecumseh Sherman, and they grew up to be brothers-in-law. Ewing died quite unnaturally when he was struck by a New York City omnibus on January 21, 1896.

There was no interest in pursuing a larger plot, or investigating any real leads. During the conspiracy trial, Samuel Chester, a friend of Booth's, testified that Booth had told him "there were from fifty to one hundred persons engaged in the conspiracy." In his inexplicably "lost confession," George Atzerodt stated, "Booth said if he did not get him quick the N. York crowd would. Booth knew the New York party apparently by a sign. He saw Booth give some kind of sign to two parties on the Avenue who he said were from New York." It was claimed, in an article titled "The Education of Linton Usher," published in the December 1938 issue of the *Indiana Magazine of History*, that Lincoln's secretary of the interior, John P. Usher, had uttered some very cryptic comments regarding the assassination to his son: "Whenever Linton importuned his father concerning the conspiracy that led to Lincoln's murder, Secretary Usher would reply that the ramifications were so far-reaching that it was well that investigations had gone no farther."

On March 30, 1939, Otto Eisenschiml wrote the well-known "muckraker" Ida Tarbell, who had written extensively about Lincoln, regarding this statement by Linton Usher. On April 12, 1939, Tarbell responded in a manner much more befitting a court historian than any kind of "muckraker." Tarbell irrationally explained, "I confess that it does not seem cryptic when you recall the experience of Indiana through the War with the various copperhead societies so strong in the Middle West. . . . They were in more or less close touch with the Confederates in Canada." Usher's statement to his son wasn't cryptic? Exactly what would be the definition of "cryptic" to Tarbell? This bold "muckraker" went on to ask, "How far was the investigation of the conspiracy which had resulted in Lincoln's death to be pushed?" and remarkably closed with the anti-conspiratorial chestnut, "He was quite right when he said the ramifications were so far-reaching that it was well that investigation had gone no farther. Personally, I agree with him, the more strongly because I believe Booth's plot was of his own making." Miss Tarbell was certainly aware of Otto Eisenschiml, as his explosive book *Why Was Lincoln Murdered?* had been published two years previously. Undoubtedly, she despised conspiracy theories. Noted Lincoln scholar Carl Sandburg, by contrast, said of *Why Was Lincoln Murdered?*, "The Lincoln shelf of books has acquired a masterpiece of inquiry, research, discussion and statement . . . so rigorous is it in analysis and so relentless and moving as a piece of story telling, that it belongs on the book shelves of those who collect masterly narratives in the field of crime."

Hundreds of pages could be spent detailing the inadequacies of the military commission's case against the alleged conspirators. The photograph used throughout the trial when asking witnesses to identify John Wilkes Booth, for example, was actually one of his brother Edwin Booth. The counsels for the defense did not question this glaring error, which would, in an honest courtroom, have thrown out the testimony of the twenty-plus witnesses who identified the person in the photograph as John Wilkes Booth.[20] Judge Advocate Joseph Holt had summed up the sham, preconceived nature of the trial with his statement, "There have not been enough Southern women hanged in this war."

The prosecution's star witnesses were less than stellar. Louis J. Weichmann, the boarder at the Surratt rooming house whose testimony helped to convict his landlady, allegedly told one Lewis Carland, after the prisoners had been executed, that a statement had been prepared for him, and that he was threatened with prosecution if he did not swear to it. James

J. Gifford, who had been in prison with Weichmann, corroborated Carland during the belated trial of John Surratt. "Did he (Weichmann) say in your presence that an officer of the government had told him that unless he testified to more than he had already stated they would hang him too?" Gifford was asked at the trial, and he replied, "I heard the officer tell him so."[21] Of Louis Weichmann, researcher Theodore Roscoe would write, "Official records on Wiechmann are confusing. One might well believe them deliberately confused. In them his name is spelled at least five different ways. Dates are curiously juggled. Wiechmann's testimony is garbled, vaguely worded, often contradictory." When he testified at John Surratt's trial in 1867, Weichmann contradicted some of his previous statements, attributing this to his being "nervous." Weichmann also admitted to being threatened if he didn't cooperate with the prosecution. Theater owner John T. Ford would state that he became convinced of Mary Surratt's innocence while serving in prison with Weichmann and Lloyd, both of whom he believed had been "coerced" by the authorities. Ford was arbitrarily jailed along with his two brothers for well over a month, for no legitimate reason, and Stanton simply ignored his pleas to be released. John W. Clampitt, one of Mrs. Surratt's lawyers, years later would report that Weichmann had been stung with remorse over falsely implicating Mrs. Surratt. Clampitt claimed that Weichmann had told him that Holt had rejected his first statement, remarking that "it was not strong enough," so Weichmann wrote another, which he subsequently swore to on the witness stand. Strangely, on his deathbed, Weichmann signed a statement swearing that his conspiracy trial testimony was really true.

Of all the defendants, Mary Surratt was the most widely empathized with. The only "evidence" presented against her came from John M. Lloyd, who rented a farm and tavern from her. Lloyd was a well-known alcoholic who claimed that Mrs. Surratt told him on the afternoon of April 14, 1865, to have two bottles of whiskey and some carbines ready, as they would be needed that night. However, according to Mrs. Offut, Lloyd's sister-in-law, the tavern keeper was "very much in liquor" at that time, and even required her assistance to remove his coat. Lloyd himself did not deny his condition on that fateful evening. "I was right smart in liquor that afternoon," he admitted during cross-examination at the trial of the conspirators, "and after night I got more so." Two years later, Lloyd reluctantly testified again, at the trial of John Surratt, declaring that "I do not wish to go into the examination of Mrs. Surratt. . . . I do not wish to state one solitary word more than I am compelled to." He swore on the witness stand that he had been hopelessly drunk that afternoon, and that he was being asked to relate things that were a part of his "confused memory." This enlightening exchange took place during the trial of John Surratt:

Q: When you went to speak to Mrs. Surratt, did you stagger?

A: That I do not recollect.

Q: Did you fall down?

A: Really, I cannot remember such a thing.

Q: What else did he say?

A: He said that it was not full enough . . . .

Q: Did he say anything to you in the way of offering a reward, or use any threat towards you, for the purpose of getting you to make it fuller?

A: When I told him what I had repeated before . . . he jumps up very quick off his seat, as if very mad, and asked me if I knew what I was guilty of. I told him, under the circumstances I did not. He said you are guilty as an accessory to a crime the punishment of which is death.

Lloyd also declared that his testimony had been forced out of him by threats of no uncertain nature. As he stated in another excerpt from Surratt's trial:

> When I was there in Carroll Prison, this military officer came there and told me he wanted me to make a statement, as near as I remember. I told him I had made a fuller statement to Colonel Wells than I could possibly do to him under the circumstances, while things were fresh in my memory. His reply was that it was not full enough.

This is a good example of what Colonel Lafayette Baker meant when, upon taking charge of the pursuit of Lincoln's alleged assassins, he had instructed his minions in an official order "to extort confessions and procure testimony to establish the conspiracy . . . by promises, rewards, threats, deceit, force, or any other effectual means."[22] When Lloyd was first arrested on April 17, 1865, Detective George Cottingham used what he termed "strategy" to obtain information from him. The alcoholic was denied liquor for forty-eight hours while being hanged from a tree by his thumbs for the entire length of time. That is indeed an interesting "strategy."[23] Years after the trial, Lieutenant D. D. Dana, in the December 12, 1897 issue of *The Boston Globe*, would admit that this had been done in order to obtain Lloyd's testimony that Booth and David Herold had stopped at the Surratt Inn on the night of the assassination.

The manner in which the authorities dealt with those persons who allegedly aided Booth and Herold during their flight was both illogical and inconsistent. Dr. Samuel Mudd, whose only crime was to set a broken leg for someone who was disguising his appearance and allow him to rest overnight under his roof, was tried as one of the eight conspirators. Others who assisted the fleeing assassin escaped punishment altogether. Samuel Cox and Thomas A. Jones, for instance, were admitted Confederate sympathizers guilty of hiding and feeding the fugitives, whom they knew to be involved in Lincoln's murder. They were incarcerated for a few weeks, then released without an indictment being brought against them. Three Confederate soldiers, Captain Willie Jett, Lieutenant Mortimer Ruggles, and Lieutenant Absalom Bainbridge, ferried Booth and Herold across the Rappahannock River after being apprised by Booth of his identity. They then hid the two wanted men on Garrett's farm. The full wrath of the law should seemingly have fallen on these rebels, but although they were taken as prisoners, none of them were ever prosecuted. The trio did not deny their involvement in harboring the fugitives, but in spite of this, one of them, Captain Jett, even appeared as a witness for the prosecution.[24]

It is not known for certain whether President Johnson actually received the leniency petition for Mary Surratt, which was signed by five members of the military commission and attached to the court transcript that was sent to Secretary of War Stanton. Some researchers have suggested that Stanton removed the plea, while others believe Johnson saw it and ignored it. At any rate, on July 6, 1865, the afternoon before the executions were to take place, Mrs. Surratt's daughter Anna and a Catholic priest, Rev. Jacob Ambrose Walter, went to the White House in hopes of personally appealing to President Johnson. Johnson's secretary, Gen. Reuben D. Mussey, along with Senators Preston King of New York and the aforementioned brutal General James H. Lane of Kansas, barred the door, however, and refused the teenage girl's desperate pleas for five minutes of the president's time.

Even though Mrs. Surratt's lawyers were able to secure a writ of habeas corpus from Andrew Wylie, a justice of the Supreme Court of the District of Columbia, at the last minute on the following morning, General Winfield S. Hancock, upon whom the writ was served, refused to obey it. Hancock, who was commanding the middle military division, appeared before Judge Wylie, accompanied by Attorney General James Speed, and stated, "I . . . respectfully say that the body of Mary E. Surratt is in my possession . . . I do not produce said body by reason of the order of the President of the

United States." The attached note of Johnson's was arrogantly blunt: "I . . . do hereby declare that the writ of habeas corpus has been . . . suspended." This would seem to be a clear indication that Johnson was well aware of the efforts to spare Mrs. Surratt from the gallows. The president's cold and illegal denial of this poor woman's constitutional right belies the contentions of those who claim he was not a willing participant in the cover-up.

While the "trial" and conviction of these pathetic souls was a legal abomination, it was an unprecedented travesty of justice to hang this middle-aged woman who, to reasonable observers, hadn't conspired to do anything. Echoing the testimony of witnesses like Lewis Carland, James J. Gifford, D. D. Dana, and John W. Clampitt, Louis Weichmann, the boarder of dubious credibility who was one of the main witnesses against Mary Surratt, was later officially branded a liar by Professor John P. Brophy of Gonzaga College. Brophy contended, in an affidavit which he took to the White House in order to seek perjury charges against Weichmann, that Weichmann had revealed to him that he had originally been arrested as one of the conspirators, and had been threatened with death unless he turned state's evidence. Brophy's long affidavit concluded: ". . . that since this trial closed, he has admitted to me that he was a liar . . . that he swore to a deliberate falsehood on the witness stand . . . that he told me that he thought Mrs. Surratt to be innocent." Johnson's secretary, General Mussey, was present once again, however, to bar the way into the president's office when the professor tried to deliver the affidavit. Brophy then took it to the *National Intelligencer,* where the editor refused to print it, on the grounds that it was "too strong."[25]

In 2010, Robert Redford directed the movie *The Conspirator,* which was based on Mary Surratt's story. It was a well-made film, but only partially detailed the horrible injustice of the "trial" she and her fellow alleged conspirators received. Mary Surratt became the first woman in American history to be executed when she was hung along with Paine, Atzerodt, and Herold on a searing hot July 7, 1865. Most people, including the executioner, Captain Christian Rath, were certain that Mary Surratt's life would be spared. Even as the four "conspirators" stood on the scaffold, and his superior officer, Gen. Winfield Scott Hancock, ordered him to proceed, a startled Rath asked, "Her, too?"[26] Adding to the macabre atmosphere, a large crowd celebrated afterward with lemonade and cakes. Rath would not speak about his role that day until forty-six years later, when the government finally permitted him to. His first-person account appeared in a 1911 issue of *McClure's* magazine, where he admitted, "The hangings gave me a lot of trouble." Rath was haunted for the rest of his long life (he lived to be eighty-nine) by nightmares involving Mary's daughter Anna Surratt.

There are many puzzling questions left unanswered about the assassination of Abraham Lincoln. How does one explain the fact that during the afternoon of April 14, 1865, John Wilkes Booth walked into the lobby of the Kirkwood House, which was the hotel where Vice President Andrew Johnson resided, and *asked for him*? When informed that the vice president was not in his room, Booth left a card with the clerk on which he had scribbled:

Dont wish to disturb you Are you at home?
J Wilkes Booth[27]

This note has provided fodder for some very intriguing speculation. Considering that Andrew Johnson's secretary, Col. William A. Browning, was a longtime friend of Booth's, and that the assassin was acquainted with the vice president himself, it's reasonable to theorize about Johnson's possible ties to the assassination.[28]

The president's widow, Mary Todd Lincoln, clearly suspected that Johnson was involved. In one of her rambling letters, written a year following the assassination, Mrs. Lincoln wrote, ". . . that miserable inebriate

Johnson. . . . He never wrote me a line of condolence and behaved in the most brutal way. . . . As sure as you and I live, Johnson had some hand in all this."[29] Mary Todd Lincoln, much like Lee Harvey Oswald's mother Marguerite, was the first to specifically question the evidence the authorities were assembling against her son; she seems to have been the first conspiracy theorist in this particular case. She was acutely aware, for example, of the note from Booth to Johnson; she wrote in the same March 15, 1866 letter to her friend Sally Orne, "Why, was that card of Booth's, found in his box, some acquaintance certainly existed." Combined with her earlier mentioned comments about the inexcusable performance of John Parker, perhaps Mary Lincoln's obvious knowledge of the minutiae surrounding the assassination played a part in her involuntary confinement in 1875 to a private mental institution.

What must have especially stung Lincoln's widow was the fact her very own son—the only one of her children to survive to adulthood—Robert Todd Lincoln, was the person who arranged an insanity trial for her, declaring, "I have no doubt my mother is insane. She has long been a source of great anxiety to me." While historians have been unrealistically kind to Abraham Lincoln, they have usually portrayed his wife as a vile creature. From the available evidence, she appears to be guilty of nothing more than having a difficult and eccentric personality. In addition to being a conspiracy theorist, Mary Todd Lincoln appeared to have been an unusually astute judge of character; in assessing Ulysses S. Grant's penchant for offering up his superior numbers of men as cannon fodder, a strategy which earned him the title "the Butcher" even in pro-Union newspapers, she wrote, "Grant is a butcher and not fit to be at the head of an army . . . He loses two men to the enemy's one. He has . . . no regard for life."[30]

As in the Kennedy assassination, there were a number of mysterious deaths connected to the murder of Lincoln. The two senators who had blocked Anna Surratt's way into President Johnson's office on the eve of her mother's execution both committed suicide. James H. Lane shot himself in 1866.[31] On November 12, 1865, ex-senator Preston King tied a bag of bullets around his neck and jumped from a ferry into the Hudson River. The couple who had accompanied the Lincolns to Ford's Theatre on April 14, 1865, Major Henry Rathbone and Clara Harris, each came to a tragic end. On December 23, 1883, Rathbone, who had married Harris and moved to Germany, attempted to kill his children. When a nurse tried to intervene, he shot his wife to death and stabbed himself. Rathbone recovered and spent the remainder of his life in a German asylum. William Petersen, the German tailor in whose house Lincoln died, took his own life. His body, loaded with laudanum, was found on the grounds of the Smithsonian Institute. John Wilkes Booth's sister Rosalie was killed in January of 1880 when she answered the door one night and a heavy object thrown from the dark hit her in the temple. Colonel William A. Browning, Andrew Johnson's personal secretary and acquaintance of Booth's, is believed to have been murdered. Lincoln family friend Dr. Anson G. Henry, who comforted Mary Todd Lincoln after the assassination and accompanied her back to Illinois in May 1865, drowned a few months later when the ship he was a passenger on sank off the northern California coast. John Lloyd's great-niece would recall his exceedingly strange death in 1892: "He was in the construction business and died of an accident that occurred on one of his building projects. He wasn't satisfied with some work that had been done and went up on a scaffold to inspect it . . . as he reached the scaffold and stood on it, the boards gave way, and he fell to the ground. The bricks tumbling down upon him crushed his head, kidneys, and other parts of his body."[32]

Sergeant Boston Corbett traveled around the country afterwards and achieved renown as "the man who shot Booth." After obtaining a job as doorman to the Kansas state legislature in 1887, he arrived with revolvers in each hand one morning and opened fire on the legislators. He was committed to an insane asylum in Topeka, Kansas, from which he escaped. After traveling to Texas to become some kind of medicine man, Corbett vanished without a trace.[33] According to researcher David McGowan, Booth's nephew Edwin Booth Clark disappeared at sea, allegedly a suicide. Patriarch of the acting clan Junius Brutus Booth, like Mary Todd Lincoln herself, seemingly went insane after the assassination. Senator John Conness, one of Lincoln's pallbearers, died in an insane asylum. McGowan claims that at least two men who physically resembled Booth, Frank Boyle and William Watson, were shot by vigilantes seeking reward money. Stanton's War Department received the bodies, and dumped at least one of them unceremoniously into the Potomac River. Secretary of State John Seward's daughter Fanny died of unknown causes at just twenty-one, a year after the assassination. Most curious of all, probable conspirator Lafayette Baker, after repeated attempts were made on his life, died in 1868, allegedly of meningitis. An exhumation of his body established that he'd been poisoned with arsenic. In McGowan's words, "Baker left behind cryptic notes alluding to a conspiracy behind the Lincoln assassination involving eleven members of Congress, twelve US Army officers, three US Navy officers, one governor, five bankers, three nationally known newspapermen, and eleven wealthy industrialists."

In 1903 Basil Moxley, who'd been a doorkeeper at Ford's Theatre and had known Booth very well, declared: "Certainly the body buried in Greenmount Cemetery was not that of Booth, for I was one of the pall bearers, and I can safely say to you that there never were any two things in this world which resembled each other less than that body did John Wilkes Booth. I had known Booth all my life. . . . I saw the body several times, and examined it, and I don't hesitate to say that the hair on the dead body was of a reddish brown colour, while Booth's was as black as a raven's wing. However, that mere detail made no difference, for we all knew at that time that the body was not that of John Wilkes Booth."[34] Provost Marshal

General James Rowan O'Beirne also came forward years after the assassination with an interesting revelation: "I can tell you something that has never been published on this case . . . something you will never find on any record. There were three men in the barn and one of them escaped. . . . It was never brought out at the testimony that there was another exit from the barn, but there was. . . . This is all I'm going to tell you at this time, and you can draw your own conclusions, but I am speaking the truth . . . we were all pledged to secrecy in those days."[35]

Conspiracy theories of Lincoln's assassination include that postulated by authors David W. Balsiger and Charles E. Sellier, in their 1977 book and film *The Lincoln Conspiracy.* The authors claim that powerful conspirators like Edwin Stanton and Lafayette Baker had replaced Booth with Confederate officer James William Boyd, who was actually the man who died in Garrett's barn. Officially, Boyd was released from prison on orders from an uncharacteristically lenient Stanton in February 1865. Boyd was supposed to meet his son James afterwards, but he never showed up, and seems to have vanished afterwards. In 1907, Finis L. Bates wrote the book *Escape and Suicide of John Wilkes Booth,* contending that Booth had escaped and moved to Texas, under the pseudonym John St. Helen. He'd supposedly made a deathbed confession but ultimately recovered and took his own life in Oklahoma in 1903. A corpse advertised as "The Man Who Shot Lincoln" was exhibited around the country in the 1920s.

In recent years, the question of just who is buried under Booth's name in Green Mount Cemetery has reappeared in the headlines. A variety of people, including Booth's descendants, petitioned for an exhumation of Booth's alleged grave in Baltimore, Maryland. But even after 130 years, the impulse to suppress was apparently too great for government to resist; a federal judge denied the motion in May 1995. One may rightfully ask establishment historians: if there is "no evidence" that the body isn't Booth's, then why not prove it? It would seem sensible that the deceased's biological descendants, and not some judicial authority, should have the ultimate say in ordering an exhumation to satisfy themselves, if not history. In December 2010, descendants of Edwin Booth reported that they had obtained permission to exhume the Shakespearean actor's body to obtain DNA samples to compare with a sample of his brother John's DNA. However, Bree Harvey, a spokesperson for the Mount Auburn Cemetery in Cambridge, Massachusetts, where Edwin Booth is buried, denied reports that the family had contacted them and requested to exhume Edwin's body. On March 30, 2013, Maryland's National Museum of Health and Medicine spokesperson Carol Johnson announced that the family's request to exhume DNA from the Booth vertebrae stored there had been rejected.[36] During the course of researching this book, I spoke more than once with Joanne Hulme, the great-great-great-grandniece of John Wilkes Booth, who continues the quest for the truth on this subject.

Joanne Hulme summed up her experiences with the following statement to me: "Having a family famous for more than one thing is truly a doubled edged sword. To be a blood relative of the Booth Family, to this day, still called the First Family of the American Stage, is an honor considering many families that have come since, the DeMilles, the Barrymores, the Fondas. But there is always the shadow of the assassin. John Wilkes Booth, despite many predictions that he was quickly becoming a star that would have out shined his father, Junius Booth, and brother, Edwin Booth, he chose differently. To this day, we still have Booth relatives acting in movies, but we remain reluctant about talking about it. Did the fantasy world that these matinee idols live in create a world of non reality where you stab a king on stage at 10:30, but he gets up at 11:00 and drives home, we will never know. The legacy of the Booth relatives is to live still on the outskirts of society forever frowned and questioned about 'this one mad act.'"

In October 2015, I spoke with Nate Orlowek, one of the most renowned Lincoln assassination experts of the present era. Orlowek has been prominently involved in efforts to exhume Booth's alleged body, and gave me the following statement:

> I have devoted over 42 years to researching the possible escape of John Wilkes Booth, and am convinced to a 90% degree of certainty that the man killed in the barn was not John Wilkes Booth. The findings of my team are so convincing that the Booth family has nearly unanimously come to the same conclusion. Many establishment historians have tried everything in their power to block any and all efforts to scientifically settle the matter once and for all. I cannot help but conclude that protecting their self-appointed sense of infallibility is more important to them than pursuing the objective historical truth—whatever that truth might be. I and my team have never been afraid of finding out the truth—even it would turn out that we were wrong. There is no shame in being wrong. But it is shameful for people who prate about being the "real historians" to squelch all attempts at arriving at the truth. Real historians (as we most certainly are, whether they like to admit it or not), like real scientists, have as their highest priority the revealing of truth, not protecting their reputations. In the end, the truth WILL come out!

There is no way of determining, more than 150 years after the event, just who was responsible for murdering Abraham Lincoln. The May 2, 1868 issue of the periodical *The People's Weekly* was discovered by chance in an old Baltimore, Maryland house in 1948, and eventually found its way into the hands of author Otto Eisenschiml. In that issue the editor, Ben Green, wrote that he had recently been approached by a stenographer (whom he did not identify) who had taken testimony at the conspiracy trial. This stenographer had supplied Green with evidence identifying "the real instigators of the Assassination of Lincoln." These "real instigators" were named as Edwin M. Stanton, Judge Advocate Joseph Holt, and Col. Lafayette C.

Baker. Green wrote that he didn't have the "time or space in this number to continue this subject," but promised to do so in the next issue. Whether he did or not is unknown, because there is no record of the next issue of *The People's Weekly* in existence today. After Eisenschiml located the May 2, 1868 number, he tried mightily to obtain the following issue of the magazine, but was never able to locate it.[37]

Some critics have speculated that when Lincoln decided (rather shockingly, considering his strong support of a central bank) to print US notes—called "greenbacks" because of their ink color—he signed his own death warrant. Lincoln apparently balked at the usurious interest rates demanded by the big banks to keep up the funding of the war effort. Lincoln wrote that these greenbacks "gave the people of this Republic the greatest blessing they have ever had—their own paper money to pay their own debts." Lincoln's directive to print over $400 million of this debt-free, interest-free money, beginning in early 1862, seems like a truly revolutionary and uncharacteristic act. The following famous response to Lincoln's creation of greenbacks was allegedly published shortly they were first issued, by Lord George Goschen in the *London Times*: "If this mischievous financial policy, which has its origin in North America, shall become endurated down to a fixture, then that Government will furnish its own money without cost. It will pay off debts and be without debt. It will have all the money necessary to carry on its commerce. It will become prosperous without precedent in the history of the world. The brains, and wealth of all countries will go to North America. That country must be destroyed or it will destroy every monarchy on the globe."

Thanks to researchers like Otto Eisenschiml and Theodore Roscoe, whose 1959 book on the assassination, *Web of Conspiracy*, elicited the usual howls from the court historians, we know that the War Department kept pertinent files on the Lincoln assassination marked "secret" until at least the 1930s. Foretelling what would come in the next century, when "national security" became a catch-all term to excuse the withholding of information about significant events, Secretary of War Stanton would maintain that the suppressed material was "not in the public interest." A pamphlet that used to be provided to visitors at the Medical Museum of the Armed Forces Institute of Pathology in Washington, DC informed the public: "Confusion and mystery still surround the shooting of Abraham Lincoln, and we probably will never know all the facts. One thing is sure . . . his murder was part of a larger conspiracy." In the words of Theodore Roscoe:

> All previous accounts of the assassination were based on official Government statements and press releases angled, slanted and otherwise doctored to suit popular consumption, and on the sketchy (although voluminous) trial reports published by the official court reporters. Thus a towering edifice of so-called history was erected on sand. It made popular reading, but it lacked the exacting foundations of true historicity. How could the facts be known or assessed when the War Department withheld them from inquiring historians and even from such authorized investigators as senators and congressmen on contemporary Congressional Committees?

The Lincoln assassination illustrates perfectly just how little the facts about important historical events have in common with the accepted analysis of them. We have barely skimmed the surface here, in regards to the inconsistencies sprinkled liberally throughout what remains of the public record. A quick perusal of the available data on Lincoln's assassination should shock the most apathetic of citizens. Nevertheless, according to the history books, what transpired at Ford's Theatre was just a senseless tragedy. Abraham Lincoln, officially speaking, was shot by a deranged Confederate sympathizer, aided by a hapless band of cohorts, for no rationally discernible purpose.

CHAPTER FIVE

POST-CIVIL WAR AMERICA

The principle for which we contend is bound to reassert itself . . . Our cause was so just, so sacred, that had I known all that has come to pass, had I known . . . all that my country was to suffer, all that our posterity was to endure, I would do it all over again.

—Jefferson Davis

RECONSTRUCTION

The consolidation of the states into one vast empire, sure to be aggressive abroad and despotic at home, will be the certain precursor of ruin which has overwhelmed all that preceded it.

—Robert E. Lee

Little-remembered Confederate Major General Patrick R. Cleburne eerily foretold what would happen after the war, writing in January 1864:

Every man should endeavor to understand the meaning of subjugation before it is too late . . . it means the history of this heroic struggle will be written by the enemy; that our youth will be trained by Northern school-teachers; will learn from Northern school books their version of the war;

142

will be impressed by the influences of history and education to regard our gallant dead as traitors, and our maimed veterans as fit objects for derision. . . . It is said slavery is all we are fighting for, and if we give it up we give up all. Even if this were true, which we deny, slavery is not all our enemies are fighting for. It is merely the pretense to establish sectional superiority and a more centralized form of government, and to deprive us of our rights and liberties.

The Confederates were an inordinately proud lot, best exemplified perhaps by Jefferson Davis's comments, in 1881, that ". . . the contest is not over, the strife is not ended. It has only entered upon a new and enlarged arena." This was after years of personal suffering, and with the full knowledge of how much the South had endured under the mantle of Reconstruction.

Thus, it was natural for the arrogant "victors" in Lincoln's bloody war to want to suppress that kind of southern pride. During Reconstruction, the federal government continued to terrorize the south for at least twelve years following Lee's surrender to Grant at Appomattox Court House. Unlike classical definitions of the word, this was much more an attempt at a psychological reconstruction of the surviving rebels than any mere effort to physically rebuild the infrastructure that had been burned and destroyed by brutal federal forces. State laws and the Constitution itself were rewritten, ostensibly in order to extend civil rights to the freed slaves. For much of the early twentieth century, even establishment historians recognized Reconstruction as an excessive, punitive punishment inflicted upon a defeated people. Andrew Johnson, once seen as a staunch defender of the Constitution in his battles with the radical Republicans of his day, is now routinely dismissed as "incorrigibly racist," to quote historian Eric Foner in his March 28, 2015 opinion piece "Why Reconstruction Matters" in the *New York Times*.

Lincoln's original, fledgling plans for Reconstruction included, interestingly enough, only limited black suffrage, for the "very intelligent" ones and "those who serve our cause as soldiers." As always, the court historians find excuses for Lincoln that "racists" like Thomas Jefferson are not allotted; Foner, for example, merely explains that "Lincoln's ideas evolved." By saddling the defeated Confederate states with draconian rules, and basically urging their former slaves to seek vengeance upon them, the federal government figuratively rubbed the South's face in it. One of many drastic examples of the despair felt by the devastated Southerners could be found in the chilling final diary entry of unrepentant Confederate exile Edmund Ruffin, who wrote, just before taking his own life:

I here declare my unmitigated hatred to Yankee rule—to all political, social and business connections with the Yankees and the Yankee race. Would that I could impress these sentiments, in their full force, on every living Southerner and bequeath them to every one yet to be born! . . . And now with what will be my latest writing and utterance, and with what will be near my lastest breath, I here repeat and would willingly proclaim my unmitigated hatred to Yankee rule—and all connections with Yankees, and the perfidious, malignant and vile Yankee race.

As early as April 1865, General Halleck would write to Ulysses S. Grant and report on the alarming number of rapes and assaults being committed by blacks against white southerners. South Carolina governor Benjamin Perry wrote out a full report on an incident in Pocotaligo, where black soldiers had entered a home, tied up a man, and "outraged" the females there. General George Meade responded by saying he was trying to control the black soldiers, but was reluctant to "offend northern sentiment."[1] These kinds of incidents would eventually lead to "Black Codes" being enacted by the southern states; these laws forbid blacks from owning weapons, serving as witnesses, or giving testimony in a court, and monitored "vagrancy."

Ironically, these codes were copied almost verbatim from those that were on the books in all northern states at that time. The miscegenation laws mirrored those in the north; interracial marriage, in fact, was illegal in every state of the union at that time. Whites who broke these codes by socializing with blacks, or engaging in sexual relations with them, faced a $200 fine and six months in jail.[2] As always, these laws applied only to the enemies of those in power; incredibly, there were still six states in the north refusing to allow blacks to vote in 1868.

By the summer of 1867, black preachers were openly urging their congregations to take what they wanted from their white neighbors. Blacks who were not members of the Union League were not permitted to vote. Those belonging to the League voted early and often; blacks as young as sixteen years old voted multiple times in the 1868 election. The ballots were counted at military bases.[3] Legislation of the most absurd kind was routinely introduced; bills requiring men to remove their hats in the presence of civil or military officers, or to mandate disenfranchised voters to remove their hat in the presence of voters. According to author Kent H. Steffgen, "In bolder instances, attempts were made to declare all marriages between whites null and void."[4] Formerly valuable property everywhere went into forfeiture. In some state legislatures, amendments "too obscene to print" were offered spontaneously.[5] All black militia units drilled constantly during elections, intimidating the public with guns and bayonets. Between the wildly corrupt white "scalawags" and the charged-up newly freed ex-slaves, "representing" the public while drunk, fighting, or even openly asleep, the "reconstructed" south was an historical embarrassment.

The northern "carpetbaggers" and southern "scalawags" formed secret societies that instructed former slaves on how to seek revenge on their onetime masters. They were given arms and encouraged to rape, kill, and pillage. Black groups like the Union League were promised the land of their former slave owners, but the government treated this promise the way it treated all the broken treaties with Native Americans. This particular broken promise became bitterly known as "Forty acres and a mule."

Rumors held that uncooperative blacks were hanged, with the crimes being blamed on the Confederates. White carpetbaggers saw to it that every state government in the south was at least three-fourths black, and blacks dominated the courts, juries, law enforcement, boards of education, and city councils. As Richard Taylor described it in his 1879 book *Destruction and Reconstruction*, graft and corruption flourished to an unbelievable extent, with warrants issued haphazardly whenever the spirit moved the often drunken "representatives." The freedom of those charged with these imaginary "crimes" often depended on the individual's financial wherewithal. Taxpayers paid for such frivolities as expensive gifts for the lady friends of the "representatives." The "robber governor" of South Carolina, white "scalawag" Frank Moses, was so notoriously corrupt that the order of the state treasurer, restoring the $1000 he lost gambling on horse races as a "gratuity," is still on file in Columbia, South Carolina. Moses had simply moved into the mansion of Wade Hampton, reputed to have been the South's wealthiest planter before the war. When the South began to wrest control back from their overseers, Moses left South Carolina penniless and died a dope addict in Winthrop, Massachusetts in 1906, after forging an impoverished existence as a petty thief and con man. His own family was so ashamed of him they changed their names to avoid being associated with him. In Georgia, things were largely the same under "scalawag" New Yorker Rufus Bullock, who rivaled Moses in corruption.

Because of the bloody carnage that led to the slaves of the south getting their freedom, and the barren land and crops left behind in so many areas, the resentment the surviving southerners felt towards their new overlords was deep and lasting. Reconstruction not only antagonized the southerners who had to live under it, it became increasingly unpopular in the north. The most radical Republican of them all, Thaddeus

Stevens, was so disillusioned with its lack of success that he remarked to a friend, shortly before he died, that "My life has been a failure . . . I see little hope for the republic." Unlike many moralists, Stevens practiced what he preached; he requested to be buried in a segregated cemetery for African American paupers, in order to "illustrate in death the principles which I advocated through a long life, Equality of man before his creator." Because Reconstruction was centered around getting southern whites to accept blacks as their equals, it began to fail miserably not only in the south, but in the north where almost all whites were just as inherently racist. Americans everywhere had more immediate concerns once financial panic hit the stock market in 1873 and created a genuine depression that lasted years.

As establishment historian Benjamin Ginsberg put it, "radical Republicans sought to drastically alter the social and political structures of the states of the former Confederacy." Radicals like Stevens and Charles Sumner insisted that the southern states be treated like conquered provinces. Stevens had never been bound by any constitutional restraints; he once described the Constitution as "a worthless bit of old parchment." The Reconstruction Act of 1867 was inspired by Oliver Cromwell's military dictatorship in England. By the time the Fourteenth Amendment to the Constitution was proposed, our leaders were so accustomed to disregarding the rule of law that it was merely declared officially passed on July 20, 1868 by Secretary of State William Seward, despite the fact it had failed to meet the constitutional requirements of three-fourths of the states voting to ratify it. This kind of blatant, unconstitutional mischief began under Lincoln and has continued almost unabated to the present day. For decades, everyone recognized the illegality of this amendment, and the unconstitutionality of Reconstruction itself. For example, a source as mainstream as *The Encyclopedia Americana* stated, "Reconstruction added humiliation to suffering. . . . Eight years of crime, fraud, and corruption followed and it was State legislatures composed of Negroes, carpetbaggers and scalawags who obeyed the orders of the generals and ratified the amendment."

Thaddeus Stevens's bill to put the southern states under military rule was vetoed by President Andrew Johnson, a move even later "liberal" historians like Henry Steele Commager agreed with. Johnson incurred the wrath of Edwin Stanton and other Radicals, and would go on to become the first American president to be impeached. Before impeaching him, the vindictive Radicals tied Johnson's hands unconstitutionally by the Tenure of Office and other acts, which forbid Johnson to remove any civil officers (an obvious reference to Edwin Stanton) without the consent of the Senate. Johnson also lost control of the military, and was forced to issue orders directly through General of the Army Ulysses S. Grant. Congress also threatened to abolish the appellate jurisdiction of the Supreme Court if it declared the Reconstruction Act unconstitutional. Few people realize, and court historians rarely remind them, that Andrew Johnson was impeached basically because of his critical speeches against Reconstruction. Considering the unconstitutional actions of so many of our presidents, first and foremost his immediate predecessor Abraham Lincoln, it is mind-boggling that Andrew Johnson suffered such a rare indignity.

The senator whose "no" vote saved Johnson from being removed from office, Edmund Ross, would be cited as one of the examples in then Senator John F. Kennedy's bestselling 1955 book *Profiles in Courage*. George Washington University professor Jonathan Turley, one of the most independent-minded journalists in the country today, lamented that, as a reward for his valor, Ross was "shunned, physically assaulted and ruined both politically and financially." Ross is not looked upon favorably by establishment historians or the mainstream media. A January 31, 1999 article in *Slate* headlined "Andrew Johnson: Saved by a Scoundrel" typified the prevailing official consensus about him. While Johnson is now seen by mainstream scholars as a "racist," Thaddeus Stevens, by contrast, was given the iconic treatment by Fawn Brodie, whose literary psychoanalysis of the Radical Republican revealed him to be more to her liking than her later biographical subject, Thomas Jefferson. Johnson further outraged Radical Republicans when he pardoned Lincoln assassination alleged conspirator Dr. Samuel Mudd in 1869.

A big financial windfall for the federal government was the South's valuable cotton crop, which they simply seized. While the estimated value of the cotton was some $100 million, the government actually received only about $30 million. "I am sure I sent some honest agents south," remarked Secretary of the Treasury Hugh McColloch, "but it sometimes seems very doubtful whether any of them remained honest very long." Plunder and debt prevailed everywhere; in South Carolina alone, the state government accumulated $14 million in debt between 1868 and 1874, largely due to mass confiscation and outright larceny on the part of the occupying military officials. This plunder and graft was hardly new; in 1862, Edward Stanly, newly appointed by Lincoln as military governor of North Carolina, lamented, "Had the war in North Carolina been conducted by soldiers who were Christians and gentlemen, the State would have long ago rebelled against rebellion. But instead of that, what was done? Thousands and thousands of dollars-worth of property were conveyed north. Libraries, pianos, carpets, mirrors, family portraits, everything in short, that could be removed, was stolen by men . . . preaching Liberty, justice and civilization. . . . I was informed that one regiment of abolitionists had conveyed North more than $40,000 worth of property. They literally robbed the cradle and the grave. Family burial vaults were broken open for robbery; and in one instance (the fact was published in a Boston newspaper and admitted to me by an officer of high position in the army) a vault was entered, a metallic coffin removed, and the remains cast out that those of a dead [northern] soldier might be put in the place."[6]

The Ku Klux Klan was born during this era, formed by desperate men who saw no other way to counter the rampant corruption and lawlessness all around them. As whites who wanted, in Abraham Lincoln's words, to retain the "superior position" over blacks, it would have been difficult enough to get them to accept any sort of equality between the races. What happened during Reconstruction hardly represented any palatable form of "equality," however. Writing in the April 1995 issue of *Special Warfare*, Professor James J. Schneider of the Army Command and General Staff College at Fort Leavenworth called Reconstruction "the darkest days in the history of the Army . . . an effort in peacekeeping, peace enforcement, humanitarian relief, nation-building and, with the rise of the Ku Klux Klan, counterterrorism . . . the Reconstruction activities of Army units were unprecedented in their time, and they sound remarkably familiar today." The occupying skills learned by US military troops during Reconstruction would be passed on to future military generations, and honed to "perfection" in postwar Germany, Iraq, Afghanistan, and other countries. High taxes were levied on ex-confederates throughout the federally occupied states, which resulted in a great loss of homes and farms. In North Carolina and Alabama, blacks who had been convicts, and were unable to read or write, were appointed as justices of the peace. The original Ku Klux Klan committed very few violent acts, and General Nathan Bedford Forrest was placed in a leadership role in the organization with the blessing of Robert E. Lee, who was adamant that their role be strictly protective.

Paul R. Petersen, author of *Reconstruction in Missouri: Worse Than the War?*, alleged that Union troops engaged in even more extreme war crimes than imagined, such as the digging up of graves in search of valuables, and the pouring of oil or salt on fields in order to prevent any future growth of crops. In Missouri after the war, Petersen reported that "roving bands of Federal vigilantes gathered in the middle of the night riding to the doorsteps of their former guerilla enemies, calling them out of their beds and shooting them down on their doorsteps in the presence of their wives and children." Guerilla Harrison Trow declared that "there was no law" now in Missouri, and that "the courts were instruments of plunder" and the "civil officers were cutthroats." William Clarke Quantrill and his band of Confederate guerillas (which included a young Jesse James) were targeted for assassination by Federal forces; some were killed on their property, and at least one was shot down in cold blood after surrendering. This was hardly new in Missouri; during the war, General John McNeil had chosen ten civilians by lottery, among only the best educated and most influential ones, and simply executed them. Learning of McNeil's actions, Lincoln actually *promoted* him.

William P. "Parson" Brownlow, the governor of Tennessee, exemplified the caliber and mindset of those who ruled the south during Reconstruction. During a convention in New York City, Brownlow made the following statement: "If I had the power I would arm every wolf, panther, catamount and bear in the mountains of America, every crocodile in the swamps of Florida, every negro in the South, every devil in Hell, clothe them in the uniform of the Federal army, and turn them loose on the rebels of the South and exterminate every man, woman and child, south of Mason and Dixon's line. I would like to see negro troops under Ben Butler crowd every rebel into the Gulf of Mexico, and drown them as the devil did the hogs in the Sea of Galilee." At an earlier meeting in Philadelphia, just after the surrender of General Robert E. Lee, Brownlow had declared: "I am one of those who believe the war ended too soon. We have whipped the South but not enough. The loyal masses constitute an overwhelming majority of the people of this country and they intend to march again on the South and intend that the 'second war' shall be no child's play. The 'second army' will, as they ought to, make the entire South as God found the earth, without form, and void." One marvels at any human being who could describe the *first* war as "child's play."

As just one of General William Sherman's countless atrocities, a number of weeping women and children in Marietta, Roswell, and New Manchester, Georgia were literally *kidnapped* by northern troops and shipped north on trains. There, they became, ironically enough, virtual slaves working for mere pennies. There was no effort during Reconstruction to send these displaced souls back to their homes. This brought to mind William Sherman's Special Order No. 254, which forced deportations of citizens out of Memphis, Tennessee. According to this "order," for every Union boat fired upon by the rebel forces, "Ten families must be expelled from Memphis." General Grant's General Order No. 11 (did these guys love their "orders" or what?) forced Jewish traders and their families to leave Oxford, Mississippi and Paducah, Kentucky. Despite the overt anti-Semitic nature of this order, Grant is still viewed favorably by establishment historians. The primarily Jewish store owners in Memphis, Tennessee were simply ordered to ship their clothing north in December 1863, under General Order No. 162. Sherman, by the way, complained about having to deal with "swarms of Jews," but again his sterling reputation with the court historians remains intact.

Philip Sheridan became a quite fitting military governor during Reconstruction for the Fifth Military District, which consisted of territory in Texas and Louisiana. As might be expected, he ruled with an iron hand, severely limiting voter registration for former Confederates, and only allowing registered voters to serve on juries. He cavalierly fired Texas governor James Throckmorton for being an "impediment to the reconstruction of the state," and replaced him with the Republican he'd defeated in the election. Andrew Johnson, further sealing his fate as the first president to be impeached, angrily removed Sheridan over Grant's objections, declaring, "His rule has, in fact, been one of absolute tyranny, without references to the principles of our government or the nature of our free institutions." Sheridan reacted with a figurative flip-off, exclaiming: "If I owned Texas and Hell, I would rent Texas and live in Hell." Considering his vile record as a military leader, I think most religious people would suspect that Sheridan received at least part of his wish. Sheridan would be utilized by President Grant several times during his abysmal administration, most notably to subdue the Plains Indians, with the same reprehensible tactics he'd perfected in the Shenandoah Valley. Whether or not he really said anything like "The only good Indian is a dead Indian," Sheridan and his Union comrade William Sherman added to their collection of atrocities during the Indian "wars," whereby they wiped out untold numbers of buffalo and forced Native Americans back on to their reservations, where they clearly believed they belonged.

The former leaders of the Confederacy were appalled by Reconstruction. Robert E. Lee told the ex-governor of Texas, F. W. Stockdale, in August 1870, "Governor, if I had foreseen the use these people desired to make of their victory, there would have been no surrender at Appomattox, no, sir, not by me. Had I seen these results of subjugation, I would have preferred to die at Appomattox with my brave men, my sword in this right hand." Jefferson Davis, meanwhile, rejected the notion that he should ingratiate himself with the federal government by declaring, "It's been said that I should apply to the United States for a pardon, but repentance must precede the right of pardon, and I have not repented." Even black activist and author W. E. B. DuBois, writing in 1915, recognized that Reconstruction "pandered to the ignorant negroes, the knavish white natives and the vulturous adventurers who flocked to the North." Historian James Ford Rhodes, writing in 1892, observed, "It was the most soul-sickening spectacle that Americans had ever been called upon to behold. Every principle of the old American polity was here reversed. In place of government by the most intelligent and virtuous part of the people for the benefit of the governed, here was government by the most ignorant and vicious part of the population for the benefit, the vulgar, materialistic, brutal benefit of the governing set."[7]

Typical of the way many historical subjects are misrepresented by scholars and historians is the treatment accorded former Confederate general Nathan Beford Forrest. Forrest went from being perhaps the South's most feared military leader to one of the founders of the Ku Klux Klan. However, what isn't reported is his later, on the road to Damascus-like conversion of philosophy. Forrest spoke the following words at an early day civil rights convention in Memphis, Tennessee:

> I want to elevate you to take positions in law offices, in stores, on farms, and wherever you are capable of going. I have not said anything about politics today . . . . You have a right to elect whom you please; vote for the man you think best, and I think, when that is done, you and I are freemen. Do as you consider right and honest in electing men for office. I did not come here to make you a long speech, although invited to do so by you. I am not much of a speaker, and my business prevented me from preparing myself. I came to meet you as friends, and welcome you to the white people. I want you to come nearer to us. When I can serve you I will do so. We have but one flag, one country; let us stand together. We may differ in color, but not in sentiment.

Why is this man still so vilified? Recently, the Memphis city council voted to exhume the bodies of Forrest and his wife and move them to another location. Given how difficult it has been for the descendants of Meriwether Lewis and John Wilkes Booth to get their loved ones exhumed, it is astonishing to consider that in this case, the government simply decided to do it, against the wishes of Forrest's descendants. It certainly ought to be illegal for any political body to vote to exhume anyone, but we live in fantastic times.

Before the court historians established a complete monopoly on academic thought, historians understood how shameful Reconstruction really was. In 1906, historian Claude G. Bowers wrote that Reconstruction represented "years of revolutionary turmoil, with the elemental passions predominant. . . . The prevailing note was one of tragedy. . . . Never have American public men in responsible positions, directing the destiny of the nation, been so brutal, hypocritical, and corrupt. The constitution was treated as a doormat on which politicians and army officers wiped their feet after wading in the muck. . . . The southern people literally were put to the torture . . . [by] rugged conspirators . . . [who] assumed the pose of philanthropists and patriots." Even the establishment's flagship newspaper, *The New York Times*, objected vehemently to the redistribution of property under Reconstruction, declaring in its July 9, 1867 issue, "An attempt to justify the confiscation of Southern land under the pretense of doing justice to the freedmen, strikes at the root of property rights in both sections. It concerns Massachusetts as much as Mississippi."

Fiery radical Frederick Douglass summed up the failure of Reconstruction this way in 1876: "You say you have emancipated us. You have; and I thank you for it. But what is your emancipation? . . . when you turned us loose, you gave us no acres. You turned us loose to the sky, to the storm, to the whirlwind, and, worst, of all you turned us loose to the wrath of our infuriated masters." No one benefited from Reconstruction. Like the bloody war that preceded it and gave birth to it, Reconstruction did not bring about a harmonious equality of the races. It did not heal the wounds of the awful War Between the States. Instead, it was a tyrannical occupation of a vanquished people, which ultimately unleashed the Ku Klux Klan and nearly a century of Jim Crow laws in retaliation. It created more racists than it reformed and it further besmirched America's "experiment" in representative government.

THE 1876 ELECTION

To vote is like the payment of a debt, a duty never to be neglected . . .
—Rutherford B. Hayes

The eight years of nearly nonstop corruption under former Union war "hero" Ulysses S. Grant are invariably attributed by court historians to an incredible naiveté on the part of the president. Grant is always portrayed as a good-hearted, trusting man whose only flaw was being a poor judge of character. After two presidential administrations inundated with a myriad of scandals, and weary of a Reconstruction that no one in America seemed pleased with, the country prepared for the 1876 election.

Democrat Samuel J. Tilden wound up winning the popular vote in the election, and also outpolled his Republican rival Rutherford B. Hayes in the Electoral College, 184 votes against 165, with 20 still remaining uncounted in the states of South Carolina, Louisiana, and Florida. Hayes would have to win all three contested states in order to have the 185 electoral votes needed for victory. In January 1877, Congress created an election commission composed of eight Republicans and seven Democrats. It was hardly a shock that each of the contested state returns were awarded to Hayes by an 8–7 vote. The Republican leadership offered the Democrats multiple consolation prizes in exchange for the presidency, the biggest of which was an agreement to end Reconstruction. Hayes was simply awarded the election, and less than two months later the military governments ruling the southern states disappeared. Ironically, an appropriations bill was passed by Congress in 1878, which included a rider that forbid the use of Army troops "for the purpose of executing the laws" without the specific authorization of Congress. This, of course, basically invalidated the entire process of Reconstruction.

The seedy manner in which the 1876 presidential election was decided should have caused all Americans to demand an investigation into obvious fraud. But as we discovered in the controversial aftermath of the 2000 presidential election, Americans have very short memories and a hesitation to confront the reality of their own disenfranchisement. They prefer instead to possess, in the words of Ambrose Bierce, "the right to vote for the man of another man's choice." Hayes wasn't a terribly corrupt man, but the results of that election should have left a bad taste in everyone's mouth. Tilden, on the other hand, had been against the war, and critical of Lincoln's heavy-handed executive leadership. As governor of New York after the Civil War, he played a crucial part in eliminating the corrupt crony ring led by "Boss" William Tweed. This quote of Tilden's hints at what type of president he might have been:

> I was never a Republican, because those gentlemen, distinguished as they are, have only one real interest, and that is the making of special laws in order to protect their fortunes. I also know they have no compassion for the masses of the people in this country who are without money and who are, many of them, without food or houses. I have always thought that only as a Democrat, reflecting Jefferson and Jackson, could justice ever be done the people because, at this moment in history, ours is the only party which is even faintly responsive to the force of ideas.

THE GARFIELD ASSASSINATION

Whoever controls the volume of money in any country is absolute master of all industry and commerce.

—James A. Garfield

James Garfield came to the presidency on the heels of being the Chairman of the House Committee on Appropriations. Upon his election to the presidency, he appointed a new collector of customs in New York, which prompted both New York senators—Roscoe Conkling and Thomas Platt—to resign in protest.

After only four months in office, Garfield stopped at the Baltimore and Potomac Railroad station in Washington, DC on July 2, 1881, on his way to give a speech at his alma mater, Williams College. In another of those strange coincidences, Robert Todd Lincoln, Garfield's secretary of war, was present on the occasion. As was customary then, Garfield had no bodyguards or security detail. Charles Guiteau, the first of the successful American "lone nuts," approached Garfield with a gun and shot him, crying out, "I am a Stalwart of the Stalwarts! I did it and I want to be arrested! Arthur is president now!" Not surprisingly, this incriminating statement initially led to the natural belief that Vice President Chester Arthur was connected in some way to the shooting. The "Stalwarts" were a Republican faction loyal to ex-president Ulysses S. Grant, and they vehemently opposed "Half-Breeds" like Garfield, who wanted reform of the notorious political patronage and spoils system.

Since Garfield was in office for such a short period of time, it is difficult to guess what would have happened if he'd served even a single full term. However, he left some consistently anti-banking remarks in the public record, leading some "conspiracy theorist" types to speculate that perhaps he was thinking of issuing more of the "greenbacks" which might have sealed Abraham Lincoln's fate. Revealing his constitutional knowledge, Garfield once said, "The chief duty of the National Government in connection with the currency of the country is to coin money and declare its value. Grave doubts have been entertained whether Congress is authorized by the Constitution to make any form of paper money legal tender. The present issue of United States notes has been sustained by the necessities of war; but such paper should depend for its value and currency upon its convenience in use and its prompt redemption in coin at the will of the holder, and not upon its compulsory circulation. These notes are not money, but promises to pay money. If the holders demand it, the promise should be kept."

Garfield's wounds shouldn't have been fatal, and he lingered on for more than two months before finally passing away on September 19. The now accepted historical fact that he was killed by medical malpractice rather than an assassin's bullet was obvious even to Guiteau, who said at his trial, "The doctors killed Garfield, I just shot him." In one of their countless inexcusable mistakes, one of the physicians treating Garfield had stuck his unwashed hands into his open wound and punctured his liver. They also probed the wrong side of his body. Guiteau had allegedly sent a great deal of previous threatening correspondence to the White House, all of it oddly ignored. During his trial, Guiteau became something of a Charles Manson-style celebrity, constantly criticizing his own defense team, quoting his testimony in lengthy poems, and passing notes to the spectators asking for advice. He even sang "John Brown's Body" to the court. His insanity defense was rejected, and Guiteau was hung on June 30, 1882, dancing merrily to the gallows and reciting his original poem "I am going to the Lordy" as a last request. The court historians tell us that, for unclear reasons, Guiteau had actually earlier given a speech before a small gathering in New York, *endorsing* Garfield's candidacy, which later resulted in him claiming credit for Garfield's victory.

One thing was for certain; the bankers didn't have to worry about Chester Arthur printing any greenbacks, or questioning their absolute authority in matters of finance. Arthur's corruption was so renowned that President Rutherford B. Hayes had fired him as part of his effort to reform the federal patronage system in New York. Arthur did wind up shocking his supporters by actually carrying the mantle of reform in several instances. Radical writer Mark Twain praised him profusely, saying, "It would be hard indeed to better President Arthur's administration."

RECONSTRUCTION FALLOUT

In 1875, there were eight black members of the US Congress. By 1887, there were none. Once military occupation of the south ceased, the embittered ex-secessionists struck back violently. The Jim Crow laws, named after a fictitious slave character popularized by white entertainer Thomas Dartmouth Rice, established an ironclad "Separate but Equal" status that resulted in "Colored" and "Whites only" drinking fountains, restrooms, restaurants, etc. This apartheid system was concentrated in the south, but gradually became unofficially established in the north as well. Poll taxes and literacy tests served to severely limit the voting rights of blacks and poor whites in the south. Unreconstructed southerners had been wounded deeply by the destruction of their land and way of life. An astute political observer should have foreseen the mighty backlash against blacks and the concept of "equality" that resulted. By 1896, the Supreme Court would rule that "separate but equal" accommodations were constitutional in its *Plessy v. Ferguson* case. As mainstream a source as the *Encyclopedia Britannica* would describe the Ku Klux Klan in a shockingly positive manner as those who "oppose the Radical Republican Party and the Union League; to defend Constitutional liberty; to prevent usurpation, emancipate the whites, maintain peace and order, the laws of God, the principles of 1776; in short, to oppose African influence in government and society and to prevent any intermingling of the races." The blowback from Reconstruction grew more and more severe; Alabama, North Carolina, and Florida passed laws during the 1880s making it a crime for a black man to change employers without permission. A black man could also be charged with a crime for speaking loudly in the company of a white woman, or having a gun in his pocket. It became a crime to fail to yield a sidewalk to white people, or sit among whites on a train.[8]

Racial relations continued to sour, as southerners took their vengeance against the north out on poor, defenseless blacks. According to statistics provided by the Equal Justice Initiative, there were nearly 4,000 lynchings of black Americans from 1877 to 1950.[9] Nathan Bedford Forrest came to regret the increasing violence of the Ku Klux Klan and repudiated the organization he helped found. He went so far as to visit black churches and apologize for the error of his ways. Just a year into his reign as the KKK's first Grand Wizard, Forrest issued General Order Number One, which stated: "It is therefore ordered and decreed, that the masks and costumes of this Order be entirely abolished and destroyed." By 1875, he was advocating that blacks be admitted to law school. In 1874, the firmly reformed racist had written the governor of Tennessee, offering to "help exterminate those men responsible for the continued violence against the blacks."[10]

While protesters pressured politicians to exhume the body of Nathan Bedford Forrest, to presumably flush it down the nearest memory hole, there has been curiously little attention paid to the statue of another KKK icon, prominently displayed in Washington, DC. Albert Pike was one of the most important Freemasons of his era, which might very well explain his special status. The most vociferous voices demanding that the statue of Pike be removed have come from members of political "extremist" Lyndon Larouche's organization. Keep in mind we are talking about a federal monument to Pike, which is administered by the National Park Service. Pike was the head of the Supreme Council of the Freemasons' Scottish Rite's, Southern Jurisdiction for thirty-two years. Pike was sculpted holding a copy of his work *Morals and Dogma*, which was so influential that until 1964 a copy was given to every Mason who completed the fourteenth degree in the Southern Jurisdiction. It is still a highly respected work among Freemasons; a new edition was published in 2011, annotated by the Scottish Rite's Grand Archivist and Grand Historian. Albert Pike, like Dr. Samuel Mudd, was pardoned for unclear actions as a Confederate general by Andrew Johnson.

An astounding anecdote surrounding Pike involves testimony allegedly given before the House Judiciary Committee in 1867 by General Gordon Granger. Granger related a meeting between himself, Albert Pike, and then President Andrew Johnson. Granger was amazed that Johnson considered himself to be subordinate to Pike, who was the higher-ranking Mason.[11]

Even more glaring is the scant attention historians and civil rights activists have paid to the fact that hundreds of thousands of blacks continued to be enslaved for decades after their supposed emancipation. There are a multitude of letters from grief-stricken black parents, describing how their children were kidnapped and forced into indentured servitude, written to a disinterested government (at least one was sent to President Theodore Roosevelt), sitting in the National Archives. Similar records, documenting subversion of the courts, forced labor camps, and a thriving system of human trafficking, can be found in local archives all across the South. According to author Douglas A. Blackmon, "By the first years after 1900, tens of thousands of African American men and boys, along with a smaller number of women, had been sold by southern state governments. An exponentially larger number, of whom surviving records are painfully incomplete, had been forced into labor through county and local courts, backwoods justices of the peace, and outright kidnapping and trafficking." This odious practice continued right up until the advent of World War II.[12]

In 1884, Grover Cleveland became the first Democrat to be elected to the Oval Office since James Buchanan. He made history as the first president ever to be married in the White House, when he wed twenty-one-year-old Frances Folsom on June 2, 1886. Frances was the youngest First Lady in US history, and became a beloved celebrity. Oddly, there was little public furor over the huge age difference between them, augmented by the fact that Cleveland had known Frances since she was an infant, and indeed had helped raise her after her father died. In 1888, Cleveland again won the popular vote, but the people's will was thwarted again, and Republican Benjamin Harrison ascended to the presidency. In 1892, Cleveland became the only chief executive to be elected to a non-consecutive second term. His vice president this time was Adlai E. Stevenson, grandfather of the two-time Democratic Party presidential nominee in the 1950s.

Cleveland had to contend with the growing influence of the Populists, who advocated free silver, a forty-hour work week, and other reforms. The panic of 1893 sent the country into an economic depression, and Cleveland angered the Populists further when he pushed for a repeal of silver coinage. The resulting protest march by "Coxey's Army," led by Jacob S. Coxey, in Washington, DC, centered around demands for a national roads program and assistance to farmers struggling to pay their debts. The few hundred disgruntled souls who made it all the way to Washington were summarily arrested for walking on the US Capitol lawn.

In February 1895, President Cleveland struck a deal with powerful financier J. P. Morgan to "save" the nation's gold reserves. Basically, Morgan's syndicate agreed to buy bonds from the government in exchange for over $60 million in gold. Populists were outraged, and made the reasonable accusation that, once again, the nation's capital had catered to the interests of the big banks and Wall Street instead of the common people.

Charles Lachman's book *A Secret Life: The Lies and Scandals of President Grover Cleveland* featured a shocking allegation of rape which had remained suppressed for over a century. In an early case of "date rape," the then thirty-seven-year-old Cleveland was accused of sexually assaulting thirty-eight-year-old department store clerk Maria Halpin on December 15, 1873. Halpin's affidavit reported that when she threatened to notify the authorities, Cleveland "told me he was determined to ruin me if it cost him $10,000, if he was hanged by the neck for it. I then and there told him that I never wanted to see him again [and] commanded him to leave my room, which he did." The forced sexual encounter resulted in a pregnancy. Halpin gave birth to a boy she named Oscar Folsom Cleveland (after Grover's best friend, whose much younger daughter would become his First Lady.) Cleveland allegedly schemed to have the boy placed in an orphanage, and

Maria was whisked off to the Providence Lunatic Asylum, although she was quickly released upon evaluation. This scandal became a presidential campaign issue, without any of the rape allegations. The refrain of Cleveland's opponents, "Ma, Ma, where's my Pa?" was answered by the victorious Democrats after the election with, "Gone to the White House, Ha, Ha, Ha." But the story behind the scandal was typically distorted by the court historians.[13]

THE POPULISTS

No one can earn a million dollars honestly.

—William Jennings Bryan

Dissatisfaction with America's entrenched two-party system began brewing in the late 1800s, culminating in the birth of the People's, or Populist, Party in 1891. The Gilded Age, as it came to be known from the title of Mark Twain's book, featured in-your-face corruption overseen by party honchos like William "Boss" Tweed. It produced a spoils system and the birth of unimaginably rich captains of industry, or as they were referred to disparagingly, the Robber Barons. Never had the gap between the haves and the have-nots been so obvious.

In the 1892 election, the Populist Party carried five states and garnered 8.5 percent of the popular vote under presidential candidate and ex-congressman James B. Weaver. Like every "third" party movement in the United States, it eventually fizzled out, but the populists who gravitated to the Democratic Party were instrumental in getting William Jennings Bryan, who was sympathetic to most of their views, nominated for president in 1896, 1900, and 1908. The original populists were primarily inspired by agrarian issues, most notably the high interest rates that banks were charging farmers. "We say in our platform that we believe that the right to coin and issue money is a function of government," Bryan stated. "Those who are opposed to it tell us that the issue of paper money is a function of the bank, and that the government ought to get out of the banking business. I tell them that the issue of money is a function of government, and that the banks ought to get out of the Government business. . . . When we have restored the money of the Constitution, all other necessary reforms will be possible, but until this is done, there is no other reform that can be accomplished."

In the 1896 presidential election, Bryan, popularly known as "The Great Commoner," focused on the silver issue. Bryan's memorable "Cross of Gold" speech inspired many of those suffering economically under the depression. Bryan was considered an enemy of the banks, and a pure advocate of peace who would resign his position of secretary of state in the Wilson administration because of his opposition to US involvement in World War I. Bryan was the first politician to "stump" during his campaigns, touring the country while traditional presidential candidates stayed home. Bryan also criticized America's burgeoning imperialist tendencies and would undoubtedly be labeled an "isolationist" today.

Unfortunately, Bryan's last moment in the limelight, during the 1925 Scopes trial in Tennessee, is probably what he is best remembered for. In suitable conspiratorial fashion, he died five days after the end of the trial. Although Hollywood and mainstream historians have ridiculed Bryan's religious beliefs, Bryan's opposition to evolution was based primarily upon his strong aversion to the "survival of the fittest" concept. He realized this philosophy could translate into a refusal to help the weakest, most helpless members of society. In contrast to his popular image as a deluded Bible-thumper, Bryan's views were influenced mostly by his criticism of Nietzsche's writings, which were already being interpreted as "might makes right" in Germany and elsewhere. Clarence Darrow, the attorney who opposed Bryan during the Scopes trial, and who enjoys a sterling "liberal" reputation with the court historians, reacted in class-less style to those who declared that Bryan had died from a broken heart by saying, "Broken heart, hell, he died of a busted belly!" In contrast to Bryan, Darrow's eugenicist leanings were best expressed in the following ugly quote: "Chloroform unfit children. Show them the same mercy that is shown beasts that are no longer fit to live."[14] Darrow was also associated with the first state propaganda bureau in US history, the Committee on Public Information (CPI), whose mission was to convince Americans to support American involvement in World War I. Like Margaret Sanger and so many other historical leftist icons, Darrow was the opposite of a classical Liberal.

SPANISH-AMERICAN WAR

The mission of the United States is one of benevolent assimilation.

—William McKinley

The age of American imperialism began in earnest in 1898 with the Spanish-American War. Establishing a familiar pattern which would continue over the next century, the American public was fed horror stories of atrocities in Cuba that swayed far too many to favor intervening on the side of the Cubans. Americans even held rallies and fund-raisers for the cause of "Cuba Libre." Again, in a foreshadowing of future false flags, on February 15, 1898, the US battleship *Maine* was sunk, killing 270 people. This cataclysmic event, necessary to whip war fever to the prerequisite pitch, was the impetus for American involvement, despite the fact even the official investigations couldn't determine who or what was to blame. Even present-day historians with the US Navy now admit that the sinking of the *Maine* was probably caused by an internal explosion rather than an attack from the Spanish.

In April, the United States declared war against Spain, with hawkish Senator Henry Teller laughingly claiming we were intervening for "liberty and freedom." Onetime Lincoln aide, now secretary of state John Hay termed the four-month conflict "the splendid little war." With the Treaty of Paris, Spain acknowledged Cuban independence. The Americans, under the Platt Amendment, reserved the right to intervene in Cuban affairs, in order to "maintain peace." The amendment also limited Cuba's authority in negotiating treaties with other nations, and conveniently provided for the leasing of important military bases to the United States.

The fledgling mainstream media outdid itself in "reporting" on the circumstances surrounding America's initial foray into imperialism. Powerful publisher William Randolph Hearst, like so many others in our society, didn't "build" anything; his father was a United States senator and provided him with a ready fortune. He did probably invent tabloid journalism, however. Hearst's *New York Journal* lobbied relentlessly for war with Spain, publishing in great, gory detail all the imagined atrocities of the enemy that would be repeated ad nauseam over the years, to shock the public into supporting whatever conflict was being promoted. As adroitly as any of today's "journalists," Hearst memorably told his artist Frederic Remington, who had insisted there would be no war with Spain, "You furnish the pictures and I'll furnish the war." Hearst's newspaper jumped all over the "attack" on the *Maine*, and popularized the chant, "Remember the *Maine*, to hell with Spain!"

Lasting far longer than the Spanish-American War was the resulting war with the insurgent Philippines. Spain had sold the Philippine Islands to the United States at the end of their conflict. This resulted in yet another war for imperialism, and the United States wound up annexing the Philippine Islands. Thousands of American soldiers died in this senseless conflict, along with hundreds of thousands of Filipino soldiers and civilians. The Filipinos continued to fight for their independence, much as the United States once had, for thirteen years until in 1915 America permitted self-government, but their full independence from American control wouldn't come until 1992. Even Andrew Carnegie was appalled at the meaningless loss of life, sending President McKinley the sarcastic message, "About 8000 (Filipinos) have been completely civilized and sent to Heaven. I hope you like it."

CHAPTER SIX

THE 1900s–1920s

I have not failed. I've just found 10,000 ways that won't work.

—Thomas Edison

As the nineteenth century turned into the twentieth, America stood strong. The age of invention, spurred by Thomas Edison and many others, gave us the light bulb, phonograph, motion picture projector, telephone, automobile, and airplane. Life was undeniably changing for everyone. Edison's brilliant young protégé Nikola Tesla would eventually break from the old man after he was almost certainly cheated monetarily. At the very least, the normally astute Edison wildly underestimated the contributions and vision of his brilliant young colleague. Tesla would go on to stray into forbidden areas of research. His revolutionary work included a fuel-less generator and the means with which to provide free energy to all. Needless to say, this kind of free energy would have toppled fortunes and made everyday life cheaper and simpler for everyone. It is telling that, over seventy years after his death, no one else has taken up his mantle. Tesla's working papers and his well-known black notebook were never found after he died in a hotel room in 1943.

While Edison can be justly criticized for many things, he epitomized work ethic and certainly put more hours into his work than most men of his wealth and fame. He also, like his friend and fellow inventor Henry Ford, understood money and distrusted banks. Edison once remarked:

If the nation can issue a dollar bond it can issue a dollar bill. The element that makes the bond good makes the bill good also. The difference between the bond and the bill is that the bond lets the money broker collect twice the amount of the bond and an additional 20%. Whereas the currency, the honest sort provided by the Constitution, pays nobody but those who contribute in some useful way. It is absurd to say our Country can issue bonds and cannot issue currency. Both are promises to pay, but one fattens the usurer and the other helps the People.

Needless to say, he would not have been a fan of Alexander Hamilton and other proponents of a strong central bank. Edison would later devise his own monetary plan, which included lending money interest-free to farmers. Henry Ford himself would state, "The one aim of these financiers is world control by the creation of inextinguishable debts."

THE MCKINLEY ASSASSINATION

Unlike any other nation, here the people rule, and their will is the supreme law.

—William McKinley

On September 6, 1901, President William McKinley was shot in Buffalo, New York, by another of those "lone nuts," Leon Czolgosz. Very few people doubt the official narrative here; to the court historians and the overwhelming majority of Americans, McKinley's assassination was a senseless act devoid of any deep political significance. Czolgosz was said to be an anarchist, inspired to act because of the excesses of the plutocrats in charge of America. The slim volume *The Secret Plot to Kill McKinley* by John Koerner, published in 2011, represented the first real attempt to question the official story of the assassination. Among Koerner's more interesting research was his revelation of the abrupt, seeming wealth of the chronically unemployed anarchist Czolgosz in the period just prior to the assassination. While the aspiring "lone nut" was unable to pay his $1.75 weekly rent, for example, he somehow managed to travel to Cleveland, and thereafter afford a $2.00 weekly rent in Buffalo. He was even seen flashing $50 bills around at his new Broadway Avenue rooming house. Koerner tied Czolgosz to the prominent anarchist group the Liberty Club, whose members included the well-known Emma Goldman.

Koerner found other anomalies: evoking comparisons to the unprecedented position of the press car in the motorcade when John F. Kennedy was assassinated, the official photographer for the Buffalo Exposition was curiously not on the scene to capture an appearance by the president of the United States. Koerner suspected McKinley's Secret Service agents of complicity, much as so many who have researched the JFK assassination suspect his presidential detail of complicity. He also described a decidedly odd, unidentified man in front of Czolgosz at the presidential reception, whose behavior appears to have aided the "lone nut" in his efforts. The commissioner of the exposition strangely ordered the room where McKinley was shot to be cleared without holding and questioning any of the witnesses there. Finally, Koerner claimed that a St. Louis doctor named Edgar Wallace Lee just burst into the operating room where McKinley had been taken after the shooting and was permitted to perform the surgery without even showing any credentials. Lee disappeared without a trace the following day. In 1914, David Caplan, a fellow anarchist who was incarcerated for bombing the *Los Angeles Times* building, allegedly told the FBI of a wider conspiracy involving others besides Czolgosz.

McKinley, even in the wake of the Spanish-American War, was seen as a reluctant imperialist, one who had to be forced to act when the USS *Maine* had sunk. McKinley actually had the temerity to ascertain the cause of the sinking before summarily declaring war on Spain. The celebrated author Taylor Caldwell envisioned a realistic scenario in her book *The Captains and the Kings*, in which the assassination of McKinley was ordered by greater powers behind the scenes, in order to elevate enthusiastic imperialist and future vice president Teddy Roosevelt to the presidency.

BULLY FOR TEDDY ROOSEVELT

The pacifist is as surely a traitor to his country and to humanity as is the most brutal wrongdoer.

—Theodore Roosevelt

Theodore Roosevelt has a sterling reputation with establishment historians. His image is that of the hale and hearty male, the rough and ready embodiment of a bygone era. Despite his reputation as a rugged, masculine outdoorsman, Roosevelt seemed to habitually suffer from a variety of illnesses and died at only sixty. As is the case with most of our allegedly "greatest" presidents, Roosevelt is unworthy of the honor.

If Teddy Roosevelt were alive today, he would be a passionate neocon like John McCain, eagerly provoking and supporting war anywhere and everywhere. He was perhaps even a more extreme imperialist than Abraham Lincoln, who seemingly only wanted to rule the people of America. Roosevelt extolled the popular propaganda that prevailed during this age of largely mythical Horatio Alger, rags-to-riches stories. He once said, "Americanism means the virtues of courage, honor, justice, truth, sincerity, and hardihood—the virtues that made America. The things that will destroy America are prosperity-at-any-price, peace-at-any-price, safety-first instead of duty-first, the love of soft living and the get-rich-quick theory of life." While he became an exuberant devotee of strenuous physical activity, Roosevelt never truly "worked" a day in his life. No Horatio Alger by anyone's definition, he was born to a philanthropist and a socialite, and like all those in his economic class, his future financial success was determined at birth.

As noted, Roosevelt was far more anxious to involve America in a war with Spain in 1898 than President McKinley. He expressed his imperialist philosophy clearly in a June 7, 1897 letter to Abraham Lincoln's former secretary, American ambassador to England John Hay, writing, "Is America a weakling, to shrink from the work of the great world powers? No! The young giant of the West stands on a continent and clasps the crest of an ocean in either hand. Our nation, glorious in youth and strength, looks into the future with eager eyes and rejoices as a strong man to run a race." At least Roosevelt walked the walk, unlike so many future war-loving "chicken hawks." His exploits leading his "Rough Riders" up San Juan Hill have become legendary (and probably exaggerated, as such exploits usually are). When McKinley's vice president Garret Hobart died suddenly in late 1899, at the premature age of fifty-five, Roosevelt conveniently slid into the vice presidential slot on the 1900 Republican ticket.

Teddy Roosevelt today is closely associated with the "Progressive" movement of his era. It is hard, however, to see just what was "progressive" about this extremely wealthy politician. Like so many of our other leaders, he was a die-hard eugenicist. Roosevelt once wrote, "Society has no business to permit degenerates to reproduce their kind. . . . Some day, we will realize that the prime duty, the inescapable duty, of the good citizen of the right type, is to leave his or her blood behind him in the world; and that we have no business to permit the perpetuation of citizens of the wrong type." In 1914, he said that "criminals should be sterilized and feeble-minded persons forbidden to leave offspring behind them." He was also a virulent racist, referring to Africans as "ape-like naked savages, who . . . prey on creatures not much wilder or lower than themselves." He once said, "A perfectly stupid race can never rise to a very high plane; the negro, for instance, has been kept down as much by lack of intellectual development as by anything else." In a 1905 statement he asserted that Caucasians were "the forward race" destined to raise "the backward race[s]" through "industrial efficiency, political capacity and domestic morality." He also declared that "The only tyrannies from which men, women, and children are suffering in real life are the tyrannies of minorities." Like Sherman, Sheridan, and other great American heroes, he hated Native Americans, once stating, "I don't go so far as to think that the only good Indians are dead Indians, but I believe nine out of ten are, and I shouldn't inquire too closely into the case of the tenth."

How does a political figure with *those* kinds of hateful comments left on the public record, and a lifelong proponent of any and every possible war, become labeled as a "progressive?" Like warmongering President Barack Obama, Teddy Roosevelt was actually given a Nobel Peace Prize. It is difficult to imagine a more inappropriate recipient. In 1906, President Roosevelt was convinced he had the authority to send Marines in to Cuba to quell an uprising following a disputed election. In 1914, to no one's surprise, he came out strongly in support of American involvement in World War I, and demanded a harsher policy towards Germany. Roosevelt lambasted Irish and German Americans for their support of neutrality. He was apparently the first politician to coin the phrase "hyphenated American," and used it to question the patriotism of others. Again walking his war walk, Roosevelt seriously attempted to lead a division of troops in France during WWI, but was stopped by President Woodrow Wilson. Solidifying his sterling "leftist" credentials, Roosevelt loved hunting big game; during his

1909–1910 expedition to Africa, he and his companions killed or trapped over 11,000 animals.

Roosevelt also has a totally unwarranted reputation as a "trust buster." In reality, he was always friendly to the powerful bankers and corporate interests; when he "broke up" Standard Oil, for instance, it merely became divided into seven corporations, all of them still controlled by the Rockefellers. Genuine progressive and high-profile attorney Amos Pinchot dubbed Roosevelt "the bellhop of Wall Street." After the "crash" of 1907, Roosevelt created one of those commissions invariably formed to study various problems, the National Monetary Commission, and stocked it with friends and cronies of J. P. Morgan and other powerful bankers. The chairman, Nelson Aldrich, would be deeply involved in the formation of the Federal Reserve only six years later. Roosevelt's friend, Colonel Ely Garrison, admitted the truth about him in his memoirs, writing, "Wall Street had no cause for hysteria at the election of Theodore Roosevelt, for any serious student of history knows that the Department of Justice's investigations of Northern Security and Standard Oil (both Kuhn-Loeb company enterprises) were initiated before Roosevelt's election and carried on without his approval." Roosevelt hated those journalists who genuinely advocated a breakup of the monopolies, and his private secretary Winiam Loeb allegedly coined the term "muckraker" to disparage them.

In the 1912 presidential campaign, ex-president Roosevelt ran as the candidate of the new "progressive" party, the Bull Moose Party. The true nature of the Bull Moose Party was revealed by the fact it was largely financed by an aide to banker J. P. Morgan. Roosevelt's third-party run ensured the election of Democrat Woodrow Wilson, and limited his supposed protégé, William Howard Taft, to a single term in office. Roosevelt's second-place finish in both the popular vote and the Electoral College represented the last time that anyone other than a Democrat or Republican finished that high in a presidential election.

THE 1913 FEDERAL RESERVE ACT

This establishes the most gigantic trust on earth. When the President signs this bill, the invisible government of the monetary power will be legalized . . . the worst legislative crime of the ages is perpetrated by this banking and currency bill. . . . From now on, depressions will be scientifically created.
—Charles A. Lindbergh, Sr.

Nothing illustrates how uninformed most Americans are more clearly than the public's blissful ignorance of our banking system. It is very difficult to enlighten most people, to get them to grasp the extent of the fraud being perpetrated upon them. Simply put, fractional based banking is no different than legal counterfeiting. The father of modern Keynesian economics, John Maynard Keynes, guru of most American politicians of the twentieth century, reacted joyously to the passage of the 1913 Federal Reserve Act in his 1920 book *The Economic Consequences of the Peace*, declaring, "By this means government may secretly and unobserved, confiscate the wealth of the people, and not one man in a million will detect the theft." Buckminster Fuller understood the extent of the problem when he said, "To expose a 15 Trillion dollar ripoff of the American people by the stockholders of the 1000 largest corporations over the last 100 years will be a tall order of business." Even sci-fi legend Robert A. Heinlein wrote, in *Expanded Universe*, "Every Congressman, every Senator knows precisely what causes inflation . . . but can't, won't support the drastic reforms to stop it (repeal of the Federal Reserve Act) because it could cost him his job."

Contrary to being advertised as a banking "reform" proposal, in order to take control away from the big bankers, the Federal Reserve Act was crafted and designed by these very same Wall Street bankers. The notorious "duck hunt" conducted at the exclusive Georgian resort of Jekyll Island in 1910 was attended by banker insiders and powerful Senator Nelson W. Aldrich, grandfather of future New York governor Nelson Aldrich Rockefeller and longtime dean of the establishment David Rockefeller. Aldrich was yet another high-profile Freemason and is laughably said to have been a "progressive." Supposedly, this secluded location offered the men a perfect atmosphere in which to develop what would become the Federal Reserve System. As the conspiracy theorists point out, the Federal Reserve actually creates money, bringing it into existence out of thin air. This is, of course, in direct violation of the Constitution, which stipulates that "Congress shall have the power to coin money and regulate the value thereof." Incredibly, after creating money out of nothing, the Federal Reserve sells this money to the government, paying only the cost of printing it, and the government pays them back at face value with *interest*. This is a pretty sweet deal for the bankers, and a world-class scam on the taxpayers. Since under fractional lending rules, only a fraction (10 percent or less) of the funds have to be on hand for loans to be made, our banks are allowed to lend individuals and businesses money that they simply don't have. Outside of the banking world, that's a crime. The Federal Reserve monetizes debt and forces the taxpayers to pay it back. Of course, this is impossible under the fractional system, since only a fraction of the principal and none of the interest exists in any tangible form.

The Founding Fathers understood that, as Mayer Amschel Rothschild once said, "Give me control of a nation's money and I care not who makes its laws." Thomas Jefferson distrusted banks, declaring, "I believe that banking institutions are more dangerous to our liberties than standing armies. If the American people ever allow private banks to control the issue of their currency, first by inflation, then by deflation, the banks and corporations that will grow up around the banks will deprive the people of all property until their children wake up homeless on the continent their fathers conquered." James Madison echoed this: "History records that the money changers have used every form of abuse, intrigue, deceit, and violent means possible to maintain their control over governments by controlling money and its issuance." Outside of Hamilton, America's Founders would be appalled by the Federal Reserve System. The battle lines had been delineated in the early years of the Republic, with Alexander Hamilton representing the interests of the big banks. "A national debt, if it is not excessive, will be to us a national blessing." Hamilton said. "The wisdom of the Government will be shown in never trusting itself with the use of so seducing and dangerous an expedient as issuing its own money." During his battles against the central bank, Andrew Jackson declared, "You are a den of thieves-vipers. I intend to rout you out, and by the Eternal God, I will rout you out!" It should be crystal clear to any American that Hamilton's side won. Vice President John C. Calhoun was yet another "conspiracy theorist" who once remarked, "A power has risen up in the government greater than the people themselves, consisting of many and various powerful interests, combined in one mass, and held together by the cohesive power of the vast surplus in banks."

One of the first and boldest critics of the Federal Reserve was Louis T. McFadden, a former banker himself who served twenty years in the US House of Representatives as a Republican from Pennsylvania. In 1932, McFadden stated, "The truth is the Federal Reserve Board has usurped the Government of the United States. It controls everything here and it controls all our foreign relations. It makes and breaks government at will." A year later, he commented, "Roosevelt has brought with him from Wall Street James P. Warburg, son of Paul M. Warburg, Organizer and first Chairman of the Board of the Federal Reserve System." Like many critics of the banking system, McFadden unfortunately flirted with anti-Semitism, but his larger points are entirely credible. Powerful establishment columnist Drew Pearson spoke for the entire mainstream media when he attacked McFadden for his supposed "support of Adolf Hitler." McFadden ostracized those within his own party, as best reflected in fellow Republican Pennsylvania senator David A. Reed's icy comment that "We intend to act to all practical purposes as though McFadden had died." Evidently, some people wanted McFadden literally dead, as shots were fired at him on one occasion and on another he was poisoned. He died suddenly and prematurely on October 3, 1936, from "intestinal flu" while attending a banquet in New York City. Later, another congressman, Wright Patman of Texas, would pick up McFadden's mantle. Patman once declared, "I have never yet had anyone who could, through the use of logic and reason, justify the federal government borrowing the use of its own money." Patman understood the banking system, unlike almost all his colleagues. "The dollar represents a one dollar debt to the Federal Reserve System." He declared. "The Federal Reserve Banks create money out of thin air to buy government bonds from the US Treasury . . . and has created out of the nothing a . . . debt which the American People are obliged to pay with interest." Patman even growled at then-Fed Chairman Arthur Burns, testifying before the House Banking Committee in the early 1970s, "Can you give me any reason why you should not be in the penitentiary?"[1]

How refreshing it would be to hear a congressman say something like what Louis McFadden said in 1936:

> Mr. Chairman, we have in this country one of the most corrupt institutions the world has ever known. I refer to the Federal Reserve Board and the Federal Reserve Banks. The Federal Reserve Board, a Government board, has cheated the Government of the United States and the people of the United States out of enough money to pay the national debt . . . Mr. Chairman, when the Federal Reserve Act was passed, the people of the United States did not perceive that a world system was being set up here . . . and that this country was to supply financial power to an international superstate—a superstate controlled by international bankers and international industrialists acting together to enslave the world for their own pleasure.

McFadden correctly identified the cause of the Great Depression when he stated:

> It was not accidental (the 1929 stock market crash). It was a carefully contrived occurrence. . . . The international bankers sought to bring about a condition of despair here so that they might emerge as rulers of us all.

The public is ignorant of the most basic fact about the Federal Reserve—that it is not "federal" or a government agency at all, but a private corporation. Efforts to even get the Fed honestly audited have consistently failed. Ron Paul tried many times. An honest audit would not only reveal massive corruption, it would raise the curtain on our fairy tale-like economy. Ron's son, Rand Paul, has followed in his father's footsteps on this issue, introducing the Federal Reserve Transparency Act of 2015. Philadelphia Fed president Charles Prosser reacted indignantly, stating, "This runs the risk of monetary policy decisions being based on short-term political considerations instead of the longer-term health of the economy." The president of the Federal Reserve Bank of Dallas, Richard Fisher, told mainstream outlet *The Hill*, "Who in their right mind would ask the Congress of the United States—who can't cobble together a fiscal policy—to assume control of monetary policy?" While Congress has certainly earned the disdain of enlightened Americans with their decades' worth of corruption and incompetence, at least we have nominal oversight over them. We have absolutely no control over non-audited bankers who are legally allowed to counterfeit the money supply.

There was a partial audit of the Fed conducted in 2012, spurred on by the efforts of Ron Paul and Bernie Sanders. Even this limited audit managed to uncover some startling facts. It was discovered that some $16 trillion had been secretly given to US banks and corporations, as well as some foreign banks. From just December 2007 to June 2010, the Fed bailed out many of the world's banks and corporations under what was referred to as a loan program. However, virtually none of the money had been repaid and it was "lent" interest-free. Senator Sanders termed it "socialism for the rich and rugged." Supposed Wall Street foe Senator Elizabeth Warren voted *against* auditing the Fed, saying, "I strongly support and continue to press for greater congressional oversight of the Fed's regulatory and supervisory responsibilities . . . but I oppose the current version of this bill because it promotes congressional meddling in the Fed's monetary policy decisions, which risks politicizing those decisions and may have dangerous implications for financial stability and the health of the global economy." Sounds very much like the excuses habitually given by banking officials. Richmond Fed president Jeffrey Lacker echoed Warren, exclaiming that such oversight would amount to "high frequency harassment of our decision-making process."[2]

As writer P. J. O'Rourke put it, "A US dollar is an IOU from the Federal Reserve bank." Senator Barry Goldwater once said, "Most Americans have no real understanding of the operation of the international money lenders. The accounts of the Federal Reserve System have never been audited. It operates outside the control of Congress and manipulates the credit of the United States." The earliest high-profile Federal Reserve critic, Congressman Charles A. Lindbergh Sr., father of the famed aviator, declared in 1923, "The financial system has been turned over to the Federal Reserve Board. That board administers the finance system by authority of a purely profiteering group. The system is private, conducted for the sole purpose of obtaining the greatest possible profits from the use of other people's money." While few modern liberals have criticized the Fed, or banks in general, maverick Congressman Dennis Kucinich acknowledged reality by saying, "The Federal Reserve is no more federal than Federal Express."

It wasn't until the 1950s that the first in-depth research on the Federal Reserve swindle was conducted, by Eustace Mullins. Mullins worked at first in conjunction with poet Ezra Pound, who was then institutionalized in a mental hospital, as America's most famous political prisoner in the postwar era. Mullins wrote, "My initial research revealed evidence of an international banking group which had secretly planned the writing of the Federal Reserve Act." Pound advised Mullins that "You must work on it as a detective story." Mullins applied to the Guggenheim and other foundations for financial aid to back his research, but even though his applications were sponsored by both Pound and well-known poet E. E. Cummings, all of the foundations refused to sponsor such research. When he tried to get the book that would eventually be known as *Secrets of the Federal Reserve* published, Mullins encountered the predictable resistance. The president of Devin Adair Publishing Company told him, "I like your book, but we can't print it. Neither can anybody else in New York. . . . You may as well forget about getting the Federal Reserve book published." Two of Ezra Pound's disciples eventually published a small edition of the book in 1952, under the initial title *Mullins on the Federal Reserve*. When a German translation was published in 1955, it was seized by government agents, who burned all 10,000 copies.

COWBOYS AND INDIANS

The destruction of the Indians of the Americas was, far and away, the most massive act of genocide in the history of the world.

—David E. Stannard

According to the most radical sources, Christopher Columbus and his fellow Spaniards were responsible for the deaths of eight million Arawaks—the indigenous population of the West Indies. Ward Churchill attributed these deaths to "torture, murder, forced labor, starvation, disease and despair." A Spanish missionary, Bartolome de las Casas, testified to witnessing the dismemberment, beheading, and rape of some 3,000 people. As author Barry Lopez summarized it, "The Spanish cut off the legs of children who ran from them. . . . They made bets as to who, with one sweep of his sword, could cut a person in half. . . . They used nursing infants for dog food." While the Spanish tended to view the natives as natural slaves, the later English settlers saw them as savages beyond any hope of salvation.

As John F. Kennedy would later charge, "the treatment of the American Indian is a national disgrace." In 1851, California governor Peter H. Burnett declared, "A war of extermination will continue to be waged between the two races until the Indian race becomes extinct." Continuing a bloody "bounty" program that began in Massachusetts, Connecticut, and New Jersey in the early 1700s, Shasta City, California offered five dollars for every Indian scalp around the time the forty-niners first arrived in the state looking for gold. To understand how successful this genocidal program was, we need only look at the fact that there were some 150,000 Native Americans in California before the forty-niners came, but by 1870 there were less than 30,000. Major newspapers editorialized in favor of exterminating the Indians. And the great Union hero General William Tecumseh Sherman said, "We must act with vindictive earnestness against the Sioux [Lakotas] even to their extermination: men, women, and children." The 1890 attack on the Wounded Knee, North Dakota Indian reservation resulted in the death of Chief Sitting Bull, who had rejected "the ways of the white man," as well as some 150 other Native Americans. In an early twentieth-century Supreme Court decision, it was ruled that the US government had the right to overturn all laws of the Cherokee Nation.

In 1928, a study conducted by the Brookings Institution found living conditions on Indian reservations to be deplorable. This did result in improved healthcare, land rights, and education for Native Americans, but many states continued to deny them the right to vote. Utah became the last state to approve Native American suffrage, in 1956. Forced assimilation policies resulted in tribal religion being outlawed, and Indian children were sent to boarding schools and forbidden to practice their traditional cultures. Native American activists like Russell Means charged that the United States government had committed genocide against Native Americans for hundreds of years.

The American government's own very conservative estimates state that between one and four million Native Americans died because of the Europeans who invaded their lands. Native Americans lost 98 percent of their land in the process. Native Americans remain largely confined to reservations, where a full quarter of them live in poverty. On some of these reservations, the unemployment rate is 80 percent. They remain under the thumb of the Bureau of Indian Affairs, and in many areas have only limited self-government. Their life expectancy is an appalling fifty-eight years, and the infant mortality rate is ten times the national average. Alcoholism and drug addiction are epidemic in their communities, and they have the highest suicide rate of any ethnic group in America.

ANTI-UNION VIOLENCE

> *Our movement is of the working people, for the working people, by the working people. . . . There is not a right too long denied to which we do not aspire in order to achieve; there is not a wrong too long endured that we are not determined to abolish.*
>
> —Samuel Gompers

As far back as 1877, the American government demonstrated its willingness to resort to violence in order to stop the newborn labor movement when US troops opened fire on striking railroad workers in several cities. Twelve people were killed by these troops in Baltimore, and another twenty-five in Pittsburgh. In 1892, Carnegie Steel declared war on its union and utilized private Pinkerton forces, which killed seven striking members, to effectively break the union. State militias would be used over the years to break the strikes of coal miners and other unions. Eugene Debs led a nationwide strike for the American Railway Union in 1894, but the normally hands-off President Cleveland sent in military troops to crush it, and Debs was sent to prison under the Sherman Anti-Trust Act. Over a thousand miners in the west were simply imprisoned without charges in 1898 in order to break a strike in Idaho.

The most notorious example of anti-union violence occurred in 1914, in what came to be known as the Ludlow Massacre. John D. Rockefeller hired special deputies, alongside the state militia, to quell a strike by some twelve thousand coal miners working for his Colorado Fuel and Iron Company. Although working conditions for all miners were unspeakably terrible, the fatality rates for those working in Colorado were double the national average. For this perpetually hazardous work, the Rockefellers paid a paltry $1.68 per day, which was issued in script, only redeemable at the company store that featured excessively high prices. The strike was precipitated by a union activist being killed in late 1913. The Rockefeller family, which effectively controlled the region, saw to it that striking workers were evicted from their homes, forcing them into the harsh winter without shelter. The conflict raged for several months, until the militia finally opened fire on a city of tents occupied by strikers and their families, and then set fire to them. Foretelling what would happen decades later at Waco, eleven children and two women were found burned to death afterward.

Head union organizer Louis Tikas had earlier met with Lieutenant Linderfelt, the officer in charge of the National Guard's assault on the Ludlow camp, to arrange a truce. Linderfelt responded by hitting Tikas with the butt of his rifle, and soldiers fired into his back as he lay on the ground, killing him. Workers failed to achieve their demands, and many wound up being supplanted by non-union replacements. All told, sixty-six people had been killed, but no one in government was ever prosecuted for their murders. In 1918, a monument was erected to those who died during the Ludlow strike.

Another dramatic instance of anti-union violence involved Industrial Workers of the World leader Frank Little, who carried the additional baggage of being an outspoken opponent of World War I. Little had proclaimed, "The IWW is opposed to all wars, and we must use all our power to prevent the workers from joining the army." Little provocatively called American soldiers "Uncle Sam's scabs in uniform." At the time of his death, Little was in Butte, Montana to help lead a miners' strike against the Anaconda Copper Company. In the middle of the night on August 1, 1917, a gang of masked men broke into his boardinghouse room, beat him, and eventually hung him from a railroad trestle. A note that read "First and last warning" was pinned to his body. No one was ever charged with his brutal murder. The almost entirely forgotten Little's tombstone reads, "Slain by capitalist interests for organizing and inspiring his fellow men." Six years earlier, in the tragic Triangle Shirtwaist Factory fire in Manhattan, 146 mostly immigrant garment workers were killed, largely because the stairwell and exit doors had been locked by owners in order to reduce theft and to discourage unauthorized or excessive employee breaks. Unions were born because of the undeniable fact that in those days workers had virtually no rights.

WORLD WAR I

At least 21,000 new millionaires and billionaires were made in the United States during the World War. Politicians and their corporate sponsors have tricked ordinary Americans into thinking legitimate enemies exist and must be confronted. The truth is there are no enemies, only business opportunities.

—General Smedley Butler

Schools all over the world teach that World War I came about as a result of the assassination of Austria's Archduke Franz Ferdinand. To the layman, that seems to be a ridiculous reason for the nations of Europe, not to mention America, engaging in a massive, unprecedented "world" conflict. While the Spanish-American War had certainly blown George Washington's "no entangling alliances" advice to pieces, with World War I America plunged forever into the globalist interventionism that has wreaked havoc all over the world and devastated our own economy.

Norman Dodd, chief investigator for the 1953 Special Committee on Tax-Exempt Foundations, led by Congressman B. Carroll Reece, later reported that the committee was permitted to study the minutes of the Carnegie Endowment for International Peace during their investigation. According to the committee, "The trustees of the Foundation brought up a single question. If it is desirable to alter the life of an entire people, is there any means more efficient than war. . . . They discussed this question . . . for a year and came up with an answer: There are no known means more efficient than war, assuming the objective is altering the life of an entire people. That leads them to a question: How do we involve the United States in a war? This is in 1909." That's quite a goal for a foundation ostensibly devoted to "peace."[3]

No war can be complete without a false flag event to start it. In the case of World War I, the triggering, emotional event was the sinking of the Lusitania. The ship was loaded with six million rounds of ammunition, courtesy of J. P. Morgan, which would be sold to England and France to aid in their efforts against Germany. England's First Lord of the Admiralty, Winston Churchill, knew where every German U-boat in the English Channel was, since British Intelligence had already broken the German war code. The German government even placed ads in the New York newspapers, warning Americans not to sail on the Lusitania, because it would be sailing through a war zone. Secretary of State William Jennings Bryan tried in vain to get President Woodrow Wilson to issue a public warning about traveling on the *Lusitania*. The plotting going on behind the scenes was revealed in a book highly favorable to Edward Mandell House, Wilson's intimate advisor. In *The Intimate Papers of Colonel House*, the following conversation between House and Sir Edward Grey, the foreign secretary of England, was quoted:

> **Grey:** What will America do if the Germans sink an ocean liner with American passengers on board?
>
> **House:** I believe that a flame of indignation would sweep the United States and that by itself would be sufficient to carry us into the war.

House was oddly referred to as "Colonel" despite the lack of any military background.

On May 7, 1915, the *Lusitania* was predictably sunk by a U-boat off the coast of Ireland. Winston Churchill's inexplicable decision to order the escort vessel assigned to accompany the *Lusitania* into the English port to return alone, leaving the *Lusitania* at the mercy of the Germans, led directly to the deaths of 1201 people. To the consternation of House, Wilson, and others, the American people weren't immediately swept up in war fervor following the sinking. Robert Lansing, Wilson's assistant secretary of state, reportedly advised, "We must educate the public gradually—draw it along to the point where it will be willing to go into the war." In two laughable "investigations" of the *Lusitania* incident, one by the English government and one by the American government, it was predictably found that the torpedoes alone, and not any exploding ammunition, caused the vessel to sink. Each "investigation" reported that no evidence of ammunition was found on board the *Lusitania*. In a review of Colin Simpson's book *The Lusitania*, the *Los Angeles Times* wrote, "*The Lusitania* proves beyond a reasonable doubt that the British government connived at the sinking of the passenger ship in order to lure America into World War I. The Germans, whose torpedo struck the liner, were the unwitting accomplices or victims of a plot probably concocted by Winston Churchill."

Woodrow Wilson campaigned for reelection in 1916 on the theme that he had "kept us out of the war." One of those who wasn't happy with America's slow entry into the war was then Assistant Secretary of the Navy Franklin D. Roosevelt. Like so many other "liberal" icons, Roosevelt never met a war he didn't like. In the early months of 1917, Roosevelt badgered Secretary of the Navy Joseph Daniels, who was strongly against American involvement in the European conflict, to convoy more American ships into the war zone. Roosevelt even became angry with Wilson when the president didn't use his executive powers to arm ships and send them out basically as sitting ducks. FDR wrote in his diary about dining at the Metropolitan Club with a group of Republican "war hawks," including his wife's uncle, Theodore Roosevelt, General Leonard Wood, J. P. Morgan, and Elihu Root, who was one of the founders of the Council on Foreign Relations. According to FDR, the primary topic discussed was "how to make administration steer a clear course to uphold rights." None of these plutocrats cared the least bit about anyone's "rights," of course, and this was obviously a euphemism for a more aggressive policy that would lead to America entering the war. Eventually, Wilson stopped dawdling and, forgetting his campaign promise, asked Congress for a Declaration of War on April 2, 1917. This would be trumpeted as "the war to end all wars," and one in which America was fighting "to make the world safe for democracy." Historian Walter Mills assessed the role of Colonel House thusly: "The Colonel's sole justification for preparing such a batch of blood for his countrymen was his hope of establishing a new world order (a world government) of peace and security."

Opponents of World War I were jailed in many countries. Congress passed the Selective Service Act in 1917. Some five hundred conscientious objectors went to prison in the United States, and others were jailed for simply speaking out against the conflict. Hundreds of those participating in the "Green Corn Rebellion," which protested the perpetual "rich man's war, poor man's fight," were arrested and three were killed. Bertrand Russell was among the most well-known critics, calling the war "trivial . . . no great principle is at stake, no great human purpose is involved on either side." He ranted about his fellow humans being "swept away in a red blast of hate." Russell described what it was like to be in such a distinct minority, "when the whole nation is in a state of violent collective excitement. As much effort was required to avoid sharing this excitement as would have been needed to stand out against the extreme of hunger or sexual passion, and there was the same feeling of going against instinct." Russell spent six months in jail in England. Antiwar resistance was greater in England; some 20,000 Brits evaded the draft, with 6,000 of them being imprisoned.[4]

The propaganda mills were cranked up, starting with George M. Cohan's song "Johnny Get Your Gun." There were fond references to "Dough Boys" and Uncle Sam became a familiar and oddly non-threatening figure to the masses. Woodrow Wilson created the Committee on Public Information shortly after declaring war. It was headed by a reliable mainstream journalist, George Creel; many of the nation's most talented writers worked alongside him to shape the public's opinion of and support for the war, including the creation of anti-German propaganda and films. They spoke at schools and churches, and encouraged citizens to spy on their neighbors and report any suspicious activities to the authorities. The American Protective League organized 12,000 local units all over the nation. The members were primarily businessmen and professionals tasked to spy on draft dodgers, gather gossip about those suspected of disloyalty, and check into people who weren't buying their Liberty Bonds. In 1918, a Collinsville, Illinois man of German-American descent was wrapped in an American flag and lynched by a mob. The leaders of the lynching were quickly acquitted by a sympathetic jury. Antiwar socialist Samuel Chovenson was stripped, tarred and feathered, and paraded through New Brunswick, Connecticut. In Berkeley, California, a group of religious pacifists were attacked by an angry mob, which burned down their place of worship and dunked them in their baptismal tank. The authorities responded by arresting and jailing the *pacifists*. A Columbia University professor was fired for his antiwar views.

The role of the establishment press was exemplified by a remarkable April 1, 1917 editorial in the "liberal" *Washington Post*. No, this was not an April Fool's joke. The editorial condemned pacifists thusly:

Large advertisements are appearing in the metropolitan newspapers, skillfully written for the purpose of stirring up class hatred and suspicion and thus dissuading Americans from enlisting in the war that is coming. . . . At this time, when the United States is on the verge of war, the Washington Post believes that the advertisements in question are an abuse of the right of free speech. It does not presume to judge other newspapers which print these advertisements, but for itself, it will not print them. . . . An effort to prevent the voluntary enlistment of American citizens for the defense of their country is treasonable in time of war. It is sedition at any time. "The hope of impunity is a strong incitement to sedition," said Hamilton. The pacifists will not long enjoy impunity. If they are wise they will cease their agitation before they are legally classified as public enemies and punished accordingly.

World War I introduced a new and horrifying scale of war. There were more than ten million deaths, and over twenty million wounded in the conflict. To give but a single stunning example of the carnage, *31 percent* of the men who graduated from Oxford in 1913 were killed. In addition, nearly seven million civilians lost their lives in this "war to end all wars." The war cost Germany over 38 billion dollars, and England spent over 35 billion. As always, the rich got richer. Conspiracy theorists have estimated that the Rockefeller family alone made more than $200 billion from the conflict. The new concept of "reparations" was born, and Germany, as the "loser" in the conflict, was forced to pay an astounding $64 billion to the countries who'd defeated them. The conference that produced the Treaty of Versailles, wherein these odious new financial penalties were adopted, was attended by some highly interesting characters. Among the British delegation was John Maynard Keynes, father of Keynesian economics. In the American delegation was the Chairman of the Federal Reserve, Paul Warburg. His brother Max Warburg was there representing the Germans. Another delegate to the conference, Lord Curzon of England, the British foreign secretary, saw through the charade and declared: "This is no peace; this is only a truce for twenty years." Curzon felt that the terms of the Treaty were setting the stage for a second world war, and he correctly predicted the year it would start: 1939. The Treaty of Versailles devastated the German economy and paved the way for Adolf Hitler. Incredibly, Germany paid out reparations for *ninety-two years*, finally ending them in 2010. Most of the reparations went to the WWI allied victors the United States, Great Britain, and France. The last surviving soldier who fought in WWI, Harry Patch, defined all war perfectly when he said, "War is organized murder, and nothing else."

The victorious nations also wrote up the charter of the League of Nations, Woodrow Wilson's longtime dream of world government. When the charter was sent to the Senate for ratification, it failed. Senator Henry Cabot Lodge blasted Wilson for fantasizing about becoming "a future president of the world." Fittingly, organized Freemasonry was strongly supportive of this first fledgling attempt at world government. France's Grand Orient Lodge advised its members: "It is the duty of universal Freemasonry to give its full support to the League of Nations." Kaiser Wilhelm II would blame the Freemasons for the war in his memoirs. The Balfour Declaration, written November 2, 1917, and sent by British Foreign Secretary Arthur James Balfour to powerful British financier Walter Rothschild, asserted, "His Majesty's government view with favour the establishment in Palestine of a national home for the Jewish people, and will use their best endeavours to facilitate the achievement of this object, it being clearly understood that nothing shall be done which may prejudice the civil and religious rights of existing non-Jewish communities in Palestine, or the rights and political status enjoyed by Jews in any other country." Arab groups, led by the Muslim-Christian Association, naturally objected to a Jewish state being created in their midst. Zionism was growing in strength, and Nazism was about to be born.

While the court historians vehemently defend so-called "good" wars like the Civil War and World War II, even they can't intelligibly explain the reasons behind World War I. It was, as *The Economist* described it, "avoidable brutality" on an impossibly grand scale. A book stressing this theme, *The War That Ended Peace: The Road to 1914*, was written by Margaret MacMillan, great-granddaughter of Lloyd George, warmongering British Prime Minster during World War I. "It was Europe and the world's tragedy in retrospect," MacMillan wrote, "that none of the key players in 1914 were great and imaginative leaders who had the courage to stand out against the pressure building up for war."[5] World War I represented the first conflict between Germany and England in a thousand years. Despite the flowery words of promising young poet Rupert Brooke, who wrote of "some corner of a foreign field that is forever England," British youth weren't fighting to defend their country or any part of their empire. Neither was Germany, or France, or any other participant. Winston Churchill described what really went on: "Nothing in human power could break the fatal chain, once it had begun to unroll. A situation had been created where hundreds of officials had only to do their prescribed duty to their respective countries to wreck the world. They did their duty."

While "progressives" like Teddy and Franklin Roosevelt were hungry for American participation in World War I, supposed right-wing "extremist" Henry Ford, now generally dismissed as an anti-Semite, was loudly calling for peace. Ford organized an amateur peace mission to Europe in 1915, and invited other prominent peace advocates to join him on the ocean liner *Oscar II*. The mainstream media unsurprisingly was hostile to the idea of peace, and mocked Ford's efforts as the "ship of fools" and "a sublimely screwy paragraph in American history." Ford, a committed pacifist, naively attempted to enlist Woodrow Wilson's support. Among the activists Ford invited who declined were Thomas Edison and William Jennings Bryan. Ford's admirable idea ultimately failed. "Colonel" Edward Mandel House called Ford "crude (and) ignorant" while expressing wonderment as to how the automaker had ever become successful. Ford memorably described the warmongering process:

> First, the people are worked upon. By clever tales, the people's suspicions are aroused toward the nation against whom war is desired. . . .
> All you need for this is a few agents with some cleverness and no conscience and a press whose interest is locked up with the interests that will be benefited by war. Then the "overt act" will soon appear. It is no trick at all to get an "overt act" once you work the hatred of two nations up to the proper pitch. . . . There were men in every country who were glad to see the World War (I) begin and sorry to see it stop. Hundreds of American fortunes date from the Civil War; thousands of new fortunes date from the World War.

Ford refused to accept the "blood money" made with the profits of war and according to one biographer returned $29 million in war profits to the government. Ford sounded like a conspiracy theorist when he wrote: "An impartial investigation of the last war, of what preceded it, and what has come out of it, would show beyond a doubt that there is in the world a group of men with vast powers of control, that prefers to remain unknown, that does not seek office or any of the tokens of power, that belongs to no nation whatever, but is international." Ford also wrote: "An old gambling trick used to be for the gambler to cry 'Police!' when a lot of money was on the table, and, in the panic which followed, to seize the money and run off with it. There is a power within the world which cries 'War!' and, in the confusion of the nations, the unrestrained sacrifice which people make for safety and peace, runs off with the spoils of the panic."[6]

It is a measure of how well the combined efforts of court historians, scholars, and establishment journalists have succeeded to consider that many of those public figures who lobbied incessantly for war, such as Abraham Lincoln, both Roosevelts, and Woodrow Wilson, are ludicrously still portrayed as devotees of peace. Meanwhile, few even know about the efforts of a genuine pacifist like Henry Ford to stop the carnage and seek peace. Ford's words and actions contained a sincere eloquence that more celebrated antiwar activists like Jerry Rubin, Abbie Hoffman, or the Berrigan brothers never possessed. Ford certainly gravitated into the world of anti-Semitism, but there was nothing "hateful" about his moving pleas for peace.

Populist Wisconsin senator Robert M. LaFollette Sr., who'd been the victim of a poisoning attempt *on the Senate floor* in 1908, was strongly opposed to our entrance into World War I and the creation of the Federal Reserve. Observing the wreckage left behind from the war during a tour of Germany, LaFollette wrote in a 1923 letter: "In the Ruhr (Germany's western industrial belt)—in and about Essen, where we visited a number of towns—the suffering is unspeakable." LaFollette went on to chastise American ally France, which was still occupying part of Germany then, by saying they were "as merciless and unfeeling as the rack and the thumb-screw."[7] LaFollette was also against the League of Nations. Another populist leader, Congressman Thomas Watson of Georgia, stated, "Is it worthwhile to remind our public servants in Washington, that this Constitution does not authorize or contemplate any other kind of war except one for self-defense?" He criticized Woodrow Wilson's "bloody Hun" propaganda, saying, "It is absurd to say we are menaced by German danger. . . . The law of nations, and our own common sense, tell us that what England, France, and Germany do to each other is none of our business." Watson made fun of the idiotic campaign slogan used to reelect Wilson: "He kept us out of war." Watson asked, "What war? Where did we have a chance to get into one? What did he do to keep us 'out?' . . . We had no cause to go in." Watson also fought valiantly against the Conscription Act, bringing a test case before federal court in 1917 to challenge its constitutionality. Watson's efforts failed, and an Iowa congressional candidate was sentenced to ten years in federal prison for merely publishing and distributing excerpts from Watson's address against the Conscription Act. Another insidious piece of legislation, the Espionage Act, banned the publication of Watson's periodicals.[8] LaFollette was burned in effigy and his own magazine was nearly banned from the mails. Watson was clearly some sort of racial separatist, but he was also a voice of reason and reform for many, many powerless people who had little say in what their leaders, elected and otherwise, did. Surely he didn't deserve the comments uttered about him by the Anti-Defamation League, which dismissed him snidely with: "Tom Watson wrote one of the dirtiest chapters of bigotry in the South."[9]

With the Espionage Act of 1917, amended to the Sedition Act of 1918, the American government rekindled ugly memories of the Alien and Sedition Acts during the administration of John Adams. These unconstitutional acts forbid the use of "disloyal, profane, scurrilous, or abusive language" about the US government, its flag, or its armed forces. Those convicted under the act usually received prison sentences ranging from five to twenty years. Only one congressman voted against the bill in the

House of Representatives: socialist Meyer London, who was also one of only fifty to vote against America's entrance into World War I. London would go on to die a decidedly unnatural death, being struck by a car on New York's Second Avenue, dying at only fifty-four. High-profile socialist Eugene V. Debs was among those convicted under the act, serving two years in prison before his sentence was commuted by President Warren Harding. As might be expected, "Far from opposing the measure, the leading papers seemed actually to lead the movement in behalf of its speedy enactment," to quote James R. Mock in *Censorship 1917*. The Supreme Court upheld Wilson's acts; few Americans realize the famous "crying 'fire' in a crowded theater" reference comes from Oliver Wendell Holmes's decision to support such blatant limits on free speech.

A now totally lost silent film, *The Spirit of '76*, was released in May 1917, just a month after America's entrance into the war. The film depicted numerous scenes of British atrocities during the Revolutionary War, and led to producer/writer Robert Goldstein being sentenced to ten years in prison under the Espionage Act, because the film portrayed the British— our World War I allies—in a negative way. Goldstein's legal appeals failed; he couldn't take the case to the Supreme Court, because in one of their most indefensible decisions, the Court had ruled in 1915 that motion pictures were not covered under the First Amendment. Goldstein was never able to resuscitate his film career, and nothing is known of him after 1938.

Attorney General A. Mitchell Palmer waged a campaign to keep the Sedition Act alive during peacetime as well. The Palmer Raids conducted between 1919 and 1920, which introduced a very young J. Edgar Hoover as the director of the Justice Department's Bureau of Investigation, would result in more than 500 anarchists and radical leftists being deported, out of over 10,000 arrested. A rare reasonable decision in June 1920 by Massachusetts District Court Judge George Anderson compelled the release of seventeen arrested aliens and denounced the raids. Anderson wrote that "a mob is a mob, whether made up of Government officials act-ing under instructions from the Department of Justice, or of criminals and loafers and the vicious classes." One prominent supporter of the 1916 Gore-McLemore resolution (one of the co-sponsors being blind Senator Thomas Gore, grandfather of Gore Vidal), designed to keep America out of the war, was Congressman Michael F. Farley. Farley served only a single term in the House, and would suffer a truly bizarre death just four years later, when he was exposed to anthrax on his shaving brush.

As General Smedley Butler wrote:

> Beautiful ideals were painted for our boys who were sent out to die. This
> was the "war to end wars." This was the "war to make the world safe
> for democracy." No one told them that dollars and cents were the real
> reason. No one mentioned to them, as they marched away, that their
> going and their dying would mean huge war profits. No one told these
> American soldiers that they might be shot down by bullets made by their
> own brothers here. No one told them that the ships on which they were
> going to cross might be torpedoed by submarines built with United States
> patents. They were just told it was to be a "glorious adventure." . . . In the
> World War, we used propaganda to make the boys accept conscription.
> They were made to feel ashamed if they didn't join the army.

Woodrow Wilson, like any good alleged "liberal," loved to deploy the military. World War I wasn't enough for him; during his administration, invasions were launched into Cuba, the Dominican Republic, Honduras, Mexico, and Panama. In his book *Presidents' Body Counts: The Twelve Worst and Four Best American Presidents*, author Al Carroll unearthed a wealth of generally unknown information. For instance, President Wilson once famously vowed, "I'm going to teach the South American republics to elect good men." This was pretty hard for those republics to do, since under the ensuing decades of US control, no elections were permitted. In the true "progressive" spirit, Wilson authorized the usage of mustard gas and phosgene against German troops, and accumulated an impressive stockpile of chemical weapons.

Like all the presidents ranked highest by the court historians, Woodrow Wilson overstepped his constitutional authority with impunity. It is little remembered that in 1914, he deployed federal troops to Colorado to suppress a labor dispute, ordering the US Army to disarm and arrest American citizens. As had been the case under Lincoln, they could be held in military custody and writs of habeas corpus issued by state courts were denied.

During his last year in office, Wilson was basically incapacitated from the effects of a stroke. Wilson's second wife, Edith Bolling Galt, whom he married in office, is thought by most historians to have actually served as de facto president during 1919–1920. The sickly Wilson died on February 3, 1924. As is strangely common in high-profile deaths, there was no autopsy performed. Ironically, Wilson is now increasingly being branded a "racist" by politically correct authoritarians. A June 25, 2015 piece in *The Washington Post* lobbied for the removal of Wilson's name from public buildings and bridges. To quote from the article:

On March 4th, 1913, Democrat Thomas Woodrow Wilson became the first Southerner elected president since Zachary Taylor in 1848. Washington was flooded with revelers from the Old Confederacy, whose people had long dreamed of a return to the glory days of Washington, Jefferson, Madison, and Monroe . . . . Rebel yells and the strains of "Dixie" reverberated throughout the city. The new administration brought to power a generation of political leaders from the old South who would play influential roles in Washington for generations to come. . . . Born in Virginia and raised in Georgia and South

Carolina, Wilson was a loyal son of the old South who regretted the outcome of the Civil War. He used his high office to reverse some of its consequences. When he entered the White House a hundred years ago today, Washington was a rigidly segregated town—except for federal government agencies. They had been integrated during the post-war Reconstruction period, enabling African-Americans to obtain federal jobs and work side by side with whites in government agencies. Wilson promptly authorized members of his cabinet to reverse this long-standing policy of racial integration in the federal civil service.

Wilson's chief sin appears to have been screening D. W. Griffith's wildly successful movie *Birth of a Nation*, based upon the novel *The Clansman*, written by Wilson's friend and former classmate Thomas Dixon, in the White House. The film, while possessing obvious racist overtones, effectively critiqued the Reconstruction period in the South and was lauded for its cinematic brilliance. Wilson was impressed enough to declare that "It is like writing history with lightning, and my only regret is that it is all so terribly true." Former supporter W. E. B. DuBois was among those who protested to Wilson directly, accusing him of being racist. Wilson refused to back down, and told the *New York Times*, "If the colored people made a mistake in voting for me, they ought to correct it." Wilson, like many leaders of the time, was a fan of eugenics, having campaigned in Indiana in 1907 for the compulsory sterilization of criminals and the mentally retarded. In 1911, while governor of New Jersey, he signed such a bill into law.

THE DEATH OF PRESIDENT HARDING

I can take care of my enemies in a fight. But my friends, my goddamned friends, they're the ones who keep me walking the floor at nights!
—Warren G. Harding

President Warren G. Harding died unexpectedly on August 2, 1923. The cause of death has variously been reported as a heart attack, pneumonia, some intestinal disorder, or the food poisoning he'd contracted during a cross-country trip the previous month that had been dubbed the "Voyage of Understanding." Secretary of Commerce Herbert Hoover's official announcement of the death attributed it to "a stroke of cerebral apoplexy." There were even rumors that Harding, a notorious ladies' man, had actually died from syphilis. Perhaps it's naive to expect that the cause of death for any president of the United States should be clear and understandable. Harding was only fifty-seven years old. Some have theorized that his wife Florence actually poisoned him. The fact that he presided over the most scandal-plagued administration since Grant's only added to the intrigue. According to PBS, "Some of his doctors warned Harding, while he was still in the US Senate, that his multiple amorous affairs might physically injure his delicate and enlarged heart." The same report managed to get a dig in at "Mr. and Mrs. Harding's favorite doctor," who "was an odd and charismatic homeopathic physician from Ohio named Charles Sawyer." Florence Harding's curious refusal to permit an autopsy, and insistence that her husband be quickly embalmed (an astonishing *hour* after his death), hardly kept suspicions at bay.[10] Dr. Ray Lyman Wilbur, the president of Stanford University, was at the hotel when Harding arrived for treatment. As he wrote in his memoirs, "We shall never know exactly the immediate cause of President Harding's death, since every effort that was made to secure an autopsy met with complete and final refusal."

While most Americans have heard of the slew of scandals in the Harding administration, invariably grouped together as "Teapot Dome," few know any details about them. Two very well-known names, Percy Rockefeller and Prescott Bush, grandfather of George W. Bush, were connected to the corruption, but strangely avoided being indicted. Just as strangely, they have avoided the scrutiny of the court historians who have written on the subject.

Gaston Means, the author of the controversial 1930 book, *The Strange Death of President Harding*, was described by PBS as "an embittered, former Harding Administration official. . . . In addition to his short stint with the Department of Justice's Bureau of Investigation, he was also a notorious confidence man and bootlegger who died in Leavenworth Prison in 1938, after being convicted for a con he tried to pull related to the Charles Lindbergh Jr. kidnapping." Like most conspiracy theorists, Means's reputation was tarnished by the media, and continues to be. In the television series *Boardwalk Empire*, he was portrayed as a would-be hit man, willing to commit murder. Who would have suspected the man had time to write the only book questioning the official narrative of the death of President Harding? Convicted of grand larceny, Means died while in Leavenworth federal penitentiary. Court historian Robert H. Ferrell later borrowed Means's title almost exactly, changing it slightly to *The Strange Deaths of President Harding*, and reassured worried skeptics that Harding had been suffering for years from hypertension and died from a conventional heart attack, not from poison or any other nefarious method.

There are numerous odd aspects to this case. According to Herbert Hoover, when he walked into Harding's room at San Francisco's Palace Hotel, the homeopathic Dr. Charles Sawyer was lying on the bed next to the deceased president. Florence Harding not only refused to permit an autopsy, she wouldn't even allow a death mask to be made. She also destroyed many of Harding's papers. Perhaps strangest of all, Dr. Sawyer would die a year later, in nearly an identical manner, while Florence Harding happened to be visiting his home. Only two months after Sawyer's death, Florence died herself, allegedly of kidney failure. Harding had supposedly made a telling comment to Hoover during that ill-fated trip, asking him whether a president who'd become aware of corruption in his own ranks had an obligation to report it An associated strange death was that of Harding crony Jess Smith, a longtime member of the so-called "Ohio Gang." On May 30, 1923, just a few months before Harding's death, Smith was found shot to death with a gun at his side. The official verdict was suicide, but Alabama senator James Thomas Heflin was among those who suspected foul play. "Nobody else knew what he knew," Heflin said, "and with him dead there was nobody to tell the story—so Jess Smith was murdered."[11] In the *Boardwalk Empire* episode noted earlier, it is in fact Jess Smith whom Gaston Means is assigned to kill. Yet another entry in the body count connected to the Teapot Dome scandal was the mysterious death of oil heir E. L. "Ned" Doheny Jr. Doheny and his longtime friend Hugh Plunkett were found together in Doheny's lavish estate in Beverly Hills on February 16, 1929, each of them shot in the head.

Very recent DNA testing finally validated the claims of Nan Britton, President Harding's lover who had long insisted he had fathered her child.[12] Warren Harding's body was transported across the country after his abrupt, still mysterious death. Much as they had for Abraham Lincoln, millions of Americans lined the train tracks in cities and towns, paying their last respects to their supremely flawed but generally liked leader. Despite the assurances of establishment historians, Harding's death has never been adequately explained, and can be filed away with all our other largely unknowable history.

PROHIBITION

Why don't they pass a constitutional amendment prohibiting anybody from learning anything? If it works as well as prohibition did, in five years Americans would be the smartest race of people on Earth.

—Will Rogers

The Eighteenth Amendment to the US Constitution effectively outlawed the manufacture, sale, and use of alcoholic beverages in January 1920. The established historical consensus is that this unwise law was instituted due to pressure from religious and puritanical forces. Conspiracy theorists raise some disquieting, normally ignored facts. The original automobiles ran on alcohol. Henry Ford's Model T offered an option whereby the driver could switch the carburetor so that the engine ran on ethyl alcohol. With such models, refueling took place at local farms that possessed stills. Among those who were adversely impacted by all this were John D. Rockefeller and his giant Standard Oil Company. The conspiracy theorists accuse Rockefeller of financing the Women's Christian Temperance Union to promote prohibition. The Prohibition era from 1920 to 1933 just happened to nicely coincide with the explosion of automobiles all across the country.

In 1926, New York City's chief medical examiner, Charles Norris, attempted to warn the public about the dangerous poisons that were in bootlegged liquor. The industrial alcohol that speakeasies used had been poisoned by the Treasury Department with methyl alcohol. When people started getting sick, the bootleggers hired chemists to make the alcohol drinkable, but the government responded by adding more deadly poisons, like kerosene, gasoline, and chloroform to the mix. By 1928, most of the liquor in New York City was admittedly toxic. During 1926 and 1927, over 1,000 people died from the alcohol poisoned by their own government.[13] Much as the "war on drugs" would create new, incredibly violent gangs, Prohibition created the Mafia and made celebrities of violent thugs like Al Capone. In 1927, Capone and his gang pulled in approximately $60 million, most of it beer profits. One group that strongly supported Prohibition was the Ku Klux Klan, then at the peak of its influence. They engaged in gunfire with bootleggers and burned down their stills.

When the Twenty-First Amendment to the Constitution repealed Prohibition in 1933, gasoline stations were an essential part of the landscape, and most automobile engines ran exclusively on gas. John D. Rockefeller allegedly spent $4 million to promote Prohibition. Judging by the incalculable profits of Standard Oil and their peers in the decades that followed, it appears to have been a brilliant investment.

SACCO AND VANZETTI

If it had not been for these things, I might have lived out my life talking at street corners to scorning men. I might have died, unmarked, unknown, a failure. . . . The taking of our lives—lives of a good shoemaker and a poor fish-peddler—all! That last moment belongs to us—that agony is our triumph.

—Bartolomeo Vanzetti

Nicola Sacco and Bartolomeo Vanzetti were two poor Italian immigrants who had been drawn naturally to anarchism. Their conviction for a 1920 robbery and murder they almost certainly didn't commit would draw the attention of the world. Numerous high-profile figures, including future Supreme Court Justice Felix Frankfurter, writer Upton Sinclair, and poet Edna St. Vincent Millay, lobbied to get them a new trial. Despite every effort to obtain justice, Sacco and Vanzetti were electrocuted on August 23, 1927.

The judge who presided over Sacco and Vanzetti's trial, Webster Thayer, had given a speech just a few weeks before in which he castigated anarchism and Bolshevism. Like so many judges before and after him, Thayer declined to recuse himself when he clearly should have. Thayer permitted the introduction of a fanciful theory, dubbed "consciousness of guilt," which was based upon the notion that Sacco and Vanzetti had "acted guilty" when arrested, and the jury was allowed to consider this as "evidence." Due to the constant threats he received after the trial, Thayer would eventually move into the private University Club in Boston, where he died six years after Sacco and Vanzetti were executed.

The case against the Italian anarchists was full of holes. No eyewitness ever placed Vanzetti at the scene of the crime, and all those who belatedly identified Sacco were uncertain, to say the least. As is customary in every high-profile trial with political overtones, the defendants received abysmally poor legal representation.

The prevailing consensus among the court historians is that Sacco was definitely guilty, while Vanzetti may or may not have been. There is no question that the political views of the defendants contributed, at the very least, to their receiving an unfair trial. As Vanzetti told the court, "the first thing the police asked me is if I was an anarchist, communist, or socialist." Sacco was badgered by prosecutors over his dodging of the draft during World War I. Thayer actually told the jury at the outset of the trial, "Although this man (Sacco) may not have committed the crime attributed to him, he is nonetheless culpable because he is the enemy of our existing institutions." Thayer's friend reported that the judge had boasted to him, "Did you see what I did with those anarchist bastards the other day?" The foreman of the jury was an ex-police officer who theatrically saluted the American flag each time he entered the courtroom. Much as would happen decades later during the trial of accused Oklahoma City bomber Timothy McVeigh, the unpopular political beliefs of the defendants were introduced into the record. Dozens of witnesses testified that Sacco and Vanzetti were nowhere near the scene of the crime. Sacco even received a letter in prison from a man who confessed to the robbery and murder.

A US Justice Department agent even swore out an affidavit, expressing his view that the Italian anarchists had been framed. "It was the opinion of the department agents here that a conviction of Sacco and Vanzetti for murder would be one way of disposing of the two men," the agent stated. "My opinion and the opinion of most of the older men in the government service has always been that the South Braintree crime was the work of professionals." But every motion for a new trial was denied. In the recent book *Sacco and Vanzetti: The Men, the Murders and the Judgment of Mankind*, author Bruce Watson was more evenhanded than most court historians, declaring, "There is far more evidence of innocence than of guilt, but unfortunately, especially with Sacco, guilt can't be ruled out. Their characters don't fit the crime. There is so much doubt surrounding their trial. The one thing I say definitively is that they deserved a second trial." No unbiased person can maintain that there wasn't at least reasonable doubt in this case.

Well-known journalist Walter Lippmann wrote, "If Sacco and Vanzetti were professional bandits, then historians and biographers who attempt to deduce character from personal documents might as well shut up shop. By every test that I know of for judging character, these are the letters of innocent men." Ballistics tests conducted in 1961 on Sacco's Colt automatic supposedly confirmed that the bullet that killed Berardelli in 1920 came from the same pistol, which was found in Sacco's possession. Critics naturally disputed these tests, noting that ballistics experts conducting it had claimed Sacco's guilt beforehand. There was also no evidence that Sacco had fired the gun. In 1988, former *Boston Globe* editorial page editor Charlie Whipple revealed a conversation he'd had with Sergeant Edward J. Seibolt in 1937. According to Whipple, Seibolt had admitted that the police ballistics experts had switched the murder weapon, but declared that he would deny this if Whipple ever printed it. In 1973, a former mobster published a confession by Frank "Butsy" Morelli. "We whacked them out, we killed those guys in the robbery," Butsy Morelli told Vincent Teresa. "These two greaseballs Sacco and Vanzetti took it on the chin." On August 23, 1977, exactly fifty years after their execution, Massachusetts governor Michael Dukakis issued a proclamation stating that Sacco and Vanzetti had been treated unjustly and that "any disgrace should be forever removed from their names."

The "roaring" '20s are remembered fondly today, as a frivolous, carefree era. The president that presided over the bulk of it, Calvin Coolidge, was perhaps as good as Americans can expect from their chief executive. He did very little while in office, and thus didn't overstep his constitutional duties or damage the civil liberties of the people greatly. Coolidge's philosophy was perhaps best expressed in his quote, "I have never been hurt by what I have not said."

In a September 1924 speech, he expounded upon his literal interpretation of the Declaration of Independence, declaring, "If all men are created equal, that is final. If they are endowed with inalienable rights, that is final. If governments derive their just powers from the consent of the governed, that is final, no advance, no progress can be made beyond these propositions." Calvin Coolidge died suddenly at age sixty on January 5, 1933, allegedly of heart failure. From the lengthy obituary which appeared in *The New York Times* on January 6, 1933, we learn not only that those who were with Coolidge that morning described him as seemingly healthy and his death about as abrupt as could be, but that "an autopsy had been discussed, but that Mrs. Coolidge was opposed to it, and that it would not be performed." It is a sad testament to how bad our leaders have generally been, to consider that simply by doing nothing Coolidge stands out favorably in comparison.

The 1920s had its conspiracy theorists as well. New York City mayor John F. Hylan said the following, in 1922:

The real menace of our republic is this invisible government which like a giant octopus sprawls its slimy length over city, state and nation. Like the octopus of real life, it operates under cover of a self created screen. . . . At the head of this octopus are the Rockefeller Standard Oil interests and a small group of powerful banking houses generally referred to as international bankers. The little coterie of powerful international bankers virtually run the United States government for their own selfish purposes. They practically control both political parties.

That statement could just as easily have been made in 1932, or 1942, or 1952, or even today.

CHAPTER SEVEN

THE DEPRESSING 1930s

There is no cause to worry. The high tide of prosperity will continue.
—Secretary of the Treasury Andrew Mellon, September 1929

The fast-paced, bootleg liquor-soaked "roaring" 1920s came to an abrupt end with the crash of the stock market on October 24, 1929. Most Americans, when they think of the Great Depression, picture soup and bread lines and financially devastated people leaping out of windows. In fact, there was nothing "accidental" about the stock market crash or the Great Depression itself. Once the Federal Reserve was created in 1913, such fantastic booms and busts were predictable. The Fed had expanded the money supply by some 62 percent between 1923 and 1929, which bid stock prices up to new, dizzying heights. As Ferdinand Lundberg explained, "For profits to be made on these funds the public had to be induced to speculate, and it was so induced by misleading newspaper accounts, many of them bought and paid for by the brokers that operated the pools." A committee in the US House of Representatives had warned that a major crash had been planned as early as 1927.

Author William Bryan described what happened in his book *The United States' Unresolved Monetary and Political Problems*:

> When everything was ready, the New York financiers started calling 24
> hour broker call loans. This meant that the stockbrokers and the cus-
> tomers had to dump their stock on the market in order to pay the loans.
> This naturally collapsed the stock market and brought a banking col-
> lapse all over the country because the banks not owned by the oligar-
> chy were heavily involved in broker call claims at this time, and bank
> runs soon exhausted their coin and currency and they had to close. The
> Federal Reserve System would not come to their aid, although they were
> instructed under the law to maintain an elastic currency.

As always, those with inside knowledge profited from the untold misery of millions. Ultimate insider Paul Warburg, one of the powerful founders of the Federal Reserve, issued a warning to his fellow elitists on March 9, 1929, when the *Financial Chronicle* quoted him thusly: "If orgies of unrestricted speculation are permitted to spread too far the ultimate collapse is certain . . . to bring about a general depression involving the whole country." After the crash, of course, these same insiders swooped down like vultures and bought what they wanted at a 90 percent discount.

While this would prove to be a worldwide depression, only Germany— with its economy already hopelessly destroyed by the mad strictures of the Versailles Treaty—could match the US unemployment rate. Signaling decades of Republican mindset to come, President Herbert Hoover was reluctant to "dole" out assistance to financially ruined Americans. The sui- cide rate rose sharply, and there were many local strikes and protests. The fertility rate dropped. Contrary to industry propaganda, movie attendance dipped dramatically.

THE BONUS ARMY

We're here for the duration and we're not going to starve.
—Walter M. Waters, Bonus Army leader

Forty-three thousand Americans, nearly half of them World War I veterans, assembled in Washington, DC, in the midst of the Great Depression, demanding the compensation that the government had promised them. On July 29, 1932, US military troops stormed several buildings occupied by the protesters, and two veterans were killed. Another fatality was a twelve-week-old baby who died from inhaling tear gas. The government "investigation" into this unconscionable death found that the baby had died of unrelated causes. Until the troops began charging at them, the Bonus Marchers had cheered them, naively thinking their fellow soldiers were on hand to offer their support. Also killed were four members of a hunger march from Dearborn, Michigan. Future military legend General Douglas MacArthur was in charge of the US forces, accompanied by six tanks commanded by another legend, then Major George S. Patton. MacArthur actually disobeyed President Hoover's order to stop the assault, making the ludicrous claim that he was preventing an attempt to overthrow the government. The Bonus Army marchers, along with their wives and children, were easily defeated by the heroic troops, who burned their shelters and belongings. Military bonuses had been an American tradition since 1776, and the World War I vets had every reason to expect them.

At MacArthur's side during the raid on the Bonus Army was his junior aide, then Major Dwight D. Eisenhower. Eisenhower felt it was wrong for the Army's chief of staff himself to lead such an attack on his fellow Americans, stating, "I told that dumb son-of-a-bitch not to go down there."[1] Nevertheless, Ike knew how to obey orders, and obligingly wrote the official report endorsing MacArthur's conduct for the Army. It is sobering to picture the mighty American military engaged in a brutal match with patriotic Americans who, in the words of journalist and eyewitness Joseph C. Harsch, were "a bunch of people in great distress wanting help. . . . These were simply veterans from World War I who were out of luck, out of money, and wanted to get their bonus . . ." Herbert Hoover was widely criticized for his handling of the Bonus Army, and the court historians tell us that this contributed to the election of Franklin Roosevelt to the presidency.

While General Smedley Butler, author of the classic book *War is a Racket*, Huey Long, and other genuine leftists supported the Bonus Expeditionary Force, as they were called, the about-to-be-elected President Franklin D. Roosevelt, not surprisingly, was against paying them the bonus they'd been guaranteed under the 1924 World War Adjusted Compensation Act (which had been passed over President Calvin Coolidge's veto). The great populist leader Senator Huey Long of Louisiana spoke out boldly on the issue of the Bonus Army, as might be expected. With his typical blunt eloquence, Long blasted Roosevelt for not supporting the veterans in a May 11, 1935 speech:

> Now the President tells us that he was a veteran of the World War too, and that he understands it somewhat better than we may think. Well it is true that Mr. Roosevelt was a veteran of the World War, and an honorable veteran. He was Assistant Secretary of the Navy. He stayed up here on Pennsylvania Avenue in the daytime and in a very fine home during the nighttime and he drew ten thousand dollars a year for his services and he was worth every cent of it. He was three thousand miles away from gunfire. Of course, he had an income besides that which made him say that he did not need the ten thousand dollars, but we paid him the ten thousand dollars anyway, and nobody's trying to take it away from him, and nobody says he wasn't worth the ten thousand dollars. But the man that he does not seem to have learned about is the man that did not stay on Pennsylvania Avenue and who did not stay in any luxurious home, but the man who scoured the seas, who walked and slept in the rain, who

stood in the mud waist deep in the trenches, who went over the top and faced the German guns, who breathed the poisonous gases, and who not only went through fourteen kinds of carnage worse than the fires of hell itself, but who, when he came back, found his occupation destroyed and the job which he had held gone.

THE LINDBERGH KIDNAPPING

I am innocent. I have never changed my story and I never will.
—Bruno Richard Hauptmann

On March 1, 1932, the infant son of famed aviator Charles Lindbergh was reported missing from his home in Hopewell, New Jersey. On May 12, the body of Charles Lindbergh Jr. was discovered only a short distance from the residence. A cursory medical examination revealed that death had been caused by a massive skull fracture.

Within hours of the baby being reported as stolen, local and state police, along with reporters and curious spectators, were allowed to roam freely about the property. Combined with the wet ground, their presence rendered any potential footprint evidence meaningless. A crude, make-shift ladder was found lying on the ground under the baby's window. Col. Lindbergh, who immediately took charge of the investigation himself, led police to an envelope that was propped up against a window in the baby's nursery. He ordered that the envelope not be touched until it could be checked for fingerprints. The envelope contained a note indicating that a group had kidnapped the child and would contact the Lindberghs later for specific ransom demands.

The search for the kidnappers included a brief affiliation between law enforcement and organized crime. More ransom letters arrived, post-marked from Brooklyn. Somehow a retired schoolteacher named John F.

Condon managed to insert himself into the middle of the case. Popularly known as "Jafsie," Condon eventually would meet with a representative of the kidnappers at a cemetery. The man he met with, known as John, told Jafsie that he was part of a group comprising three men and two women. On March 16, Condon received a package in the mail containing a sleeping outfit that Lindbergh would identify as belonging to his son. The ransom money of $50,000 was delivered to a man Jafsie "thought" was the same John, while Lindbergh only glimpsed him from a distance. They were thereafter led on a wild goose chase to a boat that didn't exist.

Over two years later, a German immigrant named Bruno Richard Hauptmann was arrested. Some $14,000 that was identified as part of the ransom money Jafsie had passed to "Cemetery John" was found in Hauptmann's home. Hauptmann's story was that he'd been given a box for safekeeping by his business partner Isidor Fisch before he went to Germany. When he learned that Fisch had died in Germany on March 29, 1934, Hauptmann opened the box, discovered it contained gold certificate bills, and decided to keep it because Fisch owed him a good deal of money. Hauptmann's rather fantastic alibi gave rise to the popular expression about something seeming "fishy."

Hauptmann, always referred to as the more Germanic sounding "Bruno," despite the fact that friends and family called him Richard ("It was a name he hated," his widow would declare), was vilified in the press and negatively impacted by growing anti-German public sentiment. His trial was a farce, with only a nominal defense offered by attorney Edward J. Reilly, whose nickname "Death House" didn't exactly inspire confidence. Reilly spent all of *forty* minutes total consulting with his famous client. The only member of Hauptmann's defense team who tried to do a decent job was C. Lloyd Fisher. When Reilly conceded the identification of the remains claimed to be the Lindbergh baby, without cross-examining the witness, Fisher shouted out, "You are conceding Hauptmann to the electric chair!" and stormed from the courtroom. Reilly was actually hired by the *Daily Mirror* in exchange for the rights to publish Hauptmann's story in their paper. Colonel Lindbergh, to his eternal discredit, took the witness stand and "identified" Hauptmann's voice as the one he'd heard, over two years earlier, utter the words "Hey, doctor," from a considerable distance. The jury wasn't told that the handwriting experts who "identified" the writing on the ransom notes as Hauptmann's originally had said there was no match.

One of the few things Hauptmann's defense team tried to do was obtain his payroll records for the day of the kidnapping so that he could prove he was at work in New York City. However, in the all too familiar pattern, the records were reported to be "missing." Thanks to Anthony Scaduto, who in 1976 wrote the first critical book examining the facts in this case, *Scapegoat*, we know that Hauptmann did indeed work the day of the kidnapping, and thus simply couldn't have arrived at the estate in Hopewell in time to kidnap the baby. David Wilentz and his prosecution team had crudely doctored the timecard records to distort the truth.

All of the physical evidence presented against Hauptmann was in fact tainted beyond any reasonable doubt. The prosecution "proved" through the testimony of a Treasury Department accountant that Hauptmann's motive for the crime was that he had gone broke speculating in the stock market between 1929 and the time of the kidnapping in March 1932. This same witness testified that, except for the $15,000 found in his garage, Hauptmann had spent almost every penny of the ransom money, most of it on further stock speculation. But another FBI accountant found that Hauptmann's stock losses from 1929 to March 1932 were merely $363.65, and that in all of his speculating over five years up to his arrest he had lost only $5,000, while he maintained $10,000 in savings and had continued to earn money during that period. This renegade FBI accountant, like numerous others willing to offer information that would contradict the official version of events, was not permitted to testify.

Ludovic Kennedy, author of the 1985 book *The Airman and the Carpenter*, hotly disputed the prosecution's ridiculous contention that Hauptman had gone through the arduous task of removing a single board from his attic, in a letter published in the February 18, 1988 issue of the *New York Times*. "In his review of *The Lindbergh Case* by Jim Fisher,[2] Mr. Francis Russell challenges the assertions of Mr. Anthony Scaduto and myself that the ladder evidence against Hauptmann was rigged. It *was* rigged." Kennedy wrote:

> The holes which the police claimed to have found in Rail 16 after Hauptmann's arrest and which they said matched identical holes in the joists of the Hauptmann attic, were not there at the time of the kidnapping. In the course of his investigations into the case Governor Hoffman of New Jersey found a photograph of the ladder taken the day after the crime. "Rail 16 can be easily identified," he wrote, "but neither in the original nor in a copy magnified ten times can the alleged nail holes be found." Apart from this, may I appeal to Mr. Russell's common sense? If, as he thinks, Hauptmann was guilty and built the ladder from the lumber which, as a professional carpenter, he always kept in stock in his garage, why should he make an exception for Rail 16? The only way then to reach the attic was to remove the linen from the linen cupboard, climb up the cleats, push open the trap door (no easy task when carrying saw, hammer and chisel) and hoist himself into the attic. There, Mr. Russell would have us believe, he solemnly began chopping up part of his landlord's flooring. What on earth would have been the point of that?

There were numerous oddities and unanswered questions about the Lindbergh case. Violet Sharpe, one of the Lindberghs' servants, told the authorities (some of whom instantly suspected an inside job) conflicting stories, and then committed suicide. Reporter Tom Cassidy would later publicly boast of having written down "Jafsie's" (Condon's) name and phone number on a board in Hauptmann's pantry. This "evidence" had been used to great effect against Hauptmann at his trial. The ransom bills, which were all marked, continued to be circulated throughout the country long after Hauptmann's arrest. The ransom notes referred to *kidnappers*, plural; "Jafsie" had described speaking over the phone to them, which included females possessing what he described as Italian accents.

The Lindberghs had a routine which never varied; up until the night of the kidnapping, they had only stayed at their estate in Hopewell on weekends. Any kidnapper(s) staking out the place would therefore not have logically acted on a Tuesday, the night the Lindbergh baby disappeared. The only witness who belatedly "identified" Hauptmann as being at the scene of the crime was eighty-seven-year-old Amandus Hochmuth, who was legally blind and incapable of identifying anyone to a legal certainty. Hochmuth originally told the police he'd seen no one around the estate that night, but at Hauptmann's trial he swore he'd witnessed Hauptmann driving a car near the home, with a ladder in it.

Whoever took Charles Lindbergh Jr. on the night of March 1, 1932, it appears they were Keystone Kidnappers. If the baby died that night, as the authorities came to believe, then why did they leave the body, unburied, so close to the estate? How did it lie undiscovered for so long, when the area had been searched thoroughly? They were certainly taking a huge risk in demanding a ransom for a child who was already dead, and whose body was left so close to the scene of the crime. Or, as some have come to believe, was there a kidnapping at all? Colonel Charles Lindbergh was known as a notorious practical joker, and some time shortly before the actual kidnapping, he allegedly hid baby Charles in a closet, informed the family he'd been kidnapped, and allowed them to despair over the situation for twenty minutes before admitting he was just kidding.[3] Nanny Betty Gow would tell author Andrew Scott Berg, in a 1993 interview, that the famed aviator had occasionally dunked the infant under the bath-water in order to "test his courage."

As awkward as it sounds, the actions of Colonel Lindbergh here deserve close scrutiny. For instance, it was oddly out of character that the fastidious aviator, scheduled to address a major fund-raiser for New York University the evening of March 1, 1932 (the night his child was supposedly kidnapped), did not show up for the event. Lindbergh attributed his absence to "mixing up" the dates. He also told his wife and nursemaid Betty Gow not to enter the nursery from the time the baby was put to bed at 7:30 until 10 p.m., when he was to be taken to the bathroom. The ostensible reason was that he feared the child would be unduly coddled. Lindbergh returned home at 8:25 p.m. that night, and although he hadn't seen his son since the previous morning, he never peeked into his room, even when he went to draw his bath in the bathroom next to the nursery shortly before 9:30 p.m.

There are so many peculiarities in this case that defy explanation. The Lindberghs' Boston terrier, known to bark at the slightest provocation, never barked that night. There were no fingerprints found at all in the nursery, even those of family members, leading one state trooper to comment that he thought someone had washed everything in the nursery before it was dusted for prints. When the body of an infant alleged to be the missing baby was found in some woods less than three miles from the Lindberghs' New Jersey home, the Colonel ordered the remains cremated instantly, before an autopsy or any pathological or toxicological tests could be performed.[4] While Anne Morrow Lindbergh would be cremated after her death in 2001, Charles Lindbergh was buried in Hawaii. It is even more difficult to understand, then, why he would opt not to bury his young son.

There are many problems with the whole kidnap scenario. As noted earlier, the Lindberghs had a set pattern, whereby they stayed with Anne Morrow Lindbergh's mother at her estate in Englewood, New Jersey during the week, when Charles would commute to work in New York, while weekends were spent at the Hopewell house. On Monday, February 29, 1932, however, Col. Lindbergh phoned Anne and instructed her not to return to Englewood that day. He was supposedly concerned about little Charles's cold and the effect a long car trip in the nasty weather would have on it. In fact, the child was feeling better than he had the previous week, when Lindbergh had allowed him to go on a car trip, in the rain, that Friday from Englewood to Hopewell. For the "old school" Lindbergh to suddenly worry about his child embarking on a car trip, with an improving cold, in a heated car (the Lindberghs' automobile was heated), is completely out of character. The Colonel's wife Anne, in a letter to her mother-in-law written March 2, 1932, indicated that little Charles was completely cured, and the fever gone, by Monday, February 29.[5] In that same letter, Anne disclosed that the first person both she and nursemaid Betty Gow suspected was none other than the "Lone Eagle" himself. Anne wrote: "At ten Betty went into the baby, shut the window first, then lit the electric stove, then turned to the bed. It was empty and the sides still up. No blankets taken. She thought C. had taken him for a joke. I did, until I saw his face."[6]

Therefore, had the home been "cased," the kidnappers would have had no reason to suspect the family would be there on any weeknight. The crude ladder found near the house, allegedly used in the kidnapping, was constructed so poorly that, if all three of its parts were used, it bypassed the bedroom windows and went all the way to the roof, making it hard for someone to step in and out of the baby's window. If only two parts were used, however (it could not be adjusted, so one either had to use all three parts or just two), the top rung rested about thirty inches below the window. It was hardly the kind of ladder even semi-intelligent criminals would use; certainly a carpenter like Richard Hauptmann could have constructed a better one. Also curious is how the kidnappers could have known where the baby's room was, or that only one of the windows in the house had shutters which didn't latch. Was it by chance, or some kind of surveillance which was somehow not detected by the staff and family of the remote estate, that they chose this window? Only one set of ladder rail holes was discovered, so whoever used it obviously knew where to climb.[7]

Also difficult to understand is why the kidnappers, even if they had miscalculated and planned the crime for a weeknight when they had no reason to believe the family would be there, would have struck in the early evening hours. The kidnapping had to have taken place sometime between 7:30, when the child was put to bed, and 10:00, when he was discovered to be missing. During that period of time, lights were on in the part of the house where the baby's nursery was, and more importantly, people were up and about and a high-strung dog that barked wildly at the approach of a stranger was also very much awake. Why wouldn't kidnappers wait until everyone was asleep? But, of course, that brings up an even more intriguing question: Why didn't anyone in the house hear anything? It is hard to believe that an individual, or group, could approach the house with a large ladder, place it against the house, mount it, take the child from the crib, go back down the ladder, and depart without causing the dog to bark, the child to cry or scream, or making any noise loud enough to attract the attention of those inside.

John F. "Jafsie" Condon was a pompous blowhard, at best, and a criminal conspirator at worst. His inconsistent testimony, from purporting to speak with Italian conspirators (plural) on the phone, to meeting a mysterious Italian woman who set up a rendezvous she never kept, to claiming that "Cemetery John" spoke with a German accent, certainly seems to implicate him in *something*. Condon could not identify Hauptmann as "Cemetery John" initially, and in fact seemed to adopt a responsible stance, telling the police that he had to be positive, since a man's life was at stake. At Hauptmann's trial, however, "Jafsie" identified Hauptmann, with great drama and fanfare. The public was rather taken by "Jafsie" and his absurd contentions. For instance, in the inevitable book he produced, *Jafsie Tells All*, he claimed to have knelt by the baby's crib and prayed for his safety. He'd been asked to spend the night at Hopewell and was, amazingly enough, given a cot and permitted to sleep in the nursery because all the guest rooms hadn't been finished. Condon noticed something that night in the nursery: a smudged handprint on the edge of the window frame. By merely glancing at the print, the decidedly non-expert Jafsie was able, in his words, to discern ". . . there is evidence of muscular development there . . . the print might have been left by a painter, a carpenter, a mechanic."[8] Condon would milk his fifteen minutes of fame for all it was worth, later spending years lecturing about the case, greatly embellishing his own role in the process.

No fingerprint expert, then or now, would ever claim to be able to tell an individual's occupation from a fingerprint. More importantly, when the nursery had been dusted, prior to Jafsie's stay there, there had not been a single fingerprint found. So much for Condon's credibility. Jafsie's descriptions of "Cemetery John" varied to a ridiculous extent: the alleged extortionist was said to be anywhere from five feet eight inches to six feet in height, with brown or blue eyes, a large or small nose, and either square or pointed facial features. Condon also visited jails in several east coast cities, viewing thousands of mug shots. Periodically, he would dramatically announce that one of them matched the man he'd given the ransom money to in the cemetery. Each time he "identified" someone, the authorities investigated and found the individuals were nowhere near New Jersey on March 1, 1932. A Lieutenant Finn of the New York City Police Department started referring to Condon as a "screwball."[9]

The eyewitness testimony against Hauptmann was more than questionable. For instance, a woman "identified" Hauptmann as the man who'd purchased a ticket from the movie theater where she was working as a cashier, paying with one of the gold certificates used for the ransom money. This incident took place on November 26, 1933, which happened to be Hauptmann's thirty-fourth birthday. As such, his wife could tes-tify vividly, as could two other friends who were there, to the fact that Hauptmann had been in their presence, as Anna had held a small party for the occasion, and they were nowhere near that or any other theater on the night in question.[10] One of the most damning pieces of evidence introduced against Hauptmann was the notorious "rail 16," wood which allegedly came from his attic and ended up as part of the ladder found at the scene of the crime. However, this belated "discovery" is hard to explain innocently, considering the police literally took over Hauptmann's home following his arrest on September 19, 1934, digging up his yard, demolish-ing the garage, and scouring the house looking for evidence. Police notes clearly show that the attic was searched several times without anything being found. Therefore, when a missing floorboard was discovered in the attic by Detective Lewis Bornmann, who'd actually moved into the home when the New Jersey State Police assumed the lease after Anna had been asked to leave one week after the arrest of Hauptmann, on September 26, 1934, most reasonable persons would place little reliability in it.[11]

Prosecutor David Wilentz, who has been accused by many critics of knowingly fabricating evidence and sending an innocent man to the elec-tric chair, made a vital and curious change in the prosecution's theory dur-ing his closing argument. Alcoholic and barely functional defense attorney Edward Reilly had questioned, in his own closing argument, why little Charles had not cried out when he was abducted. Remarking upon the fact that the Lindbergh baby had led a sheltered life and had been cared for by a very small circle of people, and didn't interact with strangers as a result, Reilly rationalized that he must have been taken by someone he knew. Wilentz was apparently so upset by this observation that he completely changed the prosecution's portrayal of the events that night. Wilentz had, up until that point, theorized that the child had died when Hauptmann dropped him from the ladder as he climbed down from the bedroom window, but now suddenly came up with an explanation for the child's silence. "This fellow took no chance on the child awakening." Wilentz declared. "He crushed that child right in that room, into insensibility. He smothered and choked that child right in that room." This absurd accusation was never questioned by the clueless jury or the completely controlled press, despite the well-known fact that there was absolutely no evidence of "choking" in the record.[12]

As for Richard Hauptmann, he alone shone throughout the whole ordeal. While the great "hero" Charles Lindbergh lowered himself to "identify" someone's voice when he'd only heard two words uttered from a distance some two and a half years previously, Hauptmann consistently maintained both his innocence and his dignity. The full measure of the man was shown when he turned down a last-minute offer from the prosecuting authorities to have his sentence commuted to life imprisonment in return for a full confession.[13] Hauptmann also turned down an offer of $90,000 from the Hearst Syndicate for his confession, which would have made his wife and son financially secure.

Nearly all of Lindbergh's activities the night of the "kidnapping" are questionable and should have been investigated. He was about an hour later than usual arriving home that night, and when he did, at 8:25 p.m., he honked the horn as he drove up, ostensibly to draw attention to his arrival. He was never questioned by the authorities as to what it was that had delayed him. Also suspicious is his mention to Anne, at approximately 9:15 p.m., of a "snapping sound" he heard coming from outside. Neither Anne nor anyone else heard this "snapping sound," and although they lived in a remote location and were expecting no visitors, Lindbergh did not go outside to investigate, as one might be expected to.[14] Yet another oddity is Lindbergh's testimony, at Hauptmann's trial, concerning his dog Wahgoosh: "I would not say that he was particularly a good watchdog" and that the dog didn't bark the night of the kidnapping, but ". . . I would not expect any from that dog." This testimony is incredible, because everyone else reported that Wahgoosh normally barked at the approach of strangers.[15]

Yet another of Lindbergh's actions is hard to innocently explain. Upon first entering the nursery, after Betty Gow had alerted him to the fact the baby wasn't in his crib, Lindbergh didn't, as one might logically do, call out or search the large house for the child, who might have just wandered off in search of a favorite toy. Instead, he stated dramatically that "Anne, they have stolen our baby." There was absolutely no reason to think this, because it wasn't until later that Lindbergh belatedly "found" the ransom note. Lindbergh thereafter made two telephone calls. The second was to the police, but the first was to his New York lawyer, Colonel Henry Breckinridge.[16] It is relevant, too, that Lindbergh accepted assistance from all sorts of kooky, shady characters, including those with ties to organized crime, but absolutely refused the help of the FBI.[17] Without any evidence to that effect, Lindbergh instantly steered the police (he, in fact, controlled the entire investigation) towards the theory that the New York underworld was involved in the kidnapping. This cool, rational man then revealed the intimate details of the case, including the contents of the ransom notes, to the most disreputable underworld con men imaginable.[18]

Authors Gregory Ahlgren and Stephen Monier developed a logical, compelling thesis which seems to answer a lot of previously perplexing questions. They note that if Hauptmann's plan was to abduct the child and hold it for ransom, and the child's death occurred accidentally when he dropped him from the ladder, how was he going to carry out that original plan? Hauptmann lived with his wife in a two-family home in the Bronx, and his son hadn't been born at the time. How was he supposed to hold the child there? No one, not even the prosecution, ever suggested that Anna Hauptmann knew anything about a kidnapping, so what was he going to tell her? Also, where was he planning to hide the child, and did he expect that somehow no one would notice it?[19] Also, according to the authors, after March 1, 1932, the lifelong practical joker Charles Lindbergh is not recorded as playing any more of his pranks.[20]

Whether there was a kidnapping or not, Richard Hauptmann was the victim of a great miscarriage of justice. The authorities were dead set on convicting him from the moment they apprehended him. From dubious witnesses, to instructing the affable German immigrant to misspell certain words that had been misspelled identically in the ransom notes in order to more easily "match" his handwriting to them, they never considered any explanation other than Hauptmann's sole guilt. FBI agent Leon Turrou told author Anthony Scaduto that the authorities even persuaded Hauptmann to try and imitate the writing in the ransom notes.

In the FBI files now available to researchers, one can find many reports by FBI agents expressing skepticism about the "evidence" against Hauptmann. FBI Director J. Edgar Hoover himself suspected that it was an "inside job," with more than one person involved. We are left with countless perplexing questions. As Detective Ellis Parker noted, could a body have decomposed so much in seventy-two days, like the one claimed to have been that of Charles Lindbergh Jr.? Parker also wondered about the lack of bloodstains, if the child had been killed or dropped during the kidnapping. What about the witness Oscar Bruchman, who told his lawyer that Isidor Frisch had asked for his help in disposing of some "hot" money? Then there were Hauptmann's supervisors at work, who initially confirmed he was working the day of the kidnapping, but then, like so many others, changed their testimony at trial. Another celebrated aviator, Amelia Earhart, later to become a historical mystery herself when her plane vanished without a trace, wrote to Governor Harold Hoffman on April 1, 1936, and declared, "Newspaper headlines such as this in the last week compel me to write a letter I have long debated. I believe many people feel reasonable doubt exists on some points in the tragic case referred to. Ceaseless argument rages among those who would have a man die because he has been condemned."

New Jersey governor Harold Hoffman sacrificed a bright political career by questioning the guilt of Hauptmann. After Hauptmann's conviction, Hoffman secretly visited him on Death Row and granted him a reprieve of his execution. In response to public outrage over the reprieve, Hoffman stated, "I share with hundreds of our people the doubt as to the value of the evidence that placed Hauptmann in the Lindbergh nursery on the night of the crime." Hoffman hired the aforementioned veteran detective Ellis Parker to conduct his own independent investigation into the case. Parker concluded that Hauptmann was innocent, but Hoffman thought that he was part of a group, declaring there was "abundant evidence that other persons participated in the crime." Hoffman was deeply critical of police superintendent Norman Schwarzkopf (father of "Stormin' Norman" of Gulf War fame) and prosecutor David Wilentz, whose zeal to convict Hauptmann led him to cross ethical lines. Hoffman's efforts were unfruitful, and Hauptmann was executed on April 3, 1936.

Harold Hoffman paid a heavy price for going against the grain in the Lindbergh case. At the time, he appeared to be a rising star in the Republican Party, having progressed from congressman to governor of New Jersey. But instead of launching a presidential bid, after his party failed to renominate him for a third term as governor, Hoffman inexplicably slid back into the position of director of the state's Unemployment Compensation Commission. In March of 1954, new governor Robert B. Meyner allegedly uncovered a large embezzlement scheme involving Hoffman, and he was suspended from his Unemployment Commission post. A few months later, on June 4, 1954, the fifty-eight-year-old Hoffman was found dead in a New York City hotel room of a purported heart attack. Conveniently, just prior to his death, Hoffman had taken the time to write out a detailed confession in which he admitted to embezzling more than $300,000 from the state. The tone was more akin to a suicide note, leaving inquiring minds to wonder how Hoffman knew he was going to die. Some sources, in fact, report that Hoffman did take his own life. In an even odder twist, more than 23,000 documents related to the Lindbergh case were discovered in Hoffman's garage in 1985, causing Anna Hauptmann to launch a wrongful death lawsuit, claiming that the documents revealed explosive information such as the fact the autopsy on the baby identified as Lindbergh's son was performed by an intoxicated coroner, and that the handwriting experts had changed their opinion as to whether Hauptmann had written the ransom notes after talking to police.

Anna Hauptmann lived into her nineties and never remarried, never even removed her wedding ring. She lobbied for decades to try and clear Richard Hauptmann's name. She was unsuccessful in her efforts to obtain legal restitution for the shameful execution of her husband, but that doesn't detract from her bravery and perseverance. To the end, she refused to say "and liberty and justice for all" when she pledged allegiance to the flag.[21] During those dark days, the authorities even falsely told her that her husband had confessed, and implicated her in the crime. They told Hauptmann, on the other hand, that his wife was being held in prison with a bunch of prostitutes and was going insane over the ordeal. Despite it all, Hauptmann clung to his heartfelt protestations of innocence, and his loyal wife never stopped believing in him. Researcher L. C. Vincent interviewed the still passionate Anna Hauptmann in 1981, and detailed her recollection that "her Richard" had been beside her in bed the night of the kidnapping, as he had been every night of their marriage. She even produced a Bible and swore upon it. She reiterated that Harold Hoffman had visited Hauptmann one final time the night before his execution, and offered to commute his sentence to life in prison, if he'd admit to some kind of involvement in the kidnapping. The ever-proud Hauptmann refused to falsely admit to anything.

Amanda Stevens, granddaughter of Jack Cunningham, who'd worked in the New Jersey Sheriff's office at the time the Lindbergh case was being "investigated," would write in a letter on Henry Makow's web site on September 25, 2015, that her grandfather had "said they were all sworn to secrecy but they all knew Hauptmann was set up." This should be taken with a grain of salt, as Jack Cunningham's name appears nowhere in the literature of this case. However, he could have been a deputy or even a file clerk and still have been aware of the general feeling within law enforcement. Anna Hauptmann received a letter from a witness who'd seen her and Richard together at the bakery where she worked on the night of the kidnapping. The letter stated:

> When I saw the picture of your husband in the paper, I knew it was the same man I saw with you. I want to help you, but I am afraid to come to Flemington. I gave that letter to the reporters. They never did anything about it . . . . One day during the trial, a reporter named Pat McGrady rode with me to Flemington. I said, "Why do they write all these terrible stories about Richard?" He said, "They the press cannot let the truth come out now because then you could sue every one of them." So ever since then I avoid the press.

There is no way of knowing how many other witnesses with information that would contradict the official story were similarly afraid to come forward.

Anna Hauptmann had to endure chants of "Kill Hauptmann!" and "Kill the German!" as she entered court each day during the farce of a trial, which H. L. Mencken labeled "the biggest story since the Resurrection." Like her husband, she naively believed that the legal system would be fair, and that justice would be done. "You sit there every day," she observed, "and those witnesses go up there and swear on the Bible and then they lie. Even policemen lying. We were brought up—you respected a policeman like a teacher." FBI documents which were released later confirmed Anna's claims that Richard was beaten while in prison. Even when her son Manfred was being taunted by his young classmates, Anna steadfastly refused to change her name, maintaining there was no shame attached to it. She would state, in a 1981 interview, that she would love to meet Anne Morrow Lindbergh and "look into her eyes and tell her that my Richard didn't kill her baby."[22]

It's shameful that our corrupt judicial system executed a man who, if he committed any crime at all, was guilty of spending money that he thought his business partner owed him anyway. The record shows that Hauptmann couldn't have been there that night if he wanted to, there was a group of kidnappers, if there was a kidnapping, and he never was given adequate legal defense. Hauptmann's defense attorney, "Death House" Reilly, confided to an FBI agent that he didn't like his client, knew he was guilty, and was hopeful he'd get the electric chair.

While books like Scaduto's *Scapegoat* and Ludovic Kennedy's *The Airman and the Carpenter* presented incontrovertible evidence that Hauptmann had not kidnapped the Lindbergh baby, the mainstream media continues to promote the official story. In 2005, the TruTV television program *Forensic Files* re-examined the physical evidence in a predictable, dishonest way. The show supported all the discredited evidence in the prosecution's case, down to the ramshackle ladder and expert "identification" match between Hauptmann's writing and the ransom notes. In 2011, Clint Eastwood's movie *J. Edgar* included a superficial portrayal of the Lindbergh kidnapping, utilizing all the flawed arguments the prosecution used, and failed to mention that Hoover himself doubted the official story.

The truth, as usual, is contrary to what is promulgated by the court historians. As Ludovic Kennedy put it, "From the day Hauptmann was arrested . . . there was not a single piece of evidence against him that was not faked, perjured or mistaken." The sad saga of Richard Hauptmann is a grim reminder that each of us may be only a corrupt police force, an unscrupulous prosecutor, and a vengeful jury away from being legally framed, simply for being in the wrong place at the wrong time. His conviction and execution represent one of the ugliest episodes in American history.

CHAPTER EIGHT

FDR CHANNELS LINCOLN

When I saw him spending all his time of ease and recreation with the big partners of Mr. John D. Rockefeller, Jr., with such men as the Astors and company, maybe I ought to have had better sense than to have believed he would ever break down their big fortunes to give enough to the masses to end poverty.

—Huey Long

Franklin Delano Roosevelt was elected president in 1932. He went on to be reelected three times, serving into an unprecedented fourth term before dying in office. He is the court historians' second favorite president; only the sainted Abraham Lincoln gets better press. He abused his executive powers nearly as thoroughly as Lincoln did, sabotaged his own forces at Pearl Harbor, and began construction of the gargantuan, unproductive, unresponsive, but all-powerful federal bureaucracy we have grown to know and love.

Following his 1932 election, Roosevelt set about implementing a series of drastic proposals, collectively referred to as the New Deal. Roosevelt's slew of "alphabet" agencies was something totally new in America. One followed after another: the Public Works Administration (PWA), Agricultural Adjustment Administration (AAA), the National Recovery Administration (NRA), Federal Emergency Relief Administration (FERA), Federal Deposit Insurance Corporation (FDIC), Civilian Conservation Corps (CCC), Civil Works Administration (CWA), Farm Credit Administration (FCA), Federal Communications Commission (FCC), Tennessee Valley Authority (TVA), Security and Exchange Commission (SEC), Works Progress Administration (WPA), and Social Security Administration, among many others. Needless to say, Thomas Jefferson and the other Founding Fathers would have been aghast at this dramatic increase in the size and scope of the federal government. While FDR was soundly criticized by most of the nation's publishers (who were generally far more conservative in those days) and business leaders, he also created plenty of enemies on the left. Populists like Huey Long felt that FDR was addressing America's severe economic woes inadequately, and becoming far too cozy with big bankers and the corporate world.

In 1933, General Smedley Butler told a congressional committee that a group of wealthy industrialists were planning a military coup to overthrow FDR, and had approached him to help lead it. Predictably, the mainstream media ridiculed Butler's outrageous conspiracy theory. On the surface, the story made little sense—why would conspirators think that such an overt anti-fascist would support and participate in a fascist coup? Butler was an unusually honorable man, and it is a certainty he was telling the truth about being approached. It seems highly unlikely, however, that powerful forces were actually planning such a coup. The story received its widest currency in Jules Archer's book *The Plot to Seize the White House* (1973). Judging from Archer's other works, he is hardly a believer in "conspiracies."

In January 1935, the Supreme Court struck down a key provision of the National Industrial Recovery Act and FDR's Railroad Retirement Act, and then invalidated several other New Deal laws, including an early effort at setting a federal minimum wage. The Roosevelt administration was irate. Attorney General Homer Cummings privately wrote the president, "We will have to find a way to get rid of the present membership of the Supreme Court." Roosevelt castigated the Supreme Court for being a relic from the "horse and buggy days." The Roosevelt administration attempted to circumvent the constitutional checks and balances by devising a so-called "court packing" scheme, whereby a new judge could be added for every elderly justice who continued to serve on the court. Despite the ensuing negative public backlash, FDR's failed power grab managed to mysteriously alter the philosophy of the existing Supreme Court. By 1937, the Court had reversed its decision on minimum wage, found Social Security and related legislation constitutional, and upheld the National Labor Relations Act. The Supreme Court had turned an ugly corner here; as one of their rulings upholding price controls stated, "Neither property rights nor contract rights are absolute."

The establishment historians tell us that FDR "saved" the country at its most perilous economic moment, much as Lincoln had "saved" the Union seventy years before. This is a typically misleading bit of propaganda. In fact, the United States remained mired in a depression until the advent of World War II. Even then, the Great Depression didn't truly end until World War II did. As even the *Wall Street Journal* admitted, it's a myth that Roosevelt "got us out of the Depression."[1] Powerful presidents—in other words, those who circumvent their constitutional authority—are greatly admired by scholars and historians. Roosevelt utilized executive orders far more extensively than any other president; he issued a whopping 3,721 during his tenure in office, more than double the number of his closest competitor, Woodrow Wilson. Only Harry Truman has even approached 1,000 executive orders since then. Many of these orders simply created dozens of offices and boards. Perhaps the ugliest was the order authorizing the placement of Japanese-American citizens in internment camps. FDR started the executive-orders ball rolling by taking the United States off the gold standard on April 19, 1933. He established the export-import bank, which triggered more commerce between the US and other nations and was an important step towards globalism.

Like Lincoln, Roosevelt engendered opposition all across the spectrum. Powerful supporters who gradually became opponents of his New Deal included William Randolph Hearst, journalist Walter Lippmann, Raymond Moley—an initial member of FDR's celebrated "brain trust"—Ambassador Joseph P. Kennedy, one-time Democratic Party presidential nominee Al Smith, Postmaster General James A. Farley, and his own vice president John Nance Garner, who broke with Roosevelt over his court-packing scheme. The America First Committee and national hero aviator Charles Lindbergh were strongly opposed to Roosevelt's foreign policy. Roosevelt was lauded as a great champion of civil rights, but he managed to deeply offend Olympic hero Jesse Owens. Following the 1936 Olympic Games in Berlin, in which Owens won four gold medals, the white American athletes were invited to the White House to meet FDR, but not Owens or the other blacks. Owens bitterly remarked, "Hitler didn't snub me—it was Roosevelt who snubbed me. The president didn't even send me a telegram." Despite this, the myth still persists that Hitler was so incensed over Owens's victories that *he* refused to meet with him. Historical revisionists have proven that Hitler in fact had been forbidden by the Olympic Committee to fraternize or even shake hands with any of the competitors. The reports about Owens being treated poorly by the German fans were untrue as well; in fact, William J. Baker, Jesse Owens' biographer, reported that Owens captured the imagination of the crowd to such an extent that they gave him several ear-shattering ovations. Later, Owens would admit that he had received the greatest ovations of his career in Berlin. It was further reported that the great "liberal" FDR segregated his servants by race and forbid them to eat together. It's a matter of public record that Roosevelt never lent his support to any anti-lynching legislation. FDR told Churchill that bringing black immigrants into the country was a nightmare waiting to happen, explaining that America already had "some eight million dark-skinned gentlemen and I don't want them coming to the United States and adding to the problem we already have with our thirteen million black men."

It was obvious early on that Roosevelt's administration was packed with the same old predictable faces. Shortly before FDR's first inauguration, Huey Long reportedly yelled at FDR brain-truster Raymond Moley, "I don't like you and your goddamned banker friends!" A few months into the Roosevelt administration, Long continued to focus on FDR's association with powerful bankers, exclaiming, "Parker Gilbert from Morgan & Company, Leffingwell, Ballantine, Eugene Meyer, every one of them are here—what's the use of hemming and hawing?" Long would derisively refer to FDR as the "Knight of the Nourmahal" (the name of FDR's yacht). Popular "radio priest" Father Charles Coughlin charged that the New Deal was "a government of the bankers, by the bankers, and for the bankers." Populist North Dakota congressman William Lemke, who would go on to run against FDR as a third-party candidate in 1936, observed, "The President drove the money changers out of the Capitol on March 4th and they were all back on the 9th." Roosevelt refused to meet with Dr. Francis Townsend, nationally known advocate of an old-age pension plan; a Townsend supporter would state, "If only he would spend as much time looking after the welfare of the people as he does playing on his yacht."

While the economy failed to revive, Roosevelt began prepping the nation for entrance into the new European conflict which would become World War II. The passage of the Lend-Lease Act in March 1941, which authorized the appropriation of funds to "the government of any country whose defense the President deems vital to the defense of the United States," was a thumbing of the nose to the America First Committee and other opponents

of American involvement in the European war, crudely slandered as "iso-
lationists" by the mainstream press. America First Committee New York
chairman John T. Flynn called Lend-Lease "an outright act of war." Left-
wingers like socialist Norman Thomas, Governor Philip LaFollette, and
writer Sinclair Lewis also assisted the America First Committee's efforts.
Invoking the style of his kindred spirit Abe Lincoln, Roosevelt labeled the
most famous non-interventionist, aviator Charles Lindbergh, as a "copperhead." Later, Roosevelt would pressure several airline companies not to hire
the famed aviator. Public opinion polls showed that a vast majority of the
American people, with memories still fresh of the pointless carnage from
World War I, opposed American involvement. FDR made another bold
move towards war in July 1941, when he sent US Naval forces to invade
Iceland. The "liberal" FDR's ridiculous rationale (that America was "protecting" Iceland so that Germany wouldn't occupy it) set the template for
all those future invasions and occupations of sovereign countries. John T.
Flynn fumed that "This audacious act may well mean the beginning of the
end of constitutional government in the United States."

The establishment's efforts to lobby for war were delineated in the
following passage from the book *Propaganda and the Next War* by Sidney
Rogerson and Liddell Hart: "To persuade her (the United States) to take
our part . . . will need a definite threat to America . . . which will have to be
brought home by propaganda to every citizen." John T. Flynn and others
objected mightily to the "appeasement" label, which has been used against
advocates of peace or even diplomacy ever since. Flynn and the America
First Committee publicized a letter written by Winston Churchill during
World War I, in which the future prime minister stated, "Nothing will
bring the Americans in on our side quicker than a little American blood
spilled." 1941 congressional hearings on the impact of British-inspired
pro-war propaganda, spurred by the America First Committee, received
strangely little publicity. Again revealing the bogus nature of America's

"two party" system was the movie industry's hiring of 1940 Republican presidential candidate Wendell Willkie to represent them in the hearings. Willkie, political "opponent" of FDR, made the same identical inference that Roosevelt and other pro-war Democrats had; that all those in favor of keeping out of the war were supporters of Hitler.

One of the most vociferous pro-war advocates in Hollywood was Charlie Chaplin. In a 1940 interview, Chaplin was asked about his unprecedented turn to the camera at the end of his film *The Great Dictator*, in which he directly called for a confrontation with the dictator he'd been lampooning. "There was no other way I could adequately express how strongly I felt," Chaplin said. "I wanted to make them (members of the audience) stop being so damned contented. This isn't just another war. Fascism means the end of our world." It hardly seemed debatable that pro-war advocates were using the film industry, newspapers, and radio to disseminate propaganda designed to lure America into the European conflict. An almost totally unpublicized anti-trust complaint by Attorney General Robert Jackson, filed in November 1940 against eight major film companies, was dropped, according to John T. Flynn and others, in exchange for "favors the movie-producing cartel agreed to extend to Roosevelt." Flynn claimed, "There is plenty of evidence of collaboration the film magnates and the government to whip up war hysteria."[2]

Powerful radio personality Walter Winchell, like almost all his peers a diehard interventionist, referred to the America First Committee as "the Hitler First-America Last-Committee." Shamefully, Pulitzer Prize-winning poet Archibald MacLeish became a paid propagandist for the Roosevelt administration after his appointment as librarian of Congress. MacLeish helped develop the "Research and Analysis Branch" of the OSS, forerunner to the CIA. He also served in the Office of War Information. In a precursor to what would later transpire under corrupt television networks, MacLeish actually impersonated the voices of supposed subjugated people in Europe, who were desperately calling on America for assistance.[3] Writer John Steinbeck was so fond of FDR's policies that he proposed the establishment of an official propaganda office utilizing the talents of the entertainment industry, and even suggested the counterfeiting of Germans marks in order to damage Hitler. A private 1939 letter from FDR to *Yale Review* editor Wilbur Cross revealed the president urging that "John Flynn . . . should be barred hereafter from the columns of any presentable daily paper, monthly magazine, or national quarterly." In fact, Flynn's professional career was dramatically impacted by his antiwar views; the previously well-regarded liberal was dismissed by *The New Republic* and then dropped as an associate editor by *Collier's* magazine, and the Scripps-Howard newspaper chain cancelled his nationally syndicated column. True liberals were aghast at the overt nature of the mainstream media's pro-war bias. Widely considered the dean of American liberals, Oswald Garrison Villard resigned as editor of *The Nation* after forty-six years, explaining, "I regret all the more that my retirement has been precipitated at this time by the other editors' abandonment of the *Nation*'s steadfast opposition to all preparations for war, to universal military service, to a great navy, and to all war." Laughably, the leader of one of the most vocal interventionist outfits, Clark Eichelberger, was a director of the League of Nations Association and the Union for Concerted Peace Efforts.[4]

In the spirit of Lincoln, and setting the template for nearly all future US presidents, Roosevelt blasted antiwar advocates as "appeasers" and "compromisers" and claimed they were proposing a course that was "perilous to our national security." FDR's Selective Service Act created the first peacetime draft in American history. Draftees were compelled to serve a twelve-month term; draft resisters were imprisoned for up to a year. In July 1941, the treacherous Roosevelt simply informed draftees that their twelve-month terms of service were being unilaterally increased. Perhaps FDR's most delusional supporter in Congress was Florida's Claude Pepper, who "represented" his constituents for over forty years. The intensely pro-war Pepper called objections to an extension of military service "quibbling," and warned that draftees might have to serve ten years or even longer, with an irrational proclamation that "This contest shall not be over until Armageddon is fought!" As had happened in the Spanish-American War and World War I, a calamitous event was about to occur, which would once again incite the masses to call for war.

PEARL HARBOR

If Tyranny and Oppression come to this land, it will be in the guise of fighting a foreign enemy.

—James Madison

On April 28, 1941, Winston Churchill wrote a secret directive to his war cabinet that read, "It may be taken as almost certain that the entry of Japan into the war would be followed by the immediate entry of the United States on our side." A few weeks later, Robert Menzies, prime minister of Australia, commented that Roosevelt ". . . trained under Woodrow Wilson in the last war, waits for an incident, which would in one blow get the USA into war and get R. out of his foolish election pledges that 'I will keep you out of war.'" Like Wilson, Roosevelt had specifically pledged not to involve America in the European conflict; at a campaign address as late as October 30, 1940, FDR vowed, "I have said this before, but I shall say it again and again and again: your boys are not going to be sent into any foreign wars." The public record clearly exposes FDR's desire for war. FDR's advisor Harold Ickes sent him a memo the day after Germany invaded the Soviet Union, which said, "There might develop from the embargoing of oil to Japan such a situation as would make it not only possible but easy to get into this war in an effective way. And if we should thus indirectly be brought in, we would avoid the criticism that we had gone in as an ally of communistic Russia." FDR was pleased with Admiral Richmond Turner's July 22, 1941 report that "It is generally believed that shutting off the American supply of petroleum will lead promptly to the invasion of Netherland East Indies . . . it seems certain she would also include military action against the Philippine Islands, which would immediately involve us in a Pacific war." On July 24, FDR told the Volunteer Participation Committee, "If we had cut off the oil, they probably would have gone down to the Dutch East Indies a year ago, and you would have had war." The following day FDR froze all Japanese assets in America, cutting off their main supply of oil. Intelligence information was withheld from Hawaii from this point forward. On August 14, at the Atlantic Conference, Winston Churchill marveled at the "astonishing depth of Roosevelt's intense desire for war" and cabled his cabinet: "(FDR) obviously was very determined that they should come in."

In an October 18, 1941 diary entry, Secretary of the Interior Harold Ickes wrote, "For a long time I have believed that our best entrance into the war would be by way of Japan." On November 25, 1941, Secretary of War Henry L. Stimson wrote in his diary, after attending an important meeting with Roosevelt, Gen. George C. Marshall, and three other ranking military advisors, that FDR. ". . . brought up the event that we were likely to be attacked perhaps (as soon as) next Monday, for the Japanese are notorious for making an attack without warning. . . . The question was how we should maneuver them into the position of firing the best first shot without allowing too much danger to ourselves."[5] The only piece of Churchill's voluminous correspondence with Roosevelt that remains classified (on the grounds of national security!) is his message sent on November 26, 1941. FDR's provocative reply, which isn't classified, was, "Negotiations off. Services expect action within two weeks." Then there was Secretary of War Stimson's confusing warning on November 27, which a Navy court would later find directed attention away from Pearl Harbor. On November 30, a foreboding headline appeared in Hawaii's *Hilo Tribune Herald* newspaper. It read simply: "Japan May Strike Over Weekend." On November 29, Secretary of State Cordell Hull showed United Press reporter Joe Leib a message stating that Pearl Harbor was going to be attacked on December 7. The December 2 edition of the *Washington Post* reported, "President Roosevelt yesterday assumed direct command of diplomatic and military moves relating to Japan." A message subsequently expunged from the record was received by the Navy on December 4, signaling an attack from Japan. The same day, General Elliott R. Thorpe was serving in Dutch-controlled Java when the Japanese diplomatic code was broken and the intercepted messages were found regarding planned Japanese attacks on Hawaii and the Philippines. He forwarded the messages to Washington, but was *ordered to stop* sending them.

Pulitzer Prize-winning author John Toland was a well-respected establishment historian until his book *Infamy* was published in 1982. A painstaking expose of Roosevelt's foreknowledge of the "sneak" attack on Pearl Harbor, the book was met with universal disdain by respectable scholars. Highly regarded court historian Barbara Tuchman reacted by calling Toland a "Nazi." Since the book dealt exclusively with the circumstances surrounding the "sneak" attack on Pearl Harbor, which had nothing whatsoever to do with Germany, this was even more ridiculous than the pronouncements of most establishment historians. Toland recounted how, at a December 5, 1941 Cabinet meeting, Secretary of the Navy Frank Knox had said, "Well, you know Mr. President, we know where the Japanese fleet is?" "Yes, I know," FDR replied. "I think we ought to tell everybody just how ticklish the situation is. We have information as Knox just mentioned. . . . Well, you tell them what it is, Frank." Knox became very excited and said, "Well, we have very secret information that the Japanese fleet is out at sea. Our information is—" and then a scowling FDR cut him off.[6] Toland also described how Roosevelt and his top aides "deliberately sat through the night of December 6, 1941 waiting for the Japs to strike." On the evening of December 6, FDR reportedly told his thirty-four dinner guests, "The war starts tomorrow." FDR aide Harry Hopkins would memorably detail how the president, upon receiving official word of the attack from Knox, expressed "great relief." Even FDR's wife Eleanor would characterize her husband's behavior afterward as "in a way more serene." In the *New York Times Magazine* of October 8, 1944 Eleanor wrote: "December 7 was . . . far from the shock it proved to the country in general. We had expected something of the sort for a long time."

When the Philippines were attacked by the Japanese some nine hours after they bombed Pearl Harbor, General Douglas MacArthur's entire air force was wiped out. Upon receiving news of the attack on Pearl Harbor, MacArthur oddly locked himself in his room and refused to meet with his air commander. He also refrained from attacking Japanese forces on Formosa after being ordered to by the War Department. As Gordon W. Prange wrote in his book *At Dawn We Slept*, "How could the President ensure a successful Japanese attack unless he confided in his commanders and persuaded them to allow the enemy to proceed unhindered?" Roosevelt's press secretary Jonathan Daniels would confess, "The blow was heavier than he had hoped it would necessarily be . . . but the risks paid off; even the loss was worth the price." FDR asked trusted establishment journalist Edward R. Murrow, in regards to the Pearl Harbor attack, "Maybe you think it didn't surprise us?" He gave the definite impression that the attack hadn't been unwelcome. FDR needn't have worried; journalists like Murrow, then and now, were conditioned not to ask pertinent questions.

Declassified British documents revealed even more clearly the extent of Roosevelt's treachery. The same documents exposed the fact that Winston Churchill—considered another heroic icon by establishment historians—was fearful that the Soviets would either collapse or accept peace terms after being invaded by Hitler in June 1941. In the "most secret" Atlantic conference record, Churchill was quoted as saying, "The President had said that he would wage war but not declare it, and that he would become more and more provocative. If the Germans did not like it they could attack the American forces." In reference to the upcoming attack on Pearl Harbor, the papers reported, "Everything was to be done to force an incident to justify hostilities." A week later, British Ambassador to Washington Lord Halifax reported to the British Cabinet that virtually everyone in the Roosevelt administration was anxious for war "and would be relieved if some incident, such as the torpedoing of an American ship, precipitated this event." During Churchill's War Cabinet meeting of August 19, 1941 it was mentioned that "Everything was to be done to force an incident." Dr. Milton Eisenhower, president of John Hopkins University, and brother of the president, charged that "Regretfully, President Roosevelt found it necessary to get the country into World War Two to save his social policies."

General Albert Wedermeyer stated that:

> Franklin D. Roosevelt, the professed exponent of democracy, was as successful as any dictator in keeping the Congress and the public in the dark about his secret commitments . . . which scoffed at the wish and will of the voters, who had re-elected Roosevelt only because he had assured them that he would keep us out of the war. In fact, there are few more shameless examples of cynical disregard of the people's will than those which came to light in Roosevelt's personal correspondence with Churchill . . . prove beyond doubt that Roosevelt, already in January 1941, had concluded a secret alliance with Great Britain, which pledged America to war.

The former War Minister of Brazil, Manuel deGoes Monteiro, disclosed that General George C. Marshall, while accompanying President Roosevelt on a 1939 trip to his country, told him that the United States was planning to enter the war alongside England. Former congressman Hamilton Fish would declare, "The shocking and amazing revelations of former Secretary of War Henry L. Stimson prove conclusively the charges made by me and other leading non-interventionists in Congress that President Roosevelt and his specially selected cabinet of ardent and militant interventionists maneuvered us into war against the will of 80% of the American people. Mr. Stimson openly states that the note sent by Secretary of State Hull on November 26th, 1941, ten days before Pearl Harbor, was a war ultimatum to Japan." Another revealing diary entry, from Secretary of War Stimson, disclosed, "We realized that in order to have the full support of the American people it was desirable to make sure that the Japanese be the ones to do this so there should remain no doubt in anyone's mind as to who were the aggressors."

In 2011, a remarkable book written by FDR's predecessor, *Freedom Betrayed: Herbert Hoover's History of the Second World War and its Aftermath*, was published. The *American Conservative* called it "a searing indictment of FDR and the men around him as politicians who lied prodigiously about their desire to keep America out of war, even as they took one deliberate step after another to take us into war." It was fully documented with first-hand source material, such as the notes from a November 25, 1941 meeting of Roosevelt's war council, during which Henry Stimson reported: "The question was how we should maneuver them (the Japanese) into . . . firing the first shot without allowing too much danger to ourselves." Secretary of the Navy Frank Knox added, "We can wipe the Japanese off the map in three months." Hoover has been maligned for decades by historians and unfairly blamed for the Great Depression. He'd been the only member of the American delegation at Versailles in 1919 to recognize how unfair the demands being placed on Germany were, and how they could lead inexorably to another war. Critical reception for Hoover's book seemed to either label it a self-serving effort by an overly sensitive Hoover (the *Wall Street*

Journal claimed the title should have been "He Knew He Was Right") or avoid any references to FDR's culpability at Pearl Harbor.

There was, of course an official "investigation" into Pearl Harbor afterwards. In fact, there were several, the most notable being the presidentially appointed commission chaired by Supreme Court Justice Owen J. Roberts. The Roberts Commission found the commanders at Pearl Harbor, Admiral Husband Kimmel and General Walter Short, guilty of "dereliction of duty." The Roberts Commission held only a few days of hearings in Washington, while spending nineteen days in Hawaii, with more vacationing than investigating taking place. Foretelling the interrogations of Lee Harvey Oswald in Dallas two decades later, all testimony taken before the Roberts Commission in Washington was unsworn and *unrecorded*. The Commission denied counsel to Kimmel. During the Hawaii sessions, Kimmel was astounded that the stenographers omitted much of his testimony and inaccurately recorded other parts. Again, this would become standard operating procedure during the "investigation" into the death of John F. Kennedy. The Commission actually refused to allow the errors to be corrected in the record. Again like the Warren Commission, whose member Senator Richard Russell had disagreed with the findings, Admiral William Standley was not allowed to write a dissenting minority report, on the grounds that doing so would harm the war effort. Standley later called Roberts's handling of the investigation "as crooked as a snake." Admiral William "Bull" Halsey was among those who called Kimmel and Short "scapegoats for something over which they had no control."

Kimmel and Short had been chosen as scapegoats right away; Kimmel was stripped of his command after the attack and demoted to the rank of two-star rear admiral. Kimmel had notified the Chief of Naval Operations back in February that "I feel that a surprise attack . . . on Pearl Harbor is a possibility." Kimmel's son was rumored to have been captured by the Japanese and burned to death during the war. Short claimed that the message he received on November 27 had said nothing about an impending air attack. He was adamant that he'd not been given adequate warning and had been saddled by a lack of resources. Anxious to clear his name and restore his rank, Short demanded to be court-martialed. In August 1944 a Naval Court of Inquiry exonerated Kimmel of all charges. The Army Pearl Harbor Board fingered General George C. Marshall and his chief of war plans, ending their report: "Up to the morning of December 7, 1941, everything that the Japanese were planning to do was known to the United States . . . except the very hour and minute when bombs were falling on Pearl Harbor." In 1999, the US Senate approved a vote to exonerate Short and Kimmel. "They were denied vital intelligence that was available in Washington," Senator William V. Roth said, while Senator Strom Thurmond dubbed them "the two final victims of Pearl Harbor." Bill Clinton, all too characteristically, declined to act on the resolution and restore the deceased men's wartime rankings. Earlier, both Presidents Nixon and Reagan had turned down requests to have Kimmel's four-star rank restored. I spoke to Manning Kimmel IV, grandson of Husband Kimmel, in July of 2016. He remains committed to restoring his grandfather's name, and is working on his own book.

Over 2,400 Americans, including sixty-eight civilians, were killed at Pearl Harbor, while nearly 1,200 were wounded. The evidence that Franklin Roosevelt not only knew that Pearl Harbor was going to be attacked, but greatly desired such an incendiary incident, is overwhelming. Despite this, the mere mention of his pre-knowledge is met with the typical howls and scorn from the respectable historical and academic communities. There are documents relating to Pearl Harbor which remain classified. Others were inexplicably destroyed. When Robert Stinnett's book *Day of Deceit* was published in 1999, it was negatively received by the court historians, even though Stinnett actually felt that Roosevelt's treachery *had been warranted*. A June 14, 2001 hit piece in *Salon* quoted a

CIA historian, Donald Steury, who dismissed the book with the blanket statement, "Basically, the author has made up his sources; when he does not make up the source, he lies about what the source says." Another pillar of the establishment, Philip Zelikow, who later served as chairman of the 9/11 Commission, also objected to the book's claims in the March-April 2000 issue of *Foreign Affairs*, the elite insider magazine published by the Council on Foreign Relations.

The idea that Roosevelt could have been guilty of such chicanery is something the court historians simply won't accept, regardless of how many documents are released due to Freedom of Information Act lawsuits by writers like Stinnett. Indeed, Stinnett unearthed numerous documents with FOIA suits, none of which are "made up" or "lies," as the CIA historian would have us believe. John Toland praised Stinnett, stating that his "Freedom of Information requests finally persuaded the Navy to release the evidence." During his 1944 presidential campaign against FDR, Thomas Dewey planned a series of speeches charging him with foreknowledge of the attack on Pearl Harbor. Again, the "loyalty" card was played, as General Marshall, then chairman of the Joint Chiefs of Staff, prevailed upon Dewey not to raise the issue. The establishment historians are fully vested in these official narratives. Franklin Roosevelt is one of their sacred icons. He is portrayed as being altruistic, daring, and concerned with the welfare of the common people. The evidence that suggests otherwise is merely shoved down the memory hole. In the conventional history books, Roosevelt is a great "liberal," lover of peace, anxious to help the poor and dispossessed.

JEANNETTE RANKIN

You can no more win a war than you can win an earthquake.

—Jeannette Rankin

Jeannette Rankin should be one of the most celebrated female figures in American history. An argument can be made that she is *the* greatest American woman who ever lived. And yet she remains an astonishingly obscure figure. Rankin was the first woman ever elected to Congress. In 1917, she was one of fifty House members to vote against American entrance into World War I. In 1941, she was the only member in the entire Congress to vote against declaring war on Japan. As an early suffragette and a lifelong pacifist, she should be a darling of the left. Like Huey Long and other true progressives, however, she receives little attention compared to establishment eugenicists like Margaret Sanger or pro-war devotees like Clarence Darrow.

After her lone courageous vote for peace following the attack on Pearl Harbor, Rankin was forced to take refuge in a cloakroom until police arrived to escort her safely to her office. She would subsequently abstain from voting for war against Germany and Italy. Rankin was attacked mercilessly by everyone from the Kiwanis and Rotary Clubs to radio commentators. Her political career was over, and she didn't run for reelection in 1942. Asked years later if she regretted her vote, Rankin steadfastly declared, "Never. If you're against war, you're against war regardless of what happens. It's a wrong method of trying to settle a dispute."

CRUSHING DOMESTIC DISSENT

Over 2,000 German-American residents had been incarcerated by President Woodrow Wilson during World War I, but FDR took this view of internal "enemies" to a new level. Over 11,500 Americans of German ancestry were interned by the US government during World War II. A small number of Italian-Americans were relocated or interned as well. They are seldom mentioned by historians and certainly never received any reparations, as did the families of the estimated 110,000–120,000 Japanese-Americans who were forced into US concentration camps. Like Lincoln before him, Roosevelt brooked no dissent from those who opposed American involvement in the war. Renowned bohemian poet Ezra Pound angered Roosevelt with his anti-Semitic accusations that Jewish bankers had manipulated America into an unnecessary war, during radio broadcasts from Italy. FDR ordered Pound indicted as a traitor in 1943, but he wasn't arrested until the fall of Italy in 1945, just after the death of Roosevelt. Pound was interned for months in a US military camp, including three brutal weeks in a small outdoor cage. Despite the best efforts of notable literary figures like Ernest Hemingway and Robert Frost, Pound spent over a decade institutionalized in Washington, DC's St. Elizabeths psychiatric hospital before finally being released. Despite his overt anti-Semitism, Pound's supporters included young Jewish beat poet Allen Ginsberg.

Roosevelt's Attorney General Francis Biddle constructed the "Biddle List" of what he considered to be "subversive" organizations. In contrast to Richard Nixon's later anemic "enemies list," Biddle's list has received little to no scrutiny from the court historians. Biddle flirted with revoking Father Charles Coughlin's mailing rights, in order to shut down his *Social Justice* magazine. Using Wilson's Espionage Act of 1917 as a precedent, Biddle sought to stop what he called "vermin publications" from criticizing FDR and his policies. Aside from Coughlin, who was an unusual far left-wing anti-Semite, Biddle's list focused on groups accused of Communist affiliations. In 1942, Biddle oversaw the prosecution, by a Lincoln-style military tribunal, of eight captured Nazi agents. Six of these Germans were subsequently executed. Biddle would continue his career pursuit of "justice" as a judge with the International Military Tribunal at Nuremberg.

Franklin Roosevelt's enemies tended not to prosper. Huey Long, in an event still shrouded in mystery and controversy, was assassinated in September 1935. My book *Survival of the Richest* includes a detailed examination of the Long assassination, as well as Huey Long's political record. One of Roosevelt's fiercest congressional critics was Senator Ernest Lundeen, a Farmer-Labor party member from Minnesota. Lundeen had been one of the fifty members of Congress to vote against the declaration of war on Germany in 1917. Remaining consistent, Lundeen was a dedicated foe of intervention in the European conflict that would become World War II. On July 11, 1940, he delivered a blistering speech on the floor of Congress, attacking the Roosevelt administration over its blatant desire to fight Germany. Lundeen died in a plane crash on August 31, 1940, little more than a month later.

Laura Ingalls (a distant cousin of the famous children's author), although completely unheralded and unremembered today, was the first woman to fly coast-to-coast, the first woman to fly from North America to South America, and she set several major flight records. According to the National Air and Space Museum in Washington, DC, "It is difficult to find a great deal of information about Laura Ingalls." Maybe it's "difficult" because Ingalls was a fierce critic of Establishment saint Franklin Roosevelt, who often used her talents to bombard public events with flyers opposing FDR's war plans. In December 1941, she was charged with being a publicity agent for the German government, and served three months in prison. Despite years of appealing for a presidential pardon, and support from flying legend Eddie Rickenbacker, she never received one and died in obscurity.

Thomas D. Schall, a member of the House of Representatives and US Senate from Minnesota, was killed by a hit-and-run driver while crossing the Baltimore-Washington Parkway on December 19, 1935. Schall exchanged a series of letters with FDR in 1934, in which he excoriated the president. In an August 24, 1934 letter, Schall wrote:

> My dear Mr. Roosevelt: Your telegram to me bears out the suggestion of the constant effort to mislead and fool the public. Your desire to make yourself appear before the people of the United States as a champion of a

free press may be as insincere as your promises to the people when you accepted the Democratic nomination at Chicago. . . . But since you assume a cloak of innocence and since your telegram to me is in the hands of the press, it becomes my duty as a sentinel of the people to do what little I can to mitigate their deception by citing specific evidence of your intention to force a censorship of the press . . . in connection with the passage of the press censorship bill by the House in the special session of Congress called by you. Under your whip it passed the House and if the Senate had not taken out the poison a publisher who had not gained your approval or the approval of some of your appointees could be sentenced to ten years' imprisonment. The evidence convicting you of a desire to censor the press twenty-five days after you swore to uphold and defend the Constitution is in print in the archives of the House of Representatives. . . . Mr. President, in my opinion, secrecy and press censorship are never necessary when motives are pure. Every Government department under you is now cloaked in censorship. Almost every bill that has been forced through Congress by you has been in itself a little censorship, a little dictatorship either giving blanket powers to you. . . . You have created some forty-seven bureaucracies. . . . These regulations cover something like 2,000 pages of dictatorship. . . . The Communications bill originally introduced by you contained a press censorship clause which was stricken out before the bill was passed but it still gives you the power to inaugurate a Government telegraphic news service, under which as one example you immediately put out of business the three radio stations of Mr. Ford.

Especially after reading Schall's words, it is entirely appropriate to question why a fifty-seven-year-old congressman would ever be crossing a busy parkway as a pedestrian. The fact that Schall was legally blind makes his alleged crossing of such a parkway truly remarkable.

One of FDR's most powerful enemies was JFK's father Joseph P.

Kennedy, who had initially supported the president and became the first chairman of the SEC and then his Ambassador to England. Kennedy's "conspiracy" mindset was clearly expressed in his comment published in the July 26, 1936 edition of *The New York Times:* "Fifty men have run America, and that's a high figure." They'd actually struck swords years earlier, when, as assistant secretary of the Navy, FDR ordered the Marines to seize ships owned by Kennedy. Kennedy nevertheless campaigned diligently for FDR in 1932, and was disappointed at not being named secretary of the treasury. While later serving in England, Kennedy established a friendship with Prime Minister Neville Chamberlain and incurred the wrath of his up-and-coming successor, Winston Churchill. Kennedy strongly opposed America's entrance into World War II. He had the most understandable motive for doing so; his two oldest sons would both serve admirably, and his first, Joseph P. Kennedy Jr., would die tragically in a plane crash. That plane crash may actually have been the first Kennedy assassination; a still furious Joe Kennedy would admonish Harry Truman later about his campaigning for "that crippled son of a bitch who killed my son." Very little research has been conducted on this mysterious incident; the official report would conclude that the cause of the plane crash remained unknown. Very few parts of the B-24 craft were found, and not even the smallest trace of young Kennedy's body was recovered. It is a bizarre historical footnote that the plane flying closest in formation to Kennedy was piloted by Eliot Roosevelt, son of FDR. Eliot Roosevelt would publicly dismiss new theories, decades later, postulating that Kennedy had been part of a secret program testing early versions of drones. The Navy's informal board of review rejected the notion that the pilot of the B-24 could have erroneously armed the circuitry, and instead suspected that jamming or a stray signal was more likely to have detonated the payload. This has led the most extreme conspiracy theorists, such as one writing on the Have to Remember blog, to hypothesize that young Roosevelt, as the pilot of the plane closest to Kennedy's, might well have been the most logical person to have caused such a detonation.

The ambitious head of the Kennedy clan was mulling the prospect of challenging FDR and running for president himself in 1940. The conventional explanation for his failure to do so is that he reluctantly accepted the fact that America wasn't ready for a Catholic president. Conspiracy theorists tend to view Kennedy's secret 1940 meeting with Roosevelt, who was furious with all the "appeasement" talk coming from JFK's father, as highly significant. Whatever transpired at this meeting, immediately afterwards Roosevelt once again had Kennedy's full support. Joseph Kennedy lost not only his son in the war; his daughter Kathleen was killed in a separate plane crash. "For a fellow who didn't want this war to touch your country or mine," Joseph Kennedy wrote a friend in Britain, "I have had a rather bad dose . . . I have had brought home to me very personally what I saw for all the mothers and fathers of the world."

While John F. Kennedy continues to be smeared as a reprehensible serial adulterer, the court historians are unusually quiet about the numerous affairs of Franklin Roosevelt. Lucy Mercer Rutherford, Eleanor Roosevelt's social secretary, has received a bit of attention, but what about "Missy" LeHand, known as FDR's "other wife?" Or Margaret Suckley, FDR's *cousin*, who was set up with a secret love nest on the Roosevelt estate? FDR's wife Eleanor was also related to him—his fifth cousin once removed. Or Princess Martha of Norway, whom FDR purportedly blackmailed into having sex with him? Then there was FDR's ugly record as assistant secretary of the Navy, especially the brutal American occupation of Haiti. In the 1920 presidential campaign, Warren Harding charged, "Practically all we know is that thousands of native Haitians have been killed by American Marines, and that many of our own gallant men have sacrificed their lives at the behest of an executive department in order to establish laws drafted by the Assistant Secretary of the Navy." In a February 1, 1920 speech before the Brooklyn Academy of

Music, FDR audaciously admitted, "Two months after the war was declared, I saw that the Navy was still unprepared and I spent $40,000 for guns before Congress gave me or anyone permission to spend the money."

Supposedly, FDR once boasted that he had "committed enough illegal acts" to be impeached and imprisoned for "999 years."[7] In 1921, a Senate subcommittee concluded that FDR had committed perjury before a Naval Court of Inquiry investigating an undercover sting entrapping homosexuals at a Rhode Island naval station. Like many a politician to come, FDR used the IRS to target his enemies, such as Huey Long, Father Charles Coughlin, Rep. Hamilton Fish, publishers William Randolph Hearst and Moe Annenberg, and Charles Lindbergh. He also intervened in a tax fraud investigation of his political protégée, Lyndon B. Johnson.[8] FDR liberally used the FBI to obtain secrets on others; his own son John stated, "Hell, my father just about invented bugging." Roosevelt's sons prospered fantastically through nepotism and their father's crony connections. While the Kennedy family has been raked over the coals in recent years, with allegations of a huge cover-up of JFK's medical problems, the fact that FDR kept his polio a secret from the public is called "a splendid deception" by these same court historians. FDR, in the finest tradition of Abraham Lincoln, had actually prepared a speech to read in one of his "fireside chats," to explain why he was going to unconstitutionally ignore a Supreme Court decision. When the Court surprisingly ruled in his favor, FDR confided to an aide, "The nation will never know what a great treat it missed in not hearing the marvelous radio address." FDR laid out his political philosophy as early as 1912, where he said in a speech that the "liberty of the community" was more important than the "liberty of the individual," and claimed that the state had the right to force "idle" men to work.

Earl Browder, general secretary of the Communist Party USA, was delighted with Roosevelt, raving, "If the New Deal could be established, it should be possible to proceed from this, step by step, without violent overturning, to socialism." H. G. Wells wrote of FDR: "The exciting thing about him, as about Stalin, is that he, too, has more of the appearance of having modern objectives, however incompletely apprehended, than anyone else in the world." According to the aforementioned Senator Thomas D. Schall, "The Russian newspapers during the last election (1932) published the photograph of Franklin D. Roosevelt over the caption 'the first communistic President of the United States.'" Teddy Roosevelt Jr., evidently not a chip off the old block, blasted FDR in 1935 thusly: "You have been faithless. You have usurped the function of Congress, hampered freedom of the press. . . . You have urged Congress to pass laws that you knew were unconstitutional. . . . You have broken your sacred oath taken on the Bible." FDR would famously remark, "Several of my best friends are Communist." The Martin Dies Committee's investigation into Communist influence in government, which was a precursor of the McCarthy era and the House Un-American Activities Committee, deeply angered FDR, who told Dies, "There is no menace here in Communism . . . there is nothing wrong with the Communists in this country." In a blatant confession of his intentions, Roosevelt declared on March 2, 1930, "Now to bring about government by oligarchy masquerading as democracy, it is fundamentally essential that practically all authority and control be centralized in our national government. The individual sovereignty of our states must first be destroyed, except in mere minor matters of legislation."[9] The KGB archives listed 221 agents in the most sensitive sections of the Roosevelt administration as of April 1941.

Roosevelt's willingness to ally the United States government with odious mobster Charles "Lucky" Luciano during Operation Husky is seldom mentioned critically by historians. Fellow murderous thug Meyer Lansky informed Commander Charles R. Haffenden of the Office of Naval Intelligence (ONI) that Luciano proposed to be placed in the front lines during the American invasion of Sicily. Luciano felt he could use his Italian contacts to convert the public into supporting such an invasion. Apparently the absurd suggestion of sending the head of organized crime into a major theater of war was seriously considered by the US government. There were astonishingly few qualms on the part of officialdom about dealing with gangsters; Lieutenant Anthony J. Marsloe declared: "The exploitation of informants, irrespective of their backgrounds, is not only desirous, but necessary when the nation is struggling for its existence." While Luciano never went to the front lines, both he and Lansky provided intelligence to the government. "The Navy wanted from the Italians all the pictures they could possibly get of every port of Sicily, of every channel," said Lansky, "and also to get men that were in Italy more recently and had knowledge of water and coastlines—to bring them to the Navy so they could talk to them." Mobster "Socks" Lanza recalled, "Joe [Adonis] would just mention the name of Lucky Luciano and say he had given them orders to talk. If the Sicilians were still reluctant, Joe would stop smiling and say, 'Lucky will not be pleased to hear that you have not been helpful.'" That truly sounds like a bad line out of an old Hollywood movie. Lansky himself would escort these characters to the offices of Naval Intelligence.

It was inferred that another powerful Mafia kingpin, Frank Costello, was also involved in this curious project during the Senate testimony of federal narcotics agent George White. In 1950, White told the Kefauver Senate committee investigating organized crime that veteran drug smuggler August Del Grazio had approached him with a deal coming from Frank Costello on behalf of Luciano. "The proffered deal," recalled Senator Estes Kefauver, "was that Luciano would use his Mafia position to arrange contacts for undercover American agents and that therefore Sicily would be a much softer target than it might otherwise be." Luciano's asking price for all this was freedom from jail and travel to Sicily for him to personally make the arrangements. The government also used Luciano in Operation Underworld, in which he supposedly helped stop sabotage on the waterfronts. The US government denied these unsavory deals with organized crime for forty years, and the mainstream media has never taken Roosevelt to task for endorsing them. Meanwhile, the Kennedys continue to be lambasted over an imaginary connection with the mob, when in fact the Kennedy administration, under zealous Attorney General Robert F. Kennedy, remains the only presidential administration to date to actually wage war on organized crime. One of those "witnesses" who helped build this illegitimate notion was mobster Frank Costello, who publicly proclaimed in 1973 that he and Joe Kennedy Sr. had been bootlegging partners. The other "evidence" tying Kennedy to bootlegging or the mob comes from—you guessed it—mafia sources.

Next to Abraham Lincoln, the one American leader who most damaged the lives of ordinary citizens was President Franklin Roosevelt. From something as comparatively innocuous as setting up the ridiculous, meaningless daylight savings time, to lying and scheming American entry into World War II, Roosevelt could only be considered "great" by a demented civilization. US Army documents revealed that the Roosevelt and Truman administrations had formulated plans to drop poison gas bombs on Japanese cities during 1945, plans that were evidently preempted by the impending atomic bombs dropped on Hiroshima and Nagasaki. Roosevelt granted diplomatic recognition to the Soviet Union, in spite of the oppression of their people, and befriended one of the most cold- blooded dictators of modern times, our World War II ally "Uncle Joe," Joseph Stalin. A sickly FDR capped his brilliant career off by giving away much of central and eastern Europe to the Soviets at the Yalta conference.

MUSSOLINI

War is to man what maternity is to a woman. From a philosophical and doctrinal viewpoint, I do not believe in perpetual peace.

—Benito Mussolini

While the Nazis and the dirty sneaky rotten Japs have drawn most of the attention when discussing the Axis powers of World War II, Italy under Benito Mussolini certainly warrants a mention. In most ways a repugnant dictator, Mussolini did, as they say, make the trains run on time. Despite his tough talk, the Italian army was the butt of numerous jokes. The one about Italian tanks only being made with a forward gear to keep their soldiers from running away from the enemy, for instance. Or the one about the Italian battle flag being a white cross on a white background. It is difficult to see how anyone outside of Italy felt threatened by Mussolini's fascists. The conventional narrative regarding Mussolini's death is that he was executed by some communists, or at least strident anti-fascists. His body, along with those of other murdered fascist leaders, was hung upside down on meat hooks from the roof of a gas station, where it was stoned by angry civilians.

The UK *Independent* would acknowledge the court historian's typical dilemma in a September 18, 1995 headline, "Scholars in a Spin Over Churchill Link to the Death of Mussolini." The "conspiracy theory" in question had been raised by eminent Italian historian Renzo De Felice, who claimed that Mussolini had not been killed by his irate countrymen, but in fact assassinated by British secret services. The Churchill-Mussolini correspondence revealed how much Churchill desired to keep Italy out of the conflict. Intriguingly, De Felice claimed that Mussolini had been carrying a mysterious black bag containing even more secretive correspondence, which conveniently disappeared following his April 28, 1945 death. Churchill was allegedly so anxious to find this black bag that he personally visited northern Italy twice afterwards in a vain attempt to locate it. British court historian, Churchill scholar Andrew Roberts, predictably dismissed the "theory" as a "sub-Hitler-diary story . . . which flies in the face of everything we know about Churchill from the period." To the court historian, of course, "everything we know" about Churchill, or Roosevelt, or any other consensus "good guy," is that he would never have been guilty of such acts, regardless of the evidence. De Felice, who was a former communist turned socialist, died around the time his book was published. The only obituary I could find, in the May 26, 1996 *Seattle Times,* reported that no cause of death was given by his wife. In that same story, it was noted that "His opinions earned him critics. In February, a gasoline bomb was thrown against his apartment in Rome but caused no damage." In 2010, the mainstream media were reporting that another respectable historian, France's Pierre Milza, was alleging that Churchill had ordered Mussolini assassinated. There was even a witness here; one Bruno Lonati confessed that he had acted as part of a two-man team with British Special Operations Agent Robert Maccarone.[10]

ALLIED WAR ATROCITIES

The only difference I can see between these men and those corpses is that here they are still breathing.
—AP photographer Henry Griffin, comparing the prisoners in Allied
POW camps to the corpses he saw at Buchenwald and Dachau.

Roosevelt's boys in the field, like most American military forces, left behind a record few should be proud of. For instance, in World War II, American troops, at the behest of the British, destroyed Monte Cassino, a monastery in Latium, central Italy. Founded in 529 by St. Benedict of Nursia, Monte Cassino was one of the great centers of Christianity and an influential landmark of European civilization. There were accusations of the killing of Italian civilians by Lieutenant Colonel George McCaffrey. There was the beating and torture of captured German submarine crew members under Operation Teardrop. Untold numbers of German POWs were simply shot and killed after being captured at Normandy under Operation Overlord.

A number of unresisting guards were shot and killed after the liberation of Nazi concentration camps. At least one Army infantry unit was given written orders to kill SS paratroopers and soldiers, not take them prisoner. Major General Raymond Huff acknowledged later that "If the Germans had won, I would have been on trial at Nuremberg instead of them." Even high-profile court historian Stephen Ambrose admitted that about one-third of the 1,000 World War II veterans he had interviewed reported seeing US soldiers shooting unarmed, surrendering German prisoners. Files declassified in 2006 revealed that American military personnel had committed 400 sexual offenses in Europe, which included 126 rapes in England. Another study came up with more alarming statistics indicating that American soldiers had raped 14,000 civilian females in Germany, France, and England. Even more recent, truly horrifying research claimed that 190,000 rapes had actually been committed by the "Greatest Generation's" All-American boys.[11]

US military behavior in Japan was hardly any better. The taking of body parts for gruesome "trophies" became common among US troops. There is one sickening photo widely available online of a severed Japanese head left hanging proudly from a tree limb. Usually, however, the mutilated remnants of human beings were taken home as "souvenirs." President Roosevelt himself was said to have been the recipient of a letter opener, presented to him by a US congressman, which had been made from a man's arm. Columnist Drew Pearson quoted FDR as responding, "This is the sort of gift I like to get."[12] Charles Lindbergh recounted in his diary how US troops in New Guinea routinely killed Japanese "stragglers" in what he termed "a sort of hobby." Many veterans told researchers that the practice of taking gold teeth from the Japanese—even if they were alive—was widespread. In 1984, during the repatriation of Japanese remains from the Mariana Islands, some 60 percent were discovered to be missing skulls. These young members of the "greatest generation" honestly pictured such macabre "trophies" as valuable gifts to be sent to their loved ones. There have been persistent reports that surrendering Japanese soldiers were gunned down by US troops. A Marine battalion capturing a Japanese field hospital allegedly slaughtered over 400, including patients and medics. Rumors of mass rapes in Japan persist as well. Interviews finally published in *The New York Times* in 2000 recounted how US marines had regularly gathered all the local women, following their victory in the Battle of Okinawa, and carried them away into the hills to be raped. The nation's flagship newspaper referred to this mass rape of Okinawan women as "one of the most widely ignored crimes of the war." Rape in Japan became so prevalent that the Japanese were forced to create the Recreation and Amusement Association, military brothels catering to Allied troops.

Evidently, there was a huge "friendly fire" cover-up at the Battle of Normandy. As many as 1,500 American men were killed by friendly fire on April 27, 1944, during a D-Day training exercise, at the hands of their British allies on a beach in Devon. As the GIs swam ashore, they were fired upon by British troops playing the part of German defenders, who had incomprehensibly been given live ammunition. Afterward, the American soldiers were thrown into quick mass graves, which were dug up after D-Day and loaded onto trains. Rail historian Ken Williams declared that his father George, who'd served in the Royal Navy at the time, still remembered seeing dozens of bodies of friendly fire victims washed ashore: "He told me how the sea turned red." Historian Charles MacDonald called it "a disaster which lay hidden from the world for forty years—an official American Army cover-up." Relatives of the dead men were given incorrect information, in fact lied to by their government. The official story was that all the deaths occurred due to a surprise attack by German E-boats, which took place the following day and killed more than 700 men off the Dorset coast. The American survivors were haunted by the incident and the ensuing cover-up, and one English soldier left a bizarre taped confession with his will, describing the heaps of dead soldiers left in the surf. Neither the Army nor the Pentagon has any records relating to this incident in its files. Admiral Donald Moon, just as happened with Pearl Harbor, was made a scapegoat and killed himself on August 5, 1944.[13]

Recently, an Australian historian has suggested that black US soldiers who rebelled against their white officers in Townsville, Queensland, were executed and secretly buried. General Douglas MacArthur was briefed on the highly classified incident. According to this historian, Josh Bavas, then Congressman Lyndon B. Johnson was tasked by the Navy to investigate the matter, but ended up destroying the report by US war correspondent Robert Sherrod because it was "too hot."[14] According to Military History Now, "friendly fire" incidents "cost thousands of lives during the Second World War." Perhaps the most tragic of these was the attack on the former luxury liner *Cap Arcona*, seemingly safe in a German harbor, at the very end of the war, on May 3, 1945—just one day before the Germans surrendered. The ship was filled with inmates from Nazi concentration camps and Allied POWs. The inexplicable assault by British planes killed almost 10,000.

Benjamin Franklin's timeless quote that "Never has there been a good war or a bad peace" has been entirely forgotten by cunning leaders and a horribly gullible public. As estimated 21–25 million soldiers from the participating nations died in World War II. Another 30 million civilians perished. If Franklin Roosevelt was a "great" president, and World War II was a "good" war, it is terrifying to imagine what "bad" ones would have been like.

CHAPTER NINE

POSTWAR AMERICA

A state of war only serves as an excuse for domestic tyranny.

—Aleksandr Solzhenitsyn

What luck for rulers that men do not think.

—Adolf Hitler

A merica was caught up in a fit of unprecedented patriotism following the end of World War II. Returning GIs would be treated with the respect and deference that veterans of other wars had never received, nor would receive again after future conflicts. In the giddy postwar boom, when a man's war record often contributed significantly to his employment prospects, a great deal of ugly information was swept under the rug. This was hardly surprising; the "greatest generation" had obeyed their government with shameful unanimity, planting "victory gardens," enduring air raid drills and sirens, rationing, the lionization of a Big Brother-like Uncle Sam, and the incessant command to "buy bonds" from Hollywood. Even the great Frank Capra stooped to directing the government-sponsored *Why We Fight* documentary series. Propaganda posters were everywhere. Even after the war, the Writers' War Board led a campaign to promote the idea of a harsh peace to be inflicted upon the German people. Luminaries such as Pearl S. Buck, Oscar Hammerstein II, Franklin P. Adams, Clifton Fadiman, Paul Gallico, William L. Shirer, Edna Ferber, Langston Hughes, Edna St. Vincent Millay, Edward R. Murrow, Clifford Odets, Eugene O'Neill, Mary Roberts Rinehart, and Thornton Wilder were all affiliated with this propaganda arm of the US government. Even writers like Dr. Seuss advocated early intervention in the war, while popular comic strips like *Little Orphan Annie* introduced the desired slant into their stories. Superman fought the Nazis in the comic books. Like his fellow extreme "leftist" Charlie Chaplin, Orson Welles shilled diligently for war on CBS Radio. Walt Disney Studios worked so closely with the US Army that military personnel were stationed on the studio lot for the duration of the war, and an officer even remained within Walt Disney's personal office. Despite this, the popular consensus has become that Walt Disney was an "anti-Semite" who actually supported the forces he certainly seemed to be allied against. The government's Office of Censorship effectively controlled what information was printed in newspapers.

THE ALLEGED SUICIDE OF HITLER

I still cannot escape the feeling that Hitler is some place where nobody expects him to be.
—Associated Press Berlin correspondent Louis Lochner

One enduring mystery from the war, which the US government strangely ignored, is just what happened to Adolf Hitler. Of all America's enemies, none was greater, or would ever be greater, than Hitler. He was lampooned mercilessly by Hollywood, as everyone from Tarzan to the Three Stooges ridiculed him and his National Socialist party. The official history books report that Hitler committed suicide, along with his wife Eva Braun, on April 30, 1945. The notoriously untrustworthy Soviet archives reported that their bodies had been taken outside the bunker and set on fire. Their burnt remains were recovered, including skull fragments, and interred in more than one location, then finally cremated totally in 1970. This establishment narrative, as is the case with all establishment narratives, is highly implausible.

The evidence that Hitler in fact survived World War II is much more compelling. A declassified FBI document revealed that an informant had told the FBI's Los Angeles office, on August 28, 1945, that he'd been paid $15,000 to help arrange Hitler's arrival in Argentina. He offered to give the FBI the names of others who were involved, and to put them in touch with someone who would take them to a ranch where Hitler was living. The same informant had earlier been interviewed by *The Los Angeles Examiner* on July 29, 1945, but his story was never published. The FBI irrationally noted their disinterest with the conclusion, "It would be impossible to continue efforts to locate Hitler with the sparse information to date."[1] Several books have been written about Hitler escaping to Argentina. Abel Basti, Argentine author of 2010's *Hitler's Exile*, collected hundreds of official documents and news reports, and interviewed local residents, all of which confirmed that Hitler had lived undercover in their midst. The Chief of American Intelligence in Berlin, Colonel W. J. Heimlich, admitted, "There is no evidence beyond that of hearsay to support the theory of Hitler's suicide. On the basis of present evidence, no insurance company in America would pay a claim on Adolf Hitler."

Secretary of State Jimmy Byrnes wrote in his 1947 book *Speaking Frankly* that Stalin had told him at Potsdam, "Hitler is not dead. He escaped either to Spain or Argentina." The Soviets, of course, can hardly be trusted on this matter. They claimed that some skull fragments found were Hitler's, but an American researcher was able to determine, during testing in 2009, that the skull was that of a young woman. Marshall Zhukov, head of the Soviet Army, had acknowledged, a month after the alleged May 4, 1945 discovery of Hitler's remains, that "We did not identify the body of Hitler. I can say nothing definite about his fate." The establishment's response to these "conspiracy theories" was predictable. An April 30, 2015 story in the *Daily Beast* definitively stated, "The origins of these rumors lie in the fact that, though scholars agree Hitler and Braun carried out a suicide pact in an underground bunker, their remains were never publicly and formally identified." This is conventional history, and the mainstream media, in a nutshell. A naysayer like myself can't help but ask: if their remains were never identified, then how do "scholars" know they had a suicide pact? While a suicide pact between fascist lovers has Hollywood written all over it, there is nothing tangible to support it. I have always wondered why a megalomaniac like Hitler would kill himself without leaving a long, detailed suicide note behind to the world.

MORE ALLIED ATROCITIES

The destruction of German cities, the killing of German workers, and the disruption of civilized community life throughout Germany [is the goal]. . . . It should be emphasized that the destruction of houses, public utilities, transport and lives; the creation of a refugee problem on an unprecedented scale; and the breakdown of morale both at home and at the battle fronts by fear of extended and intensified bombing are accepted and intended aims of our bombing policy.

—Sir Arthur "Bomber" Harris

It is not my intention to offer an apologia for the Axis forces during World War II, much as it wasn't my intention to offer an apologia for southern slave owners during the Civil War. But just as the subject of slavery in

America has been exhaustively chronicled by the mainstream media and establishment historians, the atrocities of the Nazis and Japanese have been widely detailed and continue to draw regular attention from conventional sources, including Hollywood. Few people anywhere would argue that slavery, ethnic persecution, and genocide are good things. By focusing attention on generally unreported crimes and atrocities committed by the Allies in and after World War II, I am merely showing that history is more complex than "good" guys vs. "bad" guys. The atrocities of the Axis powers are hardly "hidden" history; on the contrary, they are well known to everyone. The underpublicized atrocities of the Allies, however, are appropriate for inclusion in a book like this. Americans in general, and especially their politicians, journalists, and historians, have certainly never been reluctant to boast about our perceived values and principles. Our enemies have always been sufficiently demonized, and our heroes more than adequately heralded. Having proven to be more than willing to judge the ugly nature of others, our leaders should live up to their own high standards.

While it wasn't literally covered up, the bombing of the German city of Dresden by the Allies has been underreported and was a "war crime" if ever there was one. Young Kurt Vonnegut, later to be inspired by the experience to write *Slaughterhouse-Five*, described the scene in a letter written home on May 29, 1945:

On about February 14th the Americans came over, followed by the R.A.F. their combined labors killed 250,000 people in twenty-four hours and destroyed all of Dresden—possibly the world's most beautiful city. After that we were put to work carrying corpses from Air-Raid shelters; women, children, old men; dead from concussion, fire or suffocation. Civilians cursed us and threw rocks as we carried bodies to huge funeral pyres in the city. When General Patton took Leipzig we were evacuated on foot to ('the Saxony-Czechoslovakian border'?). There we remained until the war ended. Our guards deserted us. On that happy day the Russians were intent on mopping up isolated outlaw resistance in our sector. Their planes (P-39's) strafed and bombed us, killing fourteen, but not me. Eight of us stole a team and wagon. We traveled and looted our way through Sudetenland and Saxony for eight days, living like kings.

Thirty years later, Sir Arthur "Bomber" Harris, Royal Air Force (RAF) chief of the Bomber Command, remained unrepentant over the raids on German cities. A long-lost 1977 interview with Harris revealed him declaring, "I would have destroyed Dresden again." At the mention of the name, Harris responded, "Dresden? There is not such a place any longer" and freely admitted, "I want to point out, that besides Essen, we never actually considered any particular industrial sites as targets. The destruction of industrial sites always was some sort of bonus for us. Our real targets always were the inner cities." There were an estimated 600,000 killed during the bombing of Dresden. The bombing produced no strategic or tactical advantage for the Allies. Historically considered one of the most beautiful cities in the world, Dresden had been dubbed "the Florence of the Elbe." It was renowned for its architecture and culture, filled with priceless art treasures, and possessed no military bases, communication centers, or even heavy industry. At the time it was attacked, it had become known as "the City of the Refugees." Oxford Professor Norman Stone would write, in the UK *Daily Mail*, "We went on bombing German cities months and months after it had been clear that we would win, and that Stalin would be as potentially deadly an enemy. . . . Even now, it would cost nothing to say 'sorry' for gratuitous sadism." Most of those targeted were civilians, women, and children. In the tradition of William Sherman and Philip Sheridan, both Churchill and Roosevelt wanted to take their wrath out on the German population by razing their cities.

A German paper reported some *37,000 babies and toddlers,* and 46,000 young children, among the fatalities at Dresden. Apologists for the Allies have ludicrously attempted to equate the bombing of Dresden with the bombs dropped by German forces on the English city of Coventry, where a total of 380 were killed throughout the war. During the maliciously named Operation Gomorrah, or the bombing of Hamburg in July 1943, more than 100,000 were killed. More bombs, in fact, were dropped on the city of Berlin alone during the course of the war than fell upon all of Great Britain. Much as the South had been devastated by the "scorched earth" policy of Lincoln and his generals, all of the larger German cities were extensively destroyed during World War II. Author Douglas Botting reported, "Countless smaller towns and villages had been razed to the ground or turned into ghost towns." The city of Kassel, suffering from continuous air raids, surrendered on April 4, 1945. Out of a population of 250,000, only 15,000 remained alive.[2]

In September 1939, President Franklin Roosevelt blasted the Germans thusly: "The ruthless bombing from the air of civilians in unfortified centers of population . . . has sickened the hearts of every civilized man and woman, and has profoundly shocked the conscience of humanity. . . . I am therefore addressing this urgent appeal to every government which may be engaged in hostilities publicly to affirm its determination that its armed forces shall in no event, and under no circumstances, undertake the bombardment from the air of civilian populations." There isn't a fitting word to describe this kind of hubris, from a leader who would preside over a military force that killed an incalculable number of civilians, including *83,000 young children, babies, and toddlers* in Dresden alone.

The Allies were no less harsh with Japanese civilians. Wrote Hoito Edoin:

America has revealed her barbaric character before in the terror bombings of civilian populations in Hamburg, Berlin, and other German cities, in her destruction of priceless cultural monuments in various parts of Europe, in her sinking of innumerable hospital ships, and in countless other acts of savagery beyond mention. But the raids on Tokyo and Nagoya with the last few days have demonstrated more spectacularly than ever the fiendish character of the American enemy. For these recent raids have been the most unquestionable examples of calculated terror bombing. Raining flaming incendiaries over a vast area of civilian dwellings, the raiders can make no excuse of having aimed at military or industrial installations. It was an attempt at mass murder of women and children who had no connection with war production or any activity directly connected with the war. There can be no other result than to strengthen the conviction of every Japanese that there can be no slackening of the war effort. . . . The action of the Americans is all the more despicable because of the noisy pretensions they constantly make about their humanity and idealism. They are the first to accuse others of atrocities, raising loud protests over claims of alleged Japanese mistreatment of prisoners of war and alleged Japanese destruction in the zones of hostility. But even the most extravagant of the false American charges against the Japanese pale into insignificance beside the actual acts of deliberate American terror against civilian populations. No one expects war to be anything but a brutal business, but it remains for the Americans to make it systematically and unnecessarily a wholesale horror for innocent civilians.[3]

General Curtis LeMay, later to become one of President John F. Kennedy's strongest foes and a suspected conspirator in his assassination in the eyes of many researchers, led the 1945 firebombing campaign against Japanese cities, which killed as many as 500,000 civilians and left an estimated five million homeless.

Another Allied atrocity occurred when General Dwight D. "Ike" Eisenhower, then head of the Joint Chiefs of Staff under President Harry

Truman, gave the order on December 20, 1945, to forcibly repatriate the remaining two to five million anti-Communists in Allied hands back to their Soviet slave masters. They were rounded up at bayonet point and herded into freight cars. This wholesale murder by the US government, clearly "genocide" if ever there was such a thing, was termed "Operation Keelhaul." Allied forces knew very well that these pathetic refugees would either be killed or serve out their lives in the dreaded Russian gulags. Incredibly, included among them were some 20,000 American troops and 30,000 British troops, abandoned by Eisenhower and his British counterparts to their fate in Russia. As one American soldier who escaped bitterly recounted, "I was prepared to fight, to be wounded, to be captured, even to die, but I was not prepared to be abandoned."[4] There was such secrecy surrounding this shameful atrocity that Freedom of Information Act requests regarding it, to this day, are routinely denied on the grounds of "national security." This abandonment of American troops foretold what was to come in Korea and Vietnam. Operation Keelhaul was part of the plans devised at Yalta, where it was added as a secret codicil to the agreement. As Julius Epstein, author of the book *Operation Keelhaul*, explained, "To keelhaul is the cruelest and most dangerous of punishments and tortures ever devised for men aboard a ship. It involves trussing a man up with ropes, throwing him overboard, unable to swim, and hauling him under the boat's keel from one side to the other, or even from stem to stern. Most of those keelhauled under water are already dead when their punishment is over. . . . That our Armed Forces should have adopted this term as its code name for deporting by brutal force to concentration camp, firing squad, or hangman's noose millions who were already in the lands of freedom, shows how little the high brass thought of their longing to be free."

Author Nikolai Tolstoy was appalled by Operation Keelhaul, writing, "The Americans returned to Plattling (a town in Bavaria, Germany where an internment camp was located after World War II) visibly shamefaced.

Before their departure from the rendezvous in the forest, many had seen rows of bodies already hanging from the branches of nearby trees. On their return, even the German SS men in a neighboring compound lined the wire fence and railed at them for their behavior. The Americans were too ashamed to reply." Alexandr Solzhenitsyn called Operation Keelhaul "the last secret of World War II."

In recent years, Tom Brokaw and others have idealized World War II soldiers and their "greatest generation" brethren. They are pictured heroically in popular culture as a "band of brothers." In high-profile court historian Stephen Ambrose's book of the same name, he recounts an incident where three US soldiers were ordered by their captain to find and execute a Nazi, who was known to be hiding nearby. This was after the Germans had already surrendered. The captain, of course, had no authority to order a killing in peacetime, and one of the soldiers refused to comply. The other two shot the man. It is hard to determine who was worse; the two who executed an opponent who'd surrendered, even though they'd been told there would be no consequences if they refused, or the officer who gave them the order.

"For years we have blamed the 1.7 million missing German POWs on the Russians. Until now, no one dug too deeply. . . . Witnesses and survivors have been interviewed by the author; one Allied officer compared the American camps to Buchenwald," Peter Worthington wrote in the September 12, 1989 *Ottawa Sun*. "Starting in April 1945, the United States Army and the French Army casually annihilated one million [German] men, most of them in American camps . . . Eisenhower's hatred, passed through the lens of a compliant military bureaucracy, produced the horror of death camps unequalled by anything in American history . . . an enormous war crime," Col. Ernest F. Fisher, PhD Lt., 101st Airborne Division, Senior Historian, United States Army would declare. "My protests (regarding treatment of the German POWs) were met with hostility or indifference, and when I threw our ample rations to them over the barbed wire, I was threatened, making it clear that it was our deliberate policy not to adequately feed them," Martin Brech, ex-Private First Class, assigned as a guard and interpreter at the Eisenhower Camp at Andernach, along the Rhine River, revealed. Brech went on to say:

> When they caught me throwing C-rations over the fence, they threatened me with imprisonment. One Captain told me that he would shoot me if he saw me again tossing food to the Germans. . . . Some of the men were really only boys 13 years of age. . . . Some of the prisoners were old men drafted by Hitler in his last ditch stand. . . . I understand that average weight of the prisoners at Andernach was 90 pounds . . . I have received threats . . . when I relate the horrible atrocity I witnessed as a prison guard for one of "Ike's death camps" along the Rhine.

An anonymous camp prisoner reported, "At first, the women from the nearby town brought food into the camp. The American soldiers took everything away from the women, threw it in a heap and poured gasoline over it and burned it." An unnamed serviceman was quoted in the November 12, 1945 issue of *Time* magazine thusly: "Many a sane American family would recoil in horror if they knew how 'Our Boys' conduct themselves, with such complete callousness in human relationships over here."

As Associated Press and other mainstream media outlets reported on September 10, 2012, "potentially explosive" declassified documents revealed that the Roosevelt administration helped cover up the 1940 Soviet mass murder of Polish POWs in the Katyn forest on the western edge of Russia. More than 22,000 captured Polish officers and other prisoners were systematically shot in the back of the head. American POWs would send coded messages to Washington three years later after discovering the rows of rotting corpses in the forest. The advanced state of decay demonstrated that the Nazis—who were nevertheless blamed—couldn't have been responsible, since they'd only recently occupied the area. As AP explained, "Their testimony might have lessened the tragic fate that befell Poland under the Soviets, some scholars believe. Instead, it mysteriously vanished into the heart of American power. The long-held suspicion is that President Franklin Delano Roosevelt did not want to anger Russian leader Josef Stalin, an ally whom the Americans were counting on to defeat Germany and Japan during the war." As the story further reported, "Documents now released lend weight to the belief that suppression within the highest levels of the US helped cover up Soviet guilt. . . . which adds to evidence that the Roosevelt administration knew of the Soviet atrocity relatively early on." The victims were among the Polish intellectual elite, comprised of members of the professional class.

A congressional committee had found, during a 1952 investigation, that the Soviets were unquestionably guilty, calling the massacre "one of the most barbarous international crimes in world history." It also concluded that the Roosevelt administration had suppressed public knowledge of the incident, "out of military necessity." The recommended charges against the Soviets for this indisputable war crime were never brought.

Conservative philosopher Richard Weaver was revolted by "the spectacle of young boys fresh out of Kansas and Texas turning nonmilitary Dresden into a holocaust . . . pulverizing ancient shrines like Monte Cassino and Nuremberg, and bringing atomic annihilation to Hiroshima and Nagasaki" and considered these atrocities deeply "inimical to the foundations on which civilization is built."[5]

GLENN MILLER

The official urge to cover up and distort the truth about everything extends to even relatively innocuous events, such as the disappearance of famed bandleader Glenn Miller. Miller's plane vanished while flying over the English Channel on December 15, 1944. As we see so often, while the establishment proceeded to portray Miller as a hero (he was posthumously awarded the Bronze Star), his death continues to be shrouded in unnecessary mystery. Retired Lt. Col. Hunton Downs, an officer on General Omar Bradley's staff, spent some sixty years investigating Miller's disappearance. The official narrative that Miller's plane—no traces of which were ever found—went down in bad weather was strongly contradicted by Downs's investigation.

Downs discovered that the adjutant's signature on the official form had been falsified in the RAF records, while Miller's name had clearly been added belatedly to the passenger list. Other RAF documents yielded the astonishing report from driver Joan Heath, in which she claimed to have driven Major Glenn Miller in an Army sedan to a French airstrip on December 16–17, a day or two after Miller's plane had supposedly crashed into the channel on December 15. Downs's contention is that Miller was on a secret peace mission from Eisenhower, assigned to convince the enemy forces to surrender. According to Downs, angry Nazi officials reacted by beating Miller to death and dumping his nude body on the doorstep of a prominent Paris brothel. One of Miller's close friends, actor Broderick Crawford, allegedly revealed to Downs during a drinking session that Miller had been on "a mission for Ike" and had been "killed in the effort." Supposedly a US Army doctor signed Miller's death certificate, his body was flown to Wright-Patterson Air Force base, and he was buried in an unknown location. All of this is detailed in Downs's book *The Glenn Miller Conspiracy*.

Alternate theories claim Miller died in the brothel and/or was killed by an irate French husband. Others have postulated that Miller was yet another hapless victim of "friendly fire." What happened to the two officers who were on board the plane with Miller? As always, establishment voices emerged to counter any dreaded conspiracy theories. Dennis Spragg, of the American Music Research Center, set out to counter "the latest series of sensationalist conspiracy books," seemingly at the behest of Miller's frustrated family. According to PBS's predictably non-controversial *History Detectives* television show, the non-mysterious conclusion reached quickly by "investigators" is the most likely explanation. The court historians evidently don't find it suspicious that information about the incident was locked away, or that there was surprisingly minimal effort expended to search for a plane carrying one of the most popular entertainers in the world.

EDDIE SLOVIK

Everything happens to me. I've never had a streak of luck in my life.
—Eddie Slovik

Another sad tale from World War II was the execution of Private Eddie Slovik. When General Dwight D. Eisenhower signed the order authorizing Slovik's execution for desertion, it was the first such sentence for a US soldier since the Civil War. Slovik would be the only American executed for desertion during World War II. Slovik had been convicted of grand theft auto, and was classified as a "replacement," a designation not respected by military officers. Slovik hated guns, but was trained as a rifleman. On the way to the front lines with a fellow soldier in France, they became lost and were taken in by a Canadian unit. After being turned over to the military police, no charges were pressed against them. However, upon returning to his unit, Slovik claimed to be "too scared and too nervous" and threatened to run away if forced into combat. He ran away the next day, but quickly returned and signed a confession of desertion. He refused advice to retract his confession and enter combat, and was court-martialed and summarily convicted and sentenced to death. Slovik, who oddly didn't testify in his own defense, was astonished at the sentence, expecting to get the dishonorable discharge and jail sentence he'd seen doled out to other deserters.

It is difficult to understand why Slovik suffered such an excessive fate for an offense that wasn't all that uncommon. Over 20,000 American soldiers were tried for desertion during World War II (some sources report the figure as double that). Only forty-nine were given death sentences, and forty-eight of those sentences were commuted. So Eddie Slovik became one in 20,000. Reading some of Slovik's quotes made me envision the original "hard luck" guy, someone who couldn't catch a break. "They're not shooting me for deserting the United States Army—thousands of guys have done that," Slovik declared. "They're shooting me for the bread I stole when I was twelve years old." Slovik bitterly remarked to his wife, "The only luck I had in my life was when I married you. I knew it wouldn't last because I was too happy. I knew they would not let me be happy."[6] The obviously smitten Slovik wrote an incredible 376 letters to his wife during the year he served in the armed forces before his court-martial. It was Slovik's tragic luck to be made an example; in the words of Voltaire, "Shoot one to encourage the others."

On January 31, 1945, Slovik was executed by firing squad. None of the eleven shots killed him instantly, so he wasn't even lucky in that regard. He was buried in disgrace in a military cemetery in France, next to American soldiers who'd been executed for rape and murder. He wasn't given a coffin, interred instead in a mattress pad, and no name—only a number—originally marked his grave. Although Eddie's wife Antoinette was unsuccessful in getting her husband's remains sent home for proper burial, the Pentagon finally approved their return eight years after her 1979 death and he was interred next to her in Detroit. Antoinette's luck was no better than her husband's; she died only days before a Senate committee was scheduled to meet to consider giving her $72,000 (Eddie's original $10,000 insurance policy she'd been denied, plus interest).[7] The pleas for a pardon, from both Antoinette Slovik and others, have gone unheeded. Captain Benedict Kimmelman, who'd been a member of the court martial board, later called the execution a "historic injustice." *The Execution of Private Slovik* was a 1974 television movie starring Martin Sheen in the title role. The film was based on the 1954 book by William Bradford Huie, which had angered Dwight Eisenhower to such an extent that he tried to stop its publication. Frank Sinatra had been rumored in 1960 to be producing a film adaptation of the book, with Albert Maltz, one of those on the "Hollywood 10" blacklist, scheduled to write the screenplay, but was pressured to drop the project. In typically convoluted logic, the outrage was focused on Sinatra being a communist "sympathizer." This, of course, made absolutely no sense, as Slovik had deserted from the Allies, who were fighting on the same side as the communists in World War II. Slovik's wife wasn't even notified that he was executed; as she reported, "They told me he had died under dishonorable circumstances . . . but I didn't know until eight years later that they killed him."[8]

THE NUREMBERG TRIALS

If the Nuremberg laws were applied, then every post-war American president would have been hanged.

—Noam Chomsky

According to the postwar memoirs of Winston Churchill, Josef Stalin seriously proposed that the Allies summarily execute 50,000 German officers and technicians following the end of the war. Churchill argued against it, not on humanitarian grounds, but because it would make the Allies look bad politically. Roosevelt jokingly suggested a compromise, wherein only 49,000 German officers would be murdered. Churchill wasn't entirely sure that FDR was joking. As author James Bacque would show, in his 1989 book

Other Losses, some three million German POWs were either killed or disappeared after the war.

In her 1963 book *Eichmann to Jerusalem,* Hannah Arendt made the extraordinary argument that Nazi crimes had "exploded the limits of the law. . . . For these crimes, no punishment is severe enough." Ultimate mainstream journalist Anthony Lewis declared, "The Nuremberg trials of Nazi leaders, in open court before an international tribunal, had a profound long-term effect in bringing Germans back to democracy and humanity." Rebecca West mimicked this: "It was the virtue of the Nuremberg trial that it was conceived in hatred of war, and nurtured by those starved of peace. Of course, the trial was botched and imperfect . . . it had to deal with new crimes for which there was no provision in national law or international law." The alleged crimes for which selected Nazi leaders were convicted at Nuremberg were not unprecedented, but the idea of victors legally sentencing those they'd defeated in war certainly was. In many ways, it paralleled the "justice" meted out to the alleged conspirators in the Lincoln assassination.

The entire concept of "war crimes" is vague and impossible to reconcile with any western concept of law. The Nazi defendants at Nuremberg were charged with "crimes against peace, the planning and waging of wars of aggression," "war crimes," "crimes against humanity," and "conspiracy to commit one or more of the above acts." To put this in context, it is universally accepted that the British Royal Air Force and US Army Air Force killed approximately 600–900,000 German non-combatants when they bombed cities like Dresden and Hamburg. Somehow, this wasn't considered a "war crime."

The lust for vengeance was strong among the Allies. Churchill and Roosevelt (at the behest of his Treasury Secretary Henry Morgenthau—who proposed the diabolical "Morgenthau Plan" to literally *starve* the German population) both supported the summary execution of German leaders after the war. Morgenthau, along with his aide Harry Dexter White (later labeled a Soviet spy), strongly pushed for a harsh postwar policy towards Germany that rekindled memories of the Reconstruction era in the South. Morgenthau's diaries revealed that he sought to banish some Germans to other parts of the world, and particularly wanted to be involved in "how to bring up the next generation of children." White, meanwhile, proposed the compilation of a list of "war criminals," to which Morgenthau joked that Stalin's "list of 50,000" would make a good start. Morgenthau spoke of making the German Ruhr "a ghost area," which evoked comparisons to Sherman's March to the Sea in even the establishment press. Even Winston Churchill initially was horrified at Morgenthau's plans, terming them "cruel and un-Christian." However, after more persuasion from Morgenthau, including the promise of a huge loan to the British from America, Churchill changed his mind. Both Cordell Hull and Henry Stimson were aghast at Morgenthau's proposal. White would die suddenly at age fifty-five, from either a heart attack or overdose of drugs, depending on the source.

Polls at the time showed the public strongly in favor of holding the Germans legally accountable, with only 10 percent of them wanting to include a trial first. The same number supported the slow torture of German leaders. The chief justice of the Supreme Court at the time, Harlan Fiske Stone, was quite outspoken about the war crimes trial, calling it "a fraud." Stone would write, "Jackson is away conducting his high-grade lynching party in Nuremberg. I don't mind what he does to the Nazis, but I hate to see the pretense that he is running a court and proceeding according to common law. This is a little too sanctimonious a fraud to meet my old-fashioned ideas." In a private letter Stone wrote, ". . . I wonder how some of those who preside at the trials would justify some of the acts of their own governments if they were placed in the status of the accused." On another occasion Stone specifically wondered "whether, under this new [Nuremberg] doctrine of international law, if we had been defeated, the victors could plausibly assert that our supplying Britain with fifty destroyers [in 1940] was an act of aggression."[9] Stone would die suddenly in the middle of the Nuremberg trials. Another Supreme Court justice, William O. Douglas, wrote: "I thought at the time and still think that the Nuremberg trials were unprincipled. Law was created ex post facto to suit the passion and clamor of the time."

Some members of Congress recognized how unprecedented such a "trial" of the victors over the vanquished really was. Representative Lawrence H. Smith of Wisconsin stated, "The Nuremberg trials are so repugnant to the Anglo-Saxon principles of justice that we must forever be ashamed of that page in our history." Fellow congressman John Rankin of Mississippi agreed: "As a representative of the American people I desire to say that what is taking place in Nuremberg, Germany, is a disgrace to the United States." Senator Robert A. Taft, widely regarded as the "conscience of the Republican party," boldly declared, during an October 1946 speech at Ohio's Kenyon College: "The trial of the vanquished by the victors cannot be impartial no matter how it is hedged about with the forms of justice. . . . The hanging of the eleven men convicted will be a blot on the American record which we will long regret. In these trials we have accepted the Russian idea of the purpose of trials—government policy and not justice—with little relation to Anglo-Saxon heritage." Significantly, then Senator John F. Kennedy recognized what kind of guts it took to go against the grain so boldly, and included Taft as a "Profile in Courage" in his bestselling book. Milton R. Konvitz, prominent legal specialist at New York University, warned at the time that the Nuremberg Tribunal "constitutes a real threat to the basic conceptions of justice which it has taken mankind thousands of years to establish."[10]

Celebrating such an anti-establishment stance, especially one of so recent a nature, represented a tremendous act of courage by author and Senator John F. Kennedy as well. The trials were conducted under their own rules of evidence. The International Military Tribunal charter approved the use of normally inadmissible "evidence," declaring that "The Tribunal shall not be bound by technical rules of evidence . . . and shall admit any evidence which it deems to have probative value" and announcing, "The Tribunal shall not require proof of facts of common knowledge." In a blistering October 5, 1946 editorial, *The Economist* stated:

> Among crimes against humanity stands the offence of the indiscriminate bombing of civilian populations. Can the Americans who dropped the atom bomb and the British who destroyed the cities of western Germany plead "not guilty" on this count? Crimes against humanity also include the mass expulsion of populations. Can the Anglo-Saxon leaders who at Potsdam condoned the expulsion of millions of Germans from their homes hold themselves completely innocent?

Seventy years later, it is impossible to imagine any "conservative," let alone any "liberal," uttering even the most minor objection to the proceedings at Nuremberg.

Taking its lead from the unconstitutional actions of Abraham Lincoln, the primary Nuremberg Trial was held during 1945–1946 under the auspices of an International Military Tribunal (IMT). The governments of the United States, Great Britain, France, and our then ally the Soviet Union tried the most prominent surviving Nazi leaders. Chief US prosecutor for the IMT Robert H. Jackson, who succeeded the deceased Stone as chief justice of the US Supreme Court, admitted that the IMT was "not bound by the procedural and substantive refinements of our respective judicial or constitutional system" and also acknowledged the trial was "a continuation of the war effort of the Allied nations." Soviet Judge Iola T. Nikitchenko had presided over numerous show trials in the Soviet Union, so he was a laughable but fitting choice to preside over the solemn opening session of the IMT. Nikitchenko bluntly stated, "The fact that the Nazi leaders are criminals has already been established. The task of the Tribunal is only to determine the measure of guilt of each particular person and mete out the necessary punishment—the sentences." One thinks of Lewis Carroll's nonsensical "sentence first, verdict afterward" when reading such remarks.

As it had been during the trial of the Lincoln assassination alleged conspirators, the Nazi defendants at Nuremberg were only permitted a nominal defense. Nazi Foreign Minister Joachim von Ribbentrop delineated the obstacles against him:

> The defense had no fair chance to defend German foreign policy. Our prepared application for the submission of evidence was not allowed. . . . Without good cause being shown, half of the 300 documents which the defense prepared were not admitted. Witnesses and affidavits were only admitted after the prosecution had been heard; most of them were rejected. . . . Correspondence between Hitler and Chamberlain, reports by ambassadors and diplomatic minutes, etc., were rejected. Only the prosecution, not the defense, had access to German and foreign archives. The prosecution only searched for incriminating documents and their use was biased. It knowingly concealed exonerating documents and withheld them from the defense.

Von Ribbentrop would sum things up succinctly: "You can't have a trial without law." Defendant Julius Streicher, publisher of an anti-Jewish weekly periodical, received brutal treatment at the hands of his captors. He was severely beaten, kicked, whipped, spat at, forced to drink saliva, and burned with cigarettes. Hair from his eyebrows and chest was pulled out. Bringing to mind images we would come to know all too well during the Iraq and Afghanistan "wars," Streicher's genitals were beaten, and he was stripped and photographed. Another defendant, Hans Frank, was also savagely beaten by American soldiers after his arrest. August Eigruber, former Gauleiter of Upper Austria, was mutilated and castrated at the end of the war.[11]

Renegade historian Professor Harry Elmer Barnes, who coined the term "court historian," summed it up perfectly:

> [The Nuremberg] war-crimes trials were based upon a complete disregard of sound legal precedents, principles, and procedures. The court had no real jurisdiction over the accused or their offenses; it invented ex post facto crimes; it permitted the accusers to act as prosecutors, judges, jury, and executioners; and it admitted to the group of prosecutors those who had been guilty of crimes as numerous and atrocious as those with which the accused were charged. Hence, it is not surprising that these trials degraded international jurisprudence as never before in human experience.

John F. Kennedy quoted Supreme Court Justice William O. Douglas in his *Profiles in Courage:* "No matter how many books are written or briefs filed, no matter how finely the lawyers analyzed it, the crime for which the Nazis were tried had never been formalized as a crime with the definiteness required by our legal standards, nor outlawed with a death penalty by the international community. By our standards that crime arose under an ex post facto law." Dwight Eisenhower's brother Edgar stated, "I think the Nuremberg trials are a black page in the history of the world. . . . I discussed the legality of these trials with some of the lawyers and some of the judges who participated therein. They did not attempt to justify their action on any legal ground, but rested their position on the fact that in their opinion, the parties convicted were guilty. . . . This action is contrary to the fundamental laws under which this country has lived for many hundreds of years, and I think cannot be justified by any line of reasoning. I think the Israeli trial of Adolf Eichmann is exactly in the same category as the Nuremberg trials. As a lawyer, it has always been my view that a crime must be defined before you can be guilty of committing it. That has not occurred in either of the trials I refer to herein."

Renowned poet T.S. Eliot recognized them as "trials of the vanquished by the victors" and admitted, "I was from the beginning very unhappy about the Nuremberg trials." And John F. Kennedy himself wrote:

> The Nuremberg Trials . . . had been popular throughout the world and particularly in the United States. Equally popular was the sentence already announced by the high tribunal: death. But what kind of trial was this? The Constitution was not a collection of loosely given political promises subject to broad interpretation. It was not a list of pleasing platitudes to be set lightly aside when expediency required it. It was the foundation of the American system of law and justice and [Robert Taft] was repelled by the picture of his country discarding those Constitutional precepts in order to punish a vanquished enemy.[12]

Admiral Husband E. Kimmel, who certainly ought to have recognized a miscarriage of justice, stated, "The war crimes trials were a reversion to the ancient practice of the savage extermination of a defeated enemy and particularly of its leaders. The precedent set by these trials will continue to plague their authors." Decades later, the *New Republic* summed things up this way:

> The whole majesty of the Western heritage of the law was used to subvert that heritage in the Nuremberg Tribunal. Weighty jurists in every Western country (but not Russia) protested against this travesty of the Western legal system. So did historians. So did merely cultured and moral men and women. If the victors were to "try" the vanquished for war crimes, then they should try themselves for often committing the same crimes. Who

would try [British] Air Chief Marshal Sir Arthur Travers "Bomber" Harris, the architect of the policy of saturation bombing of German cities? But it was not only a matter of our own "war crimes." If it was right to use the apparatus of the law to punish those responsible for exceptional crimes like the Holocaust, it was wrong to use it to punish errors of judgment and statecraft such as every defeated regime seems to have committed.[13]

One of the Nazi leaders tried at Nuremberg who wasn't executed was Rudolph Hess. Decades later, he must have wished he had been. To an unbiased observer, Hess seemed like a potentially heroic figure. After bailing out of an airplane over Scotland on May 10, 1941, in an individual effort to arrange peace between England and Germany, Hess was quickly apprehended and ordered imprisoned by Winston Churchill. After spending the remainder of the war in the Tower of London, Hess was tried at Nuremburg and convicted of "planning war," a uniquely vague and heretofore unheard of charge. Spared the hangman's noose, Hess was sent to the remote Spandau prison in West Berlin, which had been commandeered by the victorious allies and christened the International War Crimes Prison. For the last twenty-plus years of his sentence, Hess was the lone prisoner in Spandau. During all his years behind bars, Hess was never allowed to be interviewed, all mention of World War II was censored from his reading materials, and his radio and later television usage was closely monitored. He was only permitted brief monthly visits from either his son or wife, not both, and always in the presence of guards. Eventually, forty-six years after his mission for peace, it appears his captors tired of his steadfast refusal to die and faked a "suicide." Among many anomalies of his death, the most glaring is the specter of a frail, ninety-three-year-old man being physically capable of hanging himself.[14] It was freely acknowledged that the prison's only reason for existence was to incarcerate Hess. "The purpose of Spandau Allied War-Crimes

Prison has ceased with the death of Rudolph Hess," the Allied Prison Administration announced. "In accordance with the decision of representatives of Great Britain, France, the USA, and the USSR, the Allied Prison Administration will be terminated and the prison will be demolished." While representatives of the other Allied nations had attempted to get Hess released from Spandau on humanitarian grounds, the Soviet Union blocked their efforts.[15]

TRUMAN DROPS THE BOMB

Put them on the defensive and don't ever apologize for anything.
—Harry S Truman

When Franklin Roosevelt died unexpectedly at age sixty-three, on April 12, 1945, his body was whisked out of Georgia, violating state law (foretelling what would happen to JFK's body in Dallas), and incredibly, there was no autopsy performed. I don't think I'm alone in thinking that the sudden death of a US president ought to warrant an autopsy, but the precedent had already been set with Warren G. Harding and Calvin Coolidge. Assuming the office of the presidency was the obscure Missourian who had no middle name, Harry S Truman.

Harry Truman was the last president elected who never graduated from college. Like Franklin D. Roosevelt, Truman was a 33rd degree Mason—the highest rank a member can achieve. Truman has a solid reputation with the court historians, who have portrayed him as a no-nonsense tough guy, with his "the buck stops here" motto. "Give 'em hell" Harry continued Roosevelt's predictable "liberal" policies, and became the first (and only) leader to authorize the dropping of atomic weapons on another nation, on August 6, 1945, when an American B-29 bomber wiped out 90 percent of the Japanese city of Hiroshima, instantly killing an estimated

80,000. An incalculable amount, at least tens of thousands, of people would subsequently perish from radiation exposure. On August 9, Nagasaki was accorded the same treatment, resulting in 40,000 more mostly civilian deaths. The United States exhibited little reluctance in employing such deadly force, and our leaders continue to attempt to justify it. They also, from the outset, instituted yet another cover-up. ". . . from late 1945 until 1952 Japanese medical researchers were prohibited by US occupation authorities from publishing scientific articles on the effects of the atomic bombs," wrote John W. Dower, in his *Hiroshima Diary: The Journal of a Japanese Physician, August 6-September 30, 1945*. In a public statement, a defiant Truman declared, "The Japanese began the war from the air at Pearl Harbor. They have been repaid many fold." In his *Public Papers*, Truman wrote, "If they do not now accept our terms they may expect a rain of ruin from the air, the like of which has never been seen on this earth." Truman's Orwellian rationale was that, by dropping the bombs, he ended the war and saved lives. War is peace. The films and photographs of the aftermath of the bombing were suppressed for decades. It would have been interesting to see how the public compared these horrifying images with those coming from Nazi concentration camps. The legacy of Hiroshima and Nagasaki should cause American leaders to hesitate in lecturing others. As Günter Grass noted, "How do we prevent Iran from developing an atomic bomb, when, on the American side, dropping atomic bombs on Hiroshima and Nagasaki is not recognised as a war crime?"[16]

Truman's own chief of staff, Admiral William D. Leahy, was mortified by the dropping of atomic weapons. "The use of this barbarous weapon at Hiroshima and Nagasaki was of no material assistance in our war against Japan," Leahy said. "My own feeling was that in being the first to use it, we had adopted an ethical standard common to the barbarians of the Dark Ages. I was not taught to make wars in that fashion, and wars cannot be won by destroying women and children." Major General J. F. C. Fuller, a renowned military historian, wrote: "Though to save life is laudable, it in no way justifies the employment of means which run counter to every precept of humanity and the customs of war. Should it do so, then, on the pretext of shortening a war and of saving lives, every imaginable atrocity can be justified." Felix Morley, one of the founders of the conservative publication *Human Events*, remarked on one particular horror of Hiroshima: the "thousands of children trapped in the thirty-three schools that were destroyed." He proposed that groups of Americans be sent to Hiroshima, to see what had been done in their name, just as Germans had been sent to witness the Nazi concentration camps. Another right-winger, Father James Gillis, editor of *The Catholic World*, termed the bombings "the most powerful blow ever delivered against Christian civilization and the moral law." *US News and World Report* owner David Lawrence was another high-profile figure outraged by the bombings. World-renowned physicist Leo Szilard stated, in 1960, that "If the Germans had dropped atomic bombs on cities instead of us, we would have defined the dropping of atomic bombs on cities as a war crime, and we would have sentenced the Germans who were guilty of this crime to death at Nuremberg and hanged them."[17] Incredibly, American forces continued to drop propaganda pamphlets onto Japan even after the atom bombs had been unleashed, warning that America had an even greater weapon at its disposal.

Some notable Americans were bold enough to speak out against the dropping of the bomb. Former president Herbert Hoover was appalled at the destruction of Hiroshima and Nagasaki, stating, "The use of the atomic bomb, with its indiscriminate killing of women and children, revolts my soul." Senator Robert Taft would later tell a reporter that he "would not be willing to authorize the use of that weapon against people, most of whom are innocent." John F. Kennedy got in a subtle jab at his father's political enemy Truman with a reference to "Japanese mothers, still binding up the wounds of Hiroshima" during an October 31, 1960 campaign speech. The only US president to go beyond that in criticizing Truman's action was Dwight D. Eisenhower, who wrote in his 1948 memoir *Crusade in Europe*, that he "disliked seeing the United States take the lead in introducing into war something as horrible and destructive as this new weapon." In a later memoir, he charged that "Japan was already defeated and ... dropping the bomb was completely unnecessary." Even the official 1946 investigation by the United States Strategic Bombing Survey determined that atomic bombs had been unnecessary in winning the war. Albert Einstein and General Douglas MacArthur disagreed that the bombings were necessary as well. JFK's secretary of defense Robert McNamara would later relate that General Curtis LeMay had once told him, "If we'd lost the war, we'd all have been prosecuted as war criminals."

The American public, on the other hand, in the midst of a patriotic fervor that would dwarf any before or after it, consistently supported Truman's actions in poll after poll. They were remarkably able to swallow the doublethink nonsense that the attacks helped end the war and somehow *saved* massive amounts of life. When Truman was awarded an honorary degree from Oxford in 1956, alumnus philosopher G. E. M. Anscombe protested, maintaining that Truman's use of nuclear weapons on civilians branded him a war criminal and remarking, "It was the insistence on unconditional surrender that was the root of all evil." Much as Lincoln had been inflexible in his demands with the Confederates, Truman's "unconditional surrender" terms were unrealistic and impossible. Establishment historians have strangely been reluctant to examine why so many Nazi leaders were tried and punished for "war crimes," while Japan's Emperor Hirohito wasn't. Hirohito, in fact, lived comfortably into his late eighties. It is also curious that the Allies' prosecution and execution of nearly 1,000 other Japanese "war criminals" has received so much less attention than the Nuremberg Trials. The gruesome medical experiments committed by the Japanese, which included the live vivisection of prisoners of war, were shamefully covered up by the United States after the war. The US granted immunity to these renowned doctors, in exchange for their data. According to one article, "Instead of putting the ringleaders on trial, it gave them stipends."[18] To cite just one example, through General Douglas MacArthur, the government granted the fiendish Dr. Shiro Ishii immunity from "war crimes" prosecution in exchange for 10,000 pages of data he had gathered from his experiments on human beings.

One little-scrutinized unnatural death of the period was that of California psychiatrist Jean Tatlock. Tatlock was known to be the mistress of Robert Oppenheimer, chief scientist for the Manhattan Project. On January 5, 1944, Tatlock's lifeless body was found *outside* her bathtub, lying on some pillows with only her head immersed in the water. There were traces of chloral hydrates—knockout drops—found in her blood. Tatlock was a left-wing activist who was a member of the Communist Party. The recent Pulitzer Prize-winning biography of Oppenheimer, *American Prometheus* by Kai Bird and Martin Sherwin, inferred that Tatlock may have in fact been murdered, although the authors were careful to admit they were speculating. Tatlock's father John Tatlock found her body, and rather curiously burned her correspondence in the fireplace. One doctor was quoted as saying, after examining the Tatlock records, "If you were clever and wanted to kill someone, this is the way to do it."

Truman's administration was mired in long-forgotten scandals. Truman became embroiled in an investigation of the IRS, led by rising senator and fellow Democrat Estes Kefauver, which unearthed rampant corruption, bribery, and influence peddling within the agency, at least some of which had benefited First Lady Bess Truman. It was in the aftermath of these disclosures that Richard Nixon delivered his often mocked "Checkers" speech. It was only through a miraculous upset that Truman defeated Thomas Dewey in the 1948 election. Allegations of corruption were such that during the 1952 midterm elections, Republicans used references to "the mess in Washington" as a rallying cry. Jules Abel wrote a full-length book devoted to the subject, *The Truman Scandals*. "The administration . . . far from taking effective action to wipe out corruption, was in some cases protecting the wrongdoers, in other cases was indifferent, and in other cases the machinery of the administration was used to block and thwart the investigators of corruption," Abel wrote. "The frauds were revealed not because of the administration, but in spite of it."

A few very notable deaths occurred during the Truman years. On December 21, 1945, sixty-year-old General George S. Patton died under highly questionable circumstances in Heidelberg, Germany. The official story that his death was the result of a low-impact motor vehicle accident, in which the other participants went uninjured, is frankly ridiculous. The recent book *Target Patton* by Robert Wilcox utilized the colorful diaries of a wartime assassin for the OSS—forerunner to the CIA—named Douglas Bazata. Bazata confessed to Wilcox that he'd been ordered to silence Patton, whom powerful forces feared would continue to speak of Allied cooperation with the Soviets that cost American lives. Bazata claimed he'd staged the accident, and when Patton began recovering from his wounds, the NKVD—later to become the KGB—poisoned him. Bazata built an incredibly "respectable" career for a former assassin; he later served on the 9/11 Commission and was an advisor to war-hawk extraordinaire John McCain's presidential campaign.[19]

James V. Forrestal, the nation's first secretary of defense, was found dead on a roof at Bethesda Naval Hospital, thirteen floors below his room on the sixteenth floor, on May 22, 1949. Forrestal was not only a staunch anti-communist, he was strongly opposed to the creation of the modern state of Israel. He'd been committed to Bethesda against his will, reportedly suffering from "operational fatigue," whatever that is. While the court historians adamantly maintain that Forrestal took his own life, his brother Henry alleged that "they" had killed the secretary of defense. Henry questioned the immediate verdict of suicide and was suspicious that hospital officials had lied to him. He also was incredulous that a man like James Forrestal would have even considered suicide, and also neglected to leave a note behind. Indeed, his brother was scheduled to pick him up and take him home that very day. David Martin has written a marvelously detailed expose on this case, which can be found on his web site dcdave.com. Bethesda Naval Hospital would later be associated with the death of Senator Joseph McCarthy and the horribly inept autopsy of John F. Kennedy. Forrestal was close friends with Joseph P. Kennedy Sr., who sought his counsel after JFK's heroics in World War II were ridiculed by the likes of Douglas MacArthur, who allegedly remarked that young Kennedy should have been court-martialed after allowing his PT-109 boat to be cut in half.

To say that Truman had a short temper is a huge understatement. The most notorious example of this occurred when the irate president wrote an incredibly petty and immature response to critic Paul Hume's review of his daughter Margaret's piano concert. "It seems to me that you are a frustrated old man who wishes he could have been successful," Truman declared. "Some day I hope to meet you. When that happens you'll need a new nose, a lot of beefsteak for black eyes, and perhaps a supporter below!" "Give 'em hell" Harry may have issued public threats to journalists, but he never resisted the will of the establishment. During his administration, the Central Intelligence Agency and the United Nations were born, and the state of Israel was created. Not surprisingly, preeminent court historian Michael Beschloss ranks Truman's decision to recognize the new state of Israel as one of his nine most courageous presidential decisions. Truman's desire to please Jewish interest groups, even at the risk of engendering Arabic hatred of America, was freely admitted to a group of Arab diplomats. "I'm sorry, gentlemen," Truman told them, "but I have to answer to hundreds of thousands who are anxious for the success of Zionism; I do not have hundreds of thousands of Arabs among my constituents."[20] Clearly, Truman acted purely out of political expediency. A 1947 excerpt from his diary, which certainly qualifies as "anti-Semitic," reads: "They (the Jews) care not how many Estonians, Latvians, Finns, Poles, Yugoslavs or Greeks get murdered or mistreated as Displaced Persons as long as the Jews get special treatment. Yet when they have power, physical, financial or political, neither Hitler nor Stalin has anything on them for cruelty and mistreatment to the underdog."

THE CREATION OF ISRAEL

We shall endeavour to expel the poor population [of Palestine] across the border unnoticed, procuring employment for it in the transit countries, but denying it any employment in our Country.
                                                    —Theodor Herzl, founder of political Zionism,
                                                              personal diary entry, June 12, 1895

Even many inside the Establishment opposed the idea of displacing inhabitants and creating a new Jewish state in the middle of all those Arabs. Secretary of State George C. Marshall was appalled at Truman advisor Clark Clifford's overt politicization of the issue, calling it "a transparent dodge to win a few votes." Thomas E. Dewey, Truman's 1948 opponent for president, on the other hand, naturally supported the creation of the state of Israel (not to mention the Marshall Plan, the Truman Doctrine, the Berlin Airlift, and most policies of the Democrats). Supreme insider Dean Acheson opposed the state of Israel as well. The ill-fated Secretary of Defense James Forrestal asserted that "United States policy should be based on United States national interests and not on domestic political considerations." Teddy's nephew Kermit Roosevelt was one of several notable figures who accurately predicted how Israel would drastically alter

American foreign policy, declaring in a February 1948 pamphlet published by the Institute of Arab American Affairs, "The process by which Zionist Jews have been able to promote American support for the partition of Palestine demonstrates the vital need of a foreign policy based on national rather than partisan interests."

Tremendous pressure was applied on other nations to support the plan to create Israel.

Powerful banker and political insider Bernard Baruch informed France it would lose US aid if it voted against partition. Top White House executive assistant David Niles pressured Liberia through rubber magnate Harvey Firestone, who told the Liberian president that if Liberia did not vote in favor of partition, Firestone would revoke his planned expansion in the country. Latin American delegates were told that the Pan-American highway construction project had a much better chance if they were to vote yes. Delegates' wives received mink coats, and Costa Rica's President Jose Figueres reportedly was the recipient of a blank checkbook. Haiti was promised economic aid if it would change its original vote opposing partition. Longtime Zionist Supreme Court Justice Felix Frankfurter, along with ten US senators and Truman domestic adviser Clark Clifford, threatened the Philippines as well. The Philippines' delegate, initially strongly opposed to the partition (he'd railed against the "dangerous principles of racial exclusiveness"), was persuaded to change his vote. Even before Israel's "founding war," Zionists had forced over 400,000 people from the area. A Swedish United Nations mediator who had rescued thousands of Jews during World War II was killed by Israeli assassins when he attempted to negotiate an end to the violence. The web site antiwar.com estimated that there were at least thirty-three separate massacres of Palestinian civilians, half of them before a single Arab army unit had entered the conflict. Hundreds of Palestinian villages were razed, and every town, village, and river was given a new Hebrew name.

With the birth of Israel, American foreign policy, already corrupted beyond any constitutional recognition, would become inexorably wedded to the "Middle East's only democracy."

ROBERT TAFT

Criticism in a time of war is essential to the maintenance of any kind of democratic government.

—Robert A. Taft

One of FDR's most powerful opponents in the US Senate, Robert A. Taft, son of former president William Taft, also became one of Truman's most high-profile enemies. Taft was a strong advocate for a non-interventionist foreign policy, which obviously was in diametrical opposition to the wishes of the establishment. His early desire for America to stay out of World War II earned him the enmity of mainstream interventionist Republicans like Wendell Willkie and Thomas E. Dewey. Much as he would courageously criticize the Nuremberg Trials, Taft was one of the few public figures that opposed the internment of Japanese-Americans. With hard-line comments like "there is only one way to beat the New Deal, and that is head on," Taft ran unsuccessful presidential campaigns in 1940 and 1948. Taft was initially seen as the Republican front-runner in 1952, but the entrance of war hero Dwight Eisenhower into the race ensured yet another defeat for the conservative Ohioan. With the full support of establishment party figures like Thomas Dewey, Senator Henry Cabot Lodge Jr., a young Richard Nixon, and California governor Earl Warren (future chief justice of the Supreme Court and head of the discredited Warren Commission), Eisenhower captured the nomination. These strident interventionist leaders depicted Taft as an isolationist, hopelessly out of touch with the demands of the new Cold war.

One of their efforts at sabotage during the convention involved a controversial "Fair Play" ruling that effectively switched a crucial number of pro-Taft delegates to Eisenhower. A bitter Taft would comment, "Every Republican candidate for president since 1936 has been nominated by the Chase National Bank."[21]

Taft later explained how the nomination had been wrested from him. "First," he declared, "it was the power of the New York financial interests and a large number of businessmen subject to New York influence who selected Gen. Eisenhower as their candidate at least a year ago. Secondly, four-fifths of the influential newspapers of the country were opposed to me continuously and vociferously, and many turned themselves into propaganda sheets for Eisenhower."[22] In his final public speech, Taft demonstrated that he was no typical "conservative," as he condemned America's involvement in the Cold War, especially the growing presence in Southeast Asia, and warned that massive increases in defense spending could lead to a "garrison state" and the erosion of civil liberties. Taft would become suddenly sick with a Jack Ruby-style of galloping cancer and died at only sixty-three on July 31, 1953.

WAR IS A RACKET

No war by any nation in any age has ever been declared by the people.

—Eugene Debs

General Smedley Butler wrote in his classic little book *War is a Racket*:

I helped make Mexico, especially Tampico, safe for American oil interests in 1914. I helped make Haiti and Cuba a decent place for the National City Bank boys to collect revenues in. I helped in the raping of half a dozen Central American republics for the benefits of Wall Street. The record of racketeering is long. I helped purify Nicaragua for the international bank-ing house Brown Brothers in 1909–1912. I brought light to the Dominican Republic for American sugar interests in 1916. In China I helped to see to it that Standard Oil went its way unmolested.

It is terribly naïve to swallow the conventional narrative that American mili-tary forces are only committed when a thoroughly demonized boogeyman or boogeymen have been responsible for enough hackneyed atrocities to awaken the otherwise gentle sleeping giant. Butler defined all wars thusly: "War is just a racket. A racket is best described, I believe, as something that is not what it seems to the majority of people. Only a small inside group knows what it is about. It is conducted for the benefit of the very few at the expense of the masses." Butler spoke of how the boys always had to "leave their dear ones behind, give up their jobs, lie in swampy trenches, eat canned willy (when they could get it) and kill and kill and kill . . . and be killed." His words could just as easily apply to World War II, or Korea, or Vietnam, or the Cold War, or any of our recent occupations of smaller sovereign nations.

Smedley Butler was perhaps the most eloquent crusader against war that America has ever had. Butler died at only fifty-eight. There is very little information available about his sudden death. Evidently, he had been sick for a few weeks, and upon being checked into a hospital was told he had "an incurable condition . . . that was probably cancer." He died on June 21, 1940. "Looking back on it, I feel that I could have given Al Capone a few hints," Butler once said. "The best he could do was . . . operate his racket in three districts. I operated on three continents."

Bank of International Settlements (BIS) president Thomas H. McKittrick would admit, during questioning by the US Treasury Department in March 1945, that "there was a little group of financiers who had felt from the beginning that Germany would lose the war; that after defeat they might emerge to shape Germany's destiny. That they would maintain their contacts and trust with other important banking elements so that they would be in a stronger position to negotiate loans for the reconstruction of Germany."[23] Many of Winston Churchill's comments echoed this theme. In a 1936 radio broadcast, Churchill proclaimed, "We will force this war upon Hitler, if he wants it or not." "Now we have forced Hitler to war so he no longer can peacefully annihilate one piece of the Treaty of Versailles after the other," Lord Halifax, English ambassador in Washington, declared in 1939.

Corporations like Standard Oil, ITT, IBM, Ford, and General Motors provided Nazi Germany with essential items like trucks, airplane motors, and technology. Industrialist Arnold Rechberg gave US Army Intelligence a sworn affidavit after the war, in which he claimed that high-ranking Nazi General Kurt Von Schleicher had told him in 1933 that Stalin had given Hitler "substantial funds." Those interested in the extent to which enemies are created, and wars managed, should read Antony Sutton's excellent books *Wall Street and the Bolshevik Revolution* and *Wall Street and the Rise of Hitler.* It is the height of hypocrisy that Hitler and the Nazis are solely associated with the odious philosophy of weeding out the "weak" and "impure" human beings from the genetic pool. The Nazi eugenicists were in full accord with much of the "liberal" western world at the time, as numerous quotes from the likes of Margaret Mead, Helen Keller, Winston Churchill, H. G. Wells, Bertrand Russell, Theodore Roosevelt, Jacques Cousteau, Linus Pauling, Woodrow Wilson, W. E. B. Dubois, Clarence Darrow, Oliver Wendell Holmes, John Maynard Keynes, George Bernard Shaw, and many others demonstrate. It was disheartening to discover that even one of my heroes, Nikola Tesla, harbored eugenicist views. To be a eugenicist was, and is, to support the notion of a "superior" race, which must eliminate the "inferior" ones. Before Hitler ever rose to power, many American states had instituted compulsory sterilization laws for those deemed "unfit" to breed. The idea of an elite "superior" ruling class, complete with infanticide and abortion for those who fail to measure up genetically, goes back to Plato's *Republic*.

After bombarding civilians and destroying priceless cultural landmarks with reckless abandon, the United States government, under the leadership of "hero" General George C. Marshall (about whom Senator Joseph McCarthy would write the widely read book *America's Retreat From Victory: The Story of George Catlett Marshall*), proposed an ambitious, tremendously expensive clean-up project to rebuild what they had destroyed. Originally dubbed the European Recovery Program, it eventually became known as the Marshall Plan. Some $13 to $18 billion was doled out to eighteen European countries over a four-year period. The plan originally included the Soviet Union, but Stalin rejected it. Out of all this would eventually emerge the European Common Market, the European Union, and NATO. After giving away so much to the Soviets at Yalta, the US now, with the abrupt dawn of the "Cold War," adopted the Truman Doctrine of Containment. Churchill, former ally to "Uncle Joe" Stalin, issued his notorious "Iron Curtain" speech, as if he hadn't been personally on hand to draw that curtain down. America became the hands-on policeman of Western Europe, establishing permanent military bases and exerting control over the "democratic" governments there. The Soviets, of course, were even more visibly exerting control over Eastern Europe. Once the Cold War was declared, America's foreign policy became truly and utterly bipartisan; "patriotic" Americans all supported "containing" communism and the massive buildup of our national defense structure, what Eisenhower would come to call a decade later the "Military-Industrial Complex." Both "left" and "right" began to back an American interventionist policy all over the world in order to stop the spread of communism.

THE CANCER EXPLOSION/VACCINATIONS/GOVERNMENT EXPERIMENTATION

If people let government decide which foods they eat and medicines they take, their bodies will soon be in as sorry a state as are the souls of those who live under tyranny.

—Thomas Jefferson

In 1900, cancer caused only 3 percent of the deaths in America. Breast cancer was basically unheard of. Both cancer and heart disease together accounted for just 18 percent of deaths. Today, they account for 63 percent. Dr. W. B. Clark would write, in the January 26, 1909 edition of *The New York Times:* "Cancer was practically unknown until the cowpox vaccination began to be introduced . . . I have seen 200 cases of cancer, and never saw a case in an unvaccinated person." From 1950–2000, the overall cancer rate would shoot up an astonishing 55 percent. This is all the more incredible when factoring in that lung cancer, attributable to the popularity of cigarette smoking for much of the twentieth century, only accounted for a fourth of the increase.

In a March 1906 letter to the secretary of the National Anti-Vaccination League, George Bernard Shaw boldly charged that "Vaccination is nothing short of attempted murder." Dr. Robert Mendelsohn wrote, "There is no convincing scientific evidence that mass inoculations can be credited with eliminating any childhood disease."[24] The developer of the polio vaccine himself, Dr. Albert Sabin, told a Senate subcommittee, "Official data shows that large scale vaccination has failed to obtain any significant improvement of the diseases against which they were supposed to provide protection." Mahatma Gandhi said, "Vaccination is a barbarous practice and one of the most fatal of all the delusions current in our time. Conscientious objectors to vaccination should stand alone, if need be, against the whole world, in defense of their conviction."

In recent years, holistic physicians and celebrities like Robert F. Kennedy Jr. and Jenny McCarthy have been castigated by the establishment for speaking out about the connections between autism and vaccines. There have been well-respected voices warning against the dangers of vaccines for a very long time. The cowpox vaccine was supposedly effective in immunizing humans against smallpox. At the time it was introduced, however, the number of cases of smallpox was already declining. England began a strict compulsory smallpox vaccination program in 1867. Those refusing the vaccine were prosecuted. By 1871, 97.5 percent of people between the ages of two and fifty had been vaccinated. The following year, England experienced the worst smallpox epidemic in its history, with 44,840 deaths resulting. Between 1871 and 1880 the incidence of smallpox actually increased, from 28 to 46 per 100,000 persons.[25] While vaccines have been trumpeted as miraculous wonders of modern medicine, in most cases the prevalence of disease had already been declining due to other factors, primarily cleaner water and improved personal hygiene. The polio vaccine wasn't introduced in England, for example, until 1956, but by then the incidence of polio had already plummeted 82 percent.

"The chief, if not the sole, cause of the monstrous increase in cancer has been vaccination," declared Dr. Robert Bell, vice president of the International Society for Cancer Research.[26] In his book *Crime of Vaccination*, San Francisco's Dr. Tennison Deane related how in Northern California during the late 1880s, he encountered a wealthy rancher who lived with his wife and seven children, with a foreman and his five children, on a 10,000-acre ranch. Until Dr. Deane appeared on the scene, none of these sixteen people had ever been vaccinated. As a passionate young physician, following the medical school doctrine of his day, Dr. Deane warned them of the danger they were subjecting themselves to, and managed to persuade six of the sixteen to get vaccinated. "A year later," wrote Dr. Deane, "an epidemic of sore throats broke out in this ranch colony which developed into diphtheria in four of the vaccinated, among them the farmer's wife, and one child died. The unvaccinated recovered rapidly from their sore throats, but the farmer's wife was paralyzed for a year and eleven years later died of cancer." Dr. Deane was so impacted by this unexpected situation that he not only kept tabs on the subsequent history of the two families on the ranch, but began noticing the connection between vaccination and other maladies in his general practice. He discovered that the other four people whom he had vaccinated on the ranch all died either of tuberculosis or cancer within four to twenty-two years from the date of vaccination, while none of the unvaccinated in either family died within that period except the farmer who, in Deane's words, "died of old age." Dr. Deane habitually asked every patient who came to him with serious throat, bronchial, or pulmonary symptoms, about their vaccination history. Inevitably he found that they'd received the cowpox vaccination against smallpox. When his book was published in 1913, he earned the wrath of his medical colleagues, who made it so difficult for him that the withdrew from the field almost altogether.

"Vaccination and sulpha drugs have been recognised as being directly responsible for the production of leukemia in humans," wrote Dr B. Duperrat of the Saint-Louis Hospital in Paris.[27] A 2010 study, carried out at Manchester's KNH Centre for Biomedical Egyptology, published in *Nature Reviews Cancer*, concluded that cancer was essentially man-made. Their study of hundreds of Egyptian mummies found only a single case of the disease, and the researchers were struck as well by the few references extant on the subject in historical literature. While the establishment responded predictably by claiming the increase in cancer was due to the fact that people are simply living long enough now to contract it, that is contradicted by the dramatic rise in childhood cancer. Professor Rosalie David, of the faculty of Life Sciences at the University of Manchester, explained, "In industrialised societies, cancer is second only to cardiovascular disease as a cause of death. But in ancient times, it was extremely rare. There is nothing in the natural environment that can cause cancer. So it has to be a man-made disease, down to pollution and changes to our diet and lifestyle." The professor added: "The important thing about our study is that it gives a historical perspective to this disease. We can make very clear statements on the cancer rates in societies because we have a full overview. We have looked at millennia, not one hundred years, and have masses of data." Professor Michael Zimmerman, a visiting professor from Villanova University, stated, "In an ancient society lacking surgical intervention, evidence of cancer should remain in all cases. The virtual absence of malignancies in mummies must be interpreted as indicating their rarity in antiquity, indicating that cancer causing factors are limited to societies affected by modern industrialization."[28]

One researcher who opposed the developing medical industrial complex was Dr. Raymond Rife, who began studying cancer in 1922. Rife invented a process called the Mortal Oscillatory Rate, and apparently cured all sixteen terminally ill cancer patients he treated in 1934. According to conspiracy theorists, Rife's laboratory was set on fire in retaliation. A Dr. Milbank Johnson, in true conspiratorial fashion, was struck down just as he was about to validate Rife's amazing 1934 cancer cures a decade later. Depending upon the source, Johnson was either poisoned (discovered when his body was exhumed), or died of a heart attack and was cremated. Author Barry Lynes would write *The Cancer Cure That Worked* in the 1980s, but Rife and his research were anathema to the American Medical Association, American Cancer Society, and big pharma. The medical community, citing the known laws of physics, simply declared that Rife's techniques could not have worked. After Rife died on August 5, 1971, his obituary described him as being embittered and penniless.[29]

How deep this rabbit hole, like all rabbit holes conspiracy researchers chase after, goes is anyone's guess. Frank Zappa wrote about "the place where they keep the imaginary diseases" before he died of cancer at fifty-two. Dr. Sidney Gottlieb, the CIA's Director of Operations of the Technical Services Staff, oversaw some of the Agency's most hideous mind-control experiments under the MKULTRA program. Under the direction of Allen Dulles, Gottlieb administered LSD and other psychotropic drugs to unwitting subjects, and utilized "techniques that would crush the human psyche to the point that it would admit anything."[30] He allegedly confessed, during a CIA hearing, to having dispersed a large quantity of viruses in Zaire's Congo River in 1960, for the express purpose of contaminating it. One of Richard Helms's last acts as CIA Director was to destroy all MKULTRA records relating to Dr. Gottlieb's mad scientist-style work.[31]

The notion that the US government would never subject its citizens to dangerous vaccinations is contradicted by an honest examination of our history. I am indebted to Michael Rivero, who lists a detailed chronology of human experimentation on his excellent WhatReallyHappened.com web site. According to a section of the public law officially establishing a Chemical and Biological Warfare Program, "The use of human subjects will be allowed for the testing of chemical and biological agents by the US Department of Defense." This law permitted the secretary of defense to "conduct tests and experiments . . . on civilian populations (within the United States)." As far back as 1845, J. Marion Sims, who is renowned as the "father of gynecology," performed medical experiments on female African slaves without anesthesia. These women usually died of infection soon afterwards. In 1895, New York pediatrician Henry Heiman infected a four-year-old boy whom he referred to as "an idiot with chronic epilepsy" with gonorrhea. A year later, Dr. Arthur Wentworth at Boston's Children's Hospital performed spinal taps on twenty children there, to see if the procedure was safe.[32] Then US Surgeon General Dr. Walter Reed used twenty-two Spanish immigrants in Cuba as test subjects to prove that yellow fever is contracted from mosquito bites. Reed established the practice of using healthy test subjects. At least he paid them. In 1906, Harvard Professor Dr.

Richard Strong inflected prisoners in the Philippines with cholera, and thirteen of them died as a result. The survivors were given cigars and cigarettes.[33] The Nazi defendants at Nuremberg cited this case as a precedent for their own medical experiments. In a very Nazi-like move, Indiana passed the world's first sterilization law in 1907, reserved for those deemed "unfit" to reproduce. In 1911, Dr. Hideyo Noguchi of the Rockefeller Institute for Medical Research published his research regarding the injection of inactive syphilis into 146 hospital patients and healthy children.

In 1913, fifteen children at St. Vincent's House in Philadelphia were injected with tuberculin, resulting in permanent blindness in some of the children. The Pennsylvania House of Representatives was aware of this tragedy, but the researchers suffered no punishment.[34] Two years later, Dr. Joseph Goldberger, under direction of the US Public Health Office, induced pellagra, a debilitating disease that affects the central nervous system, in twelve Mississippi inmates.[35] By 1935, millions had died from the disease, and the director of the US Public Health Office would reluctantly admit that officials had been aware it was caused by a niacin deficiency for quite some time, but failed to act because it mostly affected poor African Americans. Again, during the Nuremberg Trials, Nazi doctors cited this study in their defense.

Supposedly in response to the Germans' use of chemical weapons in World War I, President Wilson created the Chemical Warfare Service as a branch within the Army. From 1919 to 1922, researchers performed diabolical experiments on inmates at San Quentin State Prison, which consisted of transplanting the testicles of executed inmates and goats into the abdomens and scrotums of living prisoners. It wasn't until 1981 that a draconian Virginia state law that had resulted in an estimated 10,000 perfectly normal women being forcibly sterilized for reasons such as alcoholism, prostitution, and being the child of a retarded mother was finally ended.[36] In 1931, the Puerto Rican Cancer Experiment began under the direction of the Rockefeller Institute for Medical Research's Dr. Cornelius Rhoads. Rhoads injected his test subjects with cancer cells, and thirteen of them died. Rhoads was no misguided do-gooder; his writings revealed him to be a virulent racist who wanted to wipe out the Puerto Rican population.[37] Rising rapidly up the ladder, Rhoads later established the US Army Biological Warfare facilities in Maryland, Utah, and Panama and was named to the US Atomic Energy Commission. Rhoads was also deeply involved with radiation experiments performed on prisoners, hospital patients, and soldiers. In the 1930s, seventeen states passed laws permitting the forced sterilization of "flawed" individuals. And again, the Germans would cite these laws at Nuremberg.

Perhaps the most well-known example of medical experimentation occurred at Tuskegee, Alabama, beginning in 1932. The US Public Health Service allowed four hundred poor, black sharecroppers with syphilis to go untreated in order to study them as human guinea pigs. All of them eventually died. This was the golden era of eugenics, and the "liberal" hero Margaret Sanger, founder of Planned Parenthood, would advocate dastardly proposals, including giving "certain dysgenic groups in our population their choice of segregation (concentration camps) or sterilization." As many as 4,000 forced sterilizations were taking place in the United States every year by this time. Adolf Hitler would, in 1934, request a copy of eugenicist Leon Whitley's book *The Case For Sterilization*. Hitler wrote to another American eugenicist, Madison Grant, informing him that his book *The Great Race* was his "bible." In his notorious 1939 "Monster Experiment," Dr. Wendell Johnson placed twenty-two children at the Iowa Soldiers' Orphan Home under intense psychological duress, which resulted in their developing stutters. In 1941, Dr. William C. Black infected a twelve-month-old baby with herpes. The outraged editor of the *Journal of Experimental Medicine*, Francis Payton Rous, declared that this was "an abuse of power, an infringement of the rights of an individual, and not excusable because the illness which followed had implications for science." That same year, the *Archives of Pediatrics* mentioned, rather matter-of-factly, experiments where doctors had transmitted the severe gum disease Vincent's angina from sick children to healthy ones. Again in 1941, doctors at the University of Michigan, including the renowned Jonas Salk, sprayed wild influenza virus into the noses of mental patients.[38]

In 1942, President Franklin Roosevelt created the first biological warfare program, which was backed by the National Academy of Sciences, and a new agency, the War Research Service, was established to oversee these activities. In conjunction with this effort, Fort Detrick, Maryland opened the same year. It employed nearly five hundred scientists who worked tirelessly on developing biological weapons and defenses against them. Human subjects were used regularly. George W. Merck, of the giant Merck Pharmaceutical Company, was appointed as the head of the War Research Service. "Work in this field cannot be ignored in a time of peace," this early titan of big pharma declared. "It must be continued on a sufficient scale to provide an adequate defense."[39] Also in 1942, US military doctors infected four hundred prisoners in Chicago with malaria. The prisoners were told they were part of the war effort. The Nazis cited this experiment as well during their defense at Nuremberg. The same year, the Chemical Warfare Service began experimenting with mustard gas and lewisite on 4,000 US military personnel.

In 1943, researchers at the University of Cincinnati locked sixteen mentally disabled patients in refrigerated cabinets for 120 hours. During the Manhattan Project which resulted in the atomic bomb, US soldiers in Tennessee and patients in New York and Chicago were injected with plutonium and tested for the effects of fluoride.[40] Few Americans realize that fluoride is the key chemical component in atomic bombs. The tests demonstrated that fluoride causes damage to the central nervous system, but this didn't stop it from being force-fed into the national water supply a decade later. From 1944 to 1946, psychiatric patients at Illinois State Hospital were infected with malaria by Dr. Alf Alving of the University of Chicago Medical School. In 1945, eight hundred Atlanta inmates were infected with malaria. Starting in 1946, researchers began to tap into the readily available market of test subjects at VA hospitals. From 1946 to 1953, research sponsored by the US Atomic Energy Commission, involving doctors at Harvard Medical School, Massachusetts General Hospital, MIT, and the Boston University School of Medicine, included spiking the cereal of mentally disabled youngsters with radioactive material. A classified April 17, 1947 Atomic Energy Commission document advised, "It is desired that no document be released which refers to experiments with humans that might have an adverse reaction on public opinion or result in legal suits."[41] From 1950 to 1953, the US Army released chemical clouds over six American and Canadian cities. In the 1998 book *Acres of Skin*, Allen M. Hornblum documented how in 1950, 200 female inmates in Pennsylvania were infected with the hepatitis virus.

The CIA's MKULTRA mind-control program defined itself in a January 1952 memo thusly: "Can we get control of an individual to the point where he will do our bidding against his will and even against fundamental laws of nature, such as self-preservation?" Allen Dulles laconically complained that there weren't an adequate number of "human guinea pigs to try these extraordinary techniques." All in all, some eighty institutions, over half of them colleges, would house MKULTRA labs. Their work with LSD and heroin revolved around "discrediting individuals, eliciting information, and implanting suggestions and other forms of mental control."[42] Over 7,000 members of the military were unknowingly injected with LSD. The CIA also had Project ARTICHOKE, which utilized hypnosis and morphine in an attempt to induce amnesia. Project QKHILLTOP studied ancient Chinese methods of loosening tongues.

Beginning in 1950, the US government intentionally doused 293 populated areas with bacteria. No citizens in the areas affected were even informed, and no safety precautions or medical follow-up ever occurred. Perhaps the most memorable of these occurred over San Francisco in September 1950. The US Army showered the unsuspecting San Franciscans with bacteria over the course of eight days. As author Leonard J. Cole wrote in his book *Clouds of Secrecy*, "Nearly all of San Francisco received 500 particle minutes per liter. In other words, nearly every one of the 800,000 people in San Francisco . . . were inhaling millions of the bacteria and particles every day during the week of testing." At least one person, seventy-five-year-old Edward Nevin, died as a result of this hideous experiment. Several others contracted serious infections from the chemicals. Much of the information surrounding this sort of experimentation was only begrudgingly released during legal efforts initiated by Nevin's grandson in the late 1970s. In the trial that finally resulted in 1981, the government actually claimed that they needed no permission to spray the public without their knowledge! One government witness, a current doctor at Fort Detrick, testified that "I would still spray San Francisco again today." General William Creasy arrogantly stated, "I would find it completely impossible to conduct such a test trying to obtain informed consent. I could not have hoped to prevent panic in the uninformed world in which we live in." The judge in the case was predictably biased in favor of the government, and even berated Nevin's grandson for his lack of respect for military officials. In the hallway, General Creasy challenged young Nevin to a fistfight! After spending some $60,000 in legal fees, and draining himself emotionally, young Nevin had to witness the judge inexplicably rule in favor of the military. Nevin's appeals all the way up to the Supreme Court were denied.[43] In 1955, the CIA sprayed whooping cough bacteria over Tampa Bay, Florida.

Another infamous mad scientist, Dr. D. Ewen Cameron, who would later experiment on helpless mental patients in Canada during the MKULTRA program, published a 1950 article in the *British Journal of Physical Medicine*. He calmly described forcing schizophrenics to lie naked under 200-watt red lamps for up to eight hours at a time, placing test subjects in an electric cage that overheated their body to 103 degrees, and inducing comas by giving patients powerful injections of insulin. Cameron's work was partially funded by the Rockefeller Foundation.

At about this same time, the Department of Defense developed plans to detonate nuclear weapons in areas of the desert and secretly monitor the residents afterward for medical problems and mortality rates. Rumors persist that American military forces used germ warfare weapons in the Korean conflict, which included releases of anthrax, the plague, and yellow fever. The Eisenhower administration responded to the initial allegations by charging those who made such claims with sedition.[44] In 1951, the US Army secretly contaminated the Norfolk Naval Supply Center and Washington, DC's National Airport with a strain of bacteria thought to be particularly harmful to African Americans. In 1952, one test subject died when he was injected with mescaline at Columbia University's New York State Psychiatric Institute. In 1952, inmates from Ohio State Prison were injected with live cancer cells at the Sloan-Kettering Institute. Under Allen Dulles's MKULTRA program, the CIA doused unsuspecting prisoners, and in more absurd cases, the patrons of brothels under "Operation Midnight Climax," with LSD.[45] The needless death of Dr. Frank Olson resulted from these diabolical LSD experiments. The CIA's Project MKDELTA experimented with biochemicals "for harassment, discrediting, and disabling purposes."[46] The US Air Force established Operation Whitecoat at around the same time, which subjected test subjects to hepatitis. The Army Chemical Corps also conducted LSD research until 1958. The Army released mosquitoes infected with yellow fever into residential neighborhoods in Savannah, Georgia and Avon Park, Florida. A high incidence of fevers, respiratory disease, stillbirths, and even deaths resulted. After each test, US Army personnel would pose as public health officials as they photographed and tested the victims.[47] In 1957, the US military launched Operation Plumbbob in Nevada, which consisted of twenty-nine nuclear detonations, creating radiation responsible for 32,000 cases of thyroid cancer in the area.[48]

Starting in 1957, the CIA hired the aforementioned Dr. D. Ewen Cameron, founder of the McGill University Department of Psychiatry, to perform a series of horrific LSD studies on Canadians. What was particularly reprehensible about Cameron's experiments was the fact his test subjects were being treated for minor issues like post-partum depression or simple anxiety. The subjects were placed into vegetative states by use of drugs, electroshock, and sensory deprivation. Attempts were made to literally erase memories and rewrite psyches. The patients were also given paralytic drugs and forced to endure weeks or months of tape loops playing the same music or repetitive statements.[49] Under Operation Hardtack, some three hundred members of the US Navy were exposed to radiation when thirty nuclear bombs were exploded near the Pacific Islands.

On March 1, 1954, the United States exploded the most powerful nuclear bomb in history, in the heart of the Pacific Ocean. The bomb was lovingly named Bravo, and its explosiveness in relation to the bombs dropped on Hiroshima and Nagasaki was the same as those first atomic weapons had been in comparison to conventional weaponry. Bravo was laced with plutonium, and it vaporized three of the Bikini Islands. Marshall Islanders were saturated with radioactive fallout, and their pleas for compensation from the US government went unheeded. A report presented to the UN Human Rights Council claimed that the radiation had caused fatalities and many long-term health consequences, as well as "near-irreversible environmental contamination." The radioactive fallout from the blast was widespread and contaminated at least one Japanese tuna trawler. All this was bad enough, but the islanders were summarily converted into test subjects on the effects of radioactive fallout, conducted by the US Navy under Project 4.1. Thirty-six years later, one of the doctors involved would admit, "In retrospect, it was unfortunate that the AEC [Atomic Energy Commission], because it was a research organization, did not include support of basic health care of populations under study."[50]

This is a just a sampling. The list is long and every American should be embarrassed by it. I concentrated primarily on human experimentation within the United States. I could have discussed, for instance, the ugly 1946–1948 US research project in Guatemala, sponsored by the Public Health Service and the National Institutes of Health, where prostitutes were used to infect prisoners, mental patients, and Guatemalan soldiers with syphilis and other sexually transmitted diseases. It also involved infecting people more directly, with "inoculations made from syphilis bacteria poured into the men's penises." Among those infected were orphan children.[51] I also failed to mention ridiculous programs like Operation Big Itch and Operation Big Buzz, both of which involved the use of air-dispersed insects. No wonder all those big bug movies were so popular in the 1950s.

CHAPTER TEN

THE FABULOUS FIFTIES

In order to bring a nation to support the burdens of maintaining great
military establishments, it is necessary to create an emotional state akin to
war psychology. There must be the portrayal of external menace.

—John Foster Dulles

SENATOR JOSEPH MCCARTHY

The reason why we find ourselves in a position of impotency is not because
the enemy has sent men to invade our shores, but rather because of the
traitorous actions of those who have had all the benefits that the wealthiest
nation on earth has had to offer—the finest homes, the finest college
educations, and the finest jobs in government we can give.

—Senator Joseph McCarthy

Before his name made every dictionary in a most undesired manner, Joseph McCarthy was a powerful United States senator from Wisconsin. The majority of Americans agreed with and supported his efforts to root out Soviet influence from the upper levels of the United

States government. In just one week, thirteen million Americans signed a petition supporting him. The 2005 film *Good Night and Good Luck* solidified the mainstream view of McCarthy as a hopelessly despicable villain. Young Robert F. Kennedy was a member of Senator McCarthy's staff on the Senate Permanent Subcommittee on Investigations, and McCarthy was the godfather of RFK's daughter Kathleen. McCarthy dated two of the Kennedy sisters and was close to the patriarch of the clan, Joseph P. Kennedy. Even after drifting far to the left by the time of his assassination in 1968, Bobby Kennedy remained loyal to his old boss, labeling him "a very complicated character." Author Arthur Herman recounted an anecdote where John F. Kennedy once angrily responded to a speaker at the Harvard Spree Club who was denouncing McCarthy equally with Alger Hiss by shouting, "How dare you couple the name of a great American patriot with that of a traitor!"[1]

The conventional historical view of Joe McCarthy is that he was a crass, cynical politician who saw an opportunity to exploit Cold War fears and engaged in the most virulent kind of red-baiting, destroying untold numbers of lives in the process. Interestingly, James Forrestal was highly influential on McCarthy's thinking. As McCarthy himself wrote, "Before meeting Jim Forrestal, I thought we were losing to international Communism because of incompetence and stupidity on the part of our planners. I mentioned that to Forrestal. I shall forever remember his answer. He said, 'McCarthy, consistency has never been a mark of stupidity. If they were merely stupid they would occasionally make a mistake in our favor.'" McCarthy went after the most prominent Americans imaginable, including General George C. Marshall. Crediting Forrestal again, McCarthy stated, "Forrestal told me he was convinced that General Marshall was one of the key figures in the United States in advancing Communist objectives." Ironically, in light of what would be his own fate, McCarthy charged, "The Communists hounded Forrestal to his death. They killed him just as definitely as if they had thrown him from that sixteenth-story window in Bethesda Naval Hospital." McCarthy boldly called Forrestal's death a murder and "dedicated part of this fight to Jim Forrestal."[2]

On April 28, 1957, McCarthy entered Bethesda Naval Hospital himself. Great mystery surrounds the nature of his hospitalization. Evidently, whatever "illness" existed came as a great surprise to everyone. His wife stated that he'd sought treatment on his knee, but the mainstream media reported that he was suffering from "acute hepatitis" and had been placed in an oxygen tent. By April 30, the press reported that McCarthy had been removed from the oxygen tent and was doing better. Incredibly, two days later, on May 2, 1957, the forty-eight-year-old politician died. There were a myriad of questions swirling around the cause of death, but as could probably be anticipated by astute researchers, no autopsy was performed. The court historians have coalesced behind the view that McCarthy was a chronic alcoholic, which ignited the acute hepatitis they have decided (without any conclusive evidence) killed him. One of the most powerful mainstream columnists of the era, the ever-unreliable Drew Pearson, emphasized McCarthy's alleged alcoholism, and recklessly (absent any credible sources) charged that he'd attempted suicide four times. Since one of the few things clarified by doctors at Bethesda was the fact that McCarthy did not contract hepatitis through infection, writer Medford Evans and researcher David Martin have produced a strong argument that the disease was triggered by poison. As Medford Evans wrote in his book *The Assassination of Joe McCarthy,* "I believe they would have murdered him if they could have."

It is a testament to how simplified conventional history has become to consider that figures like McCarthy, thoroughly demonized to the point where he cannot be discussed rationally, are dismissed with the sound bite from the Army-McCarthy hearings, when he was angrily asked, by Joseph Welch, "Have you no decency, sir?" McCarthy in fact never really got bad press until he aimed his inquiry at higher targets in the government, eventually resulting in a censure over his supposedly irresponsible charges against the Army. As Paul Gottfried pointed out in an August 14, 2012 column on Lew Rockwell's website, the names of suspected communists on the list he so memorably waved during his 1950 speech in Wheeling, West Virginia, were essentially the same ones provided by Secretary of State James Byrnes in 1946. As Ann Coulter and other recent conservatives have noted, while support for McCarthy and anti- communism went hand-in-hand for a long time, the emergence of the neocons during the Reagan years brought forth a totally new kind of conservatism that rejected the strident anti-communism of Joe McCarthy and others, and instead focused on an Ayn Rand-inspired worship of the marketplace and capitalism. In fact, it has become a common rhetorical tactic of the right, as well as the left, to target critics with the label of "McCarthyism."

The establishment's hatred for Joe McCarthy is such that he is often equated with Adolf Hitler. Harry Truman angrily responded to McCarthy's February 9, 1950 speech, charging fifty-seven State Department employees with being members of the Communist Party, with "This is the first time in my experience, and I was ten years in the Senate, that I ever heard of a senator trying to discredit his own Government." President Eisenhower snobbishly deflected his troublesome fellow Republican: "I will not get in the gutter with that guy." Liberal journalistic icon Edward R. Murrow's coverage of McCarthy was perhaps even more wildly biased than Dan Rather's (and virtually everyone else in the establishment press) coverage of Oliver Stone would be, decades later, upon the release of his film *JFK*. Daniel Boorstin sneered to fellow mainstream journalist Arthur Herman in 1997 that McCarthy's death was "the fifth proof for the existence of God." This kind of universal animosity is hardly a recent development. The British newspaper *News Chronicle* reported McCarthy's death thusly: "Senator McCarthy died yesterday in Washington. America was cleaner by his fall, and is cleaner by his death." Richard Rovere evoked the predictable comparison in his book *Senator Joe McCarthy*, writing, "like Hitler, McCarthy was a screamer, a political thug, a master of the mob." Rovere demeaned McCarthy's supporters as "bat-haunted Minute Women . . . from the outmost fringes, where grievances and anxieties were the strongest and least grounded in reason, where the passion for authoritarian leadership was greatest, where the will to hate and condemn and punish could most easily be transformed into political action." Harvard sociologist Talcott Parsons decried McCarthy's "popular revolt against the upper classes." Michael Barone called McCarthy "a pathological liar, an uninformed and obscure politician."[3]

With the fall of the Soviet Union, their archives were released and shocked polite society by seemingly vindicating many of McCarthy's charges. Court historians like John Earl Haynes and Harvey Klehr, reacting to information proving the Communist Party of the United States had been secretly financed by the Soviet Union and, in fact, helped support the KGB's nefarious activities, nevertheless concluded with straight faces, "None of this, however, offers any vindication for Senator McCarthy." Put in true historical context, while American citizens had their rights trampled and were imprisoned without charges by the thousands during the Lincoln administration, none of those investigated by McCarthy's committee were denied counsel or detained without due process of law. The Communist Party itself continued to flourish legally in America at the height of the "Red Scare." Membership in the party was never considered criminal. Our conventional history has mixed in the House Un-American Activities Committee, the Rosenberg trial, and blacklisting in Hollywood with Joe McCarthy, when in fact he had nothing to do with any of that. McCarthy, instead, was focused on communist infiltration into the upper echelons of the federal government, and evidently the establishment objected, and continues to object, strongly to that. While many thousands of befuddled Americans were arrested and jailed without charges during the Civil War, a grand total of 108 Communist Party members were even convicted under the Smith Act, which Congress passed in 1941 and applied equally to fascist or communist subversion.[4] Declassified FBI files have revealed that McCarthy was essentially right about Owen Lattimore, the most famous "victim" of "McCarthyism," long portrayed favorably in the establishment press. Only the "anti-Semitic" little newspaper the *Spotlight* would report that declassified Soviet records revealed longtime Communist Party USA head Gus Hall had been paid millions of dollars over the decades by the Soviets.

An unnatural death that occurred during the height of McCarthy's influence was that of Robert M. LaFollette Jr., son of the legendary populist politician. "Young Bob" had been a senator from Wisconsin himself, and eventually lost his seat to rising Republican star "Tail Gunner Joe" McCarthy. LaFollette had spoken of his own experiences with Communists infiltrating congressional staffs, but was seemingly being targeted by McCarthy's investigation when he was found dead of an allegedly self-inflicted gunshot wound on February 24, 1953. It is the popular but unproven belief of the court historians that he killed himself to avoid testifying before McCarthy's committee.

Despite all the released documents proving that the Soviets actually did have a powerful foothold within America during the Cold War era, Joe McCarthy himself continues to be smeared, to be relegated to a cruel, constructed term of derision in dictionaries. McCarthy was genuinely working-class, from humble origins, and a war hero as well. I believe a man can often be judged by his enemies, and virtually the entire establishment of his day opposed him. Lyndon Johnson loathed McCarthy and was the impetus behind his 1954 censure by the Senate. John F. Kennedy, on the other hand, coincidentally or not, was in the hospital with back problems at the time of the censure vote.

Ironically, while the establishment did everything it could to smear and then probably kill Joe McCarthy, the most prominent voice against communist infiltration in the US government, the undeclared and impossible to define "Cold War" against communism continued unabated. An indication of just how phony most of our "wars" have been was Operation Paperclip, formulated by the Office of Strategic Services (OSS), precursor to the CIA. While the Nazis were about as completely demonized as any group in human history ever has been, our government transported 1,500 German scientists and engineers into this country following World War II. Ex-Nazis like Wernher von Braun were instrumental in developing America's space program. Hitler's master spy Reinhard Gehlen reactivated his intelligence network in the Soviet Union and his Gehlen Organization became America's sole source for intelligence on the Soviet Union for the first ten years of the Cold War.

The Pentagon, the world's largest office building, with more than seventeen miles of corridors, advertised America's new status as global policeman/superpower. Another of the unconstitutional monstrosities that were born during the Roosevelt years, it is impossible to imagine any of America's Founders approving of such an enormous central war making/war planning facility. The Pentagon actually replaced the first building complex established for "liberal" FDR's ever-expanding Department of War (well before America's official entrance into the conflict). More than 150 East Arlington, Virginia families, predominantly black, were evicted when the government appropriated their land for the massive new Pentagon. It was inevitable that America would need a stronger intelligence agency to foment and support American foreign policy.

THE CENTRAL INTELLIGENCE AGENCY

There are some things the general public does not need to know, and shouldn't. I believe democracy flourishes when the government can take

*legitimate steps to keep its secrets and when the press can decide whether to
print what it knows.*

—Washington Post publisher Katherine Graham

The Central Intelligence Agency (CIA) supplanted the OSS in 1947. Franklin
D. Roosevelt had asked New York lawyer William J. "Wild Bill" Donovan
to draft a plan for an intelligence service *before* Pearl Harbor. Donovan proposed a powerful, centralized civilian agency "which will procure intelligence both by overt and covert methods and will at the same time provide
intelligence guidance, determine national intelligence objectives, and cor-
relate the intelligence material collected by all government agencies."[5] He
also thought that this agency should have authority to conduct "subversive
operations abroad."

The CIA and the National Security Council were created under the
National Security Act of 1947. A supplemental act passed in 1949 authorized
the Agency to use "confidential fiscal and administrative procedures" and
exempted it from the usual limitations of federal spending. Incredibly, it
permitted CIA funds to be included in the budgets of other departments
and allowed it to keep "organization, functions, names, officials, titles, sal-
aries, or numbers of personnel employed" undisclosed. The conventional
historical view is that if the CIA had been around on December 7, 1941, the
dirty, sneaky rotten Japs would never have been able to "surprise" us at
Pearl Harbor.

During World War II, General "Wild Bill" Donovan had been notorious
for sending saboteurs behind enemy lines, disseminating disinformation,
and engaging in the kind of "dirty tricks" that would later become an integral part of the American political process. An early specialist in cloak-and-
dagger intrigue was Frank Wisner, the CIA's Director of Operations from
1948 until the late 1950s. Wisner allegedly went insane and committed suicide in 1965. Not only would the CIA engage in clandestine activities outside

its charter, it was largely incompetent. As author Tim Weiner showed in his book *Legacy of Ashes*, in the early 1950s the Agency wasted millions of dollars by dropping gold bars, two-way radios, and agents into Poland in an effort to support what its leading officials believed was a brewing underground movement against the Soviets. Hilariously, through double agents, the Soviets actually funneled some of the CIA's money to the Communist Party of Italy. The 1952 creation of the National Security Agency added another unconstitutional layer to the Military-Industrial Complex. The CIA covered up the needless deaths of over a hundred agents who were dropped into Manchuria after China intervened in the Korean War.

What Tim Weiner described as "the CIA's practice of purchasing elections and politicians with bags of cash" began with the 1948 Italian elections, where they spent some $65 million of American taxpayer money. The CIA sponsored literary magazines in Germany and Great Britain, promoted abstract art, and secretly funded two and a half million books and periodicals. The record of CIA "regime changes" around the world is long and shameful. They helped overthrow Iran's Mohammad Mossadegh in 1953, Guatemala's Jacobo Arbenz in 1954, were involved in the 1958 rebellion in Indonesia, installed "Papa Doc" Duvalier as the bloody dictator of Haiti in 1959, and were at least involved in the 1961 assassination of Patrice Lumumba of the Democratic Republic of the Congo, three days before JFK was inaugurated as president.

Under Operation Mockingbird, the CIA co-opted mainstream journalists, making them safe and reliable conduits of propaganda. Philip Graham, publisher of the "liberal" *Washington Post*, was an integral part of this program. The CIA itself would belatedly admit to turning at least four hundred journalists into CIA assets. With the MKULTRA program, the CIA ventured into mind control and brainwashing. An important part of this program involved giving LSD to unwitting victims, several of whom committed suicide in response. In the most infamous incident, bacteriologist and biological warfare scientist Frank Olson "jumped" from a hotel window because of this insidious drug promotion. Olson's sons Eric and Nils have not let this matter drop, and launched a lawsuit for damages against the CIA, which was dismissed in 2013. They alleged that their father was murdered after witnessing brutal interrogation sessions, which resulted in the Agency killing suspects with biological agents he had helped develop.[6] The CIA only grudgingly admitted in 1975 that Olson had even been given LSD, and initially told his family the death was from job-induced stress, but later claimed he committed suicide.

Olson worked out of Fort Detrick in Maryland in the special operations division of the Army's biological laboratory. Eric Olson declared, "The evidence shows that our father was killed in their custody. They have lied to us ever since, withholding documents and information, and changing their story when convenient" and that the CIA was guilty of a "multi-decade cover-up that continues to this day." Olson plunged to his death from a thirteenth-floor window of New York's Statler Hotel on November 28, 1953. Olson was sharing the room with a CIA doctor, who is presumably the person who made a mysterious phone call immediately after his death, in which the hotel operator overheard one party say "Well, he's gone," and the other reply, "That's too bad." The Olson case became publicized during the Senate hearings into CIA abuses in 1975, chaired by Frank Church. While President Gerald Ford officially apologized to the Olson family at the time, and they received a belated financial settlement, Eric Olson maintains that the CIA was still refusing to provide documents to the family as recently as 2014. When Olson's body was exhumed in 1993, a forensic scientist concluded that he'd probably been struck in the head and thrown from the window.[7]

KOREAN WAR

What difference does it make to the dead, the orphans, and the homeless,
whether the mad destruction is wrought under the name of totalitarianism or
the holy name of liberty and democracy?

—Mahatma Gandhi

America's rare lapse into peace didn't last long. In early 1950, an entirely new kind of "war" was born: the controlled, contrived, "no-win" variety. The United States led a United Nations force (Woodrow Wilson's life-long dream of a League of Nations belatedly came true under another name), in which Korea was split into two, with the South being controlled by the US and the north controlled by communist China and the Soviet Union. During World War II, America had agreed to permit the Soviets to occupy the northern part of Korea. Initially described as a "police action" by President Truman, this three-year "conflict" was never authorized by Congress. Most Americans probably don't realize that a formal declaration of war hasn't been made by the United States since World War II.

Under the auspices of the United Nations, our Korean intervention represented the initial American foray into "limited war." "Old Soldier" General Douglas MacArthur understandably blanched at this new, unknown concept, and was summarily relieved of his command by Truman in April 1951. When MacArthur proposed that the United States surge into North Korea and actually attempt to defeat the communists, the reliably globalist Truman fired him. Public support strongly favored MacArthur, and Truman could only lamely explain that "it is right for us to be in Korea" and rant against "communists in the Kremlin who are engaged in a monstrous conspiracy to stamp out freedom all over the world" in an April 11, 1951 address to the nation. These were the same communists that MacArthur wanted to fight, of course. Laughably, Truman spoke of making sure that "the precious lives of our fighting men are not wasted." Our pointless intervention in Korea certainly "wasted" the lives of the 54,246 Americans that were killed there, and as of April 2015 it is estimated that more than 7,800 US soldiers remain unaccounted for.[8] Korea paved the way for our disastrous involvement in Vietnam, with more "limited" goals, indecipherable enemies, and massive casualties. The "anti-communist" movement successfully divested itself of the Forrestals and McCarthys, who actually wished to root it out, and instead wasted incalculable amounts of money and resources (not to mention lives) in an unexplainable, counterproductive attempt to "contain" it.

The right-wing, truly anti-communist perspective on this undeclared "conflict" was stated succinctly in the book *Treason in High Places!* by retired USAF Lt. Col. Bud Farrell, who wrote:

When I was a young officer and a jet fighter pilot flying missions in the Korean Conflict (unknowingly under the command of a Soviet General of the United Nations Security Council), I could never understand how the enemy knew so much about us, as broadcast almost daily over the communist Pyongyang radio station in North Korea. The North Koreans knew when we were coming, how many of us there were, what type of aircraft we were flying, and even the targets we were to hit. Later I realized that the naval and ground forces suffered the same fate that we did, especially our Army and Marine infantry troops. All of our military operations had to be forwarded by radio to the Soviet Commander of the United Nations Security Council at the United Nations Building, New York City, for approval before our forces went into action against the North Koreans and Red Chinese. The Soviet Commander of the United Nations Security Council delayed the battle plans until he used the radios in the United Nations Building in New York to relay all our battle planning information to Moscow, North Korea, and Red China. The enemy then contacted and relayed these battle plans to their communist forces in the field.

While right-wing "extremists" have focused on the indisputable fact that American forces were restricted and not instructed to "win" anything, independent left-wingers have detailed the all too familiar misconduct of US troops in Korea. The left-wing narrative holds that the Koreans were ecstatic when the brutal forty-year Japanese occupation of their country ended in August 1945, but the United States refused to grant them self-determination. FDR had suggested to Stalin at Yalta that Korea be placed under their joint control before being granted independence. When the US chose the dividing line at the 38th parallel, it ensured that the vast majority of Koreans resided in the American-controlled southern zone. The United States Army military government in Korea was created, and in September 1945, 72,000 American troops arrived to occupy South Korea. A violent campaign to suppress popular Korean Peoples' Committees, allegedly "communist" inspired, resulted in more than 1,000 Koreans killed and 30,000 jailed. A police state ensued, aided and abetted by US military advisors. On just one island, Cheju, it was estimated that as many as 60,000 of the 300,000 residents were murdered in the first year.[9] Evoking fond memories of Union generals Sherman, Grant, and Sheridan, over half of the island's villages and 40,000 homes were burned down, and some 100,000 people rounded up into government compounds. All opposition to US rule was branded as "communist." Estimates of civilians killed range as high as 800,000 *before* the "police state" officially broke out in June 1950.[10] Like other small sovereign nations would discover in the years to come, this "Cold War" meant being caught in the crosshairs between whatever game American imperialists and communist totalitarian forces were playing.

The curious strategy in this Cold War became one of confronting communism indirectly, through "limited" conflicts that held no purpose or strategic value. While radicals were smeared as "communists" and had their lives and careers ruined, those most aggressively attacking communism were targeted as enemies by their "anti-communist" leaders. We know, from the research of Antony Sutton and others, that a clique of American financiers and corporate powers helped established communism in Russia, and thereafter continued to funnel money and technology to the Soviet Union. Seldom has a manufactured, artificial enemy been so transparently obvious. During the 1950s, American children rehearsed nonsensical "duck and cover" drills, and many of their parents dug their own fallout shelters. Yearly increases in the "defense" budget became a given. After all, what would befall us if the dreaded Soviets took over the world? The charade was exposed, but never to the masses. Economist and author Paul Craig Roberts visited Moscow at the height of the CIA's propaganda campaign against the Soviets, and was astonished to discover that Russia had "a Third World economy." "Extremist" researchers like Eustace Mullins claimed that the American taxpayers had been subsidizing our big, burly foe since 1917, which he detailed in his book *The $5 Trillion Cold War Hoax.*

Former senior British Intelligence officer Michael Herman revealed, in his book *Intelligence Power in Peace and War,* that the CIA and its fellow western intelligence agencies had independently manipulated Cold War tensions. Herman found that the intelligence assessments, fed to NATO governments, regarding Soviet arms programs and military capability were wildly exaggerated and consistently stressed "worst-case scenarios." The supposed "massive threat" from the Soviets was largely a fabrication. When the Cold War ended, of course, all these alarmist reports were simply funneled into the never-ending "war" on terrorism. By any measure, the people are constantly fed what H. L. Mencken once called "an endless series of hobgoblins," to perpetuate the message that the world is becoming a more dangerous place. The intelligence agencies naturally benefit from such speculation, as it reinforces the idea that they are vitally important, even with their wildly inaccurate forecasting and still top-secret budgets.

THE REECE COMMITTEE TO INVESTIGATE TAX-EXEMPT FOUNDATIONS

United States government officials, elected and unelected, with enormous financial assistance from the tax-exempt foundations, have for many years been working to implement unconstitutional regional planning.

—From the Reece Committee's 1953 Congressional Hearings

One of the most potentially important congressional investigations ever was conducted between 1952 and 1954. The House Select Committee to Investigate Tax-Exempt Foundations and Comparable Organizations was tasked to investigate how nonprofit foundations and organizations utilized their funding. While it was primarily a product of the McCarthy era, and thus focused on alleged "subversive" links, a great deal of important information was disclosed. The Committee concluded, in the report written by its director of research and former banker Norman Dodd, that huge, purportedly philanthropic institutions like the Ford Foundation, Rockefeller Foundation, and Carnegie Endowment for International Peace were devoted to causes promoting "oligarchical collectivism" and internationalism. Dodd claimed a true revolution had taken place in 1933–1936, with massive amounts of power being transferred to the executive branch of the federal government. Dodd explained that this change "could not have occurred peacefully, or with the consent of the majority, unless education in the United States had been prepared in advance to endorse it." Unfortunately, the Committee's report received scant attention, as it was released in the midst of efforts to censure Senator Joseph McCarthy.

Opponents of the committee lambasted it for "red baiting." The two Democrats on the Committee, one of which was Wayne L. Hays, who would be forced to resign from Congress in 1976 after being exposed for having an affair with his paid staffer Elizabeth Ray, refused to sign the final report, and one of the Republicans dissented from many of its conclusions. The minority report contended that Chairman B. Carroll Reece and his staff held "a deep-seated antagonism toward foundations" which might "well be characterized as pathological." The same representatives who felt comfortable in trampling over civil liberties and quelling any and all antiwar dissent nevertheless became apoplectic over the perceived lack of fairness granted powerful foundations and those who administered them. Evidently, some on the committee itself objected to the very reasonable premise being investigated, that of whether or not foundations had "used their resources for purposes contrary to those for which they were established."

Dodd would write in his report that the foundations had been "Directing education in the United States toward an international view-point." The inherent educational message "contrasts sharply with the freedom of the individual as the cornerstone of our social structure . . . it seems to substitute the group, the will of the majority, and a centralized power to enforce this." Dodd continued, "It is also interesting to note that by comparison with funds for research provided by Foundations, those now flowing from our government are so large that they dwarf Foundation contributions." The report astutely recognized that "the social scientist is gradually becoming dignified by the title 'Social Engineer.'" Finally, Dodd suggested that "the Committee give special consideration to the Ford Foundation. This Foundation gives ample evidence of having taken the initiative in selecting purposes of its own. Being of recent origin, it should not be held responsible for the actions or accomplishments of any of its predecessors. It is without precedent as to size, and it is the first Foundation to dedicate itself openly to 'problem solving' on a world scale." After citing its Center for Advanced Study, its research and training programs abroad, and its miscellaneous grants-in-aid, Dodd wrote, "When it is considered that the capital resources of this Foundation approach, or may exceed, $500,000,000, and that its income approximates $30,000,000, each year, it is obvious that before embarking upon the solution of 'problems,' some effort should be made by the trustees to make certain that their solution is 'in the public interest.'" After criticizing one of its publications for seemingly dismissing the importance of the Declaration of Independence, Dodd observed that "It is interesting that this should omit the list of grievances which originally made the general concepts of this document reasonable."

In a 1982 interview, Norman Dodd would discuss his visit with then-Ford Foundation president Rowan Gaither. Dodd claimed that Gaither made the remarkable admission that "all of us who have a hand in the making of policies here have had experience operating under directives, the substance of which is that we shall use our grant-making power so to alter life in the United States that it can be comfortably merged with the Soviet Union." Dodd clarified what the Reece Committee meant by "un-American." Contrary to a typical 1950s-era anti-communist mentality, instead Dodd defined it as "trying to effect change by unconstitutional means." He again noted how the minutes of the Carnegie Foundation for International Peace from 1908 were oddly interested in knowing, "Is there any means known more effective than war, assuming you wish to alter the life of an entire people?" It doesn't take a conspiracy theorist to question why this organization, devoted to "peace," would ask, the following year, "How do we involve the United States in a war?" They went on to specifically strive to obtain control of the State Department, where they could "control the diplomatic machinery of this country." Most damning of all was an admission that this "peace" foundation had sent President Wilson a telegram in which they cautioned him against ending the war too quickly. Following the war, their records revealed a plan to prevent America from returning to its pre-1914 ways, and controlling the dissemination of history internationally, while the Rockefeller Foundation was tasked with handling this issue domestically. They even spoke of building "our own stable of historians."[11]

Dodd explained in this interview how his aide, Katherine Casey, who had previously been skeptical, even antagonistic, towards what she perceived as an anti-foundation witch hunt, eventually "lost her mind as a result" of what she discovered in the minutes of the Carnegie Endowment. She was never able to return to her law practice, and was fortunate that Carroll Reece managed to find her a job with the Federal Trade Commission. Dodd recounted how Congressman Wayne Hays had greeted him initially with the statement, "I am opposed to this investigation. I regard it as nothing but an effort on the part of Carroll Reece to gain a little prominence, so I'll do everything I can to see that it fails." The Reece Committee was attacked by both parties; the Republican National Committee accused them of unspecified "anti-Semitism." Clearly, even in the 1950s, the Carnegie Endowment for International Peace, the Ford Foundation, the Rockefeller Foundation, and their ilk were considered "too big to fail." Since the Reece Committee investigation, there has been scant attention focused on these powerful, unaudited organizations.

THE ROSENBERGS

There had to be a hysteria and a fear sent through America in order to get increased war budgets.

—Julius Rosenberg

The now widely accepted, conventional view of the Julius and Ethel Rosenberg espionage case is that they were either both definitely guilty of spying for the Soviets, or that perhaps Ethel may have been largely innocent. As reported in stories like the one in the September 23, 2008 edition of *The Washington Post*, the two young sons the Rosenbergs left behind came to accept that their father was guilty, but feel their mother was framed. The Rosenbergs left a final message for their children: "Always remember that we were innocent and could not wrong our conscience."

The American government knew as early as 1945, when we were still allies with the Soviet Union, that the Russians were engaged in extensive spying on the United States. In July 1950, the FBI arrested admitted communist Julius Rosenberg of New York. Shortly afterwards, his wife Ethel was arrested. Ethel's brother, David Greenglass, worked as a machinist in the Los Alamos, New Mexico atomic bomb program, and was accused of providing the Rosenbergs with inside information. Both David and his wife Ruth Greenglass would testify that Ethel had typed her brother David's notes, which became the primary evidence against her. David Greenglass spent a decade in prison and later admitted he'd lied in order to protect his wife. When the 1950 grand jury records were released in 2015, it was revealed that David initially swore that he'd never discussed anything with his sister Ethel.

Once a cause celebrated cause for the left, critics of the trial still admit that the prosecution was riddled with misconduct and that Ethel, at the very least, was put to death on dubious charges. As Michael Meeropol, the eldest child of the Rosenbergs (both boys would take the name of their adoptive parents), told the *Washington Post*, the authorities used typical tactics in obtaining information from Julius: "They created a case for my mother. They put a gun to her head and said to my father, 'Talk or we kill her.'" Ilene Philipson, author of *Ethel Rosenberg: Beyond the Myths*, reacted to the release of the grand jury testimony by saying, "There was never really any solid evidence that she had been involved in any part of espionage . . . the government was using her, imprisoning her to get at Julius Rosenberg to try and persuade him to confess."[12]

One of the prosecutors in the Rosenberg case was Roy Cohn, aggressive young aide to Joe McCarthy. Shortly before his death in 1986, Cohn would allegedly reveal that the government had indeed manufactured evidence against the Rosenbergs. Federal District Judge Irving R. Kaufman presided over the Rosenberg trial, and spent a great deal of time praying in his synagogue before condemning the Rosenbergs to the electric chair. The death sentence was actually moved up a few hours on a Friday, after Kaufman consulted with a rabbi, so that the couple wouldn't continue to burn into Saturday, the Sabbath day for Jews. Much of the left had originally rallied around the belief that star witness David Greenglass was a pathological liar used by the government, and not a spy, and that the government had falsified the remaining forensic evidence against the couple. The death penalty in any case seemed extraordinarily excessive punishment; another notorious Cold War spy, Klaus Fuchs, for instance, received a fourteen-year prison sentence, served only nine years, and lived until 1988. The execution seems even more unreasonable in light of the fact the supposed spying started before the Cold War began, when the Soviets were our allies.

Typical of the new mindset on the Rosenbergs is the view expressed by high-profile attorney Alan Dershowitz, in a *New York Times* book review of August 14, 1983. Those who continue to maintain that Julius Rosenberg was framed, Dershowitz wrote, "must postulate a conspiracy so global as to include the F.B.I., the K.G.B., some officials of the American Communist Party, and dozens of individual Americans from different points on the political spectrum." Those of us who have studied these issues, however, understand just how common such conspiracies are, and thus may be excused for not rallying behind the new consensus. Despite the lack of evidence against her, Ethel Rosenberg was considered, in President Eisenhower's words, "the apparent leader of the two."

The Rosenbergs were technically convicted of conspiring to commit treason, not actual treason or espionage. Julius and Ethel Rosenberg were the perfect scapegoats for their time. The execution of this husband and wife on June 19, 1953 is yet another shameful episode in the history of our justice system.

THE TRUE COST OF COMMUNISM

The best way to control the opposition is to lead it ourselves.
—Vladimir Lenin

During times of universal deceit, telling the truth becomes a revolutionary act.
—George Orwell

In reality, America and the West engaged in a decades-long phony "war" with the Soviet Union. It was a complex psychological operation that created victims as seemingly disparate as Joseph McCarthy and the Rosenbergs. While the American war machine has seldom seen a foe it didn't feel compelled to attack, they never engaged the Soviets in combat directly at any point during the Cold War. The newspaper *Literaturnaya Rossiya* estimated, in 1992, that some 147 million deaths had resulted from Soviet communism. Harvard University Press's mainstream look at the subject, *Black Book of Communism*, went with a friendlier but still incomprehensible 100 million deaths worldwide. In contrast, under the Czars, only 467 executions took place between 1826 and 1904. Lev Bronstein, who would become known as Russian rebel leader Leon Trotsky, was quoted in the *Memoirs of Aron Simanovich* as declaring, "We must turn Russia into a desert populated by white Negroes upon whom we shall impose a tyranny . . . we meant the word 'red' literally, because we shall shed such floods of blood as will make all the human losses suffered in the capitalist wars quake and pale by comparison. The biggest bankers across the ocean will work in the closest possible contact with us . . . we shall establish the power of Zionism." In the Holodomor alone, our World War II ally Stalin murdered seven million Ukrainians, three million of them estimated to be children, during 1931–32. Ironically, Stalin's cruel strategy of confiscating the foodstuffs of the population, as "punishment" for resisting the collectivization of farms, was reminiscent of the "total war" efforts of Union generals during the War Between the States. The Soviets, however, were consistently loyal to the "capitalist" bankers. "In October, 1918, Jewish bankers in Berlin received forty-seven cases of gold from Russia. . . . The Masonic Grand Orient de France refurbished its Paris Lodge with money Lenin sent in 1919. In New York, Kuhn, Loeb received, in the first half of 1921 alone, $102 million in Russian wealth."[13] While historians like David Irving have been imprisoned for their writings on the Holocaust, *New York Times* correspondent Walter Duranty denied the Ukrainian holocaust and received a Pulitzer Prize.

Former Hollywood screenwriter Myron C. Fagan drifted into the dangerous waters of political extremism in later life. Fagan wrote and talked extensively about the Illuminati, the New World Order, and conspiracies in general. He summed up the Cold War, and most all wars, succinctly in the following statement:

> The idea was that those who direct the overall conspiracy could use the differences in those two so-called ideologies [Marxism/fascism/socialism v. democracy/capitalism] to enable them [the Illuminati] to divide larger and larger portions of the human race into opposing camps so that they could be armed and then brainwashed into fighting and destroying each other.

Despite the fraudulent nature of the Cold War, there is little question that the Soviet leaders were a brutal bunch. As Alexsandr Solzhenitsyn put it, "Bolshevism was the greatest human slaughter of all time. The fact that most of the world is ignorant of this reality is proof that the global media itself is in the hands of the perpetrators." Indeed, Hollywood has paid about as much attention to the atrocities committed by the Soviets as it has to the Founding Fathers and our war for independence. In many ways, the Soviet leaders mirrored real-life gangsters. Trotsky was killed in 1940 by Ramon Mercader, who rammed an ice pick into his head. In strangely lenient fashion, Mercader was released from prison in 1960. Vyacheslav Molotov would claim, in his 1993 memoirs, that he'd actually poisoned Josef Stalin. While any surviving Nazis evidently fled to South America, Bolshevik leader Alexander Kerensky settled in New York City, was affiliated with Stanford University's Hoover Institution, and lived until 1970. Local Russian Orthodox churches refused to bury Kerensky, because he was a noted Freemason and also because of his role in the Bolshevik Revolution. Kerensky was credited with the well-known decree that there are "no enemies on the Left."

War, General Smedley Butler so memorably said, is a racket. One of Adolf Hitler's top aides, Herman Goering, during the Nuremberg Trials, defined the farce as well as anyone:

> Naturally the common people don't want war . . . but after all, it is the leaders of the country who determine policy, and it is always a simple matter to drag the people along, whether it is a democracy, or a fascist dictatorship, or a parliament, or a communist dictatorship . . . all you have to do is to tell them they are being attacked, and denounce the pacifists for lack of patriotism and exposing the country to danger. It works the same way in any country.

We all have heard about the "Big Lie" strategy, which has been inaccurately interpreted as being advocated by Hitler, when in fact he was accusing his most despised foe—the Jews—of using it. Hitler, Stalin, Mao Tse Tung, Roosevelt, Churchill, Wilson—they all benefited from the "Big Lie," which was loyally promulgated for them by their respective court historians.

And yet we continually fall for the same propaganda.

WORLD GOVERNMENT

We shall have world government, whether or not we like it. The question is
only whether world government will be achieved by consent or by conquest.
—James Warburg, February 17, 1950 testimony before the
US Senate Committee on Foreign Relations

The most popular underlying theme behind many conspiracy theories is the contention that our leaders are constantly plotting to erase all national boundaries, and establish a one-world government. This desire for a world government is often coupled with reverential references to a "new world order." It is, in fact, one of the longest-enduring themes in the world of politics. Renowned court historian Arnold Toynbee, in a June 1931 speech before the Institute for the Study of International Affairs in Copenhagen, declared, "We are at present working discreetly with all our might to wrest this mysterious force called sovereignty out of the clutches of the local nation states of the world." Buckminster Fuller charged in his book *Critical Path* that "Great nations are simply the operating fronts of behind-the-scenes, vastly ambitious individuals who had become so effectively powerful because of their ability to remain invisible while operating behind the national scenery." This is no conspiracy theory. The great seal of the United States was established in 1782, featuring the Masonic eye over the pyramid, and the Latin phrase *Novus Ordo Seclorum*, which translates to "A New Order of the Ages." It's a small leap from there to "New World Order." Fittingly, it was under the direction of Franklin Roosevelt that the great seal was added to the back of the one dollar bill in 1935.

"What is being arranged in Washington these days is really a gigantic experiment in internationalism," reliable mainstream journalist Walter Lippmann said in April 1917. "The old notions of sovereignty no longer govern the facts. We have entered upon another phase of political unification, a phase greater in its methods to the formation of national states in the nineteenth century. This is the birth of the League of Nations." One of the twentieth century's most powerful conspirators, Winston Churchill, was a youthful conspiracy theorist, and seemingly anti-Semitic as well. In the February 8, 1920 issue of the *Illustrated Sunday Herald*, Churchill reviewed Nesta Webster's book *The French Revolution: A Study in Democracy* thusly:

> This movement among the Jews is not new. From the days of Spartacus-Weishaupt to those of Karl Marx, and down to Trotsky (Russia), Bela Kun (Hungary), Rosa Luxembourg (Germany), and Emma Goldman (United States), this world-wide conspiracy for the overthrow of civilisation and for the reconstitution of society on the basis of arrested development, of envious malevolence, and impossible equality, has been steadily growing. It played, as a modern writer, Mrs. Webster, has so ably shown, a definitely recognisable part in the tragedy of the French Revolution. . . . It has been the mainspring of every subversive movement during the 19th century; and now at last this band of extraordinary personalities from the underworld of the great cities of Europe and America have gripped the Russian people by the hair of their heads.

While Webster is shunned by polite society as a Jew-hating conspiracy theorist, her devoted fan Winston Churchill is considered one of the great heroes of the twentieth century.

"Undersecretary of State Sumner Welles tonight called for the early creation of an international organization of anti-Axis nations to control the world during the period between the armistice at the end of the present war and the setting up of a new world order on a permanent basis," the *Philadelphia Inquirer* announced in June 1942. "Countless people will hate the new world order and will die protesting against it," wrote one-world enthusiast H. G. Wells in 1939's The New World Order. Some organs in the establishment press recognized the obvious push for world government.

One of the very few critical pieces about the shadowy Council on Foreign Relations to appear in the mainstream media was published in the July 1958 issue of *Harpers*. The article stated frankly: "The most powerful clique in these (CFR) groups have one objective in common: they want to bring about the surrender of the sovereignty and the national independence of the U.S. . . . What they strive for would inevitably lead to dictatorship and loss of freedoms by the people. The CFR was founded for 'the purpose of promoting disarmament and submergence of US sovereignty and national independence into an all-powerful one-world government.'" Professor Carroll Quigley, one of Bill Clinton's idols, wrote the inadvertently conspiracy-friendly book *Tragedy and Hope: A History of the World in our Time*. One of its many enlightening passages was: "The powers of financial capitalism had another far-reaching aim, nothing less than to create a world system of financial control in private hands able to dominate the political system of each country and the economy of the world as a whole."

The most obvious manifestation of this desire for world government is, of course, the United Nations. Established in 1945 in the wake of the League of Nations, Woodrow Wilson's failed dream child, the UN hardly resulted in any sort of international peace arising. On the contrary, the world has been at war almost continuously since then. Right-wing critics immediately charged that the institution was unconstitutional, in particular articles thirty-six and forty-three of the UN Treaty, because the US Constitution was effectively amended without the approval of the states. The UN World Constitution frankly stated, "The age of nations must end. The governments of nations have decided to order their separate sovereignties into one government to which they will surrender their arms." The first president of the United Nations General Assembly, Belgium's Paul-Henri Spaak, would declare that he didn't care whether the men they needed were "God or devil, we will receive him." The United Nations Conference grew out of the Dunbarton Oaks gathering, which included a young Alger Hiss in attendance. In December 1945, the United States Congress invited the UN to place its headquarters in New York. FDR's old foe, former America First Committee leader John T. Flynn, charged that the United Nations created "special arrangements between dominant powers . . . not to protect the rights of little nations but to preserve the privileges and ambitions of a few . . . to perpetuate those very forces . . . which are the causes of all wars . . . to deny human rights to hundreds of millions of people."[14]

Not only has the United States footed an inordinate cost of the UN, the concept of Diplomatic Immunity, established legally in 1961 by the Vienna Convention, has led to United Nations representatives from other countries being outside the boundaries of American law. The least serious crimes can still be financially draining; New York City, for instance, has tried in vain for decades to recoup what amounts to millions of dollars in unpaid parking tickets from UN diplomats. The United States pays for more than one-fifth of the UN's annual budget, and more than one-quarter of the much bigger peacekeeping budget. The total cost to American taxpayers is some $3 billion per year. Given the lack of peace in the world, one doesn't have to be a conspiracy theorist to question if we're getting our money's worth. The creepiest aspect of the UN is its so-called "Meditation Room," a stark, occult-tinged place which is apparently off-limits to most visitors. The custodian of the Meditation Room is the Lucis Trust, a nonprofit service organization that publishes esoteric and new age books, and was initially known, until the 1920s, by the truly inflammatory name Lucifer Publishing Company.

CHAPTER ELEVEN

THE HISTORY OF UN-AMERICANISM

I think the most un-American thing you can say is, "You can't say that."

—Garrison Keillor

When I was first attracted to politics as a teenager in the mid-1970s, I naturally gravitated to the Left. The far Left. Civil libertarians were in vogue then, and my idols were people like writer Nat Hentoff and the Warren Commission's loudest critic, Mark Lane. I became a volunteer worker with Lane's Citizens Committee of Inquiry, which was lobbying Congress to reopen the investigations into the assassinations of John and Robert Kennedy, and Martin Luther King, Jr. I admired civil libertarians and their free speech purism. This kind of thing had resonated with me since early childhood, when I read Patrick Henry's stirring "I may not agree with what you say, but I'll defend to my dying day your right to say it."

The concept of "un-Americanism" would have been foreign to the Founding Fathers. Freedom of expression was sacrosanct with the likes of Patrick Henry, Thomas Paine, or Thomas Jefferson, who declared, "Our liberty depends upon the freedom of the press, and that cannot be limited without being lost." They would not have understood a House

Un-American Activities Committee. HUAC was created in 1938, and was not initially a "commie" hunting outfit. It was established to ferret out "disloyalty" and "subversion" on the part of fascists, communists, or anarchists. In 1969, it was given a more palatable name, the House Committee on Internal Security, until 1975, when the House Judiciary Committee took over its functions.

The first congressional foray into this morass began in 1918, with the creation of the Overman committee, named after its chairman, North Carolina Democrat Lee Slater Overman. The committee was primarily concerned with pro-German saboteurs, but as soon as World War I ended, they smoothly transitioned to investigating alleged Bolshevism in the United States. In 1930, Republican Rep. Hamilton Fish of New York started leading a committee to investigate "communist subversion" in America. The American Civil Liberties Union was among the first groups targeted by the Fish Committee. The committee suggested giving the Department of Justice more leeway in investigating communists, and advocated stronger immigration laws to keep supposed communists out of the country.[1] Years before Pearl Harbor, Congress established the Special Committee on Un-American Activities Authorized to Investigate Nazi Propaganda and Certain Other Propaganda Activities, which was active from 1934-1937. Referred to as the McCormick-Dickstein Committee, for co-chairmen Democrats John McCormack of Massachusetts (future speaker of the house) and Samuel Dickstein of New York, they concentrated on "foreign subversive propaganda." The committee investigated an attempt to overthrow Franklin Roosevelt, called the "Business Plot,"[2] in which a group of fascists unsuccessfully attempted to recruit anti-war activist General Smedley Butler. Recently, the claim has been made that Dickstein was paid $1250 a month by the Soviet NKVD, for inside information on anti-communists and pro-fascists.[3] The Dies Committee, run by Democrat Martin Dies of Texas, was the immediate precursor to HUAC, and investigated primarily communist "subversion," but also looked into some pro-Nazi organizations. It was the first to suggest interning Japanese-Americans in concentration camps.

One of the first acts by HUAC was investigating allegations of communist espionage against former State Department official Alger Hiss. Eventually, Hiss was found guilty on two counts of perjury in 1950 and served over three years in prison. While some of Sen. Joe McCarthy's allegations were substantiated by the release of KGB records after the collapse of the Soviet Union, the same archives revealed, according to two senior Soviet military officers, "Russian intelligence service has no documents proving that Alger Hiss cooperated with our service" and that he'd "never had any relationship with Soviet intelligence."[4] In 1947, HUAC investigated alleged communist subversion in Hollywood. Some in the entertainment industry invoked their Fifth Amendment right and refused to answer the committee's questions, leading them to be convicted for contempt of Congress. "The Hollywood Ten" would go on to be blacklisted by the studios. The historical ignorance displayed by both academia and the American culture in general is exemplified by the popular reference to the witch hunts, in Hollywood and elsewhere during this era as "McCarthyism." Joe McCarthy had no affiliation with the House committee, being a member of the Senate, and was focused on alleged communist infiltration into the Army and other parts of the US government. One of the more notable members of HUAC in the late 1940s was first-term California Rep. Richard Nixon.

There were attempts, prior to the twentieth century, to suppress opposition to the government, which was essentially considered "un-Americanism," even if it often was referred to by other names. The second president of the United States, John Adams, signed into law the nefarious Alien and Sedition Acts in 1798, which had been passed by the majority Federalist Congress. These Acts criminalized anyone making "false statements" about the government. That ought to sound chillingly familiar to Americans in the present age of "disinformation." Although the United States wasn't at war in 1798, Adams nevertheless called the Acts "war measures." The Acts expired in 1801, at the end of Adams' term in office. One of those jailed under the Acts was James Callender, a Jefferson-friendly journalist who would later originate the Sally Hemings legend detailed elsewhere in this book. Like so many others connected to political intrigue, Callender's death was a bit unnatural. At only forty-two years old, the heavy drinker Callender drowned in the James River on July 17, 1803. Jefferson had helped Callender financially and professionally, and referred to him in a July 15, 1802 letter to James Monroe as an object of "mere charity ... without attention to political principles." Another arrestee was Benjamin Franklin Bache, grandson of Benjamin Franklin, whose life and that of his pregnant wife was threatened, and who was physically assaulted twice. Bache died at only twenty nine while awaiting trial. Like the unconstitutional arrests under Abraham Lincoln, Alien and Sedition charges could be laughably dubious. Rep. Matthew Lyon was one of the early victims of the law, after he criticized Adams' "ridiculous pomp." The government responded by accusing Lyon of being "a malicious and seditious person, and of a depraved mind and a wicked and diabolical disposition," fined him a thousand dollars (a considerable sum in those days) and sentenced him to four months behind bars. The president's wife Abigail Adams, universally beloved by the court historians, urged her husband to respond to the "wicked and base" attacks against him and his administration. Editor Charles Holt was jailed three months for sedition, after criticizing Treasury Secretary Alexander Hamilton. Jefferson made the Acts a big part of his 1800 presidential campaign, trumpeting the people's right "to think freely and to speak and write what they think." Upon assuming the presidency, he pardoned everyone who'd been convicted under the law.[5]

In those early days of the republic, individual states still held a great deal of power. Thus, both the Kentucky and Virginia legislatures passed Resolves that rejected the Alien and Sedition Acts, establishing the doctrine of nullification. Lincoln's suspension of the writ of habeas corpus is detailed extensively elsewhere in this book. While he may not have used the term, Lincoln unquestionably attempted to portray those who opposed his policies as "un-American." In 1917, as America plunged headfirst into a disastrous globalist foreign policy, all German immigrants in America became suspect. However, the term "alien enemy" quickly came to encompass pacifist individuals and groups, opposed to our entrance into World War I. President Woodrow Wilson prohibited these "alien enemies" from owning firearms or aircraft, and forbid them from publishing an "attack" upon any part of the US government. These restrictions were tightened further later in 1917, which effectively rendered "alien enemies" all but unemployable. They were even banned from the nation's capital city of Washington, DC. While Franklin Roosevelt constructed the federal bureaucracy more assiduously, Wilson's Railway Administration Act gave control of the railroads to the federal government, and a slate of new agencies like the War Labor Board and the War Industries Board centralized power in a manner the Founders would never have approved, in the name of supporting the war effort. Price controls and fuel rationing first appeared during the WWI era. The early labor movement had many immigrant members and was a powerful force in America. Eugene Debs had received nearly a million votes running on the American Socialist Party ticket in 1912.[6]

The clash between labor and capital went farther back. Eight radical labor leaders were prosecuted by the government following the May 4, 1886 Haymarket Affair in Chicago. As the prosecuting attorney declared, "Law is on trial. Anarchy is on trial. These men [the defendants] have been selected . . . because they are leaders . . . Convict these men . . . save our institutions, our society." Four of the defendants were executed, and another killed himself to avoid it. In 1905, labor leaders formed the

Industrial Workers of the World (IWW), popularly known as "Wobblies." Early labor titan William "Big Bill" Haywood wanted all workers to unite under a single umbrella, to avoid individual trade unions fighting with each other. The Espionage Act passed by Congress in 1917, which approved heavy fines and prison sentences for very vaguely defined opposition to the war, was utilized against the IWW as well. A campaign alleging that the IWW had been infiltrated by pro-German elements resulted in US troops rounding up over a thousand men and holding them in prison for months. The response to this unconstitutional governmental overreach was best reflected in the July 15, 1917 edition of the *Los Angeles Times*, which commented, "On our own soil is an enemy . . . preaching revolution and invoking anarchy . . . the I.W.W.'s. From Butte to Bisbee, from Seattle to Leadville, that international organization, filled with foreigners, officered by convicts, and attempting vaguely to guise its sabotage behind the specious title of 'Industrial Workers of the World,' is in open warfare against our government." The government then raided IWW meeting halls across the country, and more than 160 members were arrested. In April 1918, 101 IWW defendants went on trial. Not surprisingly, all were found guilty, with Haywood and fourteen others sentenced to a draconian twenty years in prison. The trial essentially destroyed the IWW. There was little public outcry about the prosecution and stiff sentences, as the labor leaders were successfully portrayed as "radicals," "anarchists," and "un-American."[7]

In May 1918, Congress made it official and resurrected the spirit of John Adams' administration by passing a new Sedition Act. The act authorized "a fine of not more than $10,000 or imprisonment for not more than twenty years, or both . . ." for anyone who would "utter, print, write, or publish any disloyal, profane, scurrilous, or abusive language about the form of government of the United States." The next month, they revived the Alien Act as well, which targeted "aliens" who had become "a member of any anarchist organization." Only a few civil libertarians of the day, such as H.L. Mencken and Oswald Garrison Villard, publicly condemned the Acts. The first socialist elected to Congress, Victor Berger, was sentenced to twenty years for "hindering the war effort." Eugene Debs was sentenced to ten years for making an anti-war speech. The "Red Scare" officially began on May 1, 1919, when Attorney General A. Mitchell Palmer, along with several other prominent officials, received bombs in the mail, which were blamed on the communists. The Palmer Raids, which young Palmer aide J. Edgar Hoover was deeply involved in, saw five to ten thousand suspicious "aliens" arrested without warrant. Hundreds, like anarchist Emma Goldman, were deported to the Soviet Union. Supreme Court Justice Oliver Wendell Holmes upheld the constitutionality of the raids, under the same absurd pretext that justified throwing WWI protesters in jail; the "communists" were said to represent "a clear and present danger" to America. The atmosphere was such that Black lynchings increased, and Marcus Garvey was targeted for deportation by the FBI. Journalist H.L. Mencken, under suspicion himself for his German ethnicity, blasted Holmes' decision thusly; "One finds a clear statement of the doctrine that, in war time, the rights guaranteed by the First Amendment cease to have any substance, and may be set aside by any jury that has been sufficiently inflamed by a district attorney itching for higher office . . . . I find it hard to reconcile such notions with any plausible concept of liberalism."[8]

The Alien Registration Act, better known as the Smith Act, was passed by Congress in June, 1940. It established criminal penalties for advocating the overthrow of the US government by force. This act resulted in the indictments of over two hundred alleged communists, anarchists, and fascists. In 1957, the Supreme Court would declare many of the convictions unconstitutional. The media was already largely operating as an unofficial arm of the federal government, and paved the way for the Smith Act by depicting a dangerous element within America working with the Nazis.

This element was popularly referred to as a "fifth column." The House approved the Smith Act on a vote of 382 to 4, while the Senate didn't even bother with a recorded vote. The *New York Times,* sounding like the collective press secretary for Franklin D. Roosevelt, wrote, "Suddenly the European war seemed almost at our doors, and who could tell what secret agents were already at work in America? So, partly because some such bill would be adopted anyway, and partly because the step, normally distasteful, appeared inevitable, the Administration sponsored the legislation."[9] FDR's Attorney General Francis Biddle attempted to get Congress to reauthorize the Sedition Act in 1942, but they surprisingly refused, forcing the Roosevelt administration to prosecute alleged Nazi sympathizers under the Smith Act. The forgotten George W. Christians, founder of the Crusader White Shirts, advocated a "human effort monetary system" and "a paper and ink revolution for economic liberty." This bit of "un-Americanism" earned him five years in prison in 1942.[10] In 1949, ten leaders of the Communist Party USA were fined ten thousand dollars and sentenced to five years in prison, under the Smith Act. The Supreme Court upheld their convictions. The Department of Justice went on to indict over a hundred more under the Act.

The 1960s produced the largest anti-war movement in our nation's history. Our involvement in Vietnam was senseless, and it was impossible to sell it to young, draft-age people. More than half of the twenty-seven million males eligible for the draft were deferred, exempted, or disqualified from the Vietnam War. Approximately 570,000 were classified as draft offenders.[11] Over three thousand were eventually jailed. Counterculture groups like the War Resisters League counseled young people on how to evade the military. As many as a hundred thousand youngsters opted to leave the country, most often for Canada. Muhammad Ali memorably refused to go to Vietnam, declaring, "I ain't got no quarrel with them Viet Cong."

It has become a matter of some dispute as to whether or not he uttered the more colorful comment, "No Viet Cong ever called me n....r."[12] In the 1970s, conservative rocker Ted Nugent told *High Times* magazine that he'd taken crystal meth, and urinated and defecated in his pants, to avoid being drafted into the Vietnam War. Chevy Chase confessed, in 1989, that he lied to the draft board to avoid the war, including telling them he was homosexual. He stated he was "not very proud" of doing that.[13] Rush Limbaugh allegedly avoided the Vietnam War because of anal cysts. Donald Trump missed Vietnam because of bone spurs. Joe Biden never had to go because of asthma as a teenager. This was widely questioned, since Biden never mentioned asthma in an autobiography that extolled his prowess on the football field.[14] Bernie Sanders fought for years to be exempt from the draft due to a conscientious objector status, which he wasn't technically eligible for since he wasn't religious. An odd and unexplained "lengthy series of hearings, an FBI investigation and numerous postponements and delays" took so long that he eventually became too old for the draft.[15] Bill Clinton was a very visible anti-war protester at Oxford. Republicans like Mitt Romney and Rudy Giuliani were lampooned for their avoidance of Vietnam.[16]

It is instructive to compare the condemnation today of "White Supremacists," "racists," "Nazis," and "conspiracy theorists" with the sobriquets used in the past to demonize opponents of the ruling order. Communists, anarchists, fascists, and "White Supremacists" have all been referred to as "seditionists" or "traitors." Is today's alleged "Russian bot" any different from the 1950s-era "fellow traveler" or "pinko?" Politicians beginning with Abraham Lincoln have slandered those opposing literal or figurative wars as "appeasers." The American establishment transitioned effortlessly from the "Nazi sympathizers" or "fascists" of the 1930s-1940s to the "Reds" and "commie sympathizers" of the 1950s. "Better dead than red" may be a bit antiquated now, but "America—love it or leave it" has shown to have tremendous staying power. Throughout American history, those criticizing the government have had their patriotism and loyalty questioned. If that is "un-American," then "American" would be defined as unquestioned support of the policies of our leaders.

CHAPTER TWELVE

CONCLUSION

If we are to guard against ignorance and remain free, it is the responsibility of every American to be informed.

—Thomas Jefferson

It is dangerous to be right when the government is wrong.

—Voltaire

The way history is presented to Americans, from the youngest school-children to doctorate-level Ivy Leaguers, mirrors the way news is presented to the public. Much as it is difficult to find a single issue or event which the mainstream media has reported on accurately, it is just as difficult to find any historical event, or historical figure, portrayed honestly by establishment historians.

We still see everyone from history professors to late-night comedians referring to any opponent of the establishment with a mean-spirited, impossibly caricatured negativity. Dismissing opposition with juvenile name-calling is their primary method of debate. In their world, black is white and up is down. Freedom is slavery. Thus, the most bloodthirsty, consistent warmongers in any era, from Abraham Lincoln to Teddy Roosevelt to Woodrow Wilson to Franklin D. Roosevelt to Harry Truman to Lyndon Baines Johnson to Bill and Hillary Clinton to Barack Obama, are equated with "peace" and looked upon favorably by academics and the entertainment world. Henry Ford, who was a pacifist and tried desperately to singlehandedly stop our participation in World War I, is dismissed as an anti-Semite. Robert A. Taft, who was a progressive on most issues and advocated a non-interventionist foreign policy, is recalled as "Mr. Conservative" and denigrated as being hopelessly behind the times. An unwillingness to meddle in the affairs of other nations, to occupy and kill foreign civilians, is considered "outdated." Instead, we are treated to the "progressivism" of a Teddy Roosevelt, who was a vile bigot, a textbook eugenicist, and never met a war he didn't want America to become engaged in. Meanwhile, a sincerely enlightened man of his time, and one of history's finest intellects, Thomas Jefferson, is ridiculed as a racist. In the eyes of the court historians, the "greatest" presidents are those who've most completely trampled the civil liberties of their citizens, and been most eager for war.

Albert Einstein was named *TIME* magazine's "Person of the Century." Historians gloss over the fact that his 1905 treatise on the theory of relativity listed no references. He has been accused by conspiracy theorists of being a plagiarist. It's well known that Einstein was dramatically slow to develop as a child; he didn't speak until the age of three and never learned to tie his shoes. He failed an entrance exam to a simple technology school in Zurich, and worked for years as a menial clerk in a patent office. True genius Nikola Tesla strongly disagreed with Einstein, calling his relativity theory "a mass of error and deceptive ideas violently opposed to the teachings of great men of science of the past and even to common sense . . . the theory wraps all these errors and fallacies and clothes them in magnificent mathematical garb which fascinates, dazzles and makes people blind to the underlying errors. . . . Not a single one of the relativity propositions has been proved."[1] The criticisms of those published in the 1931 book *A Hundred Authors Against Einstein* were discounted on the grounds that they weren't capable of understanding such complexity.

Today, no criticism of Einstein is allowed in polite society. Einstein was a proponent of world government and was instrumental in convincing Franklin Roosevelt to fund nuclear research. Einstein is another secular saint of our civilization; the Abraham Lincoln of the scientific world.

Everywhere, convoluted, simplistic explanations for the most important historical events are promulgated, from the halls of academia to mainstream television networks. We are asked to accept the most fantastic concepts imaginable, all under the general premise that our leaders are trustworthy and have our best interests at heart. Public vitriol is channeled towards cardboard villains that more often than not appear to have been actual "good guys" fighting a corrupt system. The most awful characters imaginable are propped up as "heroes." All that's missing is an official Two-Minutes Hate, and an imaginary Goldstein as opposition leader.

When Ronald Reagan called his glittery new bomb a "peacekeeper," he wasn't inventing Orwellian doublethink. After all, the establishment continues to depict the murderous dropping of atomic bombs on Hiroshima and Nagasaki as altruistic efforts to *save* more lives. And our leaders show little compunction about lecturing Iran and other nations about developing nuclear weapons, under the rationale that such regimes are too "unstable" to be trusted with such power. Hypocrisy doesn't quite seem to cover the chutzpah there. America remains the only nation to date to use nuclear weapons on a foe. And our leaders are growing more aggressive about advocating the use of nuclear weapons again when "necessary," while in the same breath forcing others to undergo inspections and forbidding them from developing such programs.

Much as the only scandal that appears to have been investigated to any degree by mainstream journalists throughout American history was Watergate, the only war which modern-day "liberals" appear to have opposed to any large degree was Vietnam. We appear to inescapably be, in the words of General Smedley Butler, perpetually waging war, while perpetually proclaiming our desire for peace. Historically, the "liberals" of their time were adamantly in favor of the Civil War, the Spanish-American War, World War I, and World War II. Most "liberals" during the Cold War era managed the exceptional balancing act of supporting the massive military buildup against the new communist "enemy," while simultaneously attacking any aggressive anti-communist. Far too many sincere antiwar advocates, in every era, have been labeled as "anti-Semitic," as if to perpetuate the discredited stereotype that "the Jews" are responsible for all wars.

This battle has been waged for a very long time. Most of the common people seem unaware that they are being constantly besieged. Napoleon Bonaparte summed up his motivation, and the motivation for all rulers and would-be rulers: "There is only one thing in this world, and that is to keep acquiring money and more money, power and more power. All the rest is meaningless." Those of us who expose rampant corruption are not simple conspiracy theorists. We're actual citizen journalists, doing the work that highly-paid professionals won't do. J. Edgar Hoover, of all people, defined the mindset we confront perfectly when he said, "The individual is handicapped by coming face to face with a conspiracy so monstrous he cannot believe it exists." Although he was speaking specifically about communism, the point is applicable in the broader sense; most people simply cannot accept the reality of the broken, criminal system that rules us.

"People love conspiracy theories," astronaut Neil Armstrong said, during the forty-plus years he spent religiously dodging the spotlight. "The Rockefellers and their allies have, for at least fifty years, been carefully following a plan to use their economic power to gain political control of first

America, and then the rest of the world. Do I mean conspiracy? Yes, I do. I am convinced there is such a plot, international in scope, generations old in planning, and incredibly evil in intent." Congressman Larry P. McDonald wrote in the introduction to Gary Allen's 1975 book *The Rockefeller File*. Very few conspiracy theorists have ever found their way to the United States Congress, but McDonald was one of them. His words are all the more haunting considering that he was one of the victims on Korean Air Lines Flight 007, shot down by the Soviets on September 1, 1983.

I have been asked, during a few interviews, if I believe there is something bigger than politics behind all the corruption. The inference there is that a connection to Satan, or Lucifer, is the inspiration for all the misdeeds we see transpiring on a continual basis. There is certainly a lot of anecdotal evidence for something like this. Saul Alinsky, for instance, considered a mentor and hero to many modern liberals like Hillary Clinton, dedicated his book *Rules for Radicals* thusly: "Lest we forget at least an over-the-shoulder acknowledgment to the very first radical: from all our legends, mythology, and history . . . the first radical known to man who rebelled against the establishment and did it so effectively that he at least won his own kingdom—Lucifer." Many conspiracy theorists believe that the "Great Architect" whom the Freemasons refer to is revealed to high-level adepts as Lucifer. One hard-core worshiper of Lucifer was Aleister Crowley. Despite the fact he was a thoroughly despicable, incomprehensibly vile and corrupt man, Crowley was revered by a wide variety of fans, from Paul McCartney to Led Zeppelin's Jimmy Page to Michael Jackson to Liberace to L. Ron Hubbard to Jim Morrison to Sting and many other celebrities. CIA-affiliated "counter-culture" guru Timothy Leary confessed that he was continuing Crowley's work. Crowley's "work" included eating feces and sacrificing animals and even humans. Crowley inherited a fortune at the age of eleven, leaving him free to pursue a life of blasphemy and Satanism. As noted earlier in this book, Crowley's motto "Do what thou wilt," which has been bandied about frequently by deluded celebrity worshipers, actually originated with Benjamin Franklin's old Hellfire Club. As if it wasn't bad enough that Franklin Roosevelt and the American government were willing to team up with vicious mobsters during World War II, as detailed in Richard Spence's book *Secret Agent 666*, Crowley was another of FDR's curious "allies." Crowley apparently devised the "V-sign" for victory as a "magical" contrast to the Nazis' swastika, and his gesture was mimicked by Winston Churchill. Crowley wrote a pro-war propaganda poem which Charles deGaulle was so enthralled by he had it set to music and performed on BBC radio.[2] Crowley's powerful connections included Navy Intelligence Officer and future James Bond author Ian Fleming, who worked with Crowley to feed misinformation to the Germans through Rudolph Hess. To top it off, Crowley was a 33rd degree Mason.

Yet another cultural icon of our age remains nineteenth-century German philosopher Friedrich Nietzsche. Nietzsche invented the "God is dead" mantra and Crowley was only one of those said to have been inspired by him. Nietzsche influenced Hitler and the Nazis with his concept of "Superman," and there is a strong strain of anti-Semitism in his writings. Despite this, he was apparently a favorite of Hitler's dreaded enemy Josef Stalin. After inventing his own morality and contracting syphilis, Nietzsche ended his days in an insane asylum, where he screamed "I am God!" repeatedly.

To paraphrase the Bible, America's history is replete with war and rumors of war. Americans seem to have an insatiable thirst for armed conflict, and can be fooled with embarrassing ease by the same puerile propaganda that goes back more than a hundred years, and the same kind of false flags that precede each new battle. Antiwar activist Philip Berrigan once said, "Lying and war are always associated. Listen closely when you hear a war-maker try to defend his current war: If he moves his lips he's lying." Even a devout court historian and charter member of the Lincoln cult like Garry Wills can acknowledge that "Only the winners decide what were war crimes." The epitome of military careerism, General Douglas MacArthur, came to advocate that "I believe that the entire effort of modern society should be concentrated on the endeavor to outlaw war as a method of the solution of problems between nations." Much of our history is the recounting and dissection of wars. The "bad guys" are always the losers. If you believe the court historians, no "bad guys" have ever won a war. One of the greatest military commanders of all time, Stonewall Jackson, defined war as "the sum of all evils."

It's hard to discuss historical events with most people, because they are so woefully uninformed about them. The more conventionally educated they are, the less true history they know. A society that worships an unprincipled statist like Abraham Lincoln above all others isn't free. To laud the tyranny of Lincoln, or the chicanery of Franklin Roosevelt, while denigrating the legacy of Thomas Jefferson, is in direct contradiction to any ideal of a representative government serving sovereign people. The increasing tendency to label so many past American leaders as "racist" is as misguided as it is inconsistent. We can find just as much "evidence" that Abraham Lincoln, Teddy Roosevelt, or Franklin Roosevelt were ugly "racists" as the court historians can summon up against Jefferson, or Jackson, or even Woodrow Wilson. And eugenics is about as racist a philosophy as can be imagined, yet countless still respected "liberal" icons, from Planned Parenthood founder Margaret Sanger, to legendary lawyer Clarence Darrow, to author H. G. Wells, publicly espoused views that would make David Duke blush. History is vitally important, lest we forget it, as Santayana warned. But if the history we are taught is distorted and filled with inaccuracies, then no matter how thoroughly we study it, we aren't going to learn any lessons. The average American is historically illiterate.

It is difficult for everyday people to accept the fact they've been lied to so extensively. They cling to the comfortable myths about Abraham

Lincoln and other heroes of our decaying culture. "Not *everything* is a conspiracy," they'll sigh with exasperation. I have studied American history for decades, and I've found very little in establishment history books that is factual. There is instead a desperate justification for the actions of a William Sherman, or a Ulysses S. Grant, or a Theodore Roosevelt. The narrative must be defended at all costs. The mantra is that History, like the universe itself, is a product of random happenstance. Nothing is planned or created. All events must be interpreted through a present-day prism, utilizing a corrupt process that turns true liberals into "racists," and bigoted eugenicists into "liberals."

Five days before he was assassinated, one of the real heroes of American history, John F. Kennedy, said the following to the Florida Chamber of Commerce:

> I realize that there are some businessmen who feel only they want to be left alone, that government and politics are none of their affairs, that the balance sheet and profit rate of their own corporation are of more importance than the worldwide balance of power or the nationwide rate of unemployment. But I hope it is not rushing the season to recall to you the passage from Dickens' *Christmas Carol* in which Ebenezer Scrooge is terrified by the ghosts of his former partner, Jacob Marley, and Scrooge, appalled by Marley's story of ceaseless wandering, cries out, "But you were always a good man of business, Jacob." And the ghost of Marley, his legs bound by a chain of ledger books and cash boxes, replied, "Business? Mankind was my business. The common welfare was my business. Charity, mercy, forbearance, and benevolence were all my business. The dealings of my trade were but a drop of water in the comprehensive ocean of my business!" Members and guests of the Florida State Chamber of Commerce, whether we work in the White House or the State House or in a house of industry or commerce, mankind is our business. And if we

work in harmony, if we understand the problems of each other and the responsibilities that each of us bears, then surely the business of mankind will prosper. And your children and mine will move ahead in a securer world, and one in which there is opportunity for them all.

I hope that readers will understand at this point that there have been far too few John F. Kennedys and Huey Longs, and far too many Abraham Lincolns and Franklin Roosevelts, leading us down a ruinous path that contradicts our birth and heritage, and makes a mockery of all that the Founding Fathers sacrificed for.

BIBLIOGRAPHY

Basti, Abel, *Hitler's Exile*. Buenos Aires, Argentina: Sudamericana, 2010.

Carroll, Al, *Presidents' Body Counts: The Twelve Worst and Four Best American Presidents*. Annandale, Virginia: Al Carroll, 2014.

Hornblum, *Allen M., Acres of Skin: Human Experiments at Holmesburg Prison*. New York: Routledge, 1998.

Scaduto, Anthony, *Scapegout: The Lonesome Death of Bruno Richard Hauptmann*. New York: Putnam, 1976.

Sutton, Antony, *Wall Street and the Bolshevik Revolution*. New York: Crown Publishing Group, 1974.

Sutton, Antony, *Wall Street and the Rise of Hitler*. West Sussex, UK: Clairview Books, 1976.

Herman, Arthur, *Joseph McCarthy: Reexamining the Life and Legacy of America's Most Hated Senator*. New York: The Free Press, 2000.

Lynes, Barry, *The Cancer Cure That Worked*. South Lake Tahoe, CA: Biomed Publishing Group, 1987.

Watson, Bruce, *Sacco and Vanzetti: The Men, the Murders and the Judgment of Mankind*. New York: Viking, 2007.

Morgan, Captain William, *Illustrations of Masonry*. New York: Masonic Publishing and Manufacturing Co., 1867.

Quigley, Carroll, *Tragedy and Hope: A History of the World in our Time*. New York: Macmillan, 1966.

Adams, Charles, *When in the Course of Human Events*. Lanham, MD: Rowman & Littefield, 2004.

Mackay, Charles, *Extraordinary Delusions and the Madness of Crowds*. London: Richard Bentley, 1841.

Aaronvitch, David, *Voodoo Histories: The Role of the Conspiracy Theory in Shaping Modern History*. New York: Riverhead Books, 2010.

Chandler, David Leon, *The Jefferson Conspiracies: A President's Role in the Assassination of Meriwether Lewis*. New York: HarperCollins, 1995.

Balsiger, David W. and Sellier, Charles E., *The Lincoln Conspiracy*. Salt Lake City, UT: Schick Sunn Classic Books, 1977.

Kearns-Goodwin, Doris, *Team of Rivals: The Political Genius of Abraham Lincoln*. New York: Simon & Schuster, 2005.

Philipson, Ilene, *Ethel Rosenberg: Beyond the Myths*. New Brunswick, NJ: Rutgers University Press, 1993.

Masters, Edgar Lee, *Lincoln the Man*. New York: Dodd, Mead & Company, 1931.

Wilson, Edmund, *Patriotic Gore*. New York: W.W. Norton & Company, 1962.

Gibbon, Edward, *The Decline and Fall of the Roman Empire*. London: Plummer and Brewis, 1820.

Mullins, Eustace, *The Federal Reserve Conspiracy*. Union, New Jersey: Christian Educational Association, 1954.

Mullins, Eustace, *The $5 Trillion Cold War Hoax*. Staunton, Virginia: The Phoenix Project, 1996.

Mullins, Eustace, *This Difficult Individual, Ezra Pound*. New York: Fleet Publishing Corporation, 1961.

Brodie, Fawn, *Thomas Jefferson: An Intimate History*. New York: W.W. Norton & Company, 1974.

Howard, Frank Key, *Fourteen Months in American Bastilles*. London: Henry F. Mackintosh, 1863.

O'Toole, G.J.A., *The Cosgrove Report: Being the Private Inquiry of a Pinkerton Detective Into the Death of President Lincoln.* New York: Grove Press, 1979.

Means, Gaston, *The Strange Death of President Harding.* New York: Guild Publishing Corporation, 1930.

Butler, General Smedley, *War is a Racket.* Philadelphia, Pennsylvania: Smedley Butler, 1936.

Orwell, George, *1984.* London: Harvill Secker, 1949.

Ahlgren, Gregory Ahlgren & Monior, Stephen, *Crime of the Century: The Lindbergh Kidnapping Hoax.* Boston: Branden Books, 1993.

Wells, H.G., Salvador de Madariaga; John Middleton Murry; C E M Joad, *The New World Order.* London: National Peace Council, 1940.

Albarelli, H.P., *A Terrible Mistake: The Murder of Frank Olson and the CIA's Secret Cold War Experiments.* Springfield, Oregon: Trine Day, 2011.

Wiencek, Henry, *Master of the Mountain: Thomas Jefferson and His Slaves.* New York: Farrar, Straus and Giroux, 2013.

Hoover, Herbert, *Freedom Betrayed: Herbert Hoover's History of the Second World War and its Aftermath.* Stanford, California: Hoover Institution Press, Stanford University, 2011.

Edoin, Hoito, *The Night Tokyo Burned: The Incendiary Campaign Against Japan, March - August, 1945.* New York: St. Martin's Press, 1989.

Downs, Hunton, *The Glenn Miller Conspiracy.* Beverly Hills, CA: Global Book Publishers, 2009.

Bacque, James, *Other Losses: An Investigation into the Mass Deaths of German Prisoners at the Hands of the French and Americans after World War II.* London: Futura, 1991.

Kennedy, James Donald & Kennedy, Walter Donald, *The South Was Right!* Gretna, Louisiana, 1994.

Otis, James, The Rights of the British Colonies. London: J. Almon, 1769.

Manber, Jeffrey and Dahlstrom, Neil, *Lincoln's Wrath: Fierce Mobs, Brilliant*

Scoundrels and a President's Mission to Destroy the Press. Naperville, Illinois: Sourcebooks, 2006.

Byrnes, James F. Byrnes, *Speaking Frankly*. New York: Harper & Brothers, 1947.

Marshall, John A., *American Bastille: A History of the Illegal Arrests and Imprisonment of American Citizens in the Northern and Border States on Account of Their Political Opinions During the Late Civil War*. Philadelphia: Thomas W. Hartley, 1871.

Condon, John F., *Jafsie Tells All*. New York: Jonathan Lee Publishing Corp., 1936.

Kennedy, John F., *Profiles in Courage*. New York: Harper, 1956.

Koerner, John, *The Secret Plot to Kill McKinley*. Buffalo, New York: Western New York Wares, 2011.

Keynes, John Maynard, *The Economic Consequences of the Peace*. New York: Harcourt, Brace, and Howe, 1920.

Adams, John Quincy, *Letters on the Masonic Institution*. Boston: T.R. Marvin, 1847.

Robison, John, *Proofs of a Conspiracy Against All Religions and Governments of Europe Carried on in the Secret Meetings of Free Masons, Illuminati and Reading Societies*. New York: George Forman, 1798.

Flynn, John T. *As We Go Marching: A Biting Indictment of the Coming of Domestic Fascism in America*. Garden City, New York: Doubleday, Doran and Co., 1944.

Flynn, John T., *Meet Your Congress*. Garden City, New York: Doubleday, Doran and Co., 1944.

Flynn, John T., *The Roosevelt Myth*. New York: Devin-Adair Co., 1965.

Flynn, John T., *The Truth About Pearl Harbor and the Final Secret of Pearl Harbor*. New York City: J.T. Flynn, 1944.

Toland, John, *Infamy: Pearl Harbor and its Aftermath*. New York: Berkley Books, 1983.

Dower, John W., *Hiroshima Diary: The Journal of a Japanese Physician, August 6-September 30, 1945*. Chapel Hill, North Carolina: University of North Carolina Press, 1995.

McCarthy, Joseph, *America's Retreat From Victory: The Story of George Catlett Marshall*. New York: Devin-Adair, 1951.

McCarthy, Joseph, *McCarthyism: The Fight for America*. New York: Devin-Adair, 1952.

Martin, Joseph Plumb, *Memoir of a Revolutionary Soldier*. Boston: Little, Brown, 1967.

Abel, Jules, *The Truman Scandals*. Chicago: H.Regnery Co., 1956.

Archer, Jules, *The Plot to Seize the White House*. New York: Skyhorse Publishing, 2007.

Epstein, Julius, *Operation Keelhaul: The Story of Forced Repatriation From 1944 to the Present*. Greenwich, Connecticut: Devin-Adair, 1974.

Steffgen, Kent H., *The Bondage of the Free*. Berkeley, CA: Vanguard Books, 1966.

Powers, Kirsten, *The Silencing: How the Left is Killing Free Speech*. Washington, D.C.: Regnery Publishing, 2015.

Whitley, Leon, *The Case for Sterilization*. New York: Frederick A. Stokes, 1934.

Cole, Leonard A., *Clouds of Secrecy: The Army's Germ Warfare Tests Over Populated Areas*. Totowa, New Jersey: Rowman and Littlefield, 1988.

Farrell, Lt. Col. Bud, *Treason in High Places*. Boring, Oregon: F.P. Farrell, 1957.

Kennedy, Ludovic, *The Airman and the Carpenter: The Lindbergh Kidnapping and the Framing of Richard Hauptmann*. New York: Viking, 1985.

Holowchak, M. Andrew, *Framing a Legend: Exposing the Distorted History of Thomas Jefferson and Sally Hemings*. Amherst, New York: Prometheus Books, 2013.

MacMillan, Margaret, *The War That Ended Peace: The Road to 1914*. New York: Random House, 2013.

Chestnut, Mary Boykin, *A Diary From Dixie*. New York: D. Appleton and Co., 1905.

Evans, Medford, *The Assassination of Joe McCarthy*. Boston: Western Islands, 1970.

Herman, Michael, *Intelligence Power in Peace and War*. New York: Cambridge University Press, 2008.

Stenehjem, Michele Flynn, *An American First: John T. Flynn and the America First Committee*. New Rochelle, New York: Arlington House Publishers, 1976.

Eisenschiml, Otto, *The Shadow of Lincoln's Death*. Boston: Little, Brown and Company, 1937.

Eisenschiml, Otto, *Why Was Lincoln Murdered?* New York: W. Funk, Inc., 1940.

Tucker, Phillip Thomas, *Exodus From the Alamo: The Anatomy of the Last Stand Myth*. Haverton, Pennsylvania: Newbury: Casemate, 2008.

De Felice, Renzo, *Mussolini*. Torino, Italy: Einaudi, 1994.

Taylor, Richard, *Destruction and Reconstruction*. Charleston, South Carolina: BiblioBazaar, 2008.

Stinnett, Robert B., *Day of Deceit: The Truth About FDR and Pearl Harbor*. New York: Touchstone, 2004.

Ferrell, Robert H., *The Strange Deaths of President Harding*. Columbia, Missouri: University of Missouri Press, 1996.

Wilcox, Robert, *Target Patton: The Plot to Assassinate General George S. Patton*. Washington, D.C.: Regnery History, 2008.

Rogerson, Sidney and Hart, Liddell, *Propaganda and the Next War*. New York: Arno Press, 1972.

Caldwell, Taylor, *The Captains and the Kings*. New York: Fawcett-Crest, 1972.

Tenison, Deane, *Crime of Vaccination*. Charleston, South Carolina: Nabu Press, 2010 (reprint of original 1913 edition).

Roscoe, Theodore, *Web of Conspiracy: The Complete Story of the Men Who*

Murdered Abraham Lincoln. Englewood Cliffs, New Jersey: Prentice-Hall, 1959.

DiLorenzo, Thomas, *Hamilton's Curse: How Jefferson's Arch Enemy Betrayed the American Revolution—And What It Means for Americans Today.* New York: Random House, 2008.

DiLorenzo, Thomas J., *Lincoln Unmasked: What You're Not Supposed to Know About Dishonest Abe.* New York: Three Rivers Press, 2006.

DiLorenzo, Thomas J., *The Real Lincoln: A New Look at Abraham Lincoln, His Agenda, and an Unnecessary War.* New York: Three Rivers Press, 2003.

Weiner, Tim, *Legacy of Ashes: The History of the CIA.* London: Penguin, 2011.

Phillips, V.N. "Bud", *In Between the States: Bristol Tennessee/Virginia During the Civil War.* Johnson City, Tennessee: Overmountain Press, 1997.

Cisco, Walter Brian, *War Crimes Against Southern Civilians.* New York: Pelican Publishing Company, 2007.

Fleming, Walter, *The Sequel of Appomattox.* New York: Yale University Press, 1919.

Huie, William Bradford, *The Execution of Private Slovik.* New York: Dell, 1971.

Hyland, William G. Jr., *In Defense of Thomas Jefferson: The Sally Hemings Sex Scandal.* New York: Thomas Dunne Books, 2009.

Haze, Xaviant, *The Suppressed History of America: The Murder of Meriwether Lewis and the Mysterious Discoveries of the Lewis and Clark Expedition.* Rochester, Vermont: Bear, 2011.

NOTES

INTRODUCTION

1 *World Net Daily*, March 9, 2009.

CHAPTER ONE: THE BIRTH OF THE REPUBLIC

1 *The Shoemaker and the Tea Party: Memory and the American Revolution* by Alfred Young, p.120).

2 *Top Right News*, January 31, 2015.

3 *CNN*, August 22, 2008.

4 *Breitbart*, November 11, 2015.

5 *Huffington Post*, June 24, 2015.

6 *Los Angeles Times*, June 24, 2015.

7 *Los Angeles Times*, June 24, 2015.

8 *Connecticut Post*, July 23, 2015.

9 *CNN*, September 20, 2017.

10 *Huffington Post*, May 28, 2015.

11 *Elite Daily*, October 22, 2014.

12 *Daily Kos*, July 4, 2011.

13 *Chicago Tribune*, May 6, 1990.

14 *Chicago Tribune*, May 6, 1990.

15 *Los Angeles Times*, April 1, 2001.

16 *The Washington Times*, July 5, 2013.

17 *Fox News*, December 16, 2015.

18 *Letters and Other Writings of James Madison*, 1865, Vol. IV, p. 491.

19 *World Net Daily*, October 3, 2007.

CHAPTER TWO: PRE-1860: JACKSONIAN DEMOCRACY

1 *The Guardian*, August 3, 2015.

2 *Independent Journal Review*, March 2015.

3 *Washington Examiner*, June 17, 2015.

CHAPTER THREE: HONEST ABE

1 *Journal of Abraham Lincoln Association*, Winter 2003.

2 *Huffington Post*, January 26, 2013.

3 *The South Was Right!* by James Ronald Kennedy and Walter Donald Kennedy, pp. 28–29.

4 *A Youth's History of the Great Civil War in the United States, From 1861 to 1865* by Rushmore G. Horton, p. 268.

5 *State of Emergency: The Third World Invasion and Conquest of America* by Patrick J. Buchanan, p. 229.

6 *Martin Van Buren and the American Political System* by Donald B. Cole, p. 425.

7 *Lincoln Reconsidered* by David Herbert Donald, p. 180.

8 *Facts and Falsehoods Concerning the War on the South 1861–1865* by George Edmonds, p. 205.

9 *The Journal of Southern History*, November 1948, pp. 462–463.

10 *The South Was Right!*, pp. 30–31.

11 Ibid, p. 285.

12 Ibid, pp. 557–558.

13 *New York Sun*, August 6, 2007.

14 *Virginia Beach Conservative Examiner*, April 4, 2010.

15 *The Bondage of the Free* by Kent H. Steffgen, p. 92.

16 *The Secret Six* by Otto Scott, pp. 319–320.

17 *The South Was Right!*, p. 412.

18 Ibid, p. 284.

19 *Abraham Lincoln:* One Volume Paperback Edition, by Carl Sandburg, p. 233.

20 Ibid, p. 452.

21 Ibid, p. 416.

22 *Over Lincoln's Shoulder* by Bruce Tap, pp. 156–157.

23 Ibid, pp. 635–636.

24 Ibid, pp. 649–650.

25 *Journal of the Abraham Lincoln Association*, Summer 2012.

26 *Chicago Tribune*, April 14, 2009.

27 *Tyler's Quarterly Historical and Genealogical Magazine XIII (1931–1932)*.

28 The Democratic Speaker's Hand-Book by Matthew Carey, p. 33.

29 *New York Daily News*, April 3, 2015.

30 *Salon*, March 22, 2012.

CHAPTER FOUR: THE LINCOLN ASSASSINATION

1 *Why Was Lincoln Murdered* by Otto Eisenschiml, pp. 54–64.

2 Eisenschiml, pp. 32–33.

3 *The Life of Abraham Lincoln* by William E. Barton, p. 472.

4 Eisenschiml, pp. 65–75.

5 Eisenschiml, pp. 12–16.

6 Eisenschiml, p. 16.

7 Eisenschiml, p. 19.

8 *Through Five Administrations* by William H. Crook, p. 71–72.

9 "Lincoln's Missing Bodyguard," *Smithsonian* magazine, April 7, 2010.

10 (Eisenschiml, pp. 22–29.

11 *Washingtonian*, April 12, 2015.

12 Eisenschiml, pp. 138–141.

13 *The Lincoln Conspiracy* by David W. Balsiger & Charles E. Sellier, pp. 250–254.

14 *The Cosgrove Report* by George O'Toole, p. 97.

15 Eisenschiml, pp. 175–187.

16 Eisenschimil, pp. 200–206.

17 Eisenschiml, pp. 230–231.

18 Eisenschiml, pp. 235–237.

19 Eisenschiml, pp. 242–244.

20 Eisenschiml, pp. 264–265.

21 Eisenschiml, pp. 280–281.

22 Eisenschiml, pp. 284–286.

23 *The Lincoln Conspiracy* by David Balsiger & Charles E. Sellier, p. 196.

24 Eisenschiml, pp. 296–307.

25 Balsiger & Sellier, pp. 277–280, 289.

26 *Washington Post,* July 4, 2015.

27 Eisenschiml, p. 5.

28 Balsiger & Sellier, pp. 23–24.

29 *Twenty Days* by Dorothy Meserve Kunhardt & Philip B. Kunhardt, Jr., p. 66.

30 *April 1865: The Month That Saved America* by Jay Winik, p. 98.

31 O'Toole, p. 258.

32 "That Man Lloyd" by Laurie Verge, April 1988 *Surratt Courier.*

33 Balsiger & Sellier, pp. 299–302.

34 *The World's Greatest Mysteries* by Rupert Furneaux, p. 178.

35 Furneaux, p. 179.

36 *Philadelphia Inquirer,* March 30, 2013.

37 O'Toole, pp. 273–274.

CHAPTER FIVE: POST-CIVIL WAR AMERICA

1 *Dixie After the War* by Myrta Lockett Avary, p. 378.

2 *The Bondage of the Free* by Kent H. Steffgen, pp. 102–103.

3 Steffgen, pp. 110–111.

4 Steffgen, p. 118.

5 Steffgen, p. 117.

6 *Reconstruction in North Carolina* by J.G. de Roulhac Hamilton, pp. 94–95.

7 *Reconstruction* by John Hope Franklin, p. 433.

8 *Washington Monthly*, January/February 2013.

9 *The New York Times*, February 10, 2015.

10 *Huffington Post*, July 6, 2015.

11 *The New World Order* by Ralph Epperson, p. 171.

12 *Washington Monthly*, January/February 2013.

13 *The Daily Beast*, May 23, 2011.

14 *Washington Post*, November 18, 1915.

CHAPTER SIX: THE 1900s-1920s

1 *CounterPunch*, August 19, 2011.

2 *Wall Street Journal*, February 10, 2015.

3 On a much less historically known December 7th, in 1914, Pope Benedict XV suggested a temporary hiatus of the war, in honor of Christmas. While the warring countries themselves were predictably repelled at the idea, those doing the fighting were far more receptive. A "Christmas Truce" was observed beginning on Christmas Eve, as German and British troops sang Christmas carols to each other. On Christmas Day, German troops began emerging from their bunkers, and the two sides exchanged gifts like cigarettes and plum pudding. There was even a well-documented soccer match between the enemies. When another holiday ceasefire was attempted the following year, it resulted in Captain Iain Colquhoun being court martialed for permitting the enemy to bury their dead, and exchanging cigars with them. Due to the fact he was related by marriage to British Prime Minister Herbert Asquith, Colquhoun escaped with only a reprimand. (*Reuters*, December 24, 2014).

4 *The Nation*, February 27, 2012).

5 *The Economist*, November 9, 2013.

6 *Profiles in Populism*, pp. 69–72.

7 *Profiles in Populism*, p. 32.

8 Ibid, pp. 55–57.

9 Ibid, p. 62.

10 *PBS News Hour*, August 2, 2015.

11 *Time*, December 27, 1926.

12 *Saturday Evening Post*, August 14, 2015.

13 *Business Insider*, December 23, 2013.

CHAPTER SEVEN: THE DEPRESSING 1930s

1 *Smithsonian Magazine*, February 2003.

2 *New York Review of Books*, November 5, 1987.

3 *Crime Of The Century* by Gregory Ahlgren & Stephen Monier, p. 8.

4 Ibid, pp. 11–20.

5 Ibid, pp. 205–206.

6 Ibid, p. 210.

7 Ibid, p. 213.

8 Ibid, p. 87.

9 Ibid, p. 125.

10 Ibid, pp. 164–165.

11 Ibid, pp. 134–135 & 186–187.

12 Ibid, p. 188.

13 Ibid, p. 195.

14 Ibid, pp. 222–223.

15 Ibid, pp. 224–225.

16 Ibid, pp. 227–228.

17 Ibid, p. 233.

18 Ibid, p. 235.

19 Ibid, p. 242.

20 Ibid, p. 251.

21 *Philadelphia Inquirer*, October 19, 1994.

22 *The Washington Post*, October 15, 1981.

CHAPTER EIGHT: FDR CHANNELS LINCOLN

1 *Wall Street Journal*, April 12, 2010.

2 *An American First* by Michele Flynn Stenehjem, pp. 145–153.

3 *An American First* by Michele Flynn Stenehjem, p. 155.

4 Ibid, pp. 158–161.

5 *Washington Post Book World*, May 21, 1995, p. 6.

6 *Infamy* by John Toland, Chapter 14, section 5.

7 *America's Dictator: FDR the Red* by Paul David Cook, pp. 265–266.

8 *Wall Street Journal*, May 14, 2013.

9 *The Altoona Tribune*, July 3, 1937.

10 *The Telegraph*, September 2, 2010.

11 *Spiegel Online International*, March 2, 2015.

12 *Reuters*, April 18, 2012.

13 *The Guardian*, May 15, 2004.

14 *ABC News Australia*, November 22, 2013.

CHAPTER NINE: POSTWAR AMERICA

1 *Illuminati 3: Satanic Possession* by Henry Makow, pp. 137–138.

2 *Chicago Daily News*, May 15, 1946.

3 *The Night Tokyo Burned: The Incendiary Campaign Against Japan, March–August, 1945* by Hoito Edoin , p. 120.

4 *America's Abandoned Sons* by Robert S. Miller, p. 300.

5 'A Dialectic on Total War," in idem, *Visions of Order: The Cultural Crisis of Our Time* (Baton Rouge: Louisiana State University Press, 1964), pp. 98–99.

6 *The Detroit News*, August 24, 1999.

7 *Washington Post*, September 8, 1979.

8 *Los Angeles Review of Books,* April 14, 2014.

9 *Harlan Fiske Stone: Pillar of the Law* by Alpheus T. Mason, p. 716.

10 *Commentary,* January 1946.

11 *Nuremberg: A Nation on Trial* by W. Maser, pp. 51–52.

12 *Profiles in Courage* by John F. Kennedy, pp. 189–190.

13 *The New Republic,* May 20, 1985.

14 *The Spotlight,* May 23, 1988.

15 *New York Times,* August 18, 1987.

16 *The Guardian,* November 1, 2010.

17 *US News & World Report,* August 15, 1960.

18 The New York Times, March 17, 1995.

19 *The Telegraph,* December 20, 2008.

20 *The Washington Post,* February 24, 2015.

21 *NPR,* December 22, 2011.

22 *The Spotlight,* October 16, 1989, pp. 6, 7, & 12.

23 *Trading With the Enemy* by Charles Higham, p. 37.

24 *East West Journal,* November 1984.

25 *Proceedings of the Royal Society of Medicine,* November 24, 1933.

26 *Salem News,* November 29, 2011.

27 *Presse Medicale,* March 12, 1955.

28 *University of Manchester,* October 14, 2010.

29 *San Diego Union,* August 12, 1971.

30 *World Heritage Encyclopedia.*

31 *The Observer,* October 16, 1994.

32 *Children as Research Subjects: Science, Ethics, and Law* by Michael A. Grodin & Leonard H. Glantz, pp. 7–11.

33 *Acres of Skin: Human experiments at Holmesburg Prison, A Story of Abuse and Exploitation in the Name of Medical Science* by Allen M. Hornblum, p. 79.

34 *Journal of the American Medical Association,* February 28, 1914.

35 *NBC News,* February 27, 2011.

36 *The Washington Post*, February 23, 1980.

37 *Inter Press Service News Agency*, October 21, 2002.

38 *US Army Medical Department Office of Medical History.*

39 *Clouds of Secrecy: The Army's Germ Warfare Tests Over Populated Areas* By Leonard A. Cole.

40 *The New York Times*, January 19, 1995.

41 *Smithsonian Magazine*, March 8, 2017.

42 *Psychology Today*, March 21, 2018.

43 *The New York Times*, January 18, 1983.

44 "Biological Warfare in the Korean War: Allegations and Cover-up" by Thomas Powell, *Socialism and Democracy*, #31.

45 *San Francisco Weekly*, March 14, 2012.

46 *Military Neuroscience and the Coming Age of Neurowarfare* by Armin Krishnan, p. 25.

47 *UPI*, October 29, 1980.

48 *NPR*, October 12, 2012.

49 "Inside Montreal's House of Horrors," *Montreal Gazette*, January 21, 1984.

50 *Civil Beat Hawaii*, February 24, 2014.

51 *PBS*, October 1, 2010.

CHAPTER TEN: THE FABULOUS FIFTIES

1 *Joseph McCarthy: Reexamining the Life and Legacy of America's Most Hated Senator* by Arthur Herman, Introduction.

2 *McCarthyism: The Fight For America* by Joseph McCarthy, p. 7.

3 Herman, Introduction.

4 Herman, Introduction.

5 Letter from William Donovan to Franklin D. Roosevelt, November 18, 1944.

6 *Russia Today*, July 23, 2013.

7 *The Guardian*, December 8, 2015.

8 *Fox News*, December 6, 2015.

9 *The New York Times*, October 24, 2001.

10 Blog of S. Brian Wilson, January 1, 2000.

11 *Canada Free Press*, December 14, 2010.

12 *The Guardian*, July 15, 2015.

13 *Under the Sign of the Scorpion* by Juri Lina, p. 278.

14 *An American First by Michele Flynn Stenehjem*, p. 168.

CHAPTER ELEVEN: THE HISTORY OF UN-AMERICANISM

1 *Fox News*, February 15, 2021.

2 *The Hill*, January 29, 2021.

3 *NBC News*, May 31, 2014.

4 *YouGov*, April 11, 2019.

5 *Washington Post*, September 8, 2018

6 *Independent Institute*, April 1, 2002

7 *Ibid*

8 *Ibid*

9 *New York Times*, August 25, 1940

10 *New York Times*, June 9, 1942

11 Cortright, David, *Peace: A History of Movements and Ideas*. Cambridge, UK: Cambridge University Press, 2008, pp. 164–165.

12 *Slate*, June 8, 2016

13 Sherry Gershon Gottleib, *Hell No, We Won't Go: Resisting the Draft During the Vietnam War*. 1991, New York: Viking Press, p. 96.

14 *Associated Press*, September 1, 2008

15 *The Atlantic*, October 5, 2015

16 *Salon*, June 20, 2007

CHAPTER TWELVE: CONCLUSION

1 *New York Times*, July 11, 1935.

2 *The Life of Aleister Crowley* by Richard Kaczynski, p. 522.

INDEX

Aaronvitch, David, xxvii
Abel, Jules, 293
Abiff, Hiram, 44
Acheson, Dean, 295
Adams, Charles, 57, 95
Adams, John, 1–2, 5, 17, 18, 23, 41, 196
Adams, Samuel, 1, 20, 25, 29
Adams, Franklin P., 265
Adams, John Quincy, 36, 42–46
Adonis, Joe, 257
Aiken, Frederick, 123
Aldrich, Nelson, 175–177
Alford, Terry, 114
Alinsky, Saul, 356
Allen, Gary, xv
Alving, Alf, 310
Ambrose, Stephen, 7, 261, 273
Anderson, George, 197
Annenberg, Moe, 255
Anscombe, G.E.M., 291
Antoinette, Marie, 4
Aptheker, Herbert, 55
Arbenz, Jacobo, 323
Archer, Jules, 233
Arendt, Hannah, 280
Armstrong, Neil, 355
Arnold, Benedict, 3
Arnold, Samuel, 121, 123
Arthur, Chester, 158–159

Asbury, Herbert, 64
Asquith, Herbert, 372
Atzerodt, George, 118, 121, 126, 132

Bachman, John, 104
Bacque, James, 279
Bailey, John, 9
Bainbridge, Absalom, 132
Baker, Lafayette, 120–121, 123, 130, 136–137, 140
Baker, William J., 235
Balfour, Arthur James, 193
Balletto, Nick, 9
Balsiger, David W., 120, 137
Banfield, Ashley, 7
Barnes, Harry Elmer, 285
Barone, Michael, 319
Baruch, Bernard, 296
Basti, Abel, 266
Bates, Edward, 60, 124–125
Bates, Finis L., 137
Bavas, Josh, 263
Bazata, Douglas, 293
Bell, Robert, 303
Belz, Herman, 57
Berg, Andrew Scott, 218
Bernays, Edward, xiv
Berrigan, Philip, 347
Beschloss, Michae, 294

Biddle, Francis, 250
Biddle, Nicholas, 37
Bierce, Ambrose, 156
Bird, Kai, 292
Black, William C., 308
Blackmon, Douglas A., 162
Bly, John, 20
Boate, Edward Wellington, 80
Bonaparte, Napoleon, xxvi
Boorstin, Daniel, 318
Booth, Edwin, 115, 138
Booth, John Wilkes, ix, 38, 52, 94,
    114–116, 118–121, 123, 126–127,
    130–131, 133–139, 154
Booth, Junius Brutus, 136, 138
Bornmann, Lewis, 223
Botting, Douglas, 270
Bovard, James, 77, 80
Bowen, Howell Lewis, ix, 38–40
Bowers, Claude G., 154
Bowie, Jim, 49
Boyd, James William, 137
Boyle, Frank, 136
Bradley, Omar, 276
Brands, H. W., 10
Braun, Eva, 266–267
Brech, Martin, 274
Breckinridge, Henry, 225
Britton, Nan, 203
Brodie, Fawn, 5, 149
Brokaw, Tom, 35, 273
Bronstein, Lev, 335
Brooke, Rupert, 193
Brooks, David, 57
Brophy, John P., 132
Browder, Earl, 255
Brown, Jerry, 31
Brown, John, 53–55, 78, 159
Brown, Shannon, 108
Browning, William A., 133, 135

Browning, Orville H., 81, 124
Brownlow, William P. "Parson," 151
Bruchman, Oscar, 226
Bryan, William, 211
Bryan, William Jennings, 164–166, 187,
    194
Brzezinski, Zbigniew, xxix
Buchanan, James, 162
Buchanan, Pat, 64
Buck, Pearl S., 265
Buell, Don Carlos, 78
Buffalo Bill, 4
Bullock, Rufus, 146
Burke, Edmund, 35
Burnett, Peter H., 183
Burns, Arthur, 179
Burnside, Ambrose, 68
Burr, Aaron, 24
Bush, Prescott, 201
Bush, George W., xxix, 38, 65, 70, 201
Butler, Benjamin, 71, 82–83, 119, 151
Butler, Smedley, 186, 198, 213, 233,
    298–299, 337, 355
Byrnes, Jimmy, 266, 318

Caesar, Julius, 111
Caldwell, Taylor, 171
Calhoun, John C., 178
Callender, James, 5
Caplan, David, 171
Capone, Al, 204, 299
Capra, Frank, 264
Carland, Lewis, 127–128
Carnegie, Andrew, 168
Carroll, Al, 198
Carroll, Lewis, 284
Carwardine, Richard, 107
Casey, Katherine, 331–332
Cassidy, Tom, 217
Catton, Bruce, 55

Chamberlain, Neville, 255, 284
Chambrun, Marquis de, 108–109
Chandler, David Leon, 37–38
Chaplin, Charlie, 238, 265
Charles I, 80
Charles II, 13
Chester, Samuel, 126
Chestnut, Mary, 83, 87
Chomsky, Noam, 279
Chovenson, Samuel, 190
Church, Frank, 324
Churchill, Ward, 182
Churchill, Winston, xxvi, 187, 188, 189,
    193, 236, 237, 240, 241, 243, 244, 253,
    259, 260, 269, 279, 280, 281, 287, 300,
    301, 337, 339, 357
Cisco, Walter Brian, 101
Clampitt, John W., 128
Clark, Edwin Booth, 136
Clark, W. B., 302
Clark, William, 36–37
Cleburne, Patrick R., 142
Cleveland, Grover, 162–164, 171, 185
Cleveland, Oscar Folsom, 163
Clifford, Clark, 295–296
Clinton, Bill, xxvi, 6, 14, 247, 340
Clinton, Hillary, 353, 356
Cobb, Silas, 118
Cobbett, William, 19
Cohan, George M., 190
Cohn, Roy, 333
Cole, Leonard J., 311
Colfax, Schuyler, 113
Columbus, Christopher, 182
Commager, Henry Steele, 148
Condon, John F. "Jafsie," 214–215,
    217–218, 221–222
Conkling, Roscoe, 157
Conness, John, 136
Conway, Jill K., 14

Cooke, Jacob, 22
Coolidge, Calvin, 207–208, 213, 288
Corbett, Boston, 118, 135–136
Corning, Erastus, 69–70
Cornwallis, Charles, 12
Costello, Frank, 257–258
Cottingham, George, 130
Coughlin, Father Charles, 236, 250, 255
Coulter, Ann, 318
Cousteau, Jacques, 300
Cox, Samuel, 130
Cox, Walter Smith, 123
Coxey, Jacob S., 163
Crawford, Broderick, 276
Creasy, William, 311
Creel, George, 190
Crockett, Davy, 46, 49–50
Cromwell, Oliver, 55, 147
Crook, William, 116
Cross, Wilbur, 239
Crowley, Aleister, 13, 356–357
Cummings, E. E., 182
Cummings, Homer, 234
Cunningham, Jack, 229
Cuomo, Chris, 31
Czolgosz, Leon, 170–172

Dahlstrom, Neil, 59
Dalberg-Acton, John, 109
Dallek, Robert, xxvii
Dana, D. D., 130, 132
Daniels, Jonathan, 243
Daniels, Joseph, 189
Darrow, Clarence, 165–166, 249, 300,
    358
Dashwood, Francis, 13
David, Rosalie, 304–305
Davis, Jefferson, 53, 80, 85, 89–90,
    92–93, 104, 106, 125, 142–143, 153
Dawes, William, 2

de las Casas, Bartolome, 182
De Felice, Renzo De, 259–260
Dean, Henry Clay, 65–66
Deane, Tenison, 303–304
Debs, Eugene, 185, 197, 298
deGaulle, Charles, 357
Del Grazio, August, 257
Derickson, David, 58
Dershowitz, Alan, 334
Dewey, Thomas, 248, 292, 295, 297
Dickens, Charles, 359
Dies, Martin, 256
Diggins, John P., 10
DiLorenzo, Thomas, 57, 106
Disney, Walt, 49, 265
Disraeli, Benjamin, xxvi, 4
Dixon, Thomas, 200
Dodd, Norman, 329–332
Doheny, E.L. "Ned" Jr., 203
Donald Steury, 248
Donald, David Herbert, 71
Donovan, William J. "Wild Bill," 322
Douglas, Frederick, 155
Douglas, Stephen, 8, 85
Douglas, William O., 282, 285
Dower, John W., 289
Downs, Hunton, 276
Downs, Jim, 77
Dubois, W.E.B., 153, 200, 300
Dubourcq, Hilaire, 15
Dukakis, Michael, 207
Duke, David, 358
Dulles, Allen, 306, 310, 312
Dulles, John Foster, 315
Duranty, Walter, 336
Duryea, J. T., 108
Duvalier, "Papa Doc," 323

arhart, Amelia, 226
stwood, Clint, 230

Eckert, Thomas T., 113, 119, 122
Edes, Benjamin, 2
Edison, Thomas, 169–170, 194
Edmonds, George, 71
Edoin, Hoito, 270
Eichelberger, Clark, 239
Eichmann, Adolf, 280, 286
Eigruber, August, 284
Einstein, Albert, 290, 353–354
Eisenhower, Dwight, 30, 212, 271–274,
    276–277, 279, 285, 291, 297–298, 301,
    312, 318, 334
Eisenhower, Edgar, 285
Eisenhower, Milton, 244
Eisenschiml, Otto, 126–127, 139–140
Eldredge, Charles A., 124
Eliot, T. S., 286
Ellery, William, 12
Emerson, Nancy, 83
Emerson, Ralph Waldo, 54, 88
Epstein, Julius, 272
Esdaile, Scot X., 9
Evans, Medford, 317
Ewen-Cameron, Donald, 311–313
Ewing, Thomas, 125–126

Fadiman, Clifton, 265
Fagan, Myron C., 336
Faloughi, Reuben, 7
Farley, James A., 235
Farley, Michael F., 198
Farrell, Bud, 326
Fay, Theodore, 82
Feherenbacher, Don E., 97
Ferber, Edna, 265
Ferdinand, Archduke Franz, 187
Ferrell, Robert H., 202
Figueres, Jose, 296
Fillmore, Millard, 44
Findley, William, 22

Finkelman, Paul, 4
Firestone, Harvey, 296
Fisch, Isidor, 215, 226
Fish, Hamilton, 245, 255
Fisher, C. Lloyd, 215
Fisher, Ernest F., 273
Fisher, Jim, 215
Fisher, Richard, 180
Fleming, Ian, 357
Fleming, Walter, 75
Floyd, William, 12
Flynn, John T., 237–239, 341
Folsom, Frances, 162–163
Foner, Eric, 8, 143–144
Ford, Gerald, 324
Ford, Henry, xxvi, 170, 194–195, 204, 353
Ford, John T., 128
Forrest, Nathan Beford, 150, 154, 160–161
Forrestal, Henry, 293–294
Forrestal, James V., 293–295, 316–317, 326
Fort, Charles, xxxi
Frank, Hans, 284
Frankfurter, Felix, xxvi, 205, 296
Franklin, Benjamin, 1, 4, 8, 13–17, 25, 28, 33, 114, 263, 357
Franklin, William, 14
Frost, Robert, 250
Fuchs, Klaus, 334
Fuller, Buckminster, 176, 338
Fuller, J. F. C., 289

Gaither, Rowan, 331
Gallico, Paul, 265
Galt, Edith Bolling, 199
Gandhi, Mahatma, 302, 325
Gardner, Alexander, 120–121
Garfield, James, 123, 157–159
Garner, John Nance, 235

Garnett, Richard B., 100
Garrison, Ely, 175
Garrison, William Lloyd, 10
Gehlen, Reinhard, 321
Geisel, Theodore "Dr. Seuss," 265
George, Lloyd, 193
Gerry, Elbridge, 30
Gibbon, Edward, xxvi
Gifford, James J., 127–128
Gilbert, Parker, 236
Gillis, Father James, 289
Ginsberg, Benjamin, 147
Ginsberg, Alan, 250
Goering, Herman, 337
Goldberger, Joseph, 307
Goldman, Emma, 171, 339
Goldstein, Robert, 197
Goldwater, Barry, 181
Gompers, Samuel, 184
Gore, Thomas, 198
Goschen, Lord George, 140
Gottfried, Paul, 318
Gottlieb, Sidney, 306
Gow, Betty, 218–220, 225
Graham, Katherine, 322
Graham, Lindsay, 111
Graham, Philip, 323
Granger, Gordon, 161
Grant, Madison, 308
Grant, Ulysses S., 51–52, 63, 74–76, 79–80, 83–85, 90, 107, 112–113, 125, 134, 143–144, 148, 152–153, 156, 158, 201, 327, 359
Grass, Gunter, 289
Greeley, Horace, 84
Green, Ben, 139–140
Greene, Nathaniel, 19
Greenfield, Jeff, xxx
Greenglass, David, 333–334
Greenglass, Ruth, 333

Grey, Sir Edward, 188
Griffin, Henry, 260
Griffith, D.W., 200
Guelzo, Allen C., 8
Guiteau, Charles, 123, 158–159
Gutenberg, Johannes, xxv

Haffenden, Charles R., 256
Halifax, Lord, 244
Hale, Edward Everett, 71–72
Hall, Gus, 320
Halleck, Henry W., 79, 144
Halpin, Maria, 163–164
Halsey, William "Bull," 246
Hamilton, Alexander, 4, 7–8, 20, 22–24, 28, 30, 33, 40, 47–48, 110, 170, 178, 191
Hammerstein, Oscar II, 265
Hampton, Wade, 146
Hancock, John, 1–2, 12, 20, 25
Hancock, Winfield S., 131, 133
Hanscom, Simon P., 117–118
Harding, Florence, 201–203
Harding, Warren, 197, 200–202, 254, 288
Harris, Sir Arthur "Bomber," 267, 269, 287
Harris, Clara, 114, 117, 135
Harris, Ira, 114
Harrison, Benjamin, 162
Harrison, William Henry, 51
Harsch, Joseph C., 213
Hart, John, 12
Hart, Liddell, 237
Harvey, Bree, 138
Hauptmann, Anna, 223, 225, 228–230
Hauptmann, Manfred, 230
Hauptmann, Bruno Richard, 214–218, 220–230
awley, Seth C., 63
wthorne, Nathaniel, 89

Hay, John, 90–91, 95, 167, 173
Hays, Wayne L., 329, 332
Hayes, Rutherford B., 155–156, 159
Haynes, John Earl, 319
Haze, Xaviant, 37
Hearst, William Randolph, 167, 224, 235, 255
Heath, Joan, 276
Heflin, James Thomas, 203
Heiman, Henry, 306
Heimlich, W. J., 266
Heinlein, Robert A., 176
Helms, Richard, 306
Hemings, Sally, 5–7
Hemingway, Ernest, 250
Henry the Eighth, 4
Henry, Anson G., 135
Henry, Patrick, 3, 27, 29, 31, 34, 84
Herman, Arthur, 318
Herman, Michael, 328
Herndon, William Henry, 8, 58-59, 93, 108
Herold, David, 118, 121, 130–131, 133
Herzl, Theodor, 295
Hess, Rudolph, 287–288, 357
Hewson, William, 15–16
Hill, Bryant, 7
Hirohito, Emperor, 291
Hiss, Alger, 316, 341
Hitler, Adolph, 97, 106, 178, 192, 235, 238–239, 243, 259, 264–267, 274, 284, 295, 300, 308, 318–319, 321, 337, 357
Hobart, Garret, 173
Hochmuth, Amandus, 218
Hodgson, John, 59–60
Hoffman, Abbie, 195
Hoffman, Harold, 217, 226–228
Holmes, Oliver Wendell, 197, 300
Holt, Joseph, 120, 124–125, 127–128, 139
Holzer, Harold, 94

Hood, John Bell, 74
Hoover, J. Edgar, 197, 226, 230, 355
Hoover, Herbert, 201–202, 211–213, 245, 290
Hopkins, Harry, 243
Hornblum, Allen M., 310
Horton, Rushmore G., 61
House, Edward Mandell, 188–189, 194
Houston, Sam, 49
Howard, Frank Key, 62
Hubbard, L. Ron, 356
Huff, Raymond, 261
Hughes, Langston, 265
Hugo, Victor, 54
Huie, William Bradford, 279
Hull, Cordell, 242, 245, 281
Hulme, Joanne, ix, 138
Hume, Paul, 294
Hurlbut, Stephen A., 78
Hylan, John F., 208

Icke, David, 23
Ickes, Harold, 240–241
Ingalls, Laura, 251
Ingersoll, Robert G., 94
Irving, David, 336
Ishii, Shiro, 292

Jackson, Andrew, xxvi, 4, 9, 42, 45–48, 50, 52, 114, 178
Jackson, Michael, 356
Jackson, Robert H., 238, 281, 283
Jackson, Thomas "Stonewall," 72, 358
James, Jesse, 151
Jameson, W. C., 121
Jefferson, Thomas, xxvii, 3–11, 13, 16–18, 21–25, 28–29, 31, 33–34, 37–38, 41, 45, 83, 110, 144, 149, 177, 233, 302, 352–353, 358
Jett, Willie, 131

Jobs, Steve, xxviii–xxix
Johnson, Andrew, 4, 118, 123–125, 131–135, 143, 148–149, 152, 161
Johnson, Lyndon Baines, 106, 255, 263, 320, 353
Johnson, Carol, 138
Johnson, Milbank, 305
Johnson, Reverdy, 125
Johnson, Wendell, 308
Jones, Thomas A., 130
Jones, Alex, 28
Jones, John Paul, 25
Judd, Norman, 59

Kaiser Wilhelm II, 192
Katz, Jonathan, 23
Kaufman, Irving R., 333–334
Kearns-Goodwin, Doris, 57, 106
Keckley, Elizabeth, 116
Kefauver, Estes, 257, 292
Keller, Helen, 300
Kennedy, John F., xxviii–xxix, xxxii, 5, 58, 98, 114, 119, 134, 148, 171, 183, 246, 254–255, 271, 282, 285–286, 290, 294, 316, 320, 359–360
Kennedy, Robert F., 258, 316
Kennedy, Robert F. Jr., 303
Kennedy, Kathleen, 254
Kennedy, Ludovic, 217, 230
Kennedy, Joseph P., 235, 252–254, 258, 294, 316
Kennedy, Joseph P. Jr., 253–254
Kerensky, Alexander, 337
Kernan, Francis, 69
Key, Philip Barton II, 62
Key, Francis Scott, 62
Keynes, John Maynard, 176, 192, 300
Kimmel, Husband, 246–247, 286
Kimmel, Manning IV, 247
Kimmelman, Benedict, 279

King George III, 8, 11, 34
King Louis XVI, 17
King Richard III, 47
King, Preston, 131, 135
Klehr, Harvey, 319
Kloke, Dave, 107
Knapman, Paul, 15
Knox, Frank, 242–243, 245
Knox, Henry, 20
Koerner, John, 171
Konvitz, Milton R., 282
Krauthammer, Charles, xxix
Kucinich, Dennis, 181
Kun, Bela, 339
Kyl, Jon, xxxi

Lachman, Charles, 163
Lacker, Jeffrey, 181
Lafayette, Marquis de, 19, 23, 25
LaFollette, Philip, 237
LaFollette, Robert M., 195–196
LaFollette, Robert M. Jr., 320
Lamb, John, 2
Lane, James H., 79, 131, 135
Lansing, Robert, 188
Lansky, Meyer, 256–257
Lanza, Socks, 257
Larouche, Lyndon, 161
Lasky, Victor, xxxii
Lattimore, Owen, 320
Laurens, John, 23
Lawrence, David, 290
Lawrence, Richard, 46–47
Leahy, William D., 289
Leary, Timothy, 356
Lee, Robert E., 85, 91, 109, 142, 150–151, 153
, Richard Henry, 3, 29
Edgar Wallace, 171
d, Missy, 254

Leib, Joe, 242
LeMay, Curtis, 271, 291
Lemke, William, 236
Lemon, Don, 7
Lenin, Vladimir, 335–336
Lew, Jack, 47
Lewis, Anthony, 280
Lewis, Francis, 12
Lewis, Meriwether, ix, 36–40, 52, 154
Liberace, 356
Lincoln, Abraham, ix, xxvii, 8–10, 33,
    41, 51–52, 54, 56–75, 78–79, 81–101,
    105–119, 121, 124–127, 130, 133–141,
    148, 150, 158, 172–173, 195, 203, 232,
    255, 258, 283, 353–354, 358, 360
Lincoln, Tad, 92
Lincoln, Mary Todd, 58, 93, 113,
    115–116, 133–136
Lincoln, Robert Todd, 63, 115, 134
Lindbergh, Rep. Charles A., 176, 181
Lindbergh, Charles, 214–220, 223–225,
    227–228, 235, 237, 255, 261
Lindbergh, Charles Jr., 202, 214–215,
    217–220, 223–228, 230
Lindbergh, Anne Morrow, 219–220, 230
Linder, John, 27
Lippmann, Walter, 207, 235, 338
Little, Frank, 186
Little, Maxwell, 6
Livingston, William, 12
Lloyd, John M., 128–130, 135
Lochner, Louis, 265
Locke, John, 35
Lodge, Henry Cabot, 92
Lodge, Henry Cabot Jr., 297
Loeb, Winiam, 175
Lonati, Bruno, 260
London, Meyer, 197
Long, Huey, 213, 232–233, 236, 249–250,
    255, 360

Lopez, Barry, 182
Lord Curzon, 192
Lowell, James Russell, 89
Lowrie, Walter, 60
Luciano, Charles "Lucky," 256–257
Lumumba, Patrice, 323
Lundberg, Ferdinand, 210
Lundeen, Ernest, 251
Luxembourg, Rosa, 339
Lynch, Thomas, 12
Lynes, Barry, 305
Lyons, Lord, 61

MacArthur, Douglas, 212, 243, 263,
   291–292, 294, 325, 358
Maccarone, Robert, 260
MacDonald, Charles, 262
Mackay, Charles, xxvii
MacLeish, Archibald, 238
MacMillan, Margaret, 193
Madison, Dolley, 40
Madison, James, 10, 21, 23, 29, 31–33,
   40–41, 110, 177, 199, 240
Maher, Bill, xxix
Makow, Henry, 229
Malcolm X, 54
Malin, James C., 54–55
Mallard, Mary S., 103
Maltz, Albert, 279
Manber, Jeffrey, 59
Manning, Chelsea, 34
Manson, Charles, 159
Marion, Nancy E., 53
Marshall, George C., 241, 244, 247–248,
   295, 301, 316
Marshall, John A., 62–63
Marshall, John, 33
Marsloe, Anthony J., 257
Martin, David, 294
Martin, Joseph Plumb, 19–20

Marx, Karl, 55, 336, 339
Mason, George, 29, 31, 34
Masters, Edgar Lee, 65, 96
Matthews, Chris, xxix
May, John Franklin, 120
McCaffrey, George, 260
McCain, John, 111, 172, 293
McCarthy, Jenny, 303
McCarthy, Joseph, 256, 294, 301, 303,
   315–321, 326, 329, 333, 335
McCartney, Paul, 356
McClellan, George, 71, 76, 79, 90–91
McCulloch, Hugh, 149
McDonald, Larry P., 356
McFadden, Louis T., 178–180
McGowan, David, 118, 121, 123, 136
McGrady, Pat, 229
McKinley, William, 166, 168, 170–173
McKittrick, Thomas H., 299
McNamara, Robert, 291
McNeil, John, 151
McVeigh, Timothy, 206
Mead, Margaret, 300
Meade, George, 144
Means, Gaston, 202–203
Means, Russell, 184
Meeropol, Michael, 333
Mellon, Andrew, 210
Meltzer, Brad, xxx, xxxi, 36
Melville, Herman, 53
Mencken, H. L., 99, 229, 328
Mendelsohn, Robert, 302
Menzies, Robert, 240
Mercader, Ramon, 337
Merck, George W., 309
Meyer, Eugene, 236
Meyner, Robert B., 227
Millay, Edna St. Vincent, 205, 265
Miller, Dennis, xxix
Miller, Glenn, 275–277

Mills, Walter, 189
Milza, Pierre, 260
Mikkelson, David and Barbara, xxxi
Miranda, Lin-Manuel, 7
Mitchel, Ormsby M., 78
Mock, James R., 197
Moley, Raymond, 235–236
Molotov, Vyacheslav, 337
Monroe, James, 10, 17, 42, 199
Monteiro, Manuel deGoes, 244
Montgomery, J. B., 119
Moon, Donald, 263
Moore, Kathryn, 37
Moore, Michael, 3
More, Sir Thomas, xxvii
Morelli, Frank "Butsy," 207
Morgan, John Hunt, 101
Morgan, J. P., 73, 163, 175, 187, 189, 236
Morgan, William, 42–43
Morgenthau, Henry, 280–281
Morley, Felix, 289
Morris, Robert, 12
Morrison, Jim, 356
Moses, Frank, 146
Mossadegh, Mohammad, 323
Moxley, Basil, 136
Mudd, Samuel, 118, 121, 123, 130, 149, 161
Mufson, Steven, 48
Mullins, Eustace, 181–182, 328
Mumford, William, 82
Murrow, Edward R., 243, 265, 318
Mussey, Reuben D., 131–132
Mussolini, Benito, 258–260
Myers, Thomas J., 102–103
Neelly, James, 37

Nelson, James M., 93
Nelson, Thomas, 12
Nevin, Edward J. III, 311
Nevin, Edward, 311

Nicolay, John, 90–91
Nietzsche, Friedrich, 165, 357
Nikitchenko, Iola T., 283–284
Niles, David, 296
Nixon, Richard M., 247, 250, 292, 297
Noguchi, Hideyo, 307
Norris, Charles, 204

O'Beirne, James Rowan, 115, 137
O'Laughlin, Michael, 121, 123
O'Neill, Eugene, 265
O'Reilly, Bill, xxix
O'Rourke, P. J., 181
O'Sullivan, Timothy, 120
Oakley, Annie, 4
Obama, Barack, xxix, xxxi, 11, 22, 38, 65, 174, 353
Odets, Clifford, 265
Oliver, Willard M., 53
Olson, Eric, 324
Olson, Frank, 312, 324
Olson, Nils, 324
Oppenheimer, Robert, 292
Orlowek, Nate, ix, 138–139
Orne, Sally, 134
Orwell, George, xxxii, 22, 289, 335, 354
Oswald, Lee Harvey, 134, 246
Oswald, Marguerite, 134
Otis, James, 2, 25
Owens, Jesse, 235

Page, Jimmy, 356
Page, Tony, 27
Paine, Thomas, 2, 17–19
Palmer, Mitchell, 197
Parenti, Michael, 53
Parker, John F., 115–117, 134
Parker, Ellis, 226–227
Parsons, Talcott, 319
Patch, Harry, 192
Patman, Wright, 179

Patton, George S., 212, 268, 293
Paul, Rand, 180
Paul, Ron, xi, 105–106, 180
Pauling, Linus, 300
Pearson, Drew, 178, 261, 317
Penn & Teller, xxxi
Pepper, Claude, 239–240
Perry, Benjamin, 144
Petersen, William, 114, 135
Petersen, Paul R., 150
Philipson, Ilene, 333
Phillips, V.N. "Bud," 101
Pierce, Franklin, 66
Pike, Albert, 161–162
Pinchot, Amos, 175
Pitt, Brad, 114
Pitt, Sir William, xxvii
Platt, Thomas, 157
Plunkett, Hugh, 203
Poindexter, George, 47
Polk, James K., 50
Pomeroy, Marcus M., 97
Pope Benedict XV, 372
Pope, John, 64
Posner, Gerald, xxviii
Pound, Ezra, 181–182, 250
Powell/Paine, Lewis, 118, 121–122, 132
Powers, Kirsten, 31
Prange, Gordon W., 243
Prosser, Charles, 180

Quantrill, William Clarke, 151
Queen Elizabeth, 4
Quigley, Carroll, 340

Randall, James G., 56
Rankin, Jeannette, 248–249
Rankin, John, 282
Rath, Christian, 133
Rathbone, Henry, 114 , 117, 135
Rather, Dan, 318

Ray, Elizabeth, 329
Reagan, Ronald, 247, 318, 354
Rechberg, Arnold, 300
Redford, Robert, 132
Redpath, James, 54
Reece, B. Carroll, 187, 329, 331–332
Reed, David A., 178
Read, Deborah, 14
Reed, Walter, 306
Reep, Thomas P., 107
Reilly, Edward J., 215–216, 223, 230
Remington, Frederic, 167
Revere, Paul, 1–2, 34
Rhoads, Cornelius, 308
Rhodes, James Ford, 153
Rhue, Sylvia, 59
Rice, Thomas Dartmouth, 160
Rickenbacker, Eddie, 251
Rife, Raymond, 305
Rinehart, Mary Roberts, 265
Rivero, Michael, 306
Roberts, Andrew, 259
Roberts, Owen J., 246
Roberts, Paul Craig, 328
Robespierre, 18
Robison, John, 24–26
Rockefeller, David, 177
Rockefeller, John D., 185, 204–205
Rockefeller, John D. Jr., 232
Rockefeller, Nelson, 176
Rockefeller, Percy, 201
Rockwell, Lew, ix, xi, 57, 106, 318
Rogers, Will, 203
Rogerson, Sidney, 237
Roosevelt, Franklin D., xxvi, xxvii, 70,
    189, 194, 213, 232–243, 245–256, 258,
    261, 263, 270, 279, 288, 297, 309, 321,
    327, 338, 341, 354, 357, 358, 360
Roosevelt, Eleanor, 243, 254
Roosevelt, Eliot, 253
Roosevelt, Kermit, 295

Roosevelt, Theodore, xxvi, 162, 172, 173, 174, 175, 189, 300, 353, 358–359
Roosevelt, Theodore Roosevelt, Jr., 256
Root, Elihu, 189
Roscoe, Theodore, 128, 140–141
Rose, Charles, 20
Rosenberg, Ethel, 332–334
Rosenberg, Julius, 332–334
Ross, Edmund, 148
Ross, L. M., 62
Roth, William V., 247
Rothbard, Murray, xxvii
Rothschild, Mayer Amschel, 177
Rothschild, James de, 41
Rothschild, Nathan, 40–41
Rothschild, Walter, 193
Rous, Payton, 308
Rovere, Richard, 319
Rubin, Jerry, 195
Ruby, Jack, 296
Ruffin, Edmund, 144
Ruggles, Mortimer, 132
Russell, Bertrand, 18, 190, 300
Russell, Francis, 217
Russell, Gilbert, 38
Russell, Richard, 246
Rutherford, Lucy Mercer, 254

Sabato, Larry, 34
Sabin, Albert, 302
Sacco, Nicola, 205-207
Salk, Jonas, 309
Sandburg, Carl, 127
Sanders, Bernie, 180–181
Sanger, Margaret, 166, 249, 308, 358
Santa Anna, 49
Santayana, George, xxxii
Sawyer, Charles, 201–202
Sawyer, R. M., 74
aduto, Anthony, 216–217, 226, 230

Scalia, Antonin, 10
Schall, Thomas D., 251–252, 256
Schlesinger, Arthur M. Jr., 98
Schlundt, Dale, 106
Schneider, James J., 150
Schwarzkopf, Norman, 227
Scott, Dred, 86
Seibolt, Edward J., 207
Sellier, Charles E., 120, 137
Seward, Fanny, 136
Seward, John, 61–62, 65, 86, 93, 118, 147
Seymour, Horatio, 69, 71
Sharpe, Violet, 217
Shaw, George Bernard, 300, 302
Shays Rebellion, 19–22
Shays, Daniel, 19–22
Shea, Robert, 27
Sheen, Martin, 279
Sheridan, Philip, 51, 73–75, 83, 90, 152–153, 174, 269, 327
Sherman, Roger, 30
Sherman, S. C., 77
Sherman, William Tecumseh, 51, 73–78, 82, 85, 90, 102–104, 106, 126, 151–153, 174, 183, 185, 269, 281, 327, 359
Sherrod, Robert, 263
Sherwin, Martin, 292
Shirer, William L., 265
Short, Walter, 246–247
Sibley, H. H., 64
Sickles, Daniel, 62
Simms, William Gilmore, 74
Simpson, Colin, 188
Sims, J. Marion, 306
Sinatra, Frank, 279
Sinclair, Upton, 205
Sitting Bull, Chief, 183
Slovik, Antoinette, 278–279
Slovik, Eddie, 277–279

Smith, Lawrence H., 282
Smith, Brian Owen, 15
Smith, Al, 235
Smith, Jess, 203
Smyth, Albert Henry, 14
Snowden, Edward, 34
Snyder, George Washington, 24
Solzhenitsyn, Aleksandr, 264, 273, 336
Spaak, Paul-Henri, 340
Spangler, Edmund, 121
Speed, James, 124, 131
Speed, Joshua, 58
Spence, Richard, 357
Spielberg, Steven, 106
Spooner, Lysander, 73, 99
Spragg, Dennis, 276
St. Helen, John, 137
Stalin, Josef, 256, 258, 266, 269, 275, 279,
    281, 295, 300–301, 327, 335, 337, 357
Stanhope, Doug, xxix
Stanly, Edward, 149
Standley, William, 246
Stannard, David E., 182
Stansbury, Arthur J., 46
Stanton, Edwin, 62, 71, 88, 90–91,
    113–114, 116, 119–123, 128, 131,
    136–137, 139, 141, 148
Steffgen, Kent H., 145
Steinbeck, John, 239
Stephens, Alexander, 89
Stevens, Amanda, 229
Stevens, Thaddeus, 72, 91, 146–148
Stevenson, Adlai E., 163
Stewart, Kensey Johns, 68
Stimson, Henry L., 241, 245, 281
Sting, 356
Stinnett, Robert, 247–248
Stockdale, F. W., 153
Stockton, Richard, 12
Stokes, Karen, 74

Stokes, Louis, 112
Stone, Harlan Fiske, 281–283
Stone, Norman, 269
Stone, Oliver, 318
Streicher, Julius, 284
Strong, Richard, 307
Stuart, Gilbert, 40
Stuart, John T., 94
Suckley, Margaret, 254
Sulaiman, Aliyah, 7
Sumner, Charles, 72, 147
Sunstein, Cass, 22
Surratt, Anna, 131, 133–134
Surratt, John, 123–124, 128–130
Surratt, Mary, 121–123, 127–133
Sutton, Antony, 300, 328
Szilard, Leo, 290

Taft, Robert A., 282, 286, 290, 297–298,
    353
Taft, William Howard, 175
Taney, Roger, 65
Tanner, James, 114
Tansill, Robert, 60–61
Tarbell, Ida, 126–127
Tatlock, Jean, 292
Tatlock, John, 292
Taylor, Richard, 146
Taylor, Zachary, 52–53, 199
Teller, Henry, 167
Teresa, Vincent, 207
Tesla, Nikola, 169, 300, 353
Thayer, Webster, 205–206
Thomas, Clarence, 10
Thomas, Norman, 237
Thoreau, Henry David, 54
Thorpe, Elliott R., 242
Throckmorton, James, 152
Thurmond, Strom, 247
Tikas, Louis, 185

Tilden, Samuel J., 156-157
Toland, John, 242, 248
Tolstoy, Leo, xxvi
Tolstoy, Nikolai, 272
Townsend, George Alfred, 94
Townsend, Francis, 236
Toynbee, Arnold, 337
Travis, William, 49
Trotsky, Leon, 335, 337, 339
Trow, Harrison, 151
Truman, Bess, 292
Truman, General Harry, 88-89
Truman, Harry, 234, 253, 258, 272,
    288-297, 301, 318, 325, 353
Truman, Margaret, 294
Tubman, Harriet, 48
Tuchman, Barbara, 242
Tucker, Phillip Thomas, 49
Tung, Mao Tse, 337
Turchin, John B., 78-79
Turley, Jonathan, 148
Turner, Richard, 241
Turner, Robert, 9
Turrou, Leon, 226
Twain, Mark, xxvi, 159, 164
Tweed, William "Boss," 157, 164
Tyler, John, 97
Tyler, Lyon Gardiner, 97

Usher, John P., 126
Usher, Linton, 126

Vallandigham, Clement, 66-72
Van Buren, Martin, 47, 66
Vanzetti, Bartolomeo, 205-207
Ventura, Jesse, xxix
Vidal, Gore, xxv, xxxi, 21, 198
Villard, Oswald Garrison, 239
Vincent, L.C., 228
Voltaire, 352

von Ribbentrop, Joachim, 284
Von Schleicher, Kurt, 300
von Braun, Wernher, 321
Vonnegut, Kurt, 268-269

Wade, Benjamin F., 67, 97
Waldo, Cornelius, 88
Wallace, Lew, 125
Walter, Jacob Ambrose, 131
Warburg, Max, 192
Warburg, Paul M., 178, 192, 211
Warburg, James P., 178, 338
Warren, Earl, 25, 37, 76, 116, 125, 246,
    297
Warren, Elizabeth, 181
Warren, Joseph, 2, 25, 29
Washington, George, xxvii, 2-3, 9,
    20-21, 23-25, 27, 30-31, 37, 40, 48, 52,
    54, 148, 187
Washington, Martha, 22
Waters, Walter W., 212
Watkins, Louis Douglass, 74
Watson, Bruce, 207
Watson, Thomas, 196
Watson, William, 136
Wattles, David C., 62
Weaver, James B., 164
Weaver, Richard, 275
Webster, Nesta, 339
Webster, Noah, 30
Wedermeyer, Albert, 244
Weed, Thurlow, 42
Weichmann, Louis J., 127-128, 132
Weightman, Roger C., 42
Weiner, Tim, 322
Weishaupt, Adam, 24-27, 339
Well, James W., 63
Welles, Gideon, 60
Welles, Orson, 265
Welles, Sumner, 339

INDEX

Wells, H. G., 256, 300, 339, 358
Wentworth, Arthur, 306
West, Rebecca, 280
Whipple, Charlie, 207
White, Harry Dexter, 281
Whitley, Leon, 308
Wiencek, Henry, 8
Wilbur, Ray Lyman, 201
Wilcox, Robert, 293
Wilder, Thornton, 265
Wilentz, David, 216, 223–224, 227
Wilkes, John, 114
Wilkinson, James, 37–38
Willard, Joseph, 26
Williams, Robert C., xxviii
Williams, Ken, 262
Willkie, Wendell, 238, 297
Wills, Gary, 49, 56, 358
Wilson, Robert Anton, 27

Wilson, Edmund, 109–110
Wilson, Woodrow, xxvi, 4, 34, 174, 175,
    187, 189, 190, 192, 194, 195, 196, 198, 199,
    234, 240, 249, 300, 325, 340, 355, 358
Winchell, Walter, 238
Wirz, Henry, 80
Wisner, Frank, 322
Wolf-Shenk, Joshua, 58
Wood, Leonard, 189
Worthington, Peter, 273
Wylie, Andrew, 131

Yoo, John, 70
Young, Alfred, 1

Zappa, Frank, 305
Zelikow, Philip, 248
Zhukov, Marshall, 267
Zimmerman, Michael, 305